The material contained herein represents the opinions of the author construed to be the action of the National Association of Legal Assistants, Inc., unless adopted pursuant to the bylaws of the association.

Nothing contained in this book is to be considered as the rendering of legal advice for specific cases, and readers are responsible for obtaining such advice from their own legal counsel. This book and any forms and agreements herein are intended for educational and informational purposes only.

National Association of Legal Assistants, Inc. (NALA)
6450 S. Lewis Avenue, Suite 250
Tulsa, OK 74136
918.587.6828
www.nala.org
nalanet@nala.org

Published by National Association of Legal Assistants, Inc.
Editor – Leslie Metzger

This book is available at a special discount when ordered in bulk quantities. For more information, contact NALA at 918.587.6828 or at nalanet@nala.org.

ISBN: 978-0-578-45486-3

© 2021 by the National Association of Legal Assistants, Inc. All rights reserved.

No part of the publication may be reproduced, stored in a retrieval system, or transmitted in any form or by any means, electronic, mechanical, photocopying, recording, or otherwise, without the prior written permission of the publisher. Permission requests should be sent via writing to the publisher at the address or email above.

Printed in the United States of America.

Second edition

2 3 4 5 6 7 8 9 10

© 2019, 2020, 2021 NALA, Inc. All rights reserved.

Preface

This second edition of the Certified Paralegal Exam Fundamentals has been prepared and published by NALA with the help of an amazing team. Each section author is listed at the beginning of their chapter(s). While every attempt was made to avoid any errors, we regrettably admit our human flaws and realize that some may exist. Any substantial errors will be listed on www.nala.org and updated for future editions.

NALA has offered the voluntary CP credential since 1976 and has had more than 20,000 paralegals take the exam. The Certified Paralegal® (CP) Program establishes and serves as a national professional standard for paralegals that encourages the growth of the paralegal profession, attesting to the highest level of achievement.

In general, the book addresses general legal principles and broad areas of concern and is not intended to be a source of specific legal advice or solutions to particular problems. Rather, its goal is to provide the reader with an overall understanding of legal concepts associated with the CP Exam.

The purpose of the book is to assist examinees of NALA's Certified Paralegal (CP) Exam in their preparation to successfully complete the exam and earn the credential. The NALA Certifying Board is not involved in the development or delivery of any CP Exam study materials, preparation materials, or products; and the developers of those materials and products do not have access to any CP Exam content. The Certifying Board does not require, approve, endorse, or recommend any specific study materials or methods to be used by examinees.

© 2019, 2020, 2021 NALA, Inc. All rights reserved.

CONTENTS

© 2019, 2020, 2021 NALA, Inc. All rights reserved.

CHAPTER 4: CORPORATE AND COMMERCIAL LAW   85

© 2019, 2020, 2021 NALA, Inc. All rights reserved.

CHAPTER 5:
CRIMINAL LAW & PROCEDURE   117

CHAPTER 6: ESTATE PLANNING AND PROBATE — 163

CHAPTER 7: REAL ESTATE AND PROPERTY — 187

© 2019, 2020, 2021 NALA, Inc. All rights reserved.

CHAPTER 8:
TORTS   223

CHAPTER 9:
PROFESSIONAL AND ETHICAL LIABILITY   243

SKILLS EXAM CHAPTERS

CHAPTER 10: GRAMMAR
273

CHAPTER 11: SPELLING
287

CHAPTER 12: PUNCTUATION
295

© 2019, 2020, 2021 NALA, Inc. All rights reserved.

CHAPTER 13:
CLARITY OF EXPRESSION
307

CHAPTER 14:
CRITICAL THINKING
313

CHAPTER 15:
READING COMPREHENSION
317

CHAPTER 16:
ANALYSIS OF INFORMATION
323

CHAPTER 17: DECISION-MAKING   327

CHAPTER 18: PRACTICE SKILLS EXAM - SAMPLE ESSAYS   331

PRACTICE QUESTIONS ANSWER KEY   347

© 2019, 2020, 2021 NALA, Inc. All rights reserved.

© 2019, 2020, 2021 NALA, Inc. All rights reserved.

KNOWLEDGE EXAM
──── CHAPTERS ────

CHAPTER 1

The United States Legal System

Written by Todd C. Richardson, J.D.

© 2019, 2020, 2021 NALA, Inc. All rights reserved.

After completing this chapter, the paralegal will:

- Understand the impact of common law on the United States legal system

- Understand the impact of equity on the United States legal system

- Describe the multiple branches of government established under the United States Constitution

- Understand how state governments are organized

- Analyze the interplay between the federal government and state governments

- Explain how the multiple branches of the United States and individual state governmental systems create the sources of the law

- Describe the federal and state court structures

- Describe mandatory and persuasive legal authority

- Compare the concepts of jurisdiction and venue

- Understand the forms and impact of alternative dispute resolution

THE AMERICAN SYSTEM OF LAW

In the United States, government is structured according to the principles of federalism under which citizens are regulated by separate governments, federal and state. Paralegals should be familiar with the structure of government as well as the sources of law arising from this structure. The concepts and principles discussed in this chapter provide a basic underpinning for every area of law and will assist in preparing for the Certified Paralegal (CP) Exam.

COMMON LAW AND ITS ORIGINS

United States law is based primarily on the English common law, a system in which laws develop through the courts by case decisions. Common law is generally uncodified, meaning that there is no centralized compilation of court opinions, although cases are often published chronologically. The basis of common law is the concept of precedent through the doctrine of *stare decisis*. Essentially, the doctrine of stare decisis is the proposition that when an issue has been previously considered by a court and a ruling has been issued, the court will defer to its previous decision. Therefore, common law creates stability, predictability, and consistency for subsequent parties similarly situated involving the same legal issues.

Another influence on the American legal system is equity jurisprudence from the English system. Initially, English commoners could only have their disputes resolved in the king's court of common pleas. By the 13th century, the relief available in civil cases filed in common-law courts had become very limited. Causes of action had to be pled within very narrow and technical confines in order for a legal writ to be issued. Likewise, relief in common-law courts was limited to the payment of damages and the recovery of the possession of property. However, common-law court actions and forms of relief did not evolve to reflect the changes in society and the needs of a more complex world. Indeed, as the common-law courts developed, they lost much of their discretion and abandoned the idea of tempering law with equity. Out of the rigid constraints of the common-law courts arose the need for more flexible remedies.

Litigants in time turned to the king with petitions seeking justice because the law courts were unable

---

 © 2019, 2020, 2021 NALA, Inc. All rights reserved.

to afford effective remedies. Eventually, these petitions were directly referred to the Lord Chancellor, a principal minister of the king. By the middle of the 14th century the Court of Chancery was recognized as a new and distinct legal system. The Court of Chancery evolved into a separate system known as equity, in which cases were decided by chancellors based on principles of fairness rather than technical rules. Although the law and equity courts have been merged in modern practice, vestiges of these two systems still have a great impact on the law. The titles of pleadings can reflect the forms of law and equity. A complaint is filed in a traditional law action, while a petition is filed in a traditional equity action. In addition, the right to a jury trial may be impacted if a cause of action was traditionally sought in either law or equity, and the types of remedies the court can award may also be impacted by the traditional origins of an action.

At both the state and federal levels, the law of the United States mainly derives from the English common law in force at the time of the American Revolution. The substance of pre-revolutionary English common law has been formally adopted by all states, with the notable exception of Louisiana, by the enactment of "reception statutes." Reception statutes generally provide that the common law of England is the foundational law of a state to the extent that it is general and not local and is not inconsistent with the constitution and law of the United States or the legislative acts of the states. Some states adopted English common law as of July 4, 1776, while other states were deliberately vague as to the cut-off date. As a result of differing constitutions, statutes, and case law emanating from each state, there have been 50 separate systems of law developed in areas governed by state law.

Unlike the states, there is no formal reception statute at the federal level specifically adopting English common law. Justice Brandeis notably wrote for the Supreme Court in *Erie Railroad Co. v. Tompkins* that "[t]here is no federal general common law." There are two theories justifying the existence and scope of federal common law. The first theory suggests that federal courts are vested with the implied judicial power of common-law courts to formulate persuasive precedent. The second is an alternate theory that suggests the federal common law exists only to the extent that Congress has delegated to the federal courts the power to make common law. In any event, it is fairly well agreed upon that federal courts are justified in making federal common law to the extent and with the same constraints as state courts.

CONSTITUTIONS

A constitution is generally defined as the fundamental principles or precedents of a nation or state, which determine the powers and duties of the government and guarantee certain rights to the people subject to it. Constitutions may be either written or unwritten. In the hierarchy of the law, constitutions are at the top and all other forms of law are below it and must conform to it. Statutes, ordinances, regulations, and executive orders must all conform to the constitutions under which they originate.

The United States Constitution provides the basic framework of government, protects individual rights, and is the basis upon which all other laws are created. The United States Constitution was specifically drafted "to form a more perfect union" of the previous 13 colonies and "secure the blessings of liberty." A major concern in the drafting of the Constitution was to remedy the weaknesses of the Articles of Confederation which preceded it by strengthening the central federal government within proper constraints. The Constitution initially focused on the structure of the federal government and the division of powers between the federal government and the states.

During the adoption process of the United States Constitution, the original document was amended to include specific guarantees of individual rights relating to liberty, justice, and the reservation of unenumerated rights and powers. These amendments (1-10) came to be known collectively as the "Bill of Rights." These amendments were primarily drafted by James Madison in response to the demands of many states for greater protection of individual rights. The Federalists, including Thomas Jefferson, wanted a strong national government and argued that individual guarantees need not be included because all power not specifically delegated to the federal government was kept by the people and the states. The Anti-Federalists, including George Mason, advocated for a weaker federal government and argued that a bill of rights was necessary to safeguard individual liberties. Although the Bill of Rights was added as amendments to the original constitutional text, it has become the paramount source of protecting individual freedoms. Initially, the Bill of Rights only applied to actions of the federal government and to federal court cases. However, most aspects of the Bill of Rights were eventually made applicable to the states through the due process clause of the 14th Amendment. The incorporation process has evolved under a process of "selective incorporation" where the United States Supreme Court has incorporated parts of certain amendments as cases arise, rather than incorporating an entire amendment at once.

© 2019, 2020, 2021 NALA, Inc. All rights reserved.

Rights and Protections of the Bill of Rights

Amendment	Right or Protection
I	• Freedom of speech • Freedom of the press • Freedom of religion • Freedom of assembly • Right to petition the government
II	• Right to bear arms
III	• Protection against housing soldiers in civilian homes
IV	• Protection against unreasonable search and seizure • Protection against the issuing of warrants without probable cause
V	• Protection against trial without indictment • Protection against double jeopardy • Protection against self-incrimination • Protection against property seizure
VI	• Right to speedy trial • Right to be informed of charges • Right to be confronted by witnesses • Right to call witnesses • Right to legal counsel
VII	• Right to trial by jury
VIII	• Protection against excessive bail • Protection against excessive fines • Protection against cruel and unusual punishment
IX	• Rights granted in the Constitution shall not infringe on other rights
X	• Powers not granted to the Federal Government in the Constitution belong to the states and people

Supremacy Clause

Article VI of the United States Constitution contains a provision referred to as the "Supremacy Clause." The Supremacy Clause provides that federal law is the supreme law of the land. This clause means that judges in every state must follow the Constitution, laws, and treaties of the federal government in matters that are directly or indirectly within the federal government's control. Essentially, the Supremacy Clause is a conflict-of-laws rule specifying that certain national acts take priority over any state acts that conflict with national law. However, the primacy of federal law is not absolute. The Founding Fathers, in drafting the Constitution, intended to strengthen the federal government, but they did not intend to abolish the power of the states. The federal government's power was limited under the Constitution with specific powers carved out. Remaining powers not specifically enumerated remained with the states and the people. These retentions and reservations of rights to the states and the people were enshrined in the Ninth and Tenth Amendments.

The Supremacy Clause is given effect by the doctrine of federal preemption. The preemption doctrine holds that state regulation is precluded or invalid by federal regulation in three situations:

- When Congress expressly states its intent to preempt state regulation

- When a state law is inconsistent with federal law, even though no express preemption has been made by Congress

- When Congress by its enactment of a comprehensive legislative scheme sufficiently occupies a field so that it is reasonable to infer that it left no room for the states to supplement the federal law

Enumerated Powers

The United States Constitution creates a limited and defined federal government of enumerated powers, not one of general powers such as those of the states. Article I, Section 1 of the United States Constitution provides that all legislative powers are vested in the Congress of the United States. Article I, Section 8 of the United States Constitution sets forth the enumerated powers specifically delegated to the federal government. These powers include:

- That Congress shall have power to lay and collect taxes, duties, imposts, and excises, to pay the debts and provide for the common defense and general welfare of the United States; but all duties, imposts, and excises shall be uniform throughout the United States

- To borrow money on the credit of the United States

- To regulate commerce with foreign nations, and among the several states, and with the Indian tribes

- To establish a uniform rule of naturalization, and uniform laws on the subject of bankruptcies throughout the United States

- To coin money, regulate the value thereof, and of foreign coin, and fix the standard of weights and measures

- To provide for the punishment of counterfeiting the securities and current coin of the United States

- To establish post offices and post roads

- To promote the progress of science and useful arts, by securing for limited times to authors and inventors the exclusive right to their respective writings and discoveries

- To constitute tribunals inferior to the Supreme Court

- To define and punish piracies and felonies committed on the high seas, and offences against the law of nations

- To declare war, grant letters of marque and reprisal, and make rules concerning captures on land and water

- To raise and support armies, but no appropriation of money to that use shall be for a longer term than two years

© 2019, 2020, 2021 NALA, Inc. All rights reserved.

- To provide and maintain a navy

- To make rules for the government and regulation of the land and naval forces

- To provide for calling forth the militia to execute the laws of the Union, suppress insurrections, and repel invasions

- To provide for organizing, arming, and disciplining the militia, and for governing such part of them as may be employed in the service of the United States, reserving to the states respectively, the appointment of the officers, and the authority of training the militia according to the discipline prescribed by Congress

- To exercise exclusive jurisdiction in all cases whatsoever, over such district (not exceeding 10 miles square) as may, by cession of particular states, and the acceptance of Congress, become the seat of the government of the United States, and to exercise like authority over all places purchased by the consent of the legislature of the state in which the same shall be, for the erection of forts, magazines, arsenals, dock-yards, and other needful buildings

- To make all laws which shall be necessary and proper for carrying into execution the foregoing powers, and all other powers vested by this Constitution in the government of the United States, or in any department or officer thereof

Amendments

The United States Constitution can be revised, corrected, or improved by a process of amendment. To date, 27 amendments have been adopted. Article VI of the United States Constitution provides two methods of initiating a constitutional amendment:

1. Congressional Resolution. Two-thirds majorities of both houses of Congress are required with no role for the President; and

2. State Legislatures/Convention. Two-thirds of the state legislatures can convene a convention of the states to propose amendments.

Once an amendment has been proposed under one of the above two methods, the amendment is subject to ratification. Congress determines which of the following two methods will be used for the ratification process:

1. The legislatures of three-quarters of the states, or

2. Three-quarters of state ratifying conventions.

BRANCHES OF GOVERNMENT

In setting up the structure of the federal government, the Founding Fathers applied the theory of separation of powers. Influenced by the social and political philosopher Montesquieu, the framers of the United States Constitution divided the federal government into legislative, executive, and judicial branches. Each branch is separate from the other and was established with specific duties and methods of selection. The purpose of separating governing power into various branches is to guard against concentrating too much power into any one body of government.

Legislative Branch

Pursuant to Article I of the United States Constitution, the legislative branch consists of two separate bodies or chambers, the House of Representatives and the Senate. Together, these two bodies constitute Congress. Congress has the primary power to enact laws, raise and appropriate funds, declare war, and impeach officials from the executive and judicial branches. In addition, the Senate has the right to provide advice and consent to the president on appointments of judges, ambassadors, and important executive officers. The Senate also has the power to ratify treaties.

Initially, the Constitution provided that members of the House of Representatives were directly elected by citizens of the United States while members of the Senate were selected by the individual states to represent each state as a separate entity. The 17th Amendment changed the method of selection of senators from the states to direct election by the people in each state. Therefore, all members of Congress are now elected directly by the citizens of the United States. Under Article I of the Constitution, each state is allotted the same number of senators (two). The number of representatives for each state is based on the state's population. Members of the House of Representatives serve two-year terms, while senators serve six-year terms. The entire House of Representatives is subject to election every two years while only one-third of the Senate is subject to election each two-year cycle. The Constitution does not set any term limits on members of Congress.

Therefore, currently in Congress there are 100 senators, 435 elected members of the House of Representatives, plus an additional six non-voting delegates who represent the District of Columbia as well as Puerto Rico and other U.S. territories. The determination of how many House members each state is entitled to is based on an apportionment process which relies on the results of a national census conducted every 10 years.

In order to enact legislation, bills must first be introduced into the House or Senate by a representative or senator. Under Article I, Section 7, Clause 1 of the United States Constitution, "the origination clause," all bills raising revenue must originate in the House, although the Senate may propose or concur with amendments of those bills originating from the House. Proposed legislation is then assigned to a committee or committees for review and consideration. After committee review, both chambers must pass the same version of a bill by majority vote. If adopted, the bill goes to the president, who can either sign the bill into law or reject it using the veto power authorized by the Constitution.

In the case of a regular veto, the bill is returned to Congress. Congress can override a veto by a two-thirds vote of both houses. Both the veto power and Congress's ability to override a veto are examples of the system of checks and balances intended by the Constitution to prevent any one branch from gaining too much power.

Executive Branch

Article II of the United States Constitution establishes the executive branch, with the president as its head. The executive branch has the power to enforce the laws of the nation. The president is the commander and chief of the armed forces and head of state. The executive branch includes the vice president, cabinet, executive departments, and other federal agencies, commissions, and committees. The president can sign or veto legislation and can issue executive orders, presidential memorandums, and proclamations. The executive branch is also responsible for carrying out the nation's foreign policy, conducting diplomacy, and appointing ambassadors. Additionally, the president has the authority to nominate judges to the federal court system, subject to the consent of the Senate. The president and vice president are not directly elected by the people, but rather are elected through an Electoral College process where each state is allocated electors based on its representation in Congress, both the House and

© 2019, 2020, 2021 NALA, Inc. All rights reserved.

Senate. Under United States constitutional law, the president of the United States possesses the power to control the entire executive branch under the unitary executive theory. The president serves a four-year term of office subject to a term limit of 10 years. The 22nd Amendment provides for a limit of two terms of office plus two years or less if a person serves part of the last president's term.

Judicial Branch

Article III of the United States Constitution provides that "judicial power of the United States shall be vested in one Supreme Court, and in such inferior Courts as the Congress may from time to time ordain and establish." The framers of the Constitution did not specify how the judicial branch should be organized, leaving significant discretion to Congress to determine the structure of the federal judiciary. While Article III specifically authorizes the establishment of the United States Supreme Court, the actual number of justices on the Supreme Court is left to Congress.

Congress established the basic framework for the federal judiciary by adopting the Judiciary Act of 1789 in which the court system was set up and guidelines for the operation of the United States Supreme Court were adopted. The Act established federal district courts as the trial-level courts in each federal district. The act also created the United States circuit courts of appeals as intermediate appellate courts between the district courts and the United States Supreme Court. The United States Supreme Court is the court of last resort in the federal judicial system.

The exact nature and scope of review of the federal courts was originally vague. That changed in 1803 with *Marbury v. Madison,* a Supreme Court case which established the Court's power of judicial review, by which the courts determine the constitutionality of executive and legislative acts. Judicial review is another key example of the checks and balances system in action.

Members of the federal judiciary are nominated by the president of the United States and confirmed by the Senate. Federal judges serve for life, subject to retirement or removal from office through impeachment by Congress. Currently the federal judiciary includes the Supreme Court with nine justices, 13 circuit courts of appeals, and 94 federal judicial district courts.

Interplay Between the Three Branches of Government

An understanding of the relationship between the three branches of the federal government is essential for the legal professional in order to fully comprehend the sources of law and division of responsibilities and limitations of each branch of government. As noted earlier, the Founding Fathers were greatly influenced by the 18th century French social and political philosopher Montesquieu and the concept of "separation of powers." Montesquieu in his work, *Spirit of the Laws,* asserted that political authority should not be concentrated but should be divided into legislative, executive, and judicial branches. This division of power and responsibilities, he maintained, would effectively promote liberty if these three branches operated separately and acted independently.

In framing the United States Constitution, the Founding Fathers created a political system dividing the powers of government to prevent the concentration of power and to provide checks and balances between the branches.

This separation takes the form of:

- The legislative branch is responsible for enacting laws and providing the money necessary to operate the government. The Constitution empowers the legislative branch to override presidential vetoes with a super majority; to impeach members of the executive and judicial branches, including the president; to investigate actions of the executive branch; to propose amendments to overturn judicial opinions; to provide Senate approval of presidential appointments to the judicial and executive branches; to approve ambassadors; and to ratify treaties.

- The executive branch is responsible for implementing and administering the laws enacted by the legislature. The Constitution empowers the president to veto laws adopted by Congress, make foreign treaties, appoint federal judges, and serve as commander in chief of the military. In addition, the president is empowered to exercise the pardon power to violations of federal law as a check on the judicial branch.

- The judicial branch is responsible for interpreting the Constitution and laws and applying these interpretations to cases and controversies brought before the courts. The courts are empowered to declare laws unconstitutional, declare executive actions or orders unconstitutional, and judges are not subject to dismissal by the president.

STATE GOVERNMENTS

Under the system of federalism established by the United States Constitution, governance is shared between the national and state governments. The Founding Fathers in drafting the Constitution envisioned that state governments, not the federal government, would be the primary government impacting citizens on a day-to-day basis. The Constitution established that certain powers were exclusive to the federal government while others were concurrent with the states. As the United States developed, the balance of power moved steadily from the states to the federal government giving rise to increased interaction between the states and the federal government.

Article IV, Clause 1 of the Constitution guarantees to every state in the Union a republican form of government. This "guarantee clause" ensures that all the states must operate under the same basic republican governmental philosophy. In addition, the 10th Amendment, part of the Bill of Rights, provides that powers, that are not delegated to the federal government and are not prohibited by the Constitution, are reserved to the states respectively or to the people.

While the United States Constitution establishes the federal government, the document is silent as to the structure of the governments of the states. States set up their governmental structures which are authorized by their own constitutions. State constitutions are often modeled on the United States Constitution and outline the structure of government, establish bills of rights, and create the branches of government. In addition, state constitutions tend to cover a wide array of issues important to each state. Historically, state constitutions have been subject to more frequent revision, amendment, or replacement. State constitutions divide government power into three branches: legislative, executive, and judicial.

Legislative Branch

Mirroring the structure of the federal government, the legislative branch of states in the United States consists of state legislatures. With the exception of Nebraska, 49 of the state legislative bodies are bicameral, meaning they have two legislative chambers. Nebraska has a unicameral legislative body, meaning they have only one legislative body, known as the "Senate." The remaining 49 state legislative bodies have an upper and lower chamber. In all the remaining states the upper house is known as the "Senate." Lower house names vary from "House of Representatives," "House of Delegates," "State Assembly," "Assembly," and "General Assembly." An important power of state legislatures is the authority to create political subdivisions such as counties and cities within each state.

 © 2019, 2020, 2021 NALA, Inc. All rights reserved.

Executive Branch

The executive branch in state governments is headed by an elected governor. The executive branches in each state are organized in various ways. Most states utilize a cabinet form of government with departments, agencies, boards, and commissions tasked with different functions. Most states elect other executive branch members to serve alongside the governor. These can include a lieutenant governor, attorney general, secretary of state, commissioner of agriculture, commissioner of education, chief financial officer, and other key positions depending on the structure of the individual state. This plural form of the executive branch is in contrast with the unified executive branch in the federal government where only the president and vice president are subject to election.

Judicial Branch

In the United States, there exist a wide variety of structures in state court systems. Each state has a court of last resort, variously referred to as a "supreme court" or "court of appeals." Some states separate their highest court into civil and criminal divisions for appeals. States also have a variety of trial level courts which are titled by various names with specific jurisdictional limitations. Some states also provide for a layer of intermediate appellate courts between the trial courts and the courts of last resort. The method of selection and length of terms also vary from state to state. Some states provide for the direct election of judges and justices while others provide for systems of appointments. In addition, some states provide for a mixed system of appointed as well as elected judges. State courts primarily rule on matters of state law.

Interplay Between the Federal Government and State Governments

Article IV, Section 1 of the United States Constitution requires all states to give "full faith and credit" to the public acts and judicial proceedings of other states. Section 2 provides that citizens of each state are entitled to all "privileges and immunities" of citizens in other states. The interplay between the federal government and the state governments rests on the establishment of exclusive powers of the federal government, exclusive powers of the state governments, and powers which both the states and federal governments exercise concurrently. The following is a chart setting forth the nature of the powers involved in the interplay between the federal and state governments:

Exclusive Federal Powers	Exclusive State Powers	Concurrent Powers
Declare war	Provide for public safety, health, and welfare	Lawmaking and enforcement
Raise armies	Conduct elections	Taxation
Conduct foreign affairs	Establish local governments	Borrow money
Regulate mail	Maintain militia	Establish courts
Regulate interstate and foreign commerce	Regulate intrastate commerce	Eminent domain
Coin money	Ratify constitutional amendments	Charter banks
Establish rules of naturalization		

The relationship between the federal government and states has changed with time. Initially, the states were in a strong position in determining local matters and predominated in the day-to-day governance of their citizens. The federal government gained prominence in the relationship between states and the federal government culminating in President Franklin D. Roosevelt's New Deal. The trend has been towards a "New Federalism," where power is devolving once more to the states to resolve issues and to restore more autonomy and power to the states. An era of cooperative federalism has also evolved, where the federal government cooperates with state and local governments in resolving issues.

Sources of Law

In studying the American legal system, the next step in a full understanding of how the system of law impacts the paralegal is understanding how these various elements then result in "the law." By understanding the nature and role of each element of federal and state government, the legal professional will then have a fuller insight into how law is made and how it is applied and researched.

Primary Sources and Secondary Sources

In the United States, laws come primarily from the federal and state constitutions, statutory law from Congress and state legislatures, local laws and ordinances, common law and case law, administrative rules and regulations, and executive orders and treaties. These sources of law are deemed "primary" because they provide first-hand, original information from bodies or individuals with legitimate law creating authority. On the other hand, secondary sources are not first-hand sources with binding authority but rather are analysis or reviews of the law by legal scholars or indexes and finding tools used to assist in researching the law.

Paralegals are often called upon to conduct legal research. Legal research can be an interesting part of the job. Paralegals may conduct legal research using books, but it is increasingly common for legal research to be conducted using computerized legal services such as Westlaw® and Lexis®. It is important to understand the distinction between primary sources, which come from an entity with legal authority to make the law, and secondary sources, which compile and analyze the law and are often used as finding tools.

Constitutions

A constitution embodies the basic principles and laws of a nation or state, which defines the powers and duties of the government and guarantees certain rights to the people in that political body.

The United States Constitution is a written document that delineates the powers of the federal and state governments and the relationships between the branches of government in the federal system. The Constitution also identifies certain rights and protections of individual liberties. The provisions of the United States Constitution are controlling and are the supreme law of the country with precedence over state laws and state constitutions. The Constitution itself is a source of law because it is the supreme law of land. In addition, the United States Constitution is a primary source of law because the Constitution creates and allocates power between the three other sources of federal law: the legislative, executive, and judicial branches. Under the doctrine of judicial review, the meaning and intent of the Constitution are interpreted by the courts.

Statutes

Another primary source of law are statutes passed by Congress or state legislatures. These legislatures are a source of law because they have been given the power to enact statutory law. Statutory law is the codified body of laws containing specific acts or statutes passed by the legislature. Statutes passed by

© 2019, 2020, 2021 NALA, Inc. All rights reserved.

legislatures are general in nature and reflect general public policy as determined by the elected members of the legislature. As a source of law, statutes are interpreted by a set of rules of construction. It is the job of the courts to interpret the meaning and application of specific provisions of a statute. In interpreting statutory meaning, courts utilize the following in determining what the text of a statute means:

- Courts will generally first look at the ordinary meaning of the statute's text.

- Courts will interpret specific provisions of a statute by looking at the broader statutory context.

- Courts will apply canons of construction which provide a framework of presumptions on how courts ordinarily interpret statutes.

- Courts may examine the legislative history of a specific statute.

- Courts may also consider how the statute has or will be implemented.

Case Law

Judicial decisions or case law is an important source of law in the American legal system. The common law is a source of substantive law, and court opinions reflect the common law as well as interpretations of constitutional provisions, statutes, and administrative rules. The United States operates with a dual court system: state courts and federal courts. Under the doctrine of judicial review, courts have the power to determine the constitutionality of a statute or other governmental actions. In addition, courts make law when they resolve disputes by reviewing cases or controversies. The result of these court opinions is a body of law from cases known as common law. Court cases are issued by courts chronologically and are not arranged by any topical or subject matter arrangement as they are published. There are various finding tools which identify cases dealing with specific areas of the law.

Doctrines of *Stare Decisis* and Precedent

The keystones of judicial review and the common law are the concepts of *stare decisis* and legal precedent. In deciding a case, courts must have an actual case or controversy before them in which to apply the law to the facts in order to arrive at a resolution. The doctrine of *stare decisis* is simply defined as "to stand by things decided" and means that courts look to past judicial opinions involving similar issues to guide their decisions in later cases. The past opinions are known as precedent. These prior cases become authority for judges deciding similar issues later.

Mandatory Authority and Persuasive Authority

Under the doctrines of *stare decisis* and precedent, while prior cases are authority for resolution of later similar cases, not all court decisions are binding authority on all other courts. While courts are expected to follow their own prior rulings and also follow prior rulings from higher courts within the same court system, courts are not always compelled to follow prior decisions from courts in other states or on issues over which the court has primary jurisdiction. Under the federal system, all courts are obligated to follow the rulings of the United States Supreme Court. Likewise, lower courts within a state are obligated to follow the rulings of higher courts in their systems. However, state courts are not obligated to follow precedent from courts in other states. Mandatory authority are cases which a lower court must follow when issued by a higher court in the same court system or by the United States Supreme Court. In determining an issue, courts may, however, rely on decisions from other jurisdictions as a theoretical basis for their own decisions. While not bound by the other courts' decisions, these cases from other jurisdictions may serve as persuasive authority to support a court's conclusions. While the doctrine of precedent is strong, a court may overturn its own precedent if there is a compelling reason to do so.

Court Rules

Important primary sources of law that may not initially come to mind are procedural rules promulgated by courts. Essentially, court rules govern the conduct of business in the court systems and include time limitations, pleadings, and other procedural requirements. While not as prominent as other primary sources of law, such as constitutions, statutes, and case law, court rules are equally important because they govern all aspects of the administration of justice. Failure to follow these rules can result in drastic and sometimes fatal results to litigation. While some court rules may govern mundane aspects of filing and proceedings in a case, some rules, such as jurisdictional time limits to appeal, may result in appeals being dismissed with prejudice, thus depriving clients their day in court. Court rules vary from state to state and from the federal court system to the state systems.

The rulemaking authority of a court depends on how the court itself was created. In the federal system, the United States Constitution created the judicial system in general terms but gave Congress the power to determine the structure and nature of the court system. Technically, under this method of creation, Congress has the ultimate authority to promulgate court rules. However, as a practical matter, Congress has delegated the rulemaking authority to the Supreme Court. In turn, the Supreme Court has delegated the rulemaking process to committees of the Judicial Conference. If a rule or revision to a rule is proposed by the Conference, the Supreme Court may review and officially adopt the rule or change. Congress has the opportunity to reject, modify, or defer implementation of the proposed rule. If no objection is made, the rule takes effect. Some state constitutions also grant their legislatures the final authority over court rules. Importantly, under this authorization of power, legislatures retain the ultimate power to determine court rules. The level of involvement of the legislatures varies from state to state.

In contrast, some state courts have the exclusive power to promulgate court rules. This power can come from either explicit grants of rulemaking authority by the courts under state constitutions or from the inherent constitutional rulemaking powers under state constitutions.

One area of ongoing debate is the nature of rules governing evidence. In the federal system and in states where the power to regulate court procedures are given to the legislature, this is not an issue. This issue is most prominent in states where the courts are specifically given the right to regulate procedures in the court system, and the legislatures are given the power to create substantive law. It is argued that procedural law governs the practice and procedure or the "machinery of the judicial process," while substantive law includes those rules and principles which fix and declare the primary rights of individuals respecting their persons and property. Evidence codes contain a mix of the "machinery of the judicial process" and the primary rights of individuals. Traditionally, when these issues arise, the courts and legislatures have worked together. However, there exist tensions on whether the evidentiary rules are substantive, and subject to legislative enactment, or whether they are procedural, and subject to court control.

ADMINISTRATIVE LAW

Administrative law refers to the body of law and legal principles that deal with the creation, administration, and regulation of federal, state, and local governmental agencies. Administrative regulation as a system of law is not specifically provided for in the United States Constitution. Rather, the rulemaking authority of governmental agencies comes from powers granted by Congress, state

    © 2019, 2020, 2021 NALA, Inc. All rights reserved.

legislatures, or municipal entities through statutory law or ordinances under which regulations are promulgated.

The rise of administrative law has grown exponentially and has increased the power and independence of governmental agencies over the lives of citizens. This "fourth branch" of government now has an increased practical impact on daily life more than the legislative, executive, and judicial branches combined. The increased range of administrative law was recognized and enhanced by the United States Supreme Court in 1984 in *Chevron U.S.A., Inc. v. Natural Resources Defense Council, Inc.*, where the Court held that agencies were entitled to considerable deference in their interpretations of laws. However, it should be noted that the *Chevron* deference standard appears to be subject to revision by current federal courts. See e.g., *Waterkeeper Alliance v. EPA*, 853 F.3d 527, 534 (D.C. Cir. 2017) (quoting *Entergy Corp. v. Riverkeeper, Inc.*, 556 U.S. 208, 218 n.4 ("[i]f Congress has directly spoken to an issue then any agency interpretation contradicting what Congress has said would be unreasonable."))

On the state level, there are many examples of Administrative Court hearings. For example, in California, if a former employee has unemployment benefits denied by a former employer, the former employee can challenge that denial. The California Employment Development Department, the agency which oversees unemployment claims, would then give both the former employee and former employer the opportunity to be heard in front of an Administrative Judge. Because there is no jury in an Administrative Court hearing, the judge alone would decide whether or not the former employee is entitled to unemployment benefits. This Administrative Court hearing is less formal and allows nonlawyers to represent individuals or employers in its Administrative Court hearings.

Legislative Rulemaking Authority

In 1947, Congress enacted the Administrative Procedure Act (APA), which governs the process by which administrative agencies create and enact regulations. Likewise, most states have created state level administrative agencies under their own constitutions in which they have delegated rulemaking authority. Generally, states have adopted legislative schemes governing how state agencies operate, promulgate rules, and conduct administrative hearings and appeals. In addition, states also delegate a portion of their generalized police powers to local governments limited by geographical boundaries.

Quasi-Legislative Function

An important purpose of administrative agencies is the development and issuance of regulations, which are primary sources of law and have the impact of law. Administrative agencies have a "quasi-legislative" function under which agencies generally follow specific procedural steps in adopting and issuing regulations. These steps usually include public notice, public comment, adherence to general guidelines, and explanation of the legislative source of the agency's authority for enforcing statutes and regulations.

Quasi-Executive Function

In addition to exercising quasi-legislative functions in promulgating regulations, administrative agencies also perform "quasi-executive" functions in enforcing the regulations they have passed. Agencies investigate complaints and identify conduct they deem violates their regulations. Agencies commonly investigate activities subject to their regulations and may issue citations for violations, as well as issue advisory opinions stating generally how the agency views particular conduct.

Quasi-Judicial Function

Finally, administrative agencies may act in a "quasi-judicial" capacity to resolve disputed claims and examine evidentiary facts to reach binding decisions. Generally, agency action is quasi-judicial when a hearing is held, the parties participate, a hearing officer presides and can subpoena witnesses, and the administrative body has the power to take remedial steps. While administrative hearings are generally less formal than court proceedings, due process requires notice and an opportunity for a fair and full hearing.

Appeal

The scope of administrative actions is broad but is subject to judicial review. Persons challenging administrative actions must establish the statutory authority which gives subject matter jurisdiction to the court in which they seek review. The Administrative Procedure Act (APA) incorporates a basic presumption that a party who has been injured by agency action is entitled to judicial review unless there is "clear and convincing evidence of contrary legislative intent." The reviewing court decides all relevant questions of law, interprets constitutional and statutory provisions, and determines the meaning or the applicability of the terms to the agency action. This review includes a determination of whether the agency action was supported by substantial evidence or unwarranted by the facts to the extent the facts are subject to a trial de novo by the reviewing court.

In determining the propriety of an appeal, it must first be established whether the agency action sought to be reviewed resulted in an "injury in fact." Second, is whether the interest the party seeks to protect is arguably within the zone of interests protected by the constitutional or statutory provision. Even if a party establishes standing to seek review of an administrative action, the party must first exhaust all administrative remedies before the claim will be ripe for judicial review. Courts generally will accept an agency's findings of fact made in the agency's quasi-judicial capacity, while courts are free to examine whether the agency's action exceeded the authority granted to them by statute. Courts may overrule agency actions which are found to be "arbitrary, capricious, an abuse of discretion, or otherwise not in accordance with law." Essentially, for federal courts, the Administrative Procedure Act provides that an agency decision shall stand as long as it is supported by substantial evidence. In contrast, while some states follow the same scope of review as the federal system, other states provide for a trial de novo based on state constitutional requirements.

JURISDICTION AND VENUE

Before an action or case can be heard, there are requirements that must be met. These requirements include:

- Jurisdiction
- Venue

Jurisdiction

Jurisdiction is the authority of a court to hear and decide a specific action. There are several types of jurisdiction including:

- **Personal Jurisdiction**. The authority of a court to hear and decide a dispute involving the particular parties before it. Personal jurisdiction is geographical. Courts have personal jurisdiction

   © 2019, 2020, 2021 NALA, Inc. All rights reserved.

over parties who reside or do business within a particular country, state, district, circuit, or county. State and federal courts may also exercise "long arm" jurisdiction over non-resident defendants under statutory authority or a court's inherent jurisdiction. Generally, "minimum contacts" between the defendant and forum state must be established.

- **Subject Matter Jurisdiction.** The authority of a court to hear and decide a particular dispute before it.

- **Original Jurisdiction**. The authority of a court to hear and decide a case in the first instance.

- **Appellate Jurisdiction.** The authority of a court to review a prior decision decided by a lower court or tribunal.

- **In Rem Action.** An "in rem" proceeding is a lawsuit or legal action which is directed towards property rather than a particular person. Jurisdiction is determined by the location of the property and generally must be brought in the court which has jurisdiction over that location. Judgments are enforced upon the property (not a person) and are binding on all persons having claimed title to the property.

- **Quasi In Rem Action**. "Quasi in rem" is a legal action based on property of a person absent from the jurisdiction. Courts use their "in rem" jurisdiction over property to compel a litigant, over whom the court has no personal jurisdiction, to appear in court by attaching the property. Litigants must submit to the court's jurisdiction in order get the litigant's property back.

- **Federal Court Jurisdiction and State Court Jurisdiction**. The American legal system consists of two types of courts, federal and state. State courts are established by each state and may consist of varieties of trial and appellate courts. Federal courts are generally authorized under the United States Constitution. The Constitution specifically provides for a Supreme Court but leaves the specific details of the structure of the federal judiciary to Congress. Federal courts consist of trial and appellate courts and specialty courts dealing with matters such as admiralty, tax, armed forces, federal claims, international trade, and veterans' claims.

State courts exercise broad jurisdiction over state law matters, including criminal cases, family disputes, contracts, and torts. State courts may also exercise concurrent jurisdiction with federal courts in certain areas. State courts do not have jurisdiction to hear lawsuits against the United States government and those involving specific federal laws, including patent and copyright disputes, bankruptcy, certain admiralty claims, antitrust, and federal crimes. Federal court jurisdiction is limited to cases provided for by the Constitution or specifically authorized by Congress. These include:

- Cases involving violations of the Constitution and federal laws; referred to as "federal question" jurisdiction

- Cases in which the United States is a party

- Cases between citizens from different states when the amount in controversy exceeds $75,000; referred to as "diversity" jurisdiction

- Cases dealing with bankruptcy, admiralty and maritime claims, antitrust, federal crimes, patent disputes, and copyright disputes

Venue

Venue is the proper or possible location for a lawsuit to proceed. The purpose of venue is to ensure all

---

possible fairness and convenience for parties to litigation. Unlike jurisdiction, which is the power of a court to hear a case, venue deals with the place where the case should be heard. In criminal cases, proper venue is the locality where the crime occurred. In civil cases, venue is generally determined by the defendant's principal residence or where they do business, where a contract was to be carried out, or the location where the cause of action accrued. Unlike jurisdiction, which is an essential element for a court to hear a case, venue is generally based on convenience and can be changed "in the interests of justice" to a court with the same jurisdiction to hear the underlying action.

ALTERNATIVE DISPUTE RESOLUTION

Alternative dispute resolution refers to the processes that can be used to resolve conflicts or claims without having to go to court. These dispute resolution processes can resolve many types of disputes including family, employment, business, personal injury, housing, and environmental claims. The use of alternative dispute resolution is on the rise, and parties often prefer to pursue a non-judicial resolution to save time and money, preserve privacy, and retain more control over the process.

- **Negotiation** is a process where parties engage in good faith discussions of their disputes with the goal of coming to a mutually agreeable resolution.

- **Case Evaluation** is a non-binding process where the parties present facts, and issues are determined by an experienced neutral case evaluator.

- **Mediation** is a private process where a neutral third party, called a mediator, assists the parties in discussing and trying to resolve their disputes. Mediation may be court ordered but is considered "voluntary" because the parties are not required to come to an agreement.

- **Arbitration** is a private process where the parties agree that an impartial intermediary chosen by the parties can decide about a dispute after receiving evidence and hearing arguments. The parties agree in advance to abide by the arbitrator's resolution. Arbitration proceedings are generally more formal than mediation proceedings. Often arbitration agreements between the parties are agreed to before a dispute arises. There are two types of arbitration, private and judicial. Private arbitration is usually agreed upon by the parties, and the arbitrator is limited to settling disputes and issues provided for in the parties' agreement. In private arbitration, the parties can agree that the arbitration decision be either binding or non-binding. Judicial arbitration is a non-binding form of arbitration from which a dissatisfied party may choose to go to trial. Some jurisdictions mandate that arbitration is mandatory prior to trial proceedings. However, because such arbitration is non-binding, judicial arbitration is often used to facilitate negotiations between the parties.

- A **mini-trial**, such as mediation and arbitration, is not a trial proceeding but rather is a settlement process where the parties present summarized versions of their cases to a neutral advisor and representatives from each side who have authority to settle the dispute. These presentations are made in a private forum. After the presentations by the parties, the parties' representatives attempt to settle the dispute. If the representatives fail to settle the dispute, the neutral advisor at the parties' request may serve as a mediator and issue a non-binding opinion as to the likely outcome in court.

© 2019, 2020, 2021 NALA, Inc. All rights reserved.

Chapter 1: Practice Questions

1. **United States law is based primarily on:**

   A. The Code Napoleon

   B. The United Nations Charter

   C. English common law

   D. Colonial charters

2. **Which doctrine stands for the proposition that prior rulings of a court serve as precedent for future decisions?**

   A. *Res ipsa loquitur*

   B. *Trespass quare clausum fregit*

   C. Act of state

   D. *Stare decisis*

3. **Which was not a right delineated in the Bill of Rights?**

   A. Right to free speech

   B. Right to bear arms

   C. Right to safe housing

   D. Right to trial by jury

4. **What doctrine maintains that state laws that interfere with federal laws are invalid pursuant to the supremacy clause?**

   A. States' Rights

   B. Preemption

   C. War Making

   D. Sovereign immunity

5. **Which is not one of the three branches of government in the federal government?**

   A. Legislative branch

   B. Administrative branch

   C. Executive branch

   D. Judicial branch

6. **Congress may override a presidential veto of legislation.**

   A. True

   B. False

7. **The regular term of office for United States senators is:**

   A. Ten years

   B. Two years

   C. Four years

   D. Six years

8. **Members of the United States Supreme Court serve terms of:**

   A. Five years

   B. Ten years

   C. Twenty-five years

   D. Lifetime

9. **The regular term of office for House of Representatives members is:**

   A. One year

   B. Two years

   C. Five years

   D. Six years

10. **The regular term of office for United States president is:**

    A. Four years

    B. Six years

    C. Eight years

    D. Ten years

11. **Presidents of the United States are elected by which method?**

    A. The Electoral College

    B. Lottery

    C. Popular vote

    D. A vote of each state legislature

12. **What is the source of the United States Supreme Court's power of judicial review?**

    A. The Declaration of Independence

    B. *Marbury v. Madison*

    C. *Gideon v. Wainwright*

    D. English common law

© 2019, 2020, 2021 NALA, Inc. All rights reserved.

13. **Which branch of government is constitutionally responsible for enacting laws?**

    A. Legislative

    B. Executive

    C. Department of Agriculture

    D. Judicial

14. **Which branch of government is constitutionally responsible for implementing laws?**

    A. Legislative

    B. Executive

    C. Judicial

    D. Department of Defense

15. **Which branch of government is responsible for interpreting the Constitution?**

    A. Legislative

    B. Department of Agriculture

    C. Executive

    D. Judicial

16. **Which is not a concurrent power which can be exercised by both the federal and state governments?**

    A. Taxation

    B. Establish courts

    C. Eminent domain

    D. Declare war

17. **Which is not a primary source of law?**

    A. Constitutions

    B. Legal digests

    C. Statutes

    D. Case law

18. **Administrative agencies exercise which function in promulgating regulations?**

    A. Quasi-Legislative

    B. Quasi-Executive

    C. Quasi-Judicial

    D. Quasimodo

19. **Administrative agencies exercise which function in enforcing regulations?**

    A.   Quasi-Legislative

    B.   Quasi-Executive

    C.   Quasi-Judicial

    D.   Quasimodo

20. **Which legislation establishes the parties' right to judicial review of administrative action?**

    A.   The Federal Judicial Act

    B.   The Administrative Procedures Act

    C.   The Federal Aviation Act

    D.   The Administrative Omnibus Act

21. **Jurisdiction over a particular person is:**

    A.   Personal jurisdiction

    B.   Subject matter jurisdiction

    C.   Appellate jurisdiction

    D.   Quasi-in rem action

22. **The authority of a court to hear and decide a particular dispute is:**

    A.   Personal jurisdiction

    B.   Subject matter jurisdiction

    C.   Appellate jurisdiction

    D.   Quasi-in rem action

23. **What amount in controversy must be alleged for a federal lawsuit based on diversity jurisdiction?**

    A.   Exceeds $25,000

    B.   Exceeds $35,000

    C.   Exceeds $50,000

    D.   Exceeds $75,000

24. **In a criminal prosecution, proper venue is:**

    A.   The state in which the victim resides

    B.   The state in which the defendant resides

    C.   The locality where the crime occurred

    D.   The locality in which the crime has the most impact

© 2019, 2020, 2021 NALA, Inc. All rights reserved.

25. **Which is not considered a form of alternative dispute resolution?**

    A. Arbitration
    B. Mini-trial
    C. Civil lawsuit
    D. Negotiation

© 2019, 2020, 2021 NALA, Inc. All rights reserved.

Civil Litigation

Written by Deana M. Waters, M.Ed., ACP

© 2019, 2020, 2021 NALA, Inc. All rights reserved.

JURISDICTION

The American government is based on the concept of federalism, or a dual system of government where power is shared between federal and state governments. This dual approach applies to the federal and state judicial systems. In each system, there are trial, appellate, and supreme courts. Deciding whether a claim should be brought in federal or state court depends on subject matter jurisdiction and personal jurisdiction. Jurisdiction is the power of a court to hear a controversy brought before it.

Subject Matter Jurisdiction

Subject matter jurisdiction varies depending on whether the claim is brought in federal or state court, and the subject of the claim. In state courts, a trial court may only hear a certain type of case, such as civil, criminal, or contract. The state court's subject matter may be further limited based on the monetary value of a civil claim or whether the crime was a misdemeanor or felony. There may be other limited courts that hear only certain matters. States also have an appellate or intermediate court that hears appeals from trial courts, and a supreme court. A typical state court system hierarchy may look like this:

<table>
<tr><td colspan="4"><h2 style="text-align:center">Alaska Supreme Court</h2><ul><li>All civil appeals</li><li>Appeals from Court of Criminal Appeals</li><li>Appeals from Workers' Compensation Appeals Commission</li></ul></td></tr>
<tr><td colspan="4">Court of Criminal Appeals
(Intermediate Criminal Appeals)</td></tr>
<tr><td colspan="2">Superior Court</td><td colspan="2">District Court</td></tr>
<tr><td>Civil</td><td>Criminal</td><td>Civil</td><td>Criminal</td></tr>
<tr><td>All domestic relations, probate and real property claims</td><td>Felony or misdemeanor crimes</td><td>Small Claims and evictions</td><td>Misdemeanor crimes</td></tr>
<tr><td>Monetary disputes over $100,000</td><td>Appeals from District Court</td><td>Monetary disputes under $100,000</td><td>Minor violations</td></tr>
<tr><td>Appeals from District Court</td><td></td><td></td><td></td></tr>
<tr><td>Appeals from state administrative agencies</td><td></td><td></td><td></td></tr>
</table>

The federal court system has a similar structure with trial courts that hear the initial claim, circuit courts that hear appeals from trial courts, and the United States Supreme Court. In addition, there are specialty courts at the federal level that exercise specific jurisdiction in bankruptcy, patent or trademark infringement, and Internal Revenue Service claims.

The United States Supreme Court is the highest court in the American legal system. As such, it exercises original jurisdiction in certain matters and has limited jurisdiction in others. Original jurisdiction is a court's power to hear and decide a case before any appellate review. A trial court must necessarily have original jurisdiction over the types of cases it hears. Limited jurisdiction courts can only hear certain types of matters. In the chart above, the civil district court has limited jurisdiction. For matters involving

© 2019, 2020, 2021 NALA, Inc. All rights reserved.

a dispute between states or ambassadors or public officials, the U.S. Supreme Court is the first court to hear the claim. In other claims that may involve a federal question or constitutional issue, the U.S. Supreme Court acts as the final appellate court.

The federal trial courts exercise general jurisdiction and can hear cases arising as a federal issue. General jurisdiction refers to the court's authority to hear any kind of case arising in its geographic area. Federal issues usually deal with a federal law or constitutional issue. In other cases, the federal court may have pendent jurisdiction. Pendent jurisdiction allows a federal court to hear a non-federal, or state claim, provided there is also a federal claim arising out of the same incident. Sometimes a claim is brought in state court and a federal issue emerges. In this situation, the defendant may remove the claim from state court to federal court.

When the claim does not have a federal question, it still may be brought in federal court if there is diversity jurisdiction. There are four categories where diversity jurisdiction is appropriate:

- Between citizens of different states

- Between a citizen of a state and citizens or subjects of a foreign state

- Between citizens of different states and in which citizens or subjects of a foreign state are joined as parties

- Between a foreign state as the plaintiff and citizens of a state or different states

The first category is most often used in diversity jurisdiction. In addition to meeting the citizen requirement, the amount in controversy must exceed $75,000.

In any court, the party bringing the claim must have a genuine controversy for the court to decide. Courts will not hear moot or hypothetical questions and will not give advisory opinions. To bring a claim in federal trial court, the party must have standing. Standing is the legal right to sue. Typically, a plaintiff must have some stake in the controversy. For example, in a personal injury accident, the plaintiff is the party who was injured and suffered damages as the result of the defendant's negligence. The plaintiff's standing to sue for negligence is clear. But in other situations, a party's standing may be muddled. In situations where a party's standing is less clear, the party must prove that they will suffer damage or lose a legal right.

Personal Jurisdiction

Personal jurisdiction refers to the court's power to bring a person before it and make a decision that is binding upon that person. In state courts, a potential defendant must be a resident of the state or judicial district or have significant business connections to the state for that court to have personal jurisdiction. Personal jurisdiction is an element of due process, which is guaranteed in the United States and states' constitutions.

The concept is the same for federal court. In order to bring a defendant to federal court, the person must reside or do business in the federal district. When the defendant does not reside in the judicial district, the court may still exercise personal jurisdiction over the defendant through long-arm statutes. These laws allow a court to reach out past judicial boundaries and bring the defendant into the jurisdiction of the court depending on the quantity and quality of contact the defendant has with the district. An example is a vendor who sells defective merchandise in a state. There are no connections, other than the business contacts, between the vendor and the location. The court may bring the defendant into its personal jurisdiction based on the vendor's purchase of a business license or the payment of taxes within the locale.

Venue

Venue refers to the geographic location of the court. Venue is proper when the claim is brought in the judicial district where the incident occurred, where the defendant resides, or where the defendant may be served the complaint and summons. Venue may be changed on two grounds: inconvenient venue or improper venue. The defendant has the burden of proving that the forum is not proper or is inconvenient.

FEDERAL RULES OF CIVIL PROCEDURE

The Federal Rules of Civil Procedure (FRCP) govern how an action proceeds through the court system. The purpose of uniform rules is to "secure the just, speedy, and inexpensive determination of every action and proceeding" (FRCP 1). Federal district courts may also have local rules that apply only in that jurisdiction. State courts have specific rules regarding actions filed in their jurisdictions.

Parties

Parties are the individuals or entities who are involved in the controversy. The plaintiff is the party who brings the claim, or files the complaint. The defendant is the party who responds to the claim, or files a response to the complaint.

Real Party in Interest

FRCP 17 discusses a real party in interest. A real party in interest is the person who has the right the lawsuit is seeking to enforce. This is the plaintiff. A real party in interest is also the person or entity that the lawsuit is seeking to recover from or order it to perform an act. This is the defendant. While a child, a deceased person, or a ward may be the interested party, their status prohibits them from pursuing an action. In these situations, a person with representative capacity, such as a parent, executor, or guardian, become the real party in interest.

Joinder of Parties

In cases where the real party in interest is not named in the claim, the real party may be joined, or brought into the litigation under FRCP 19 and 20. Joinder of a party is required under Rule 19 if that party's presence is 1) required to grant complete relief, or 2) the party has interest in the litigation such that the party's presence is required to protect those interests. If an indispensable party cannot be served or if joinder would undermine the jurisdiction of the court, the court must decide whether to proceed without the indispensable party or dismiss the case. In making this decision, the court must consider whether a dismissal will prejudice the parties already before it, if an order may minimize the prejudice, if a judgment entered without the absent party can be adequate, and if the plaintiff will have an adequate remedy if the claim is dismissed.

As an example, to illustrate compulsory joinder, consider *Padgett v. Theus*, 484 P. 2d 697 (Alaska 1971). In this unusual case, appellees (party responding to an appeal) Jim and Pearl Theus entered into a somewhat unusual contract with Earl Bell and appellants (party making an appeal) Vern L. Padgett and Investment Enterprises, Inc. The Theuses promised to convey (or transfer) 12 parcels of land to

© 2019, 2020, 2021 NALA, Inc. All rights reserved.

Investment Enterprises. Vern Padgett promised to lend Investment Enterprises $10,000. The corporation in turn promised to transfer one-third of its stock to the Theuses and to lend Jim Theus $10,000. Investment Enterprises further promised to transfer one-third of its stock to Earl Bell, for unstated consideration, and to transfer one-third of its stock to Vern Padgett. When this deal soured, Jim and Pearl Theus sued Vern Padgett and Investment Enterprises. Earl Bell was not named in the suit although he was an "indispensable party" and should have been joined.

Given the late raising of the issue by the appellants and the conduct of Bell, which includes knowing facts of the loan arrangement, participating in settlement negotiations, and testifying at trial, the Alaska Supreme Court declined to set aside judgment because of the failure to join the indispensable party.

A party, whose presence is not required, may still be joined under FRCP 20. Permissive joinder allows a party to be joined in the litigation if there is a question of law or fact common to all parties arising out of the action, and each plaintiff has a right to relief, jointly, severally, or alternatively, against each defendant.

Besides compulsory and permissive joinder, a person may be brought into litigation by interpleader, intervention, or substitution. Interpleader under FRCP 22 allows a person with claims that may cause double or multiple liability to the plaintiff to be joined as defendants. Defendants with a similar liability may join persons as plaintiffs through cross-claims or counterclaims. The court may allow a person to intervene in the litigation. Intervention as a matter of right is allowed when one is given an unconditional right to intervene by federal law or when one claims an interest in the subject of the action and the denial of intervention may impair or impede the person's ability to protect its interest. If a party dies after suit has been filed and that party's claim is not extinguished with death, the court may allow the substitution of a party. Under FRCP 25, a motion to substitute may be made by any party within 90 days after the notification of death. If the right to be enforced survives as against the remaining parties, the action will continue, but will proceed in favor of or against the remaining parties. If a party becomes incompetent during the litigation, the court may permit the substitution of the party's representative, such as a guardian. When the party is a public officer who dies or leaves office during the litigation, the individual's successor is automatically substituted as a party.

Pleadings

While it is typical for practitioners to refer to all documents in a client file as "pleadings," FRCP 7 identifies certain documents specifically as pleadings. Only these pleadings are allowed:

- A complaint

- An answer to a complaint

- An answer to a counterclaim designated as a counterclaim

- An answer to a cross-claim

- A third-party complaint

- An answer to a third-party complaint

- If the court orders one, a reply to an answer

Pleadings are documents that state a claim for relief, either as the initiating plaintiff or as a third-party claimant, or respond to the allegations in a complaint, counterclaim, cross-claim, or third-party complaint. Documents that request the court to issue an order or take some action are motions, motions are discussed later in this chapter.

Every pleading must contain information required by FRCP 10. This includes a caption that identifies the court and its district, the names of the parties, the title of the document, and a file or case number. While not required by the rules, when filing multiple page documents, it is helpful to include a footer that contains this information as well as page numbers for the document. In the complaint at the end of this chapter, note that the court's jurisdiction and location are clearly stated, as is the identity of the parties. The document has a space for a case or file number (here identified as the Cause No.) and the title of the document is clear.

Complaint

A complaint is the document that typically begins the process of civil litigation. The complaint must state the jurisdictional basis showing the court in which the claim is filed has jurisdiction to hear the matter (FRCP 8(a)(1)). As discussed above, federal courts have jurisdiction based upon subject matter or personal jurisdiction. State courts usually have similar jurisdictional requirements.

In addition to stating the jurisdictional basis, a complaint must provide a statement showing that the pleader, or plaintiff, is entitled to the relief sought. This part of the complaint will usually identify enough facts of the incident to put the responding party on notice of who is filing the claim and what specific relief is being requested. In most civil cases, the relief is monetary compensation, but it can also be an order to compel the defendant to act or to refrain from acting. The request for relief can also state alternative forms of relief like injunctive relief or a declaratory judgment (a judgment that defines a legal relationship between parties).

Finally, the complaint must be signed by the attorney representing the party, or by the party if unrepresented. The signature component of a complaint certifies that to the best of the person's knowledge, information, and belief, formed after an inquiry reasonable under the circumstances:

- It is not being presented for any improper purpose, such as to harass, cause unnecessary delay, or needlessly increase the cost of litigation.

- The claims, defenses, and other legal contentions are warranted by existing law or by a nonfrivolous argument for extending, modifying, or reversing existing law or for establishing new law.

- The factual contentions have evidentiary support or, if specifically so identified, will likely have evidentiary support after a reasonable opportunity for further investigation or discovery.

- The denials of factual contentions are warranted on the evidence or, if specifically so identified, are reasonably based on belief or a lack of information (FRCP 11(b)).

Look at the complaint (Appendix A) included at the end of this chapter. In the opening paragraphs, one can see a brief statement of the facts that led to the filing of the complaint (the plaintiff is objecting to a religious statue placed on public land leased to a private organization). Paragraphs three and four detail the jurisdictional basis and venue. Because this is a claim related to a federal matter (i.e., a Constitutional issue) and the subject of the controversy is physically located within the geographical boundaries of the district, the U.S. District Court for Montana has jurisdiction to hear the matter and the venue is proper in this particular court.

Paragraphs six through 15 more specifically identify the plaintiff and defendant in this action. The majority of the complaint provides notice of what action led to the filing of this complaint, what harm

© 2019, 2020, 2021 NALA, Inc. All rights reserved.

has been suffered by the plaintiff, and why the plaintiff is entitled to the requested relief.

The closing paragraphs in this complaint are the plaintiff's request for relief. One will notice the plaintiff is not seeking monetary compensation; rather it is seeking a judgment to declare the religous statue in violation of the Establishment Clause of the Constitution and an order to remove the statue. The plaintiff also requested reasonable attorney fees and costs associated with bringing this action. This form of relief is typically requested in a complaint, and if it is not requested here, a plaintiff waives the right to fees and costs.

Service of Process

Service of process is an essential element of due process. The United States Constitution guarantees due process to citizens through the Fifth Amendment, which states "No person shall…be deprived of life, liberty, or property, without due process of law." This amendment applies to the federal government and has been extended to the states through the 14th Amendment. Due process is the notion that one is entitled to receive adequate notice of a legal proceeding, has the right to appear and defend against claims before an impartial tribunal, and has the right of appeal to a higher court. In a civil action, a defendant risks losing property or the liberty to use that property. The plaintiff is required to provide notice of the claim, including enough facts to inform the defendant of the nature of the claim, and the court must allow the defendant the opportunity to appear and defend against those claims. If service of process is defective in any way, due process is not being satisfied.

After the complaint has been filed with the court and the appropriate filing fee paid, the court will issue a summons. The summons is an order from the court directing the defendant to appear and/or respond to the allegations in the complaint. As such, the summons must identify the court and parties, provide the name and contact information for the plaintiff's attorney (or the plaintiff if unrepresented), state the time period in which the defendant has to appear and respond to the complaint, and notify the defendant of the consequences for failing to appear or respond. Generally, if the defendant does not enter an appearance or respond to the allegations in the complaint, the plaintiff may motion the court to enter a default judgment against the defendant.

There are several options to serve the complaint and summons. The plaintiff is responsible for serving the complaint and summons within the time allowed under FRCP 4(m). This time is usually 90 days. If service is not accomplished or a waiver not filed within that time, the court may dismiss the case without prejudice or order a specific date by which to accomplish service. The plaintiff may request an extension of time to serve the summons and complaint on a showing of good cause.

In most cases, any person over the age of 18 who is not a party to the case may serve the defendant. The plaintiff may request service by United States Marshall or another specially appointed person under FRCP 4(c)(3). When serving an individual, corporation, or association, the plaintiff may notify the defendant that an action has been filed and request a waiver of service by the defendant. The notice and request must be in writing and addressed to the individual, or an officer or agent of the defendant. The notice and request must provide the following:

- Name of the court where the complaint was filed.

- A copy of the complaint, two copies of the waiver form found in FRCP 4, and a prepaid means for returning the form.

- State the consequences of waiving and not waiving service.

- State the date when the request is sent.

- Give the defendant a reasonable time to return the waiver.

The notice and request for waiver must be sent by first-class mail or other reliable means. When the plaintiff files the waiver, service is accomplished. The waiver only waives the time period in which to serve the summons and complaint; it does not waive jurisdiction or venue.

If a waiver is not obtained, the plaintiff may serve an individual, other than a minor or incompetent person, within a judicial district of the United States by following the state laws for service within the state where the federal district is located, or by delivering a copy of the summons and complaint personally to the defendant or leaving a copy at the defendant's usual place of abode. Substitute service, or leaving the summons and complaint with another person of suitable age who also resides at the defendant's usual residence, is acceptable service under the federal rules. When the defendant is a corporation or other business entity, service is usually made on an officer of the business or an agent specifically appointed to accept service on behalf of the corporation.

When the defendant is outside of United States or its territories, service must be made pursuant to an internationally agreed upon means of service that is reasonably calculated to give notice, such as authorized by the Hague Convention. If the foreign country where the defendant is located does not participate in an international agreement regarding service, then service is usually made according to the laws of that country.

Once service is accomplished, the plaintiff must provide the waiver of service or proof of service to the court. Proof of service is typically made by affidavit of the person making the service. From this point to the end of the litigation, all documents filed with court or exchanged between the parties must be served on all parties to the litigation under FRCP 5. In federal court, service of pleadings or motions is fairly easy through the court's electronic filing system. Other documents, such as discovery, notices, or offers of judgment, may be served by delivering or mailing copies to the opposing party. Documents may be served by electronic mail if the party consents to this method of service. Proof of service under Rule 5 is made by a certificate of service embedded in or attached to the served document, or by an affidavit of service accompanying the served document.

Answer

After the summons and complaint are served and the proof of service or waiver filed with the court, the defendant must appear and/or defend against the action. This is usually done by filing an entry of appearance and an answer. Depending on the circumstance, the defendant may enter a limited appearance for the purpose of protesting jurisdiction or venue.

A defendant must serve an answer within 21 days of service of the summons and complaint. If the defendant has waived service, this deadline is extended to 60 days (90 if served outside of the United States) after the notice and request for waiver is sent. If the defendant is the United States or its agencies, officers, or employees sued in their official capacity, the deadline to respond is generally 60 days. There are two ways to respond to a complaint: by a responsive pleading or by a motion.

A defendant must respond to each claim for relief stated in the complaint, or risk having that claim deemed admitted. The answer typically responds to each claim in the complaint, statement by statement. Responses include admit, deny, admit or deny in part, and deny for lack of knowledge. The defendant may also assert affirmative defenses in the answer. An affirmative defense is a fact or set of facts not alleged by the plaintiff that if proven true will defeat or mitigate an allegation by the plaintiff. An affirmative defense must be stated in the answer or it is waived. Examples of affirmative defenses are:

- **Assumption of Risk**: the plaintiff was informed of potential risks and consented to proceed with

 © 2019, 2020, 2021 NALA, Inc. All rights reserved.

action that caused damages.

- **Contributory/Comparative Negligence**: the plaintiff's own negligence contributed to damages.

- **Duress**: the defendant was coerced or forced into an act.

- **Failure to Mitigate Damages**: the plaintiff acted or failed to take an action that would have reduced or eliminated damages.

- *Res Judicata*: the controversy has already been decided by another court.

- **Statute of Frauds**: the contract in dispute is not memorialized in writing.

- **Statute of Limitations**: the plaintiff failed to file a claim within the allowed time.

There are many other affirmative defenses that can be found with a simple internet search. Similar to the FRCP 11 requirements for a complaint, defenses must be grounded in existing law, or there must be a good faith argument for extending, modifying, or reversing the existing law. In addition, denials of factual contentions must be supported by specific evidence or based on a reasonable belief or lack of information.

An answer must include the relief that the defendant is requesting. The relief is typically dismissing the plaintiff's complaint and awarding costs or attorney fees associated with defending the claim. Like complaints, if a request for costs or fees is not included in the answer, this relief will be waived. The defendant may also assert claims against the plaintiff or a co-party by a counterclaim or cross-claim, or bring in another party through a third-party complaint.

Preliminary Motions

A defendant may also challenge a defect in the complaint by filing a motion. These preliminary motions are governed by FRCP 12 and may challenge any of these defects as a response to the complaint:

- Lack of subject matter jurisdiction. Rule 12(b)(1).

- Lack of personal jurisdiction. Rule 12(b)(2).

- Improper venue. Rule 12(b)(3).

- Insufficient process. Rule 12(b)(4).

- Insufficient service of process. Rule 12(b)(5).

- Failure to state a claim upon which relief can be granted. Rule 12(b)(6).

- Failure to join a necessary party under Rule 19. Rule 12(b)(7).

Some defects, such as lack of personal jurisdiction, may be raised at any point in the litigation, while most of the others must be claimed before a responsive pleading is filed or the defect may not be waived. The defendant may also make a Motion for a More Definite Statement or a Motion to Strike. These motions challenge the content, or lack of content, in the complaint.

Any party can bring a Motion for Judgment on the Pleadings, but usually the plaintiff makes the motion. In order to grant this kind of motion, the court must find that the pleadings provide sufficient evidence to render a decision, there are no facts in dispute, and the moving party is entitled to the relief claimed as a matter of law. Motions for Judgment on the Pleadings are rare and are usually brought in contract or declaratory judgment cases. For example, a merchant brings an action to recover a debt from the defendant. The parties had a valid contract. In the answer, the defendant admits that a debt is owed and agrees to the amount owed. There is no factual dispute and the merchant is entitled to the relief requested in the complaint. In this situation, either party may motion the court to enter a judgment in favor of the plaintiff.

Counterclaims and Cross-Claims

A counterclaim may be asserted by the defendant under FRCP 13. The counterclaim may be compulsory or permissive. A compulsory counterclaim must arise out of the same transaction that is the basis for the complaint, and the claim does not require the addition of other parties over whom the court cannot obtain jurisdiction. The defendant is required to raise these claims in the same litigation, or the claim may be barred. For example, Justine Hamilton is injured in a car crash. She sues David Peterson and alleges that he is responsible for her damages. David, who was also injured and incurred damages from the same crash, must counterclaim against Justine if he wants to recover for his injuries. If he does not, his right to bring suit may be extinguished.

A permissive counterclaim is one that may be brought in conjunction with the pending litigation, but the claim does not need to be related to the occurrence giving rise to the underlying complaint. Let us assume David loaned Justine money to purchase a car. After the car crash, Justine was unable to pay back the loan. David may counterclaim in the underlying suit to recover the money that he loaned to Justine.

A coparty may also cross-claim against another coparty under FRCP 13(g). A cross-claim must arise out of the transaction or occurrence that is the subject matter of the original action or of a counterclaim. In our car crash example, assume that Lisa Cooper was a passenger in David's car. Lisa is a bartender at a local club where David had several drinks before the crash. Justine joins Lisa as a defendant; Lisa then sues David for the injuries she sustained because of David's negligence.

Third-Party Claims

A defendant may bring in a third party, who may be liable for some or all of the claims. In this situation the defendant, as a third-party plaintiff, may serve a complaint and summons on a non-party, who becomes the third-party defendant. The defendant/third-party plaintiff must obtain the court's permission to file a third-party claim more than 14 days after the defendant's answer is due.

The third-party defendant:

- Must assert any defense against the third-party plaintiff's claim under Rule 12.

- Must assert any counterclaim against the third-party plaintiff under Rule 13(a), and may assert any counterclaim against the third-party plaintiff under Rule 13(b) or any cross-claim against another third-party defendant under Rule 13(g).

- May assert against the plaintiff any defense that the third-party plaintiff has to the plaintiff's claim.

- May also assert against the plaintiff any claim arising out of the transaction or occurrence that is the subject matter of the plaintiff's claim against the third-party plaintiff(FRCP 14).

The plaintiff may also assert a claim against the third-party defendant arising out of the same transaction or occurrence that is the subject of the underlying claim. To illustrate, recall Justine's claim against David. Assume that David (the defendant) files a third-party complaint against Acme Garage. Acme is the mechanic who replaced David's brakes the day before the accident. Acme then becomes the third-party defendant. Acme may assert the same defenses listed above. Suppose Acme then wanted to sue Fast Brake

 © 2019, 2020, 2021 NALA, Inc. All rights reserved.

Company, who manufactured the brakes installed on David's car. A third-party defendant may bring a claim against a non-party who may be liable for claims against it. For claims asserted against a plaintiff, the plaintiff may also bring in a third-party claim if FRCP 14 would allow a defendant to do so.

Amending Pleadings

In litigation, it may be necessary to amend a pleading. FRCP 15 describes the procedure to change a pleading. Pleadings may be amended early in the litigation as a matter of course. This is usually done with complaints and answers. A party may amend a pleading within 21 days after service of the complaint, responsive pleading, or motion under FRCP 12. For example, in Justine's suit against David, she may amend the complaint within 21 days of service to correct a material fact, such as the location of the accident, the date it occurred, or the extent of her injuries. David may amend his answer within 21 days of service to admit an allegation he previously denied. For all other amendments, the party must obtain the permission of the other party or the court to change a pleading. The time to respond to an amended pleading is usually the time remaining to respond to the original pleading, or 14 days after service, whichever is later.

Discovery

After the defendant answers the complaint, the next phase in litigation begins. This is the discovery phase. Discovery is the process of gathering information that will prove or defeat the claims brought in the complaint, or the defenses asserted in the answer.

The purpose of discovery is to provide each party with the same information so there are no surprises or unknown evidence at trial. It levels the playing field so neither party has a distinct advantage over the other. Prior to the discovery amendments to the rules of civil procedure in 1946, neither party had an obligation to share information with the other. This led to "trial by ambush." Surprise witnesses or evidence that was not known until trial left the opposing party unable to prepare for or rebut the testimony or evidence. While trial by ambush makes for good plot twists in crime dramas, it increased the amount of time spent at trial and decreased the effectiveness of the judicial process. With the advent of formal discovery rules in the late 1940s, each party gathers and shares information in a uniform and systematic way.

The scope of discovery under the federal rules and most state rules is intentionally broad. "Parties may obtain discovery regarding any nonprivileged matter that is relevant to any party's claim or defense. Information within this scope of discovery need not be admissible in evidence to be discoverable" (FRCP 26(b)). Under this section of Rule 26, any information that is not privileged and relevant to the party's claim or defense, but not necessarily admissible, is subject to discovery. This gives a party an almost unlimited range of information it can gather during discovery.

The parties may conduct discovery informally or under the formal rules of civil procedure. Informal discovery consists of investigation or document gathering by a party that does not require the involvement, or even notice, to the other party or the court. Interviewing witnesses, taking photographs, or obtaining documentary evidence are examples of informal discovery. These same tasks can be performed in formal discovery as well. Paralegals may conduct much of the discovery with the appropriate delegation and supervision by the attorney. Many times, the paralegal has a better working knowledge than the attorney of what information has been gathered, what information is missing, who has the information, and how the information pertains to the case. Paralegals are usually responsible for organizing, indexing, and storing the vast amount of discovery that is generated in litigation.

Formal discovery utilizes the methods set out in FRCP 27 through 36. Depositions, interrogatories, requests for production, mental or physical exams, and requests for admission are covered under these rules and will be discussed in more detail below. Formal discovery is directed to the opposing party. Depositions are the only formal discovery that may be used to gather information from non-parties such as a records custodian or a witness. As such, the party receives notice that discovery is occurring and has recourse to judicial oversight if the requesting party is overstepping the bounds of the law. Either party may object to the discovery request or response, in which case the court may have to consider evidence and issue a ruling. Otherwise, the discovery process is largely conducted by the parties.

Discovery Planning

After the answer is served, the court will generally schedule a pretrial conference where the parties will frame the issues to be litigated, plan and schedule discovery, admit or stipulate to facts already known, adopt special procedures for complex litigation, plan and schedule trial, and resolve any other issues that may prevent the speedy and inexpensive disposition of the action. The court will use this information to formulate its pretrial or scheduling order. The scheduling order sets out the various deadlines in the litigation, such as the close of discovery or when witness lists must be filed. This order is usually issued 60 to 90 days after the complaint has been served.

Disclosure of Information

In most jurisdictions, parties have a duty to disclose certain types of information to the other party. Under FRCP 26, unless exempted by other rules, each party must disclose the following: the names and contact information for each individual who may have discoverable information; a copy or description of documents, electronically stored information (ESI), or tangible things that may be used to support the party's claims or defenses; a computation of damages being claimed; and any insurance agreements that may be available to satisfy a potential judgment. Mandatory disclosures are typically exchanged within the time frame established by the court's scheduling order.

The goals of mandatory disclosures of information are to:

- Narrow the scope of litigation early in the case.
- Identify areas for further investigation.
- Identify potential witnesses.
- Frame the issues that are really in dispute.
- Encourage settlement early in the litigation.
- Level the playing field by each party having access to the same information.

Depositions

A deposition is the oral questioning of a party or witness under oath. Depositions are governed by FRCP 27 through 32. The deposition is taken before a court reporter, an officer of the court, or other person authorized by the court. The deposition is recorded, either stenographically, or by audio or video means, and a verbatim transcript of the deposition is prepared by a court reporter. The federal rules limit the number and the length of depositions that can be taken in a federal matter. Deposition testimony may be used at trial to impeach or discredit a witness, or if the deponent is unavailable at trial, to provide that

© 2019, 2020, 2021 NALA, Inc. All rights reserved.

witness's testimony.

The attorney setting the deposition provides written notice to the other party or witness. A non-party's participation may be compelled by a subpoena under FRCP 45. A Notice of Deposition may request that the deponent bring certain documents to the deposition. At the deposition, which may be held at a court reporter's office, the attorney's office, or in the case of an expert, at the expert's office, the deponent is sworn in by the reporter or officer and the questioning begins. Examination and cross-examination proceed similar to trial. The attorney calling the deponent starts the examination. The opposing counsel may then cross-examine the witness. Both attorneys have the opportunity to ask rebuttal questions of the deponent. An attorney may object to a form of questioning, but the witness is generally instructed to respond, unless the response may reveal privileged information. Objections made during a deposition are not heard until shortly before trial when the attorneys may seek a ruling from the court. Occasionally, the attorneys may consult with the judge by phone during the deposition. After the deposition is concluded, a transcript is prepared by a court reporter. The deponent has the opportunity to review the transcript and correct it as necessary. If there are changes to form or substance of the transcript, the deponent must sign a statement identifying the changes.

Written depositions may also be conducted under FRCP 31. This form of discovery is rarely used. In written depositions, questions are provided to the deponent prior to the deposition. At the scheduled deposition, the deponent appears before a court reporter or officer, and answers those questions under oath. The deponent may be subpoenaed and compelled to attend under FRCP 45. Like an oral deposition, the opposing counsel has the opportunity to submit cross-questions to be answered by the deponent. This form of deposition is useful to obtain testimony or gather documents from a records custodian. When planning a written deposition, remember that the deponent has time to craft a response and follow up questions may not be asked during the written deposition.

Depositions are best used to tie a party or witness to specific details. If the deponent varies a response at trial, the deposition may be used to impeach the witness or damage the witness's credibility. Benefits of using a deposition in discovery include the ability to immediately follow up on questions or obtain clarification on the deponent's responses and evaluating the "jury appeal" of a party or witness by examining body language, responses, or habits. Depositions may be used to discover information from a party as well as a non-party witness or records custodian. Testimony that is preserved through a deposition becomes useful if that witness is unavailable at trial. Since a subpoena may command a witness to appear at a deposition within 100 miles of the person's residence or place of employment, depositions may need to be arranged in other locations. Some jurisdictions may allow telephonic participation.

In preparing a client for a deposition, the paralegal should review with the client all previous testimony, depositions, answers to interrogatories, written and oral statements, and any other material that could be used for impeachment, as well as documents that the witness may be asked to identify or authenticate. It is also a good idea to review the probable testimony of other witnesses to see if any inconsistencies may exist. The paralegal or the attorney should counsel deponents to answer only the question asked, to request restating or clarification if the question is unclear, to never argue with the questioning attorney or lose their temper, and to ask for breaks when needed.

Paralegals can assist their attorneys to prepare for depositions by drafting questions to be asked of the deponent and gathering exhibits and documents about which the deponent will be testifying. Paralegals may or may not be asked to attend the deposition with their attorneys. Remember, the paralegal's role is to support the attorney and client. As nonlawyers, paralegals may not question the deponent or participate in the deposition. However, they may pass potential questions to the attorney, keep track of responses and documents, and observe the deponent's performance as a witness.

Interrogatories

Interrogatories are written questions directed to the opposing party who must answer under oath. The responding party has 30 days to respond or object to the interrogatories. The number of interrogatories, including discreet subparts, propounded to each party is limited to 25 by FRCP 33 unless otherwise stipulated or ordered by the Court. State jurisdictions may have a different limit. Interrogatories may be propounded throughout the discovery process, but responses cannot be due after the close of discovery. Careful calendaring is essential. The scope of interrogatories is broad and generally follows FRCP 26. Interrogatories may inquire into any matter that is not privileged, which is relevant to the subject matter involved in the pending action if the information sought appears reasonably calculated to lead to the discovery of admissible evidence.

Interrogatories must be answered by the person to whom they are directed. If the party is a corporation or governmental agency, the interrogatories may be answered by an agent or officer of that entity. The responding party may object to the interrogatory and refuse to respond. The grounds for objections must be stated with specificity. If an objection is not made in the response, it may be deemed waived.

Interrogatories are useful for gathering basic information, such as the identity of parties or witnesses, the identity of any experts and their areas of expertise, and the identity and location of documents, records, or other tangible evidence. Interrogatories may also be used to discover the opposing party's position on disputed evidence. Since the number of interrogatories are limited by court rules, be cautious in using them. Information that could be obtained informally should not be gathered through an interrogatory. Interrogatories may not be the best discovery method to learn detailed facts, impressions of witnesses or parties, or versions of an event. This type of information is better obtained through depositions.

Request for Production

A request for production under FRCP 34 allows a party to request documents, ESI, tangible evidence, or the opportunity to inspect or test property or things. The scope of this rule is similar to other discovery rules–it is broad and allows discovery of information that will lead to admissible evidence. Information that is in a party's possession, custody, or control is subject to this rule. The rule applies to tangible, physical documents and things, as well as information that is generated, transmitted, or stored by electronic means. A party may also request to inspect or test tangible items or request entry to property in the possession or control of the responding party for the purpose of inspecting or testing the property or objects on the property.

A request must describe with "reasonable particularity" the item to be copied or inspected. If a party requests entry upon land, the request must state a reasonable time, place, and manner for the inspection or performing related acts. If the request is for ESI, it should state the form responsive information is to be produced. Unlike interrogatories, there is no limit on the number of requests a party may propound on another. Responses are due within 30 days after service of the request.

When responding to a request for production, the responding party should produce the information as it is kept in the normal course of business. If a form of ESI has not been stated in the request, the responding party may produce the information in its usual form. Typically, the responding party provides copies of documents or ESI, but it may also permit an inspection of the information. If the responding party objects to the production of the information, it may state the specific objection and withhold the information related to the objection.

This rule is often used in conjunction with the deposition of a non-party to obtain documentary or physical evidence in addition to testimony. Similar to a non-party deposition, the responding party can

 © 2019, 2020, 2021 NALA, Inc. All rights reserved.

be compelled to produce documents by a subpoena duces tecum under FRCP 45.

Mental/Physical Exam

When the mental or physical condition (including the blood group) of a party is in controversy, the court may order the party to submit to a physical or mental examination under FRCP 35. The order may be made only upon motion for good cause. Notice of the exam, which specifies the time, place, manner, conditions, and scope of the examination, is given to the person to be examined and to all parties. The scope of the exam must be related to the controversy in litigation.

The report of examiner must contain detailed findings, conclusions, results, diagnoses, and prognosis of the person examined. The examinee may not claim patient-physician privilege as to this exam as it relates to the controversy being litigated. Upon request, the party or person who was examined is entitled to a copy of the physician's report. Conversely, the person examined must also produce prior or later reports related to same condition in controversy, if the party has access to those reports. If the report is not provided, the court may order the party in possession of the report to produce it and may exclude the examiner's testimony at trial if the report is not produced.

Request for Admission

A request for admission is a written request asking the opposing party to admit the truth of matters relating to a fact, the application of law to a fact, an opinion about a fact, or to admit the genuineness of a document. The scope of a request for admission under FRCP 36 is similar to Rule 26. That is, the admission must lead to the discovery of admissible evidence. There is no limit to the number of requests for admission that a party may propound, but the request must fall within the purpose of the matter at hand. If the request relates to the genuineness or authenticity of a document, the questioned document should be attached to the requests.

The responding party has 30 days from the date of service to respond to a request for admission. The party or its attorney must sign the answers. If the party fails to timely respond or object to a request, that request is deemed admitted. The fact, application of law, opinion, or authenticity of a document is conclusively established. This makes a request for admission a powerful tool in the discovery process.

In responding, the party may admit or deny the request. In denying the request, the party must state in detail the basis for the denial. It may also admit in part and deny in part. The party may assert a lack of knowledge as its response, but only after it has made a reasonable inquiry and the information it can obtain is insufficient to answer the request. In objecting to a request, the party specifically state the grounds for the objection.

Failure to Participate in Discovery

When a party fails to participate or resists discovery, FRCP 37 sets out the procedure to compel disclosure or discovery. Rule 37 is broad and provides a remedy for most situations where a party does not cooperate with discovery. This rule is used when a party refuses to participate in discovery process, fails to answer, gives an incomplete or evasive answer, refuses to produce documents, or refuses to permit entry to property. The aggrieved party motions the court for an order to compel the opposing party to disclose information, answer a discovery request, or participate in a deposition. The moving party must certify to the court that they made a good faith effort to obtain discovery without court order.

The court has several sanctions available to remedy the failure of a party to participate. If the court grants the motion to compel discovery, or if the non-complying party produces the information after the filing of a motion to compel, the court may order reasonable attorney fees or other monetary fines to be paid by the non-complying party to the moving party. When a deponent fails to appear at a deposition, the court may find the deponent in contempt of court. If the court denies the motion to compel, it may issue a protective order to the non-complying party preventing the disclosure or discovery. When the non-complying party refuses to participate after the court issues a discovery order, the sanctions become harsher. The court may:

- Allow designated facts to be taken as established for the purposes of the action.
- Prohibit that party from introducing designated matters in evidence.
- Strike the pleadings, dismiss action, or issue default.
- Find party refusing Rule 35 exam in contempt.
- Order attorney's fees to moving party.

Evidence Rules in Discovery

The discovery process, while broad and able to produce various information, still relies on the evidence rules governing civil procedure. In general, Fed. R. Evid. 502 protects privileged information or attorney work product prepared in anticipation of litigation. Privileged information includes confidential communications between an attorney and client, a physician and patient, a husband and wife, or a clergy and parishioner. Fed. R. Evid. 502 protects a litigant from the mandatory disclosure of this type of confidential information. Work product is material that a lawyer (or paralegal) prepares for trial. Examples of work product include pre-suit investigation reports, handwritten notes, or communications with expert witnesses.

Evidence rules pertaining to hearsay apply in discovery. Generally, hearsay is a statement by a declarant that is made outside of the current litigation that a party offers as evidence to prove the truth of the matter asserted in the statement. A witness's prior statement under oath or statement offered against an opposing party are not hearsay (Fed. R. Evid. 803). Fed. R. Evid. 803 and 804 define several exceptions to the general hearsay rule.

Electronically Stored Information (ESI) in Discovery

With the increased use of electronic media to produce, store, or transmit information, practitioners must pay special attention to preserving, collecting, and producing ESI in the discovery process. Mandatory disclosures under FRCP 26 and the discovery methods described in Rules 33 and 34 include ESI. A party has an affirmative duty to preserve potentially relevant ESI when litigation is anticipated. Failure to preserve or produce ESI is subject to sanctions under FRCP 37(e).

Motion Practice

At any time during the litigation process, a party may file a motion seeking an order from the court. A motion is simply a written request to the court to order an action. In motion practice, the moving party will file and serve a motion, which is usually accompanied by a memorandum of law supporting the motion. The responding party has 21 days in which to stipulate or agree with the motion or oppose the motion. An opposition to a motion also includes a memorandum of law. After the opposition is filed and served, the moving party has seven days to reply to the opposition. The reply cannot bring up

 © 2019, 2020, 2021 NALA, Inc. All rights reserved.

new requests or introduce new evidence. Certain dispositive motions, such as a motion for summary judgment, have extended deadlines to oppose and reply. The court may set an oral argument to hear the merits of the motion, or it may decide based solely on the arguments and evidence presented in the documents. The court may grant the motion, in which case, the moving party obtains the relief it requested, or the court may deny the relief requested.

Trial Process

When discovery concludes, the parties prepare for trial. At this point, the litigation team begins coordinating witnesses, compiling exhibits, and developing trial strategy. Most disputes are resolved without trial as discussed below.

Termination Without Trial

There are several ways a case can be terminated without going to trial. The plaintiff may voluntarily dismiss the complaint. This can be done once without prejudice, meaning the claim may be refiled in the future. The plaintiff may file a notice of dismissal before the opposing party answers or files a motion for summary judgment. The parties may have reached an agreement through alternative dispute resolution or decided after mandatory disclosures to dismiss the claim. In this case, the parties stipulate to dismiss the action.

There are several ways to dismiss a claim involuntarily. One is when the plaintiff fails to pursue the action. Other ways to dismiss a claim involuntarily are a Rule 12(b) motion or a judgment on the pleadings, described previously. A variation on these procedures is summary judgment under FRCP 56. To obtain a summary judgment, the moving party must show there is no genuine dispute as to any material fact and that the moving party is entitled to judgment as a matter of law. This motion may be filed at any time during the litigation, but no later than 30 days after the close of discovery. The motion must be supported by "materials in the record, including depositions, documents, ESI, affidavits or declarations, stipulations (including those made for purposes of the motion only), admissions, interrogatory answers, or other materials" (FRCP 56(c)(1)(A)). This information is usually not available until some discovery occurs. After considering the motion, opposition, and supporting evidence in the light most favorable to the non-moving party, the court must determine if there is any genuine dispute for a jury to decide. If there is not, the court will grant summary judgment, ending the litigation. If there is a genuine dispute, the motion is denied and case proceeds to trial.

If the complaint is not dismissed, and the matter proceeds to trial, the court usually schedules a pretrial conference. The purpose of this conference is to confirm the issues in dispute, resolve any disagreements on witnesses, evidence, or other matters, and confirm the trial schedule. FRCP 16 controls both the scheduling conference at the start of litigation and the trial scheduling conference.

At trial, each party presents the testimony and evidence supporting the party's claims or defenses to the jury. The jury, or the judge in a bench trial, decides which facts are true and decides which party should win. The judge will decide what law applies to the case. The verdict will state which party is liable and what amount of money, if any, will be awarded to the prevailing party.

The United States Constitution guarantees a jury trial in the Seventh Amendment. The concept of trial by one's peers dates back to the Magna Carta, and this English law tradition continues in the United States. A party must request a jury trial under FRCP 38. In the demand for jury trial, a party may specify the issues to be tried by a jury. FRCP 48 sets the minimum number of jurors at six and the maximum at 12. Not every case is entitled to a jury. Equity cases or tax court do not permit juries. At the state level, most domestic relation matters are not heard by a jury.

The jury pool is drawn from a representational cross-section of the community where the trial is held. Potential jurors could be selected from voter registration rolls, motor registrations lists, or other sources that could produce a cross-section. Jury selection, or *voir dire*, is the process of determining qualified jurors. Attorneys for each party may question potential jurors as to their knowledge of the parties, the case or the witnesses, or the potential jurors' ability to hear the case impartially. Each party may challenge a potential juror for cause, meaning the juror knows a party, attorney, or prospective witness, or has shown during *voir dire* that the juror cannot be impartial. There is no limit to the number of challenges for cause. Peremptory challenges, on the other hand, are limited to three per party (FRCP 24). A peremptory challenge does not require cause for dismissing the juror. An attorney may want to remove individuals who support a particular cause or who are politically conservative. In other cases, the attorney may want sympathetic jurors who have experiences similar to a party in the case at trial. For example, in a personal injury case, the plaintiff's attorney would want a juror who has been involved in an accident before, while the defense would want this juror removed from the panel. The defense could remove this juror with a peremptory challenge. However, a juror may not be removed by peremptory challenge solely on the basis of a protected characteristic, such as race, nationality, or gender, under *Batson v. Kentucky*, 476 U.S. 79 (1986).

After jury selection, the parties present their opening statements. The opening statement explains the background of the claim or defense, how the evidence will be presented, and what it will prove. Attorneys may not argue the merits of their case in the opening statement. The plaintiff's attorney makes a statement first, followed by the defense. The opening statement is crucial to prepare the jury for what to expect during the presentation of evidence. Paralegals may outline an opening statement or prepare an audiovisual presentation to show the jury.

When opening statements are completed, the plaintiff's attorney presents evidence and testimony. This is direct examination. During direct examination, the attorney questions the witness to set the foundation for the introduction of admissible evidence and present facts to the jury. The defense then has the opportunity to question a witness, which is called cross-examination. If the testimony reveals facts that were not covered in the direct examination, the plaintiff's attorney may redirect. If a redirect occurs, the defendant's attorney may re-cross-examine the witness. After the presentation of its evidence, the plaintiff rests. The defendant's attorney presents testimony and evidence using the same pattern of direct, cross, redirect, and re-cross examination. If new evidence is raised during the defenses presentation of evidence, the plaintiff may present evidence in rebuttal. During this phase of trial, witnesses testify and lay a foundation for the admissibility of proposed exhibits. Many times, it is the paralegal's role to track admitted or withdrawn exhibits, to pass documents to the attorney during questioning a witness, and to observe the demeanor of the jury as testimony is presented.

Once each party has presented its case-in-chief, they may present closing arguments to the jury. During closing, an attorney may argue the strength of its case or the weakness of the opposing party's evidence. This is the point in trial where attorneys may appeal to the emotions of the jurors and use their power of persuasion to convince a juror to rule in their favor. Again, a paralegal may assist in drafting a closing argument or preparing an audiovisual presentation for the jury.

After each party has rested, the court will instruct the jury on the law to be applied in the case. Usually, each party will propose jury instructions before the trial starts and the judge will decide what instructions will ultimately be given to the jury. The instructions may include how the jury is to weigh evidence, determine witness credibility, or establish the burden of proof for the particular case. Jurors may also be instructed to not speak about the case or research facts on their own.

© 2019, 2020, 2021 NALA, Inc. All rights reserved.

The burden of proof in most civil matters is a preponderance of the evidence. This is a far lower standard than "beyond a reasonable doubt" used in criminal trials. To be proved by a preponderance of the evidence, the jury must believe the matter is more likely true than not true. This standard is often illustrated by an example of tipping scales. At the start of trial, both sides of the scales are even. At the end of trial, the jury may believe the evidence presented by one party outweighs the evidence presented by the other and determine the scales have tipped in favor of the party with the most convincing evidence.

After the jury is charged, or given instructions, it meets in private to deliberate and reach a verdict. In most civil cases, a majority decision of the jury is sufficient to find for one party or the other. A jury may return a general verdict, which simply identifies the prevailing party, or it may return a special verdict, which provides a written finding for each allegation of the case. The type of verdict depends on the jury instructions issued by the court. When the jury returns a verdict, the court issues a judgment. This is usually a final judgment and is appealable to a higher court. The judgment becomes part of the official record and is the last action taken in the case.

As a final judgment, the prevailing party can enforce the judgment, usually after time to request a new trial or file an appeal has passed. In most civil actions, the judgment identifies the prevailing party, the outcome of the trial, and the amount of money owed by the non-prevailing party. The judgment does not state a time period in which to pay the judgment.

If the judgment-debtor (non-prevailing party) does not voluntarily pay judgment, the judgment-creditor (the prevailing party) may obtain a writ of execution to levy (collect by legal authority) against the personal property or assets of the debtor. FRCP 64 describes the procedures for enforcement of judgments and follows the execution procedures of state where the federal court is located. Remedies include garnishment of debtor's bank accounts or wages, seizing assets such as personal or real property, or seizing the debtor. FRCP 69 discusses the procedure to conduct post-trial discovery to determine the location or amount of assets available to satisfy the judgment. If the debtor has no assets, the individual is said to be judgment proof. Once the judgment has been paid in full, either voluntarily or through execution, a satisfaction of judgment is filed with the court.

Appeal Process

Either party may appeal the final trial court judgment to the appellate court. In the federal system, a judgment from the U.S. District Court (trial court) or decisions from administrative agencies are appealed to the U.S. Circuit Court of Appeals. There are 13 circuit courts that hear appeals from the trial courts in the United States, U.S. Territories, and Washington D.C. Sometimes the losing party believes the court committed an error that prejudiced the outcome. Sometimes the winning party was not awarded as much as they think they should have won. In some state courts, requesting a new trial is the first step in the appeal process; this is not the case in federal court. In an appeal, the party bringing the appeal is the appellant and the party defending against the appeal is the appellee.

The first step in appeal is to file a notice of appeal within 30 days of entry of the final judgment, or 30 days after a motion under Rules 50, 52, or 59 are denied per Fed. R. App. P. 4(a)(4). The other party may file a cross appeal within 14 days after the notice of appeal is filed. The appellee may motion the trial court for a stay of the judgment issued by that court, or for an order suspending or modifying an injunction while the appeal is pending under Fed. R. App. P. 8. If the stay is granted, the appellant may be required to pay a supersedeas bond or other form of security. This ensures the prevailing party will be paid if the appellant loses the appeal.

The scope of appellate review may be de novo, de novo on the record, or on the record. De novo review is typically performed in appeals from a court or agency where there is no record. The appellate court tries the case as if there were no prior proceedings. Witnesses are allowed, and evidence is taken. In this type of review, the appellate court is not bound by any findings or conclusions from the lower court or agency.

In de novo on the record appeals, the appellate court's review is limited to record of the trial court. The appellate court does not hear witnesses or consider new evidence. The record is reviewed to ensure the trial court's decision was not "clearly erroneous." Most appeals from state trial courts fall under this category of review.

On the record review is usually done with appeals from administrative agencies. In these appeals, the findings of fact reached by the lower court (or agency) are given greater deference. However, the appellate court is not bound by the conclusions of law in this type of review.

After the appeal is filed, the record from the trial court is prepared. The record consists of the pleadings, transcript of testimony and proceedings, admitted exhibits and docket entries, or orders. Sometimes a surety or bond must be deposited with the appellate court.

Fed. R. App. P. 28 dictates the format and contents of the briefs filed by the appellant and appellee. The appellant's brief includes a table of authorities, a jurisdictional statement, statement of issues on appeal, the procedural history of the case, a statement of facts relevant to the issues on appeal, and the legal argument supporting the appeal. Also included in the appellant's brief is the standard of review the appellate court is being asked to use. The basis for the standard of review include procedural errors, such as objections that were improperly ruled upon, or admitting evidence that was prejudicial, or the incorrect application of law. The appellant files the brief first, followed by the appellee. The appellee's brief is similar to appellant's brief as to the contents of the document.

If there is a procedural defect with the appeal, such as untimely notice of appeal or failure to file a record, the appellate court may dismiss the appeal. Otherwise, the appellate court reviews the appeal and makes its disposition. The appellate court may affirm the lower court's decision. That is, it finds no error with the lower court's application of law and no procedural errors were made by the trial court. Most appeals are disposed of this way.

The appellate court may reverse the lower court's decision. If the appellate court determines the lower court's findings of fact are clearly erroneous, the law was misapplied, or there were prejudicial errors, it may change the lower court's decision. In some appeals, the appellate court may reverse a portion of the trial court decision and remand the matter back to the trial court for further proceedings.

Paralegals involved in appellate practice may be responsible for arranging the trial transcript or reviewing the trial court record. They may also research the law and assist in drafting briefs.

© 2019, 2020, 2021 NALA, Inc. All rights reserved.

APPENDIX A

Richard L. Bolton, Esq.
Boardman & Clark, LLP
1 South Pinckney Street, 4th Floor
P.O. Box 927
Madison, WI 53701-0927
Telephone: (608) 257-9521
Facsimile: (608) 283-1709
Email: rbolton@boardmanclark.com
(Pro Hac Vice Pending)

Martin S. King, Esq.
Reid J. Perkins, Esq.
Worden Thane P.C.
111 North Higgins, Suite 600
P.O. Box 4747
Missoula, MT 59806
Telephone: (406) 721-3400
Facsimile: (406) 721-6985
Email: mking@wthlaw.net
Email: rperkins@wthlaw.net

Attorneys for Plaintiff

IN THE UNITED STATES DISTRICT COURT
FOR THE DISTRICT OF MONTANA
MISSOULA DIVISION

FREEDOM FROM RELIGION FOUNDATION, INC., a Wisconsin non-profit corporation
 	
        Plaintiff,
 	
    vs.
 	
CHIP WEBER, Flathead National Forest Supervisor, UNITED STATES FOREST SERVICE, An Agency of the United States Department of Agriculture
 	
        Defendants.
	Cause No. _____
	
	COMPLAINT

The plaintiff, Freedom From Religion Foundation, Inc., alleges as its Complaint:

Complaint   1

© 2019, 2020, 2021 NALA, Inc. All rights reserved.

1.   This is an action by plaintiff brought against the defendant alleging violation of the Establishment Clause of the First Amendment to the United States Constitution.

2.   The plaintiff seeks a declaration under 28 U.S.C. §2201 that the continued authorization to put a six-foot tall statue of Jesus Christ in the Flathead National Forest, on a 25 by 25 foot plot of land owned and administered by the United States Forest Service, violates the Establishment Clause of the First Amendment to the Constitution of the United States.   Plaintiff further requests the Court to enjoin the defendant from continuing to allow the statue of Jesus Christ, a patently religious figure, to remain on land owned and administered by the Forest Service.

3.   The Court has federal question subject matter jurisdiction pursuant to 28 U.S.C. §1331. The Court also has the authority to issue a declaratory judgment under 28 U.S.C. §2202. The Court further has the authority to order injunctive relief under 28 U.S.C. §1343 and F.R.C.P. 65.

4.   Venue is appropriate in the District Court for the District of Montana, pursuant to 28 U.S.C. §1391, because the defendant resides within this judicial district and because the actions giving rise to the claims occurred within the district.

5.   The United States has waived sovereign immunity pursuant to 5 U.S.C. §702.

6.   The plaintiff, Freedom From Religion Foundation, Inc. ("FFRF"), is a non-profit corporation organized under the laws of the state of Wisconsin that advocates for the separation of church and state and educates on matters of non-theism.

7.   FFRF has more than 17,000 members, residing in every state of the United States and the District of Columbia, including more than 100 members in the State of Montana.

8.   FFRF represents and advocates on behalf of its members throughout the United

Complaint   2

                                       © 2019, 2020, 2021 NALA, Inc. All rights reserved.

States.

9.   FFRF's membership includes individuals who have had direct and unwanted
exposure to the statue of Jesus Christ in the Flathead National Forest, and such members will have
direct and unwelcome exposure to the statue of Jesus in the future, as frequenters of the Flathead
National Forest, more specifically at the location on Big Mountain, near Whitefish Mountain
Resort's Chair Two, site of the Jesus statue; other members of FFRF have altered their conduct to
avoid Big Mountain because of the Jesus statue.

10.   The defendant, Chip Weber, is the Forest Supervisor for the Flathead National
Forest, with a principal office located at 650 Wolfpack Way, Kalispell, Montana 59901.

11.   The defendant's office is located within the geographic authority of the District
Court for the District of Montana.

12.   The defendant is an employee of the United States Forest Service, an agency of the
United States Department of Agriculture; he has been authorized and delegated authority to take
the actions complained of in his official capacity.

13.   Tom Tidwell is the United States Forest Service Chief.

14.   Tom Vilsack is the Secretary of the United States Department of Agriculture.

15.   The United States Forest Service manages public lands owned and administered by
the United States.

16.   The Flathead National Forest is owned and administered by the United States
Forest Service.

17.   The Flathead National Forest, including Big Mountain, lies in the heart of the
Rocky Mountains, west of the Continental Divide and just south of the Canadian border.

18.   The Flathead National Forest is a premier destination for visitors looking to

Complaint   3

experience natural landscapes of the American West, according to the Forest Service.

19.   Despite the fact that Big Mountain was, and remains, owned and administered by the United States Forest Service, the Knights of Columbus applied for a permit to erect a religious shrine overlooking the Big Mountain ski run, in 1953.

20.   The Knights of Columbus application stated that the applicant "proposes to erect a Statue of our Lord Jesus Christ" on public land owned by the Forest Service.

21.   The idea for a shrine at the top of a ski run originated with requests from Catholic skiers for such a religious shrine; the Knights of Columbus then pushed the idea forward to eventual dedication on Big Mountain, as reported in contemporaneous sources.

22.   The Knights of Columbus is an exclusively Roman Catholic organization for which "church-related activities are central to our [its] work as an organization of Catholic laymen."

23.   Membership in the Knights of Columbus is limited to practicing male Catholics who "accept the teaching authority of the Catholic church on matters of faith and morals, aspire to live in accord with the precepts of the Catholic church, and are in good standing in the Catholic church."

24.   The Knights of Columbus has placed religious shrines at locations throughout the United States, including on its own extensive real estate holdings.

25.   The Forest Service granted the application of the Knights of Columbus on October 15, 1953, authorizing the Knights to erect a religious shrine on public land without payment.

26.   The Forest Service has continued thereafter to sanction without payment the prominent presence of the six-foot statue of Jesus Christ overlooking the Big Mountain ski run since 1954.

Complaint   4

   © 2019, 2020, 2021 NALA, Inc. All rights reserved.

27.   As recently as February 3, 2000, the Forest Service authorized the Knights of Columbus to continue "to provide a site for a religious shrine" on Big Mountain.

28.   After objection by FFRF to the Forest Service's authorization of a religious shrine on public land, however, the defendant determined in 2011 that the placement of the statue of Jesus Christ on Big Mountain is indeed inappropriate and must be removed.

29.   The Forest Service decision on August 24, 2011, "had to do with the large number of Supreme Court decisions and recent case law that set the precedent regarding monuments with religious themes or icons with religious themes."

30.   The defendant decided after careful consideration that authorization of a religious shrine conflicted with Supreme Court decisions prohibiting such religious displays on public land.

31.   The defendant concluded in his decision letter of August 24, 2011, that the statue of Jesus Christ should be removed from public land no later than October 31, 2012.

32.   The defendant immediately faced criticism from religious groups; supporters of the religious shrine on Big Mountain tried to overwhelm the defendant with opposition to his decision, including intense lobbying by United States Representative Denny Rehberg, replete with public rallies at the base of the Jesus statue.

33.   Mr. Weber gave in to the pressure exerted by advocates of the Christ statue, and on October 21, 2011, the defendant withdrew his earlier decision of August 24, 2011, and announced plans by the Forest Service to formally assess public sentiment for re-authorizing the religious shrine on Big Mountain.

34.   Representative Rehberg applauded the defendant's about-face, noting that "public outcry from the community -- and the entire country -- can be a remarkable lubricant for getting the wheels of government turning."

Complaint   5

© 2019, 2020, 2021 NALA, Inc. All rights reserved.

35.   The defendant's capitulation to supporters of the Christ statue followed with unconvincing rationales being advanced by the Forest Service to justify the continued presence of this religious shrine on public property.

36.   In the defendant's letter of October 21, 2011, withdrawing his earlier decision, Mr. Weber referred to "new information" indicating that the Jesus statue is eligible for listing on the National Historic Register.

37.   The Forest Service, however, actually first suggested the "new information," to the Montana State Historic Preservation Office, in a letter dated September 1, 2011, wherein the Forest Service requested that the Montana Historic Preservation Office "concur" in a statement that the statue of Jesus was eligible for listing on the National Register of Historic Places.

38.   The Forest Service letter of September 1, 2011, candidly describes the religious history of the shrine at issue:

> The statue was emplaced on Big Mountain and dedicated on September 5, 1954, by the Knights of Columbus (K of C). The Knights chose to put a shrine in the area after being approached by Winter Sports, Inc. (WSI) and some participants in the 1949 and 1951 National Ski Championships, which took place at Big Mountain. Many of the skiers were veterans of the fighting in Europe in WWII, where they observed many such shrines and thought there should be one here as well. The statue is located on FS-administered lands under a Special Use Permit first issued to the K of C in 1953 for a spot of ground measuring 25 feet by 25 feet. According to the permit application, the Knights wished to "erect a shrine overlooking Big Mountain ski run." A committee was formed, led by L. J. Reed, to select a site and design a shrine and then have it erected. Other members of the committee were Frank Davis, Wayne Dirkson, Charles Smith, Ed Lyonais, Kenneth O'Brien, Bud Drew, Curtiss Barnhardt, Fred Dennis, Charles Rogers, Tony Hecimovitch, and Father Cronin. The Knights first approached Winter Sports about placing the shrine within the Village, but after being turned-down by WSI, they turned to the Forest Service for a permit to place the shrine near the top of the ski runs. The final location was chosen because of its spectacular views over the valley below and for its proximity to the original

Complaint   6

© 2019, 2020, 2021 NALA, Inc. All rights reserved.

main lift and run.

39.   The Forest Service letter to the Montana Historic Preservation Office further acknowledges that monuments and religious properties are not eligible for listing on the National Register of Historic Places if associated with important persons or events or religious values: "The statue of Jesus cannot be considered eligible for its association either with the soldiers who fought in WWII, nor for its association with Jesus."

40.   The Forest Service, therefore, proposed to the Montana Historic Preservation Office that the statue be deemed to have no association with Jesus or WWII veterans.

41.   The Forest Service suggested instead that the Jesus statue be re-characterized as something other than a religious shrine or a war memorial.

42.   Following the lead of the Forest Service, the Montana State Historic Preservation Office "concurred" that the Jesus shrine "is not believed to be a religious site because unlike Lourdes or Fatima, people do not go there to pray."

43.   Advocates of the religious shrine then responded zealously to the Forest Service's request for public comment, with the American Center for Law and Justice, a conservative Christian advocacy organization, submitting more than 70,000 names of supporters; Representative Rehberg also submitted approximately 10,000 comments he solicited through his "VeteransJesus.com" website.

44.   The defendant also received many comments opposing religious monuments on public land, including from FFRF.

45.   The defendant subsequently tallied up the support for the Jesus shrine and issued a new decision on January 31, 2012; the defendant's written decision principally rejected non-existent environmental issues that no one had raised.

Complaint   7

46.   The defendant's decision reauthorized the special use permit to the Knights of Columbus so as to maintain "a statue of Jesus Christ located on National Forest land near the top of Chair #2 within the Whitefish Mountain Resort permit boundary."

47.   The defendant omitted from his decision any discussion or explanation of the Supreme Court precedent prohibiting religious monuments on public land, which decisions he previously relied on as the basis for non-renewal of the Jesus permit.

48.   The self-executing prohibitions of the Establishment Clause, in fact, are not contingent on public opinion polls orchestrated by federal officials as to whether to obey the Constitution.

49.   The continued presence of the Jesus shrine on Forest Service property, therefore, violates the Establishment Clause of the First Amendment to the United States Constitution by giving the appearance of the government's endorsement of Christianity in general, and Roman Catholicism, in particular; the defendant's actions also diminish the civil and political standing of non-religious and non-Christian Americans and constitutes governmental preference for religion and Christianity.

50.   The continued presence of the statue of Jesus Christ, intended as a religious shrine, gives the unmistakable appearance of governmental endorsement of religion, as does the defendant's orchestrated justification for maintaining a religious monument on public land.

51.   The presence of a religious shrine on federal property constitutes governmental approval of an inherently religious message.

52.   The actions of Mr. Weber, in perpetuating a religious shrine on federal property, give the public appearance of government endorsement of religion, including an unmistakable symbolic link between the government and religion.

Complaint   8

© 2019, 2020, 2021 NALA, Inc. All rights reserved.

53.   The defendant's actions violate the fundamental principle of the separation of church and state by impermissibly advancing, endorsing and promoting the establishment of religion in violation of the United States Constitution.

54.   The actions of Mr. Weber in contriving to justify the Jesus shrine on federal property, in response to public opinion, further violates and makes a sham of the Establishment Clause protections.

55.   The Establishment Clause prohibits governmental endorsement of religion, even on a majoritarian basis; the Establishment Clause protects the liberty of conscience of minorities, including the consciences of non-believers, who constitute at least 15% of the United States population.

56.   The Establishment Clause, moreover, is violated by governmental endorsement of religion even in respect to religious shrines of longstanding on public lands.

57.   The plaintiff, FFRF, for its part, includes members who are non-believers opposed to such government endorsement of religion.

58.   Members of FFRF include persons who would have standing individually to object to the defendant's endorsement of religion in this case, based upon their past and prospective exposure to the figure of Jesus Christ on Forest Service property, as well as based on the decisions of individual members of FFRF to forego activities on Big Mountain in order to avoid the Jesus shrine.

59.   The actions of the defendant in violating the Establishment Clause are injurious to the interests of the plaintiff FFRF, and to its members, and warrant relief from the Court.

WHEREFORE, the plaintiff demands judgment as follows:

A.   Declaring that the religious shrine, including a statue of Jesus Christ, on United

Complaint   9

States Forest Service property violates the Establishment Clause of the United States Constitution;

B.   Ordering the defendant to withdraw approval for the Knights of Columbus to keep a religious shrine with a statue of Jesus Christ on Forest Service property;

C.   Ordering the defendant to direct the Knights of Columbus to remove the religious shrine from Forest Service property;

D.   Awarding plaintiff its reasonable costs and disbursements of this action, as allowed by law; and

E.   Ordering such further relief as the Court deems just and equitable.

Dated this _8th_ day of February, 2012.

Martin S. King, Esq.
Reid J. Perkins, Esq.
Worden Thane P.C.
111 North Higgins, Suite 600
P. O. Box 4747
Missoula, MT   59806
Telephone: (406) 721-3400
Facsimile: (406) 721-6985

Richard L. Bolton, Esq.
Boardman & Clark LLP
1 South Pinckney Street, 4th Floor
Madison, WI   53701-0927
Telephone: (608) 257-9521
Facsimile: (608) 283-1709

Attorneys for the Plaintiff

F:\DOCS\WD\9999\960\A1338530.RTF

Complaint   10

© 2019, 2020, 2021 NALA, Inc. All rights reserved.

11/20

1. **In most civil cases, the burden of proof is:**

   A. Preponderance of the evidence

   B. Clear and convincing evidence

   C. Beyond a reasonable doubt

2. **Under FRCP 36, if a party served with a request for admissions does not respond within 30 days, the fact(s) involved are deemed to have been:**

   A. Admitted

   B. Admissible

   C. Denied

   D. Expunged

3. **After a complaint is filed with the clerk of court, it is essential that the defendant or defendants be notified of the claim and be advised how much time is allowed to file an answer. This is accomplished by serving a copy of the complaint on the defendant(s) along with a:**

   A. Subpoena

   B. Summons

   C. Affidavit

   D. Proof of service

4. **Which federal civil rule lists the affirmative defenses to a pleading?**

   A. FRCP 6

   B. FRCP 8

   C. FRCP 10

   D. FRCP 12

5. **An affirmative defense is a fact or set of facts other than those alleged by the plaintiff which, if proven by the defendant, defeats or mitigates the legal consequences of the defendant's otherwise unlawful conduct. Which of the following is not an affirmative defense?**

   A. Contributory negligence

   B. *Res judicata*

   C. *Respondeat superior*

   D. Statute of limitations

6. The sanctions stated in FRCP 37 for failing to cooperate with discovery provide a trial judge with the authority to penalize a litigant who routinely ignores an opponent's requests for discovery. Which of the following is the harshest sanction?

   A. Court may dismiss case.

   B. Court may strike a pleading.

   C. Court may issue a protective order.

   D. Court may prevent introduction of evidence.

7. Which motion asks the court to enter judgment as a matter of law if the moving party proves there is no genuine dispute as to any material fact and is entitled to the relief requested?

   A. Motion for directed verdict

   B. Motion in limine

   C. Motion to show cause

   D. Motion for summary judgment

8. What is a brief speech made by the attorneys for the plaintiff and the defendant where they outline what will happen in the case and what evidence the jury can expect to see?

   A. Closing argument

   B. Cross-examination

   C. Direct examination

   D. Opening statement

9. Which discovery method may be used for party and non-party witnesses?

   A. Deposition

   B. Interrogatories

   C. Mental/physical exam

   D. Request for Admission

   E. Request for Production

10. If a case primarily involves issues that are controlled by state law, but there also exists a "federal issue" which is inextricably intertwined with the "state law" issues, the federal court may accept the case under what is called:

    A. Personal jurisdiction

    B. Supplemental jurisdiction

    C. Subject matter jurisdiction

    D. Original jurisdiction

© 2019, 2020, 2021 NALA, Inc. All rights reserved.

11. During *voir dire,* an attorney may remove a prospective jury member using a peremptory challenge for the following reason:

    A.   The attorney believes the juror is biased.

    B.   The juror knows a party.

    C.   The juror is a certain race, religion, or gender.

    D.   The attorney believes the juror is uneducated.

12. What motion is filed if you want the court to act on a case where the defendant had failed to answer the complaint?

    A.   Motion to Compel

    B.   Motion for Default

    C.   Motion to Strike

    D.   Motion for Summary Judgment

13. What do you call a response to a counterclaim?

    A.   Answer

    B.   Cross-claim

    C.   Reply

    D.   Third-party answer

14. What type of verdict provides the jury's findings as to each issue in dispute?

    A.   Directed verdict

    B.   General verdict

    C.   Special verdict

    D.   Unanimous verdict

15. Which party has the burden of proving an affirmative defense?

    A.   The defendant

    B.   The plaintiff

    C.   Neither party

    D.   Both parties

16. Which is not a goal of a trial scheduling conference?

    A.   Confirm issues in dispute

    B.   Challenge jurors

    C.   Confirm trial schedule

    D.   Resolve evidentiary disputes

© 2019, 2020, 2021 NALA, Inc. All rights reserved.

17. **In a trial, one of the last actions the court performs is:**

    A. Hear closing arguments

    B. Issue jury charge and instructions

    C. Rule on evidentiary challenges

    D. Issue a final judgment

18. **Which type of joinder allows a party to join the litigation if there is a common question of law or fact, and each plaintiff has a right to relief?**

    A. Compulsory joinder

    B. Discretionary joinder

    C. Intervening joinder

    D. Permissive joinder

19. **Substitution of parties is not appropriate when:**

    A. A party dies after the complaint is filed.

    B. A party lacks standing.

    C. A party becomes incompetent or incapacitated after the complaint is filed.

    D. A party who is public official loses reelection.

20. **What is a person whose interest in the controversy before the court is such that the court cannot render an equitable judgment without having jurisdiction over that party?**

    A. An indispensable party

    B. A dispensable party

    C. A permissive party

    D. A third party

© 2019, 2020, 2021 NALA, Inc. All rights reserved.

CHAPTER 3

Contracts

Written by Jeanie C. Johnson, ACP

© 2019, 2020, 2021 NALA, Inc. All rights reserved.

A paralegal's skill set should include an understanding of contracts. After completion of this chapter, paralegals will be able to explain the six elements involved in the formation of contracts, the classification and types of contracts, parties' contractual obligations and rights, and the enforceability of contracts. Further, ethical considerations for paralegals with an emphasis on contracts will also be discussed. This chapter will also stress an understanding of relevant contract terminology.

WHAT IS A CONTRACT?

A contract is defined as "an agreement with specific terms between two or more persons or entities in which there is a promise to do something in return for a valuable benefit known as consideration." There are several ways to form a contract: 1) express, 2) implied, or 3) quasi-contract. There are also six elements to a contract which include: 1) offer, 2) acceptance, 3) consideration, 4) mutuality of obligation, 5) competency and capacity, and in certain circumstances, 6) a written instrument.

Formation of a Contract

Contracts can be formed by specific words, either oral or written. This type of contract is known as an express contract. An implied contract is an agreement created by actions of the parties, but it is not written or spoken.

Example:

> Marty takes his dog to the veterinarian. The veterinarian's actions suggest that she will do her best to examine and treat Marty's dog in exchange for the payment of a fee. Marty's actions indicated that he intends to receive treatment for his dog in payment of a fee to the veterinarian.

Another type of contract is a quasi-contract. A quasi-contract is a binding obligation that is imposed by the Courts to avoid injustice or unjust enrichment. A quasi-contract occurs in situations in which there is an obligation under a contract, although the elements of the contract have not been fulfilled.

Example:

> Sally orders a pizza to be delivered to her and she pays for the pizza prior to delivery. The pizza is delivered to another house and someone else enjoys Sally's pizza. In this situation, a quasi-contract could be initiated. The pizzeria could be court ordered to reimburse Sally for the amount she paid for the pizza.

Offer

An offer is a promise to act or refrain from acting in exchange for a return promise to do the same. The offer must be an objective expression of a promise. The offer must be communicated to the offeree. The offeror is the party to the agreement that makes the offer. The offeree is the party to the contract who either accepts or rejects the offer. The terms of the offer must be definite and certain and are called the "Essential Terms." The Essential Terms of an offer include: identity of the offeree and subject matter, the price to be paid and the time of payment, delivery or performance, the quantity involved, and the nature

 © 2019, 2020, 2021 NALA, Inc. All rights reserved.

of the work to be performed.

Examples:

> Dave owns a car that needs painting. Mike, a painter, offers to paint Dave's car for $500. The offer is conditioned on Dave paying Mike the $500 upon completion of the job.
>
> Dave offers to pay Mike $500 to paint his car and is conditioned on Mike successfully performing the job.

In either example listed above, the offeree's power of acceptance is formed when the offeror delivers an intent to enter a contract in certain and definite terms that are conveyed to the offeree.

On the other hand, no contract is formed when parties to preliminary negotiations respond to each other's invitations and requests. Advertisements, catalogs, brochures, and announcements to the public related to the sale of merchandise at a specified price are not considered offers to enter into a binding contract, rather they are considered invitations to make a deal. If an advertisement were considered an offer, the seller of the advertised goods and services would be accountable for limitless contracts with customers who view the advertisement or read the catalog.

The rejection of an offer terminates the offeree's power of acceptance and ends the offeror's liability for the offer. A rejection of an offer may be in the form of an expressed refusal to accept or an implied refusal. An express refusal to accept an offer is one that is made verbally or in writing expressly rejecting the offer.

Example:

> Lou makes an offer to Chris to buy his motorcycle. Chris calls Lou on the phone and rejects the offer. This is an express refusal to accept an offer. An example of an implied refusal is if the offeree makes a counteroffer that is materially different than the original offer.

Most jurisdictions recognize the offeror's right to withdraw or revoke the offer as a reasonable means of terminating the offer.

Offers that are not rejected, withdrawn, or revoked usually continue until the specified time has elapsed. If there is no time limit specified on how long an offer is good for, the offer is rejected, withdrawn, or revoked when a reasonable time has elapsed. When trying to determine what a reasonable time would be, courts try and determine what a reasonable person would consider sufficient.

Acceptance

Acceptance of an offer is the express agreement to its terms. The offer generally sets out the manner of acceptance, however, if the offer is silent on the manner of acceptance, then it may be made in a manner reasonable under the circumstances. An acceptance is only valid if the offeree knows the offer, the offeree demonstrates an intention to accept, and the acceptance is expressed as an indisputable and absolute agreement to the terms of the offer.

An offer of acceptance can be made in a variety of ways including: in writing, by phone, in person, or even by handshake. An offer may specify a method of acceptance. If the terms of the offer are silent on the method of acceptance of the offer, then acceptance of the offer must be made in a reasonable manner. For example, a consumer accepts a merchant's offer by taking possession of an item and paying for it at the cash register.

An offer that may only be accepted by the performance of or the non-performance of an act is known as a unilateral contract. An offer that may only be accepted by a return promise of performance is called a bilateral contract. Unilateral and bilateral contracts will be discussed later in this chapter.

A party's conduct can imply an acceptance of the offer.

Example:

> A homeowner orders a stove to be delivered and installed. The stove is delivered and it is too large for the kitchen. If the homeowner has paid for the stove and does not notify the company that the stove does not fit or does not attempt to return the stove, the homeowner has effectively communicated a legally binding acceptance of the non-conforming good.

Likewise, a party's silence or inaction cannot infer a party's acceptance of an offer. An exception can occur when two parties have a prior course of dealings where the offeree has led the offeror to believe that the offeree will accept all goods shipped by the offeror unless the offeree sends notice to the offeror to the contrary. In this instance, the offeree's silence or inaction creates a legally binding acceptance upon which the offeror can rely.

Consideration

Consideration is something of value that each party brings to the table to induce the other to enter into an agreement. The law refers to this as an exchange of values of consideration. Consideration is not always money. Consideration may consist of a promise to perform an act that one is not legally required to perform or a promise to refrain from an act that one is legally entitled to do.

Example:

> If a dad promises to buy his son a house if the son refrains from smoking cigarettes and drinking alcohol for five years, the law deems both the dad's promise and the son's self-control lawful consideration.

Courts will rely on the promise or performance of an offeree and the promise or performance of the offeror to analyze whether a contract is supported by sufficient consideration. No consideration is found unless the offeree suffers a legal detriment in making the return promise or performance as requested by the offeror. Legal detriment is defined as a change in position by one to whom a promise has been made, or an assumption of duties or liabilities not previously imposed on the person due to the person's reliance on the actions of the one who makes the promise. Legal detriment is considered if the offeree gives up a legal right in fulfilling a promise or performance. Love and affection are not deemed sufficient consideration to support a contract because there is no legal duty for one person to give or refrain from giving these things to others. Likewise, a promise to perform an act that has already been done in the past fails to be sufficient consideration.

 © 2019, 2020, 2021 NALA, Inc. All rights reserved.

Mutuality of Obligation

Mutuality of obligation is often referred to as a "meeting of the minds." Mutuality of obligation requires that every party to the contract agrees to the specific terms of the contract. It occurs when one party makes an offer, and the other party accepts that offer.

Mutuality of obligation is linked closely with consideration. With consideration, both parties must perform the obligations in the contract. If either party fails to perform, the court will treat the contract as invalid, which allows for neither party to perform. When a party makes a promise and the other party accepts the promise to perform, neither party can have the unlimited option to void the contract.

Not all contracts are required to be in writing and signed by the parties. A verbal agreement is valid even though it is not memorialized in writing. However, the elements of offer, acceptance, and consideration must be present in a verbal agreement. The Statute of Frauds sets which contracts must be in writing. When two parties sign a contract, the act of signing represents a mutual obligation to one another. Without an obligation, the court would not consider the contract to be a legally binding document. However, there is an exception to mutuality of obligation. Mutuality of obligation does not exist on unilateral contracts.

Example:

> Max promises to pay $500 to Bill in exchange for Bill painting Max's house. When Max makes his promise to Bill, it is clear that the payment of the $500 is in exchange for the act of painting the house, not just the promise of painting it. This unilateral contract binds both parties but is not an exchange of one promise for another. Only Max is bound by the agreement because he is the only one making a promise.

COMPETENCY AND CAPACITY

Anyone who enters into a contract must have complete legal capacity to be held liable for the promises and performances that person has agreed to undertake. A minor, someone who is mentally incapacitated, or someone who is intoxicated lack the capacity to enter into a contract.

A minor is a person under the age of 18 or 19, depending on specific state law. A contract entered into by a minor is valid until the minor takes an affirmative action to disavow the contract. Minors who disavow their contracts may not be held liable for the breach of the contract. The courts assume minors are too immature, naïve, or inexperienced to negotiate contracts on equal terms as adults, so the courts protect them from being held accountable.

When a party to a contract does not understand the nature and consequences of the contract that party has entered into, the courts will treat that party as lacking mental capacity to form a binding contract. However, a party will not be relieved from any duties until either a court rules on the issue of the party's mental capacity or if a court order exists declaring the person incompetent or insane. Like agreements with minors, contracts entered into with a mentally incapacitated person are voidable at the discretion of the incapacitated person. However, a guardian or personal representative may approve the agreement for that person, which in turn converts the contract into a legally binding document.

Contracts that are entered into by an intoxicated or impaired person can either be enforceable, meaning held to the fullest extent of the law, or voidable by the impaired person. The court will look at two criteria that need to be present in order to make the contract voidable. First, if the intoxication was severe enough that the person entering into the contract was incapacitated, and second, the non-impaired party was aware of the intoxication at the time the contract was made. Courts are not sympathetic to defendants that avoid contractual obligations on the grounds they were intoxicated. On the other hand, if the evidence shows that the sober party was trying to take advantage of the intoxicated person, courts will typically void the contract. Persons who are impaired from prescription medication are treated like persons who are mentally incompetent or insane and are usually relieved from their contractual duties, more willingly than persons who are impaired from non-prescription drugs or alcohol.

Void and Voidable Contracts

A contract is void if it cannot be enforced by either party. The law treats this type of contract as if it had never been formed. A contract is considered void when it requires one of the parties to the contract to perform an act that is impossible or illegal. Some examples of voidable contracts are contracts that are entered into for illegal purposes, such as prostitution or murder for hire, the requirement of performing something impossible, or acts against public policy. These types of contracts are considered void because they are too unfair, or they infringe on a person's rights (like who to marry or the right to work). An example of a contract that is void is a contract between a drug dealer and an individual who is buying illegal drugs. This contract is voidable because the terms are illegal and neither party could go to court to enforce the contract.

Voidable contracts are valid agreements, but one or both of the parties to the contract can void the contract at any time. As a result, you may not be able to enforce a voidable contract:

- Contracts entered into when one party was a minor. (The law often treats minors as though they do not have the capacity to enter into a contract. As a result, a minor can walk away from a contract at any time.)

- Contracts where one party was tricked or forced into entering it.

- Contracts entered when one party was incapacitated (drunk, insane, or delusional).

© 2019, 2020, 2021 NALA, Inc. All rights reserved.

The following comparison chart provides additional information regarding the difference between void and voidable contracts:

Basis for Comparison	Void Contract	Voidable Contract
Meaning	The type of contract which cannot be enforceable is known as a void contract.	The contract in which one of the two parties has the option to enforce or rescind it, is known as voidable contract.
Nature	The contract is valid, but subsequently becomes invalid due to some reasons.	The contract is valid, until the party whose consent is not free, does not revoke it.
Reasons	Subsequent illegality or impossibility of any act which is to be performed in the future.	If the consent of the parties is not independent.
Rights to party	No	Yes, but only to the aggrieved party.
Suit for damages	Not given by any party to another party for the non-performance, but any benefit received by any party must be restored back.	Damages can be claimed by the aggrieved party.

Source: https://keydifferences.com/difference-between-void-and-voidable-contract.html

The following summarizes the differences between a void contract and a voidable contract:

Void Contract	Voidable Contract
A contract which lacks enforceability is void.	A contract which lacks the free will of one of the parties to the contract is voidable.
A contract which was valid at the time when it is created, but later on, it becomes invalid, is void.	Conversely, if a contract is valid until the aggrieved party does not revoke it within stipulated time is voidable.
When it is impossible for an act to be performed by the parties, it becomes void, as it ceases its enforceability.	When the consent of the parties to the contract is not free, the contract becomes voidable at the option of the party whose consent is not free.
In a void contract, no party can claim any damages for the non-performance of the contract. On the other hand, the aggrieved party can claim damages for any loss sustained.	

Source: https://keydifferences.com/difference-between-void-and-voidable-contract.html

THIRD-PARTY CONTRACTS

When two parties enter into a contract for the benefit of another, this is referred to as a third-party contract. The party benefitting from the contract is referred to as the third-party beneficiary. A third-party beneficiary is a person who may have the right to sue on a contract, despite not having originally been an active party to the contract. Paralegals must be aware of the distinctions of delegation, assignment, and novation in third-party contracts, as well as the three types of third-party beneficiaries: (1) creditor, (2) donee, and (3) incidental.

Delegation

Delegation of duties occurs when one party to a contract arranges to have a third-party perform the party's contractual obligations. Delegation of duties is allowed under various state statutes. Delegation of duties is proper only if the principal of the contract authorizes the performance by another. This authorization can be expressed or implied. The liability of the third-party reverts to the original party that delegated their duties under the contract.

Third-Party Beneficiary and Assignment

Normally, only parties to a contract have rights and duties under the terms of the contract. An exception to this is made in the case of third-party beneficiary contracts. If a contract is intended to benefit a third-party, this party is called the third-party beneficiary. A life insurance policy is a type of third-party beneficiary contract.

Example:

> If Joe takes out an insurance policy on his life, names his wife Mary as the person who will receive the insurance proceeds on his death, and the insurance company promises to make the payment to Mary, then Mary is the beneficiary of the insurance proceeds and is considered a third-party beneficiary to the contract with the insurance company. If Joe dies, and the insurance company does not pay the proceeds to Mary, Mary has a right to bring a lawsuit against the insurance company even though she was not a party to the contract.

An assignment of rights in a contract happens when one party to the contract assigns or transfer their rights in the contract to another party. The person to whom the rights are transferred is called the assignee. The person who is assigning their rights under the contract to the other party is called an assignor.

Example:

> Mack agrees to sell his car to Sean for $5,000. Sean does not have $5,000 but agrees to sign a contract whereby Sean agrees to pay Mack $250 a month for 20 months. Later, Mack assigns his rights under the contract to Mary, and Sean now has to make the payment owed under the contract to Mary. In this situation Sean is the obligor, Mack is the Assigner, and Mary is the Assignee. In an assignment, a new contract is not required.

Novation

Novation is similar to an assignment in that one party is transferring all of their rights under the terms of a contract to another party. The novation contract must be signed by all original parties to the contract and by the third party who is taking the place of one of the parties to the contract. The original contract

© 2019, 2020, 2021 NALA, Inc. All rights reserved.

is then extinguished. When the third party comes in to take the place of the original party, the third party assumes the same rights and obligations of the original party. Once the novation has been signed, the withdrawing party's obligations and rights are discharged under the terms of the original contract.

Third-Party Beneficiaries: Creditor

A third-party creditor beneficiary is a non-party to a contract who receives benefits when a promise is made to satisfy a legal duty.

Example:

> John owes the Bank $500. John then lends $500 to Doug. Doug promises to use the money to pay John's debt. Doug makes the promise to be enforced (he is the promisor). John is the debtor (the promisee), to whom the promise is made. The contract is between John and Doug. The Bank (creditor) is the third-party beneficiary to the contract. If Doug refuses to pay the Bank the $500, then the Bank may sue Doug and prevail, although the Bank is not a party to the contract. The Bank may also sue John as the debtor as he agreed to pay the original $500 to the Bank. Then John may sue Doug for breach of contract for refusing to pay the Bank.

Third-Party Beneficiaries: Donee

A donee beneficiary of a contract is a non-party to the contract who benefits from a promise that is made for the purpose of making a gift to the donee.

Example:

> Luke plans to give Mark $500 as an anniversary present. Luke plans to sell a computer for $500 to a purchaser who promises to pay Mark the $500 directly. Mark is the donee beneficiary of the purchaser and may enforce a claim against the purchaser. Mark has no claim against Luke, as Luke has no legal duty to Mark but is only giving Mark a gift. However, Luke will be able to sue the purchaser for refusal to pay Mark because it would breach their terms of their contract for the sale of the computer.

Third-Party Beneficiaries: Incidental

An incidental beneficiary is a beneficiary that incidentally benefits from the terms of a contract between other parties and is not the intended beneficiary. For example, a grandchild may benefit from a parent receiving a gift that could be used for the entire family or which the grandchild inherits from the parent.

The two kinds of third-party beneficiaries are: intended beneficiaries and incidental beneficiaries. An intended beneficiary is a third-party beneficiary who is not the promisor or promisee who stands to benefit from the contract's performance. Intended beneficiaries have rights in the event of a breach of contract. In order to bring an action for breach, the intended beneficiary must prove:

- A contract exists between A and B.

- The clear or manifest intent of A and B that the contract primarily and directly benefits the third-party (or class of persons to which that party belongs).

- Breach of the contract by either A or B.

- Damages to the third-party resulting from the breach. An incidental beneficiary has no enforceable rights under a contract.

STATUTE OF FRAUDS AND OTHER PROVISIONS

Statute of Frauds is a statute that requires certain contracts to be in writing and signed by all the parties bound to it to be enforceable. The purpose is to prevent fraud or other injury. The most common types of contract to which this statute applies are:

- An agreement by a personal representative to pay the debts of an estate out of the personal representative's own funds.

- Contracts that involve the sale and transfer of land, however, an exception is where partial performance has occurred. For example, if a purchaser has paid all the payments for land under a land contract and the seller refuses to convey title, courts may intervene and take the contract out of the Statute of Frauds and require specific performance.

- Collateral contracts, such as promises to answer for the guaranty of the debt of another person.

- Promises made in consideration of marriage, i.e., prenuptial agreement.

- Contracts that cannot be performed within one year. The date of the agreement is used to calculate the one-year period.

- Contracts for the sale of goods valued at $500 or more.

As for satisfaction of the writing requirement, the essential terms of the contract must be set out, such as:

- The identity of the parties.

- The identity of the subject matter.

- The essential terms.

- The recital of the consideration.

- The signature of the party to be charged.

Breach of Contract

When a party fails to perform its obligations on a contract, a breach of contract has occurred. There are numerous reasons why a contract can be breached and include but are not limited to:

- Not finishing a job.

- Failure to make a payment in full or on time.

- Failure to deliver the goods or perform the services.

- Substituting lesser goods.

 © 2019, 2020, 2021 NALA, Inc. All rights reserved.

- Substituting different goods.

Material Breach

A material breach of a contract is the failure of a party to uphold their end of a contract in a way that renders the contract seemingly pointless. If a party to the contract does something that would defeat the whole purpose of the contract, then a court would find the breach to be material. This type of breach would not include a breach of superficial terms.

Minor Breach

A minor breach, also referred to as a partial breach, is a breach of contract that is less severe than a material breach and gives the harmed party the right to sue for damages but does not usually excuse them from further performance.

The main difference between a material breach and a minor breach is the severity of the breach. A material breach is much more serious and makes performing on the contract difficult or impossible. A minor breach is small enough that the contract can be performed satisfactorily.

CONTRACT DEFENSES

There are several contract defenses available for defendants who are sued for breach of contract. A defendant may assert that there was no breach of contract because a contract was never formed due to absence of the six elements of a contract as discussed above. If a contract lacks offer, acceptance, consideration, mutuality of obligation, or writing (when required), then a contract was never formed. Other defenses available to a defendant are:

- Unconscionability
- Mistake
- Fraud
- Undue Influence
- Duress
- Misrepresentation

Unconscionable

Unconscionable contracts are those contracts that are so offensive that it offends the conscience of all reasonable people. These contracts go against public policy. If two individuals enter into a contract and one individual is 50 years old and the second individual is 19 years old, the older individual will have more knowledge regarding the legal concept of a contract due to age. This is an example of an unconscionable contract relating to bargain power. Unfair terms would include one-sided terms or provisions that are favorable to one party or another. Hidden language in unrelated provisions, small font, or provisions added to the contract after the contract has been signed are deemed unconscionable.

Mistake in Value

The mistake in value defense is when parties make assumptions concerning the value of the subject matter of the contract.

Example:

> Dawn agrees to purchase 10 acres from Tyler for $15,000. An agreement is signed between Dawn and Tyler. It is discovered that the 10 acres is in fact $15,000 per acre. A mistake was made, and it supports a rescission of the contract.

Fraud

Fraud is defined as a deliberate misrepresentation of a material fact made by one party to another with knowledge of the falseness and for the purpose of inducing the other person to act, and upon which the other person relied with resulting injury or damage. There are two types of fraud. Fraud in the inducement is where fraud exists with regard to the entire contract. The person is deceived into signing the contract due to fraudulent circumstances. For example, one party signs because they believe the person was a real estate agent when they actually are not a real estate agent. Fraud in the factum is where fraud exists as to a fact or description contained in the contract. For example, if a party signs the contract when they believe they are purchasing 50 items, but the other party's intent is to sell them 100 items, then there is a fraud in the factum. In order to prove fraud, one party to the contract must be able to prove that the other party knowingly misrepresented a material fact in the contract with an intent to deceive. Further, the party that believes fraud has occurred must have relied upon the misrepresentation and suffered a loss.

Undue Influence

Undue influence occurs when one party to a contract is able to influence the decisions of another party and takes advantage of another party through a position of trust. Undue influence always involves two parties and one of the parties to the contract must be in a superior position over the other party.

Example:

> Matthew is a successful businessman. Matthew's lawyer has been pressuring Matthew to enter into a business contract that is not very advantageous to Matthew. Matthew's lawyer has pestered him over a long period of time, and Matthew feels pressured to enter into the contract in order to keep a good working relationship with his lawyer. This is a case of undue influence. There is a presumption that Matthew's lawyer has influence over him. However, Matthew must prove that the influence was undue in order to have an actionable claim against the contract.

Duress

A coercive threat of sufficient gravity that induces the other party to assent to an agreement to which they would not have assented to otherwise is known as duress. Blackmail, violence, and threats may all

© 2019, 2020, 2021 NALA, Inc. All rights reserved.

constitute duress to void a contract.

Example:

> Nicolas owns an auto repair shop. One day a large, frightening-looking man comes into the auto repair shop and demands that Nicolas sign a contract to buy his auto parts from this man or his family will be harmed. Nicolas, fearing for the safety of his family, signs the contract. Nicolas has made the contract under duress.

Misrepresentation

Misrepresentation refers to a statement made by one party to a contract to induce another party to enter into the contract. The misrepresentation must be both false and fraudulent in order for damages to apply. Negligent misrepresentation is a statement of fact that is false as the result of a party's negligence, induces another to act, and results in injury to the party relying on the statement. An example of negligent misrepresentation is when a real estate agent is trying to sell a house. The purchaser wants a house that is in a neighborhood that is quiet. The agent claims that the house is in a quiet and peaceful atmosphere, when in fact there is a youth baseball park located behind the house that causes excessive noise in the neighborhood. The agent has made a false statement that convinced the purchaser to enter into a contract to buy the house.

CONTRACT REMEDIES

Once a plaintiff shows both a material breach by the defendant and no material breach by the plaintiff, a remedy is available to address the breach. The purpose of a contract remedy is to put the plaintiff where the plaintiff would have been if the contract had never been breached. There are five simple remedies for breach of contract. They are money damages, restitution, rescission, reformation, and specific performance.

Money Damages

If money damages are awarded by a court, they can include a sum of money that is given to the plaintiff as compensation for financial losses caused by the breach. The type of breach determines the amount of the damages that may be recovered. Damages must be proved and cannot be speculative. Money damages may be classified as compensatory (general or special), punitive, nominal, or liquidated.

Compensatory Damages

These damages are to ensure the injured party receives what was expected from the bargain. The injured party should be placed back in the position as if the contract had been fully performed.

Example:

> Bob agrees to buy Jake's house for $70,000. On the scheduled date of closing, the house is valued at $73,000. If Jake refuses to sell his house, Bob's general damages loss as result of Jake's breach will be $3,000.

Consequential Damages

In addition to compensatory damages, a plaintiff may be able to recover other losses incurred as a consequence of the breach, provided that they were reasonably foreseeable at the time the contract was made. These damages are not a direct result of the incident itself but are consequences of the incident. A coat manufacturer enters into a contract with a department store to produce 1,000 coats by the end of August, so the department store would have the coats for the winter season. When the end of August comes, the department store discovers that the manufacturer has not produced the 1,000 coats as agreed. The coat manufacturer has breached the contract with the department store and now the department store has to absorb the costs that were involved with the original coat manufacturer, as well as hire a different company to manufacture the coats at a higher cost as it is now a rush to have the coats by winter. The direct damages are the initial costs the department store has with the original coat manufacturer. The consequential damages are the costs the department store had to pay to hire an additional company to manufacture the coats at a higher rush rate. The department store can sue the original coat manufacturer for direct and consequential damages for breach of contract.

Punitive Damages

These are damages that are designed to punish or penalize the defendant for bad conduct above and beyond a simple breach of contract. A court will use punitive damages to set an example so that others do not perform the same act. Punitive damages are rare in a breach of contract case because the court assumes both parties entering into the contract were fully aware of the risks. As an example, if a plaintiff sues an insurance company, and can prove that the insurance company breached its requirement of good faith and fair dealing, the courts may award punitive damages.

Factors that are used to determine punitive damages include: how egregious the defendant's actions were; whether any precedents exist in other lawsuits that have awarded punitive damages; the difference in the plaintiff's injuries and losses compared to the amount of damages claimed (will the compensatory damages cover the losses); if it is hard to place a value on the harm done to the plaintiff; if there is continuing medical care for the injuries; and how offensive the defendant's actions were against the plaintiff.

Nominal Damages

Nominal damages may be awarded by a court when a defendant has breached the contract, but no monetary loss is proved. Nominal damages are usually in the amount of $1.00 - $2.00. The amount of money is small, but it is still important because it proves that the plaintiff had a legal right to bring a lawsuit against a defendant for the wrongful behavior of the defendant.

 © 2019, 2020, 2021 NALA, Inc. All rights reserved.

Example:

> Barnes Company contracted with Smith Company to have Smith Company manufacture 10,000 chairs. In reality, Smith Company does not have the capacity or equipment to manufacture 10,000 chairs but hires Jones Company to manufacture the chairs. Barnes Company makes a call to Smith Company and discovers they are not manufacturing the chairs. While Barnes Company did not actually suffer a loss, Smith Company deceived them. In this case nominal damages could be awarded for the deception.

Liquidated Damages

Liquidated damages are those damages that are predetermined if either party breaches the contract. Liquidated damages are used when the parties understand that proving damages, like lost profits, in the event of a breach may be difficult. Courts usually uphold liquidated damages if they are reasonable.

Measure of Damages

The measure of damages is a way to compute damages that are to be awarded to an injured party in a contract. The intent is to place the injured party where they would have been if the contract had been performed.

Sale of Goods

The Uniform Commercial Code (UCC) consists of nine articles and is a set of laws that governs the sale of goods, lease of goods, negotiable instruments, bank deposits, fund transfers, letters of credit, bulk sales, warehouse receipts, bills of lading, investment securities, and secured transactions. Contract law is governed by common law and the UCC. Under the UCC, the remedy to a seller is governed under UCC §2-703, and the remedy to a buyer is prescribed in §2-711 of the UCC.

Pursuant to UCC §2-703, if the buyer rejects or revokes acceptance of the goods or fails to make a payment due on or before the delivery, the seller may:

- Withhold delivery of such goods

- Stop delivery by any carrier

- Resell and recover damages

- Recover damages for non-acceptance

- Cancel

- Recover ordinary contract damages for non-acceptance

Per the UCC §2-711, when the seller fails to make delivery of the goods or when the buyer rightfully or justifiably rejects the goods or revokes acceptance of the goods, the buyer's remedies are to:

- Cancel.

- "Cover" by purchasing substituted goods on the open market and recovering from the seller the difference between the contract price and the substituted goods.

- Recover the specific goods identified in the contract if the buyer has paid all or a portion of the purchase price.

- Recover damages for non-delivery of the goods, which is the difference between market prices at the time that the buyer learned of the breach and the contract price. This includes consequential damages.

- Obtain specific performance where the goods are special or unique as spelled out in UCC §2-0716.

Contracts for Sale of Land

The measure of damages for a breach of contract involving the sale of land is compensatory. The measure is the difference between the contract price and the fair market value of the land at the time that the land was to be conveyed.

Construction Contracts

If the contractor breaches a contract:

- Before construction – only profits can be recovered by the contractor (contract price less cost of materials)

- During construction – the builder can recover profits plus cost of partial construction

- After construction – the builder can recover the contract price plus interest

If the builder breaches a contract, the owner can recover for:

- Failing to begin – price over contract price to complete

- Stopping mid-projects – cost of completion

- Late completion – cost related to loss of use (pay rental or hotel expenses for owner)

Restitution

Restitution is the remedy designed to return the injured party back to the position they were before the contract was formed. Injured parties seeking restitution may not request to be compensated for lost profits or other earnings. However, any money property that was given to the defendant under the contract must be returned. Restitution is sought when the contract is entered into by one party that lacks capacity or is incompetent.

Rescission

Another remedy is the right of rescission. Rescission is the unwinding of the contract between the parties. This is done to bring the parties back to the positions they were in before they entered into the contract. Any benefit received as a part of the contract must be returned.

© 2019, 2020, 2021 NALA, Inc. All rights reserved.

Example:

A borrower has a right to cancel certain types of loans, such as a home equity line of credit or a mortgage refinance. The borrower may cancel the loan until midnight of the third day after closing. This gives the borrower a three-day waiting period to think about the loan and reconsider. If the borrower exercises the right of rescission, any fees paid with regard to the loan are to be refunded to the borrower by the lender.

Reformation

Reformation is the remedy that allows courts to change the substance of the contract to correct inequities that were suffered. This happens when the parties enter into the contract and not all of the provisions of the contract match what the parties understood the agreement to be. The court can reform that contract to settle a dispute.

Example:

One party sells a parcel of land to another party. In the contract, the value of the land is stated. However, the value is incorrect, either by mistake or one party was trying to mislead another party. This contract could be taken to a court of law and reformed, where the court corrects the wording to reflect the actual value. However, if fraud occurred, reformation may not be a solution, as there may be penalties for the party perpetuating the fraud and compensation for the person who was harmed.

Specific Performance

Specific performance is a remedy whereby a court issues an order requiring a party to a contract to complete a specific obligation or act of the contract. This is an alternative to the court awarding damages and is commonly used as injunctive relief.

Example:

A construction company agrees to construct a barn for Joyce that is 36 feet wide and 50 feet long. However, when the barn is complete the measurements are 24 feet wide and 36 feet long. The court may issue an order for the construction company to reconstruct the barn to the original contracted size of 36 feet wide and 50 feet long.

Tort Actions

A tort is a wrong, civil wrong, or a wrongful act whether intentional or accidental from which an injury occurs. Contract law and tort law are similar in that they both involve breach of duties. A civil wrong is a non-criminal cause of action under the law of a governing body. Tort actions and breaches of contract are civil wrongs for which there is a legal remedy for harm caused. Tort actions are put in place to address a breach of duty of either party to a contract.

Example:

> A physician warrants that his treatment is safe but performs the surgery negligently, disabling the patient for life. The patient could sue for malpractice (tort) or for breach of warranty (contract).

© 2019, 2020, 2021 NALA, Inc. All rights reserved.

CHAPTER 3: PRACTICE QUESTIONS

1. **The taking back of an offer by the offeror is:**

    A. Revocation
    B. Rejection
    C. Cancellation
    D. Consideration

2. **A contract that amounts to nothing and has no legal effect is:**

    A. Bilateral
    B. Voidable
    C. Void
    D. Unilateral

3. **A contract that contains a promise by both parties is:**

    A. Express
    B. Implied
    C. Bilateral
    D. Unilateral

4. **What occurs when one party to a contract does not do what that party agreed to do?**

    A. Breach
    B. Fraud
    C. Consideration
    D. Ratification

5. **People sometimes enter into contracts without saying a word. What type of contract is this?**

    A. Voidable
    B. Express
    C. Unenforceable
    D. Implied

6. **The offeree's refusal of an offer ends that offer. This is known as:**

    A. Rejection
    B. Revocation
    C. Implication
    D. Expression

---

7. An offer must be definite, communicated to the offeree, and:

   A. Signed

   B. Implied

   C. Seriously intended

   D. Timely

8. Deliberate deception to secure unfair or unlawful gain is:

   A. Misrepresentation

   B. Libel

   C. Unilateral mistake

   D. Fraud

9. Overcoming a person's will through force is:

   A. Fraud

   B. Duress

   C. Extortion

   D. Ratification

10. Alex persuaded his grandmother, Clara, to sell him her car for $1,000. They both knew the car was worth much more than that. However, Clara did not need the car anymore and loved her grandson, so she agreed to sell him the car. The next day Clara found out that Alex was planning to sell the car to a friend for $6,000. Clara can void the contract because of:

   A. Duress

   B. Fraud

   C. Undue influence

   D. Mistake

11. A legal means of enforcing a right or correcting a wrong is a(n):

   A. Breach

   B. Remedy

   C. Avoidance

   D. Beneficiary

© 2019, 2020, 2021 NALA, Inc. All rights reserved.

12. A minor who claims to be over the age of majority commits:

A. Fraud

B. Misrepresentation

C. Extortion

D. Larceny

13. Consideration in a contract means that:

A. A person has the mental capacity to enter into a contract.

B. The two parties deal with the contract in a polite manner.

C. The contract is legal and fully valid.

D. Something of value is being exchanged by the two parties.

14. A court's award that reimburses a buyer for reasonable expenses when the seller has breached a contract is:

A. Incidental

B. Actual

C. Real

D. Illusory

15. Illegal agreements are:

A. Voidable

B. Void

C. Limited

D. Enforceable

16. Can a contract be ended by mutual agreement by the parties?

A. Yes

B. No

17. As long as all terms have been carried out properly and completely, the most common way a contract is discharged is by:

A. Agreement

B. Avoidance

C. Performance

D. Exaction

18. Damages agreed upon by the parties when they first enter into a contract are called:

   A.   Actual damages

   B.   Incidental damages

   C.   Anticipatory damages

   D.   Liquidated damages

19. Damages that may be awarded by a court when a defendant has breached a contract, but no monetary loss is proved, are called:

   A.   Incidental damages

   B.   Anticipatory damages

   C.   Nominal damages

   D.   Consequential damages

20. Damages that ensure the injured party receives what the injured party expected from the bargain are:

   A.   Anticipatory damages

   B.   Compensatory damages

   C.   Punitive damages

   D.   Incidental damages

21. An incorrect/false statement made by one party to a contract to induce another party to enter into a contract is:

   A.   Misrepresentation

   B.   Fraud

   C.   Libel

   D.   Mistake

22. Which of the following is NOT one of the three required elements of a contract?

   A.   Acceptance

   B.   Offer

   C.   Seal

   D.   Consideration

© 2019, 2020, 2021 NALA, Inc. All rights reserved.

23. **The act of one party transferring all rights, obligations, and benefits under the terms of the contract to a third-party is called a(n):**

    A.   Assignment

    B.   Novation

    C.   Delegation

    D.   Beneficiary

24. **An unwinding of a contract is called:**

    A.   Reformation

    B.   Specific performance

    C.   Rescission

    D.   Restitution

RESOURCES

- www.dictionary.law.com

- https://legal-dictionary.thefreedictionary.com/Legal+Detriment

- https://www.legalmatch.com/law-library/article/void-vs-voidable-contract-lawyers.html

- https://definitions.uslegal.com/f/fraud/

- Restatement (Second) Torts §552

Corporate and Commercial Law

Written by Kelly A. LaGrave, ACP

© 2019, 2020, 2021 NALA, Inc. All rights reserved.

Paralegals will find that having a basic knowledge and understanding of corporate and commercial law is beneficial because the principals of business law touch almost every other field of law. Upon completion of this chapter, readers will be able to:

- Define and explain the formation of various forms of business entities.

- Discuss the advantages and disadvantages of various forms of business entities.

- Discuss the various fiduciary duties that owners and management have toward their business entities.

- Describe the differences between various types of commercial transactions.

- Understand antitrust issues faced by businesses in the United States.

In the business world, model and uniform acts have been drafted by respective corporate bodies which serve as guidelines or templates to be used by states to draft their own specific business statutes. The use of model and uniform acts by each state in the United States standardizes statutes as much as possible, which aids businesses in doing business across state lines. However, note that no state typically adopts the model or uniform act in its entirety, and specific state statutes should be reviewed within the state in which an entity is doing business prior to formation or doing business. (See reference list at the end of this chapter regarding model and uniform acts.)

BUSINESS ORGANIZATIONS

Although the catalog of business organizations is extensive, most business entities formed in the United States fall under one of the following types of entities: sole proprietorship, general partnership (or co-partnership), limited liability partnership, limited partnership, corporation, and limited liability company. However, paralegals should be aware that there are numerous other types of business entities in the corporate world which include, but are not limited to, the following:

- Limited Liability Limited Partnership (LLLP) provides traditional limited liability to the limited partners and limited liability to the general partners to the same extent permitted to a partner in a limited liability partnership (LLP).

- Joint Venture is a form of temporary partnership organized to carry out a particular business enterprise for profit. Often, the joint venture is terminated as of the conclusion of the specific project.

- Publicly Traded Partnerships Trust (PTP Trusts) is a partnership in which ownership interests are regularly traded on an established securities market and are treated for federal tax purposes as corporations.

- Real Estate Investment Trust (REIT) is a financial device in which investors purchase shares in a trust that invests in real estate ventures.

- Regulated Investment Company (RIC) is a mutual fund or REIT that is eligible to pass the taxes on capital gains, dividends, and interest payments onto the clients or individual investors.

- Foreign Sales Corporation (FSC) is used by U.S. Exporters to reduce federal income tax on export related income. The U.S. Exporter sets up an FSC in certain foreign countries or in U.S. possessions to obtain a corporate tax exemption on a portion of its earnings generated by the sale or lease of export property.

© 2019, 2020, 2021 NALA, Inc. All rights reserved.

- Insurance Company is specifically formed to sell insurance policies to individuals, whether directly or indirectly through insurance agencies or employers.

- Cooperative is a corporation or association organized for the purpose of rendering economic services, without gain to itself, to its shareholders or members who own and control it. Participants in an industry (i.e., farming) may combine their resources and efforts in a consolidated facility to enable the sale of their products.

SOLE PROPRIETORSHIP

A sole proprietorship is an unincorporated business conducted in a single owner's individual capacity, and without the organization of a separate legal entity for holding and conducting the business. Typically, sole proprietorships are started by individuals who run their own small business (e.g., a lawn care service provider, handyman, etc.). In business practices, sometimes an individual may not want to incur the expense of setting up another type of entity until they become established, so they will start with a sole proprietorship.

There is no specific legal documentation required to form a sole proprietorship. In most states, a notice filing or certificate should be filed with the county clerk in each county in which the owner is doing business or in the county in which the sole proprietor resides. Certificates usually are for a specific time period (i.e., five years) and can be continually renewed if the business continues.

Advantages

Since no legal documentation is required to form a sole proprietorship, startup is very easy, and costs related to the startup are minimal. Management of the entity is controlled by the sole owner who makes all the business decisions. The owner of the sole proprietorship retains all profits made by the business.

All income and/or losses of the sole proprietorship are treated as individual income to the sole owner. Any business income and/or loss of the sole proprietorship is reported on a separate Schedule C, which is attached to the sole owner's individual tax return. A separate federal, state, or local tax return is not filed for the sole proprietorship.

Disadvantages

There are a multitude of disadvantages to doing business under this structure of business entity. The individual owner takes all the risk for the business and has unlimited personal liability. If the business fails, the owner is personally responsible for all debts of the business. Personal assets of the individual owner can be subject to judgment in a lawsuit. If the sole proprietorship needs additional capital to continue the business, the owner can be limited financially by their personal assets. In addition, lending institutions can be uncomfortable with this form of business unless the owner has enough personal assets to use as collateral. Both factors can result in limited availability of alternative sources of capital for the business. Finally, the business terminates upon the death of the owner.

GENERAL PARTNERSHIP OR CO-PARTNERSHIP

A general partnership is an unincorporated legal entity formed between two or more persons to carry on a business for profit, whether or not the persons intended to form a partnership. In some state

© 2019, 2020, 2021 NALA, Inc. All rights reserved.

jurisdictions, a general partnership is called a co-partnership. Owners in the partnership are called partners.

In most states a statement, notice, or certificate of partnership may be filed with the secretary of state or county clerk in each county in which the partnership is doing business. These statements are optional, voluntary, and, unless canceled earlier, typically expire five years from the date of filing. Under the Uniform Partnership Act (UPA), which includes revisions that are referred to as the Revised Uniform Partnership Act (RUPA), the law of the jurisdiction in which a partnership has its chief executive office governs relations among the partners and the partnership. Incentives to file a certificate or notice usually come from lenders or transferees of partnership property.

Partners should enter into a written partnership agreement which governs the relationship among the partners and between the partners and the partnership. A partnership agreement will outline issues such as who manages, how a partner's withdrawal is handled, how a new partner is added to the partnership, etc. To the extent that the partnership agreement does not otherwise provide, RUPA or the applicable state statute will govern the partnership.

The partnership must obtain a Federal Employer Identification Number (EIN) from the Internal Revenue Service (IRS). To obtain an EIN, the partnership completes IRS Form SS-4 Application for Employer Identification Number and one of the partners executes the form and then forwards the form to the IRS for processing. By going to the IRS website (www.irs.gov) an entity can obtain a copy of the form to complete and mail to the IRS, or the entity can obtain the EIN online directly with the IRS.

Advantages

There are a few advantages to this partnership form of business. Partnerships are relatively easy to form. All partners can participate in the management of the partnership. Adding more partners can provide additional capital if needed to continue and grow the business of the partnership. For tax purposes a partnership is considered a "pass through tax entity." The partnership income and/or loss is reported on a separate Schedule K-1 that is prepared for each partner of the partnership and then attached to each partner's federal tax return. Each partner then pays the taxes on any income produced by the partnership. However, although the partnership must file tax return Form 1065 with the IRS annually, the partnership itself is not taxed. The tax return filing is an informational filing only.

Disadvantages

There are many disadvantages to doing business under the general partnership form of entity. As with a sole proprietorship, each partner in the partnership has personal risk and unlimited liability for all actions of the partnership. Also, with multiple partners, the authority of the management of the partnership is divided amongst the partners. If the partners do not agree on the direction of the business of the partnership, then it can be detrimental. If the partnership business fails, and the partnership has no assets, each partner can be held personally responsible for all the debts of the partnership, and the personal assets of each partner can be subject to judgment in a lawsuit.

Under RUPA, if a partner withdraws from the general partnership or dies, the partner becomes "disassociated" and the partnership does not necessarily dissolve. However, in some state jurisdictions, a partnership can be considered dissolved upon the death or withdrawal of a partner. If the partnership is to continue doing business after the death or withdrawal of a partner, a review of the relevant state statutes must be reviewed in order to determine how to proceed to maintain the ongoing business of the partnership.

© 2019, 2020, 2021 NALA, Inc. All rights reserved.

LIMITED LIABILITY PARTNERSHIP

A limited liability partnership (LLP) is a general partnership formed by two or more persons in which the partners have less than full liability for the action of other partners but have full liability for their own actions. An LLP is the most recent form of general partnership (see RUPA, §§1001-1003). Owners in the LLP are called partners, and all partners participate in management of the partnership.

In addition to filing a Certificate or Notice of Partnership with the county in which the general partnership is doing business, the general partnership will also need to file an additional statement, notice, or application with the state in which the partnership is doing business making an election to be treated as an LLP. This additional filing makes the general partnership a limited liability partnership. The partners of the LLP should enter into a written partnership agreement and obtain an EIN from the IRS. RUPA requires that the partnership also file the LLP form annually with the state where the original statement was filed. It should be noted that if the annual filing is not made, the partnership may no longer be considered an LLP during the time that no filing is on record with the state.

Advantages

An LLP is relatively easy to form, and partners can provide additional capital when needed. The LLP is formed in the same way as a general partnership except for the additional annual filing for LLP status.

For tax purposes, the LLP is treated the same as a general partnership. Income and/or loss are reported on a separate Schedule K-1 attached to each partner's tax return. The partnership itself is not taxed but must file an annual information return with the IRS on Form 1065.

The main advantage to filing as an LLP is that the LLP affords the partners in the partnership some limited liability with regard to the actions of the other partners, and it provides a corporate-style liability shield, which protects partners from vicarious personal liability for all partnership obligations incurred while the partnership is an LLP. Most states, however, have adopted a partial liability shield protecting the partners only from vicarious personal liability for all partnership obligations arising from negligence, wrongful acts, or misconduct, whether characterized as tort, contract, or otherwise, committed while the general partnership has made the election to be treated as an LLP.

Note that the partial liability shield of electing to be treated as an LLP does not alter a partner's liability for the partner's own personal misconduct. The primary effect of the LLP filing is to sever a partner's personal liability to contribute to the partnership when assets are insufficient to cover its indemnification obligation to a partner who incurs a partnership obligation in the ordinary course of business.

Disadvantages

The disadvantages are similar to those of a general partnership. Each partner has personal risk and some liability for the debts of the partnership, and general liability for their own actions. The authority of the LLP is divided among the partners, and in some states, the partnership is dissolved upon the death or withdrawal of a partner.

The LLP must also be sure to continue to make its annual renewal registration filing and pay the renewal fees. Renewal fees typically are the same as the registration fees. If the annual renewal is not filed, then the state may revoke the LLP status of the general partnership. A revocation only terminates the general partnership's status as an LLP and is not an event of dissolution of the partnership.

© 2019, 2020, 2021 NALA, Inc. All rights reserved.

DOMESTIC AND FOREIGN JURISDICTIONS

For limited partnerships, corporations, and limited liability companies, the initial state of formation is called its state of domestic jurisdiction. The location of the domestic jurisdiction of an entity is typically determined by looking at issues such as location of the business, state tax laws, and favorable business case law. Other than its state of domestic formation, if an entity is also going to do business in another state of the United States, the District of Columbia, Puerto Rico, the United States Virgin Islands, or any other territory or insular possession subject to the jurisdiction of the United States (Foreign Location), the entity will need to file the required documentation with such Foreign Location. Once filed, the entity is considered qualified to do business as a foreign entity in the Foreign Location. A business entity can qualify to do business as a foreign entity in as many Foreign Locations as its business requires.

An entity's level of activity in a Foreign Location is a good indicator to determine if the entity will need to qualify to do business as a foreign entity. Although not a complete list, the following are some of the items that may need to be evaluated in order to determine if an entity will need to qualify to do business in a Foreign Location:

- Does the entity have a retail or store front presence in the Foreign Location?

- Does the entity have employees in the Foreign Location?

- Does the entity pay state sales taxes in the Foreign Location?

- Does the entity own real property in the Foreign Location?

- Does the entity have many contracts with in-state entities in the Foreign Location?

- Is the management of the entity located in the Foreign Location?

Each Foreign Location has its own statutes, rules, and case law which must be reviewed to determine if the entity is required to qualify to do business as a foreign entity. If an entity is doing business in a Foreign Location and is not properly qualified, there could be considerable consequences including financial penalties for not properly qualifying and the prohibition from suing in the courts of the Foreign Location.

LIMITED PARTNERSHIP

A limited partnership (LP) is formed by two or more persons under the laws of the state in which the LP forms. An LP has at least one general partner and at least one limited partner. Unlike a general partnership or LLP, the existence of an LP does not begin until a Certificate of Limited Partnership is filed with the appropriate governmental entity in the LP's state of domestic jurisdiction. An LP can also qualify as a foreign LP in other Foreign Locations by filing a Certificate of Authority to Transact Business in such Foreign Location. An LP also has certain naming conventions it must adhere to when forming. The name of the LP must contain the phrase "limited partnership" or the abbreviation LP or L.P.

Depending upon management duties, owners in the limited partnership are called either general partners or limited partners, and ownership interests are called partnership interests. The general and limited partners of the LP must also enter into a written partnership agreement, which governs the relationship among the general and limited partners and the LP. Finally, the LP must obtain an EIN from the IRS.

© 2019, 2020, 2021 NALA, Inc. All rights reserved.

Advantages

From a management perspective, the general partner(s) can run the business in the manner they believe is in its best interest. General partners do not have to obtain consensus or permission from limited partners on how the LP is going to be managed. If an LP needs to obtain additional capital to further its business, adding additional limited partners can provide the needed capital, while not dividing up management authority.

For limited partners in an LP, they have limited personal liability for the actions of the LP, and their personal assets are not subject to payment of LP debts or judgment in a lawsuit. A limited partner's potential loss is that of their capital contribution to the LP.

LP income and/or losses are reported on a separate Schedule K-1 which is attached to each partner's tax return (both the general and limited partners). As with a general partnership, the partnership itself is not taxed, but must file Form 1065 with the IRS annually.

Disadvantages

Limited partners in an LP do not have a say in the management of the business; they have no management powers. If a limited partner participates in the management of the business, their interest in the LP becomes a general partner interest and not a limited partner interest. This can be a disadvantage to a limited partner who does not like the way that the LP is being managed. As with a general partnership, the general partners have unlimited personal liability.

The Uniform Limited Partnership Act (ULPA) requires annual report filings. (Check local state statutes for this requirement.) Depending upon the specific state statute, the Certificate of Limited Partnership filed with the state may require detailed information that will become public information (e.g., the names of all the partners, their addresses, and the amount they contributed). Some partners may not want their personal information made public.

CORPORATIONS

A corporation is formed under the laws of the state in which it is organized and is a separate entity from its owners.

Owners in a corporation are called shareholders or stockholders, and the corporation is managed by a board of directors elected by the shareholders. The board of directors elects or appoints officers to run the daily operations of the business.

A domestic corporation must file Articles of Incorporation (or a Certificate of Incorporation, in some states) with the state where it is formed. A foreign corporation files an Application for Certificate of Authority, or a similar document, with the Foreign Location in which it is going to do business.

A corporation does not exist until the Articles of Incorporation are filed with the appropriate state authority (or upon a future date specified in the document, usually not more than 90 days). Depending upon specific state requirements, the Articles of Incorporation will typically need to include – at a minimum – the following information:

- The name of the corporation, which must include one of the following corporate designator words: Corporation; Corp.; Incorporated; Inc.; Company; Co.; Limited; or Ltd. (with or without punctuation).

- The name and address of each incorporator. Although only one person is required to incorporate a corporation, having multiple incorporators is not prohibited. An incorporator does not need to be a future shareholder, officer, or director of the corporation. The incorporator prepares and signs the Articles of Incorporation and has the document filed with the state of domestic jurisdiction.

- The name of the registered agent (or resident agent or statutory agent) and the address of the registered office. The registered agent is the person who receives legal notices on behalf of the corporation (such as service of process). In every jurisdiction within the United States, the registered agent must either be a legal entity formed in that jurisdiction or a resident of that state, and they must have a physical address in that state (a P.O. Box is not sufficient).

- Purpose of the corporation. Although a corporation can list a specific purpose, for profit corporations, most state statutes allow for a general-purpose clause to be used such as "any and all purposes as allowed under the Michigan Business Corporation Act."

- Number of authorized shares, the par value of the shares, and the designation of classes of stock and series or shares within a class of stock (if applicable). Authorized shares are the number of shares of stock that the corporation is authorized to issue to its shareholders. A corporation does not have to issue all their authorized shares. Par value is defined as the face or stated value of a share of stock. The Model Business Corporation Act and the statutes of most states have eliminated the concept of par value. Shares of stock can be issued in series or classes. Examples of these are voting and nonvoting shares, and preferred shares.

- The term of the corporation (if other than perpetual). Unless specified otherwise, a corporation is deemed to go on continuously until such time as an event occurs (i.e., a merger, consolidation, or dissolution).

Once the Articles of Incorporation are filed with the state of domestic jurisdiction, the incorporator(s) approves the initial bylaws of the corporation and appoints the first board of directors, which shall consist of one or more individuals. The bylaws outline the method and manner for governing the corporation (i.e., prescribes how to elect officers and directors, how to issue stock, what kind of notice is required to hold meetings, etc.).

Once the incorporator has formed the corporation and elected the first board of directors, the Board of Directors will, at a minimum:

- Confirm the actions of the incorporator(s).

- Elect officers as prescribed by the bylaws and/or the respective state statute. Under the MBCA and most state statutes, the officers must be at least a President, Secretary, and Treasurer, and then any other officers as specified in the Corporation's Bylaws.

- Issue stock to the shareholders.

- Authorize a corporate bank account.

- Grant officers of the corporation authority to execute documents.

- Authorize the corporation to obtain an EIN from the IRS.

- Authorize the officers to enter into contracts.

- Authorize any other necessary actions.

When stock is being issued to shareholders, it is possible for a shareholder to elect Internal Revenue

© 2019, 2020, 2021 NALA, Inc. All rights reserved.

Code (IRC) §351 stock. Incorporating can be partly or wholly tax-free if technical rules are satisfied. No gain or loss is recognized if property is transferred to a corporation solely in exchange for stock of that corporation, and if the shareholder(s) is in control of the corporation immediately after the transfer.

In issuing stock, a shareholder will pay a certain amount (capitalization) for their shares of stock (i.e., what did the shareholder give or pay to the corporation in exchange for the receipt of their shares of stock in the corporation?). If a shareholder transfers real or personal property to the corporation in exchange for their stock, then the shareholder is said to have made a tax-free transfer under IRC §351.

The type of property (property as defined under IRC §3511) transferred tax free includes cash, tangible property, and intangible personal property (e.g., stock, partnership interests, patent rights, and working interests in oil and gas properties).

If a shareholder is going to obtain stock under IRC §351, there are a few technical rules that must be followed. Treasury Regulation §1.351-3(a) requires any person who receives stock of a controlled corporation in a §351 exchange to include a "complete statement of all of the facts pertinent to such exchange" with the tax return for the year in which the exchange is consummated. The statement needs to include a description of property transferred, the stock received, any other property received, and any liability assumed by the controlled corporation.

Treasury regulations also require the tax return to be accompanied by a description of the property received from the shareholder, including a statement of the basis of such property to the shareholder, certain information with respect to the capital stock of the corporation, the amount of money passed to the shareholder, the value and the basis of any other property which passed to the shareholder, and certain information concerning any liabilities assumed by the corporation in the exchange.

Finally, every taxpayer who participates in the IRC §351 exchange must keep permanent records in substantial form which include all the information required (Treasury Regulation §1.351-3(c)).

Typically, the Board of Directors will reference the IRC §351 exchange in the board's minutes and provide a letter of explanation with a copy of the IRC §351 code to the shareholder, and the shareholder's accountant or CPA. A bill of sale also needs to be prepared and executed by the shareholder indicating the transfer of the respective assets to the corporation.

In addition to an IRC §351 exchange, a shareholder may make an IRC §1244 stock election, which applies to shares of stock issued by a small corporation that qualify for ordinary loss treatment. When sold, §1244 stock can be offset against ordinary income without having to carry it forward. Thus, a shareholder can deduct the entire capital loss in the same tax year against ordinary income. This section permits ordinary loss treatment when either the holder of §1244 stock sells or exchanges such stock at a loss or when such stock becomes worthless.

Section 1244 stock is defined in IRC §1244(c)(3) as being common stock in a domestic corporation if the following conditions apply:

- At the time such stock is issued, the corporation was a small business corporation.

- Such stock was issued by the corporation for money or other property (other than stock and securities).

- The corporation, during the five most recent taxable years ending before the date the loss of such stock was sustained, derived more than 50 percent of its aggregate gross receipts from sources other than royalties, rents, dividends, interests, annuities, and the sales or exchanges of stock or securities.

In general, a corporation under IRC §1244(c)(3) is treated as a small business corporation if the aggregate amount of money and other property received by the corporation for stock, as a contribution to capital and as paid-in surplus, does not exceed $1 million. Minutes of the Board of Directors meeting should indicate that the stock being issued to the shareholders is being issued pursuant to IRC §1244.

There are minimum annual requirements that corporations must follow in order to maintain their corporate integrity. Shareholders must meet annually to elect the Directors to their Board of Directors, and the Directors must then meet annually to elect officers of the corporation. The Board of Directors should approve year-end financials and authorize bonuses and contributions to pension plans, if applicable.

Most states require filing an annual report with the respective state agency where the articles have been filed, along with the relevant filing fee. Failure to file an annual report may result in the state involuntarily dissolving the corporation. Annual state, federal, and local tax returns must be filed on behalf of the corporation.

For shareholders to shield themselves from personal liability, the corporation must maintain itself as a separate and distinct entity from that of its shareholders. A corporation must be adequately capitalized, and the funds of the corporation must be kept separate from the funds of the owners. The corporation should not commingle its funds with that of its owners. The corporation must follow the corporate formalities as described above, along with acting as a separate and distinct entity from its owners. If a court finds that the corporation has not acted as a separate and distinct entity, then the court can "pierce the corporate veil," and the shareholders can be deemed to be personally liable.

Advantages

There are several advantages to forming a corporation. A corporation provides limited liability to the shareholders of the corporation. Ownership interests of the shareholders (shares of stock) are easily transferable to others. The corporation's existence is separate from the shareholders of the corporation, so a change in a shareholder does not affect the corporation's existence.

There are also tax advantages to forming a corporation. A corporation can deduct certain expenses from income prior to paying corporate income tax. Certain types of corporations can receive special tax treatment for income or capital gain on the sale of stock (Subchapter S corporations, Subchapter C corporations, and corporations that make a §1244 stock election).

Disadvantages

Unless the corporation has elected to be treated as an S corporation, if the corporation makes a profit and declares a dividend to its shareholders, its income is taxed as corporate income tax and the shareholders must also include any dividend declared and paid to them on their individual income tax returns; thus, the income is taxed twice (double taxation). Compared to a sole proprietorship, general partnership, or limited partnership, a corporation can be costly to organize and requires more extensive record keeping.

Subchapter S Corporation

A Subchapter S corporation is a small business corporation that has chosen a tax status that allows it to be taxed as a partnership to avoid corporate income tax. To qualify as a Subchapter S, the corporation

© 2019, 2020, 2021 NALA, Inc. All rights reserved.

must comply with all the following:

- The corporation cannot have more than 100 shareholders (family members from as many as six generations count as one shareholder).

- The corporation may have only "natural persons" as shareholders (certain trusts qualify as natural persons).

- The corporation must be a domestic corporation (not formed in another country such as Canada).

- The corporation can issue only one class of stock.

- Nonresident aliens cannot be shareholders of the corporation.

- The corporation must timely file IRS Form 2553 with the IRS (a one-time filing). The form must be signed by each shareholder and an officer of the corporation. Timely filing means it must be filed before the 16th day of the third month of the tax year that the election is to take effect, or at any time during the preceding tax year. If a tax year is less than two months long, an election is made timely if it is made no later than two months and 15 days after the beginning of the tax year. An election made after the 15th day of the third month but before the end of the tax year is effective for the next year. If a late election is made, and failure to file can be shown due to reasonable cause, then relief may be requested from the IRS.

If a corporation elects to be treated as an S corporation, care must be taken when issuing new stock or transferring shares to new owners, so that the S election is not involuntarily revoked because the corporation no longer meets all the preceding requirements.

Subchapter C Corporation

A Subchapter C corporation is a regular private corporation that pays income taxes and distributes taxable dividends to shareholders because it has chosen not to be treated as a Subchapter S corporation. As a Subchapter C, the corporation can issue "qualified small business stock." Shareholders who hold qualified small business stock for at least five years can exclude up to half of any gain from the sale or exchange of the stock.

Close Corporations

In some jurisdictions, individuals can form close corporations. A close corporation is owned by a small number of shareholders and is typically the form used by a family business. The corporation can dispense with some of the formalities, such as annual shareholder meetings and the election of a board of directors. Shareholders are typically given management control.

Although some states may not have a specific "close corporation statute," many have provisions authorizing shareholder agreements, which can be used to dispense with some of the corporate formalities required under a regular corporate state statute.

PROFESSIONAL SERVICE CORPORATIONS

Professional service corporations (PC) are formed by those licensed in certain professions. Lawyers and doctors must form as professional service corporations. Depending on state statutes, other types of licensed professionals may be required to or have the option to form as a PC, such as certified public accountants, engineers, architects, etc. Depending on the respective state statute, a PC may:

- Render only one professional service, and each shareholder must be licensed in that profession.

- Render one or more professional services, and each shareholder must be licensed in one of the professional services of the corporation.

A PC gives the licensed professional the benefits of a corporation, while not altering the law regarding the liability of a licensed professional. A PC is formed in much the same way as a corporation, and the specific state statute should be reviewed to determine if the business of the corporation would require the corporation to file as a PC.

For a PC, the Articles of Incorporation will require a very specific purpose clause relative to the profession of the licensed professional. The name of the PC must include the words "Professional Corporation" or "PC." Most states require filing an annual report that typically will list the shareholders of the corporation and attest that they are all licensed in the profession or professions of the corporation.

Nonprofit Corporations

A nonprofit corporation is one by which the owners – if any – are not permitted to receive any profits of the corporation. Nonprofits are commonly formed for education, charitable, and religious organizations.

Social clubs, churches, civic organizations, day care centers, foundations, outreach organizations, museums, humane societies, hospitals, schools and centers for personal enrichment, homeowner associations, counseling centers, and trade associations are some of the various types of nonprofit corporations.

All funds of the nonprofit corporation must be used to further the purposes for which the corporation is formed. Nonprofit corporations can make a profit – the profits are used by the business to further its mission and/or purpose. Profits cannot be distributed to any of its shareholders or members (as applicable).

A nonprofit corporation can be organized on either a stock or nonstock basis. If the nonprofit corporation does not issue stock, then it typically is organized either on a directorship or membership basis. Members or shareholders, as applicable, of a nonprofit corporation are entitled to elect a board of directors and to vote on matters on which members or shareholders are entitled. Directors in a directorship corporation are the only individuals authorized to vote.

Many states do not require the use of a specific naming convention for the name of the nonprofit corporation, but specific state statutes should be reviewed when preparing the Articles of Incorporation for a nonprofit corporation. A nonprofit will need to enter into Bylaws, obtain an EIN from the IRS, potentially file annual reports with the state, and will need to file annual tax returns. If a nonprofit is tax exempt, it must file IRS Form 990 (or 990-EZ or 990-PF) annually. If the entity is not tax exempt, then it will file Form 1120 annually. If a tax-exempt nonprofit does not timely file its Form 990 with the IRS, the IRS may revoke the nonprofit's tax exempt status.

If a nonprofit corporation solicits charitable contributions, it may need to obtain a license with the Charitable Trust Division of the respective State Attorney General's office (or a similar bureau of the government) from the jurisdiction in which the entity is obtaining contributions. Not all states require a license, but if an entity is obtaining website contributions, care should be taken to make sure that a charitable solicitation license is obtained from any state jurisdiction where a contribution is received, if required under state law.

 © 2019, 2020, 2021 NALA, Inc. All rights reserved.

Tax Exemption of Nonprofit Corporations

Nonprofit corporations are not automatically tax exempt. In order to obtain tax exemption, a nonprofit corporation must file the necessary documentation with the IRS to obtain federal tax exemption. There are many types of tax exemptions granted by the IRS under the IRC. The following is a list of the various tax exemptions:

- §501(c)(1) – Corporations Organized Under Act of Congress (including Federal Credit Unions)

- §501(c)(2) – Title Holding Corporations for Exempt Organization

- §501(c)(3) – Charitable, Religious, Scientific, and Literary Organizations

- §501(c)(4) – Civic Leagues and Social Welfare Organizations

- §501(c)(4), (9) or (17) – Employee Benefit Associations or Funds

- §501(c)(5) – Labor Organizations and Agricultural or Horticultural Organizations

- §501(c)(6) – Trade Associations and Business Leagues

- §501(c)(7) – Social Clubs

- §501(c)(8) and (10) – Fraternal Societies

- §501(c)(11) – Teachers' Retirement Fund Associations

- §501(c)(12) – Benevolent Life Insurance Associations, Mutual Ditch or Irrigation Companies, Mutual or Cooperative Telephone Companies, or Like Organizations (if 85 percent or more of the organization's income consists of amounts collected from members for the sole purpose of meeting losses and expenses)

- §501(c)(13) – Cemetery Companies (owned and operated exclusively for the benefit of their members or which are not operated for profit)

- §501(c)(14) – State Chartered Credit Unions and Mutual Reserve Funds

- §501(c)(15) – Mutual Insurance Companies or Associations

- §501(c)(16) – Cooperative Organizations to Finance Crop Operations

- §501(c)(18) – Employee Funded Pension Trusts (created before June 25, 1959)

- §501(c)(19) and (23) – Veterans' Organizations

- §501(c)(21) – Black Lung Benefit Trusts

- §501(c)(22) – Withdrawal Liability Payment Funds

- §501(c)(25) – Title Holding Corporations or Trusts with Multiple Parents

- §501(c)(26) – State-Sponsored High-Risk Health Coverage Organizations

- §501(c)(27) – State-Sponsored Workers' Compensation Reinsurance Organizations

- §501(c)(28) – National Railroad Retirement Investment Trust (45 U.S.C. 231n(j))

- §501(c)(29) – Qualified Nonprofit Health Insurance Issuers

- §501(d) – Religious and Apostolic Associations

- §501(e) – Cooperative Hospital Service Organizations

- §501(f) – Cooperative Service Organizations of Operating Educational Organizations

- §501(k) – Child Care Organizations

- §521(a) – Farmers' Cooperative Associations

- §527 – Political Organizations

Three of the most common tax exemptions that a nonprofit organization may obtain from the IRS are:

- 501(c)(3) is organized and operated exclusively for religious, charitable, scientific, literary, or educational purposes, or for testing for public safety, to foster national or international amateur sports competitions, or prevention of cruelty to children or animals.

- 501(c)(4) is organized and operated primarily to further the common good and general welfare of the people of the community (such as by bringing about civic betterment and social improvements).

- 501(c)(6) is organized and operated by chambers of commerce, business leagues, real estate boards, and boards of trade. The National Association of Legal Assistants is a 501(c)(6).

501(c)(3) ORGANIZATIONS

In order to obtain and maintain its exemption, a 501(c)(3) organization cannot have any part of its net earnings inure to benefit any private shareholder or individual, and no substantial part of its activities can consist of carrying on propaganda or otherwise attempting to influence legislation (i.e., lobbying).

To request exemption under 501(c)(3), the nonprofit corporation will need to file IRS Form 1023 with the IRS in order to receive a tax determination letter from the IRS. Form 1023 requires the nonprofit to provide a wealth of information on its financial and management structure. In addition, the nonprofit corporation will need to provide copies of the Articles of Incorporation, Bylaws, financial data, and printed materials or publications regarding the nonprofit entity.

Generally, if an organization files its application within 15 months after the end of the month in which it was formed, and if the IRS approves the application, the effective date of the organization's 501(c)(3) status will be the date it was organized. If the IRS requires major changes to be made to the Articles of Incorporation, the effective date of the 501(c)(3) status may be the date the amendment to the Articles of Incorporation are filed.

The IRS will require the Articles of Incorporation of the nonprofit corporation to contain certain provisions in order to meet exemption requirements in the IRC. The following are a few of the provisions that the IRS requires to be included in the Articles of Incorporation:

- The nonprofit corporation will not discriminate based on race, color, creed, or national origin.

- The nonprofit corporation will not engage in certain political activities.

- A description of what happens to the assets of the nonprofit corporation in the event of its dissolution (e.g., assets of a 501(c)(3) must go to another 501(c)(3) organization). For additional information on the requirements for dissolution, see IRS Publication 557 for sample language.

 © 2019, 2020, 2021 NALA, Inc. All rights reserved.

Additional evidence may also be required to show the IRS that the nonprofit corporation has complied with other state statutes as a condition to filing its Articles of Incorporation (e.g., approval of the state department of education if the nonprofit is formed as a school).

Benefits to Obtaining 501(c)(3) Tax Exemption

Nonprofit corporations may file for 501(c)(3) status because they want to obtain certain incidental benefits, such as public recognition of tax exemption status, advance assurance to donors of the deductibility of contributions, exemption from certain state taxes or certain federal excise taxes, and nonprofit mailing privileges.

A complete list of all current 501(c)(3) tax exempt organizations can be found by going to the IRS website (www.irs.gov/charities).

501(c)(4) Organizations

In order to obtain and maintain its exemption, a 501(c)(4) organization cannot have any part of its net earnings benefit any private shareholder or individual. If the organization engages in an excess benefit transaction with a person having substantial influence over the nonprofit, an excise tax may be imposed on the person and any managers agreeing to the transaction. Under 501(c)(4), a social welfare organization may further its purposes through lobbying as a primary activity without jeopardizing its exempt status. This type of organization can engage in some political activity if such activity is not its primary purpose.

To request exemption under 501(c)(4), the entity will be required to file Form 8976 (Notice of Intent to Operate) and Form 1024-A in order to receive a tax determination letter from the IRS. As with Form 1023, Form 1024-A requires the nonprofit to provide a wealth of information on its financial and management structure. In addition, the nonprofit corporation will need to provide copies of the entity's Articles of Incorporation, Bylaws, and financial data.

Benefits to Obtaining 501(c)(4) Tax Exemption

Nonprofit corporations may file for 501(c)(4) status because they want to obtain certain incidental benefits, such as public recognition of tax exemption status, advance assurance to donors of the deductibility of contributions, exemption from certain state taxes or certain federal excise taxes, and nonprofit mailing privileges.

501(c)(6) Organizations

In order to obtain and maintain its exemption, this type of organization cannot have any part of its net earnings inure to benefit any private shareholder or individual, and no substantial part of its activities can consist of carrying on propaganda or otherwise attempting to influence legislation (i.e., lobbying).

To request exemption under 501(c)(6), the nonprofit corporation will need to file IRS Form 1024 with the IRS in order to receive a tax determination letter from the IRS. Form 1024 requires the nonprofit to provide a wealth of information on its financial and management structure. In addition, the nonprofit corporation will need to provide copies of the entity's Articles of Incorporation, Bylaws, and financial data.

Generally, if an organization files its application within 15 months after the end of the month in which it was formed, and if the IRS approves the application, the effective date of the organization's 501(c)(6) status will be the date it was organized. If the IRS requires major changes to be made to the Articles of Incorporation, the effective date of the 501(c)(6) status may be the date the amendment to the Articles of Incorporation are filed.

It should be noted that even if 501(c)(6) status is granted by the IRS, donors to this type of entity will not be able to take a charitable contribution deduction on their taxes.

Benefits to Obtaining 501(c)(6) Tax Exemption

Organizations will file to obtain 501(c)(6) tax exemption in order to obtain certain incidental benefits, such as public recognition of tax exemption status, exemption from certain state taxes, and nonprofit mailing privileges.

PUBLICLY TRADED CORPORATIONS

A corporation is publicly traded if its shares of stock are traded to the general public on a public stock market exchange. A stock exchange is a market in which securities are bought and sold. There are many stock exchanges around the world including, but not limited to, the New York Stock Exchange, NASDAQ, Japan Exchange Group, London Stock Exchange Group, or Euronext. To find out if a corporation is publicly traded, the paralegal can find a list of all publicly traded companies on the Securities and Exchange Commission (SEC) free web database called EDGAR. Each publicly traded corporation must file a variety of reports with the SEC on EDGAR, all of which are available to the public.

There are a lot of reasons a company may decide to go public.

- To raise a large amount of capital to assist with future expansion.

- As a strategy for founders and venture capitalists, or insiders, to capture profits by exiting a company or selling a percentage in order to make a lot of money. This strategy can also be used by a founder to reduce their risk.

- To provide an opportunity for employees of private companies, who have worked hard to grow the company, to cash in their rewards and make money. (i.e., Google's first employee's net worth is approximately $800,000,000.)

- To acquire more companies. It can be easier to find buyers for a corporation if a corporation's stock is listed on a public exchange.

- To attract top talent by providing stock options.

- To increase the value of the company. Good health, then higher valuation, leads to increase in share price and, in turn, increases net worth of shareholders. Also trading on a public exchange can attract the attention of big financial institutions, banks, and hedge funds. This makes getting loans easier.

- To establish brand equity.

- To encourage management changes which can move the company forward. No longer are the private shareholders in control. Publicly held companies must work toward growth for their public

© 2019, 2020, 2021 NALA, Inc. All rights reserved.

shareholders which can increase shareholder value.

U.S. Securities and Exchange Commission (SEC)

The SEC is an independent federal government agency. The mission of the SEC is to "protect investors, maintain fair, orderly and efficient markets, and facilitate capital formation." The SEC was created by Congress in 1934 as the first federal regulator of securities markets. The SEC oversees the securities exchanges, security brokers and dealers, investment advisors, and mutual funds. Publicly traded companies must file a variety of reports with the SEC, including quarterly financials, annual reports, information change reports (i.e., company insiders), and future forecasts.

Initial Public Offerings

For a private company to go public, they must offer their shares for sale through an initial public offering (IPO). The IPO provides investment capital for the corporation by offering shares of stock for sale to the public for the first time.

In an IPO, the corporation will bring in an underwriting firm or investment bank to help decide how the sale of shares will be handled: from the best type of security to issue, what the offering price will be, the number of shares that will be sold, and how long the shares will be offered for sale. A corporation prospectus will be prepared which will outline information on the corporation, including financial information and expected future operations. Once prepared, the prospectus is filed with the SEC and an offering date is set.

Sarbanes-Oxley

The Sarbanes-Oxley Act of 2002 (Pub L. 107-204, 116 Stat. 745, enacted July 3, 2002), also known as SOX, is a U.S. federal law that outlines expanded requirements for the management and Boards of Directors of U.S. public companies, along with public accounting firms. Some of the provisions of SOX also apply to privately held companies.

SOX was enacted as a result of various major corporate and accounting scandals of larger corporations in the 1990s, in which billions of dollars were lost by investors when the share prices of the affected companies collapsed. There were several major corporations involved in the scandals, including but not limited to, Enron, WorldCom, and Tyco International. In response to the scandals, SOX was enacted by the federal government to provide safeguards to try and eliminate these types of accounting scandals from happening in the future.

SOX contains 11 sections addressing:

1. The establishment of the Public Accounting Oversight Board.

2. The standards for external auditor independence.

3. The individual responsibility of senior executives for the accuracy of corporate financial reports.

4. Enhanced reporting requirements for financial transactions.

5. The establishment of codes of conduct for securities analysts and required disclosure of conflicts of interest.

---

6. SEC's authority to censure or bar securities professionals from practicing.

7. The requirement of the Comptroller General and the SEC to perform various studies and report their findings.

8. The establishment of the Corporate and Criminal Fraud Accountability Act of 2002.

9. The establishment of the White-Collar Crime Penalty Enhancement Act of 2002.

10. The requirement of the Chief Executive Officer to sign the corporation's tax return.

11. The establishment of the Corporate Fraud Accountability Act of 2002.

LIMITED LIABILITY COMPANIES

In 1977, Wyoming initiated a national movement by enacting the first limited liability company act in the United States. The movement started slowly, as it took the IRS more than 10 years to announce that a Wyoming LLC would be taxed as a partnership. Since that time, all 50 states have enacted their own versions of LLC acts.

An LLC is a cross between a corporation and a limited partnership. Owners in an LLC are called members. The LLC is managed either by managers appointed by members or by the members of the LLC. The managers or members may elect or appoint officers to run the day-to-day operations of the business. Unless otherwise specified in the Operating Agreement or Articles of Organization of an LLC, the managers need not be members of the LLC.

The allure of an LLC is its unique ability to bring together in a single business organization the best features of all other business forms. Owners of a properly structured LLC can obtain both a corporate-styled liability shield and the pass-through tax benefits of a partnership. General and limited partnerships do not offer a corporate-styled liability shield, and corporations, including Subchapter S corporations, do not offer shareholders all the passthrough tax benefits of a partnership.

The IRS implemented the Check the Box Rule Under Decision 8697 of 12/18/96. The final "check-the-box" regulations were implemented to simplify the task of classifying entities as either an association (taxable as a corporation) or a partnership. Prior to these rules, drafters had to be careful as to how they drafted Operating Agreements, so that the LLC did not have too many corporate characteristics causing them to be taxed as a corporation rather than a partnership. Drafters of Operating Agreements had to have no more than two of the following corporate characteristics: continuity of life, free transferability of interests, centralization of management, and limited liability.

Therefore, unless an LLC files an election with the IRS on Form 8832, the default election is as follows:

- A multiple-member LLC will be taxed as a partnership for federal tax purposes, and no election is required to be filed with the IRS.

- A single-member LLC will be considered a disregarded tax entity for federal tax purposes (in which case it is treated as a pass-through conduit such as a sole proprietorship) unless it elects to be classified as an association (also known as a corporation).

With the advent of check-the-box regulations, most states revised their LLC acts.

The domestic LLC must file Articles of Organization with the appropriate state authority where the LLC is going to form, while a foreign LLC files an application for Certificate of Authority to Transact Business

---

 © 2019, 2020, 2021 NALA, Inc. All rights reserved.

with the state where the LLC is going to do business. Depending on the specific state statute, the articles or application must be signed by an organizer, a member of the LLC, or an agent. The LLC does not exist until the Articles of Organization are filed with the appropriate governmental agency.

Articles of Organization typically include the following:

- Name of the LLC, including one of the following terms: limited liability company; LLC; limited company; or LC. In some states, "Limited" may be abbreviated as "Ltd." and "Company" may be abbreviated as "Co." (with or without punctuation).

- Name of the registered agent and the address of the registered office.

- Purpose of business (some states allow a general purpose).

- The term of the LLC (specific period or perpetual).

- How the LLC is to be managed – whether it will be managed by members or managed by managers.

Ownership interests in an LLC are called membership interests. Members must approve and execute an operating agreement and elect managers and officers (if applicable). If the LLC has multiple members, it must obtain an EIN from the IRS. If the LLC has only one member and the LLC is not electing to be classified as an association, the LLC will not need to obtain an EIN. The exception to this rule is if the LLC is going to have employees and will be paying withholding taxes, then the LLC will need to obtain an EIN.

Most states require that an annual report be filed in the state where the LLC is formed and/or qualified to do business.

Advantages

There are several advantages in using the LLC form of entity. There is minimal paperwork required to form the entity, minimal annual requirements, and no statutory requirement for meetings to be held by the members or managers. All members of the LLC have very limited liability for the actions of the LLC. Because of the IRS check-the-box regulations, one of the main attractiveness of the LLC form of business is its extreme flexibility.

The members of an LLC and the LLC itself must enter into an Operating Agreement. The Operating Agreement can provide for either very broad or very flexible management, can be very restrictive regarding the right to vote of the members, or can provide provisions forcing a buy-out of a member upon death or incapacity.

The income and/or losses of the LLC are reported on a separate Schedule K-1 attached to each member's tax return. The LLC itself is not taxed, but like the partnership, it must file IRS Form 1065 annually.

Disadvantages

There are a few disadvantages for LLCs that should be considered when forming this type of entity.

Not all countries across the globe recognize the LLC form of entity. Therefore, if the LLC is going to be doing business outside of the U.S., it is important to confirm whether the jurisdiction recognizes the LLC form of business entity.

There are instances in which members in an LLC may have to pay self-employment tax on the net income received from the LLC under IRS Code 1402(a)(13). However, if a member does not participate in the management of the LLC, then the member may be able to avoid paying self-employment tax. A tax analysis should be done to determine if the payment of self-employment taxes will have to be made by the member(s).

LLC acts do not allow for right of withdrawal of a member unless the Operating Agreement allows for membership withdrawal.

LLCs do not protect an individual from their own negligence in acting on behalf of the LLC.

Finally, a member in an LLC will be given a Schedule K-1 at the end of the year which allocates the member's share of revenue and losses. Therefore, the member may have to pay taxes on LLC gain that was not actually distributed to them. This can be handled in the Operating Agreement by specifying that if a member has a tax obligation due to the gain allocated by the LLC, then the LLC will make a distribution to the member in an amount to cover the tax that will be owed by the member.

PROFESSIONAL LIMITED LIABILITY COMPANIES

The Professional Limited Liability Company (PLLC) is formed in the same way as a profit LLC as referenced above. Specific state statutes should be reviewed to determine if the business of the LLC would require the entity to file as a PLLC.

The difference between a profit LLC and a PLLC is that the PLLC is made up of one or more licensed professionals. It gives licensed professionals the benefits of an LLC while not altering the law regarding the liability of a licensed professional.

Depending upon state law, a PLLC may:

- Render a single professional service.

- Render two or more professional services.

- Require that each member and manager be licensed in one of the professional services of the PLLC.

For a PLLC, the Articles of Organization will require a very specific purpose clause relative to the profession of the licensed professional. The name of the PLLC must include the words "Professional Limited Liability Company" or "PLLC." Most states require filing an annual report that typically will list the members of the entity and attest that they are all licensed in the profession or professions of the PLLC.

With all the business entity choices available today, careful consideration must be made as to what type of entity would offer the maximum advantage to those forming the business. While the choices seem confusing, it is worth taking them one at a time and cultivating an understanding of the trades and balances represented by each alternative.

FIDUCIARY DUTY

Fiduciary duty is considered the highest standard of care that a fiduciary has to a principal or beneficiary. A fiduciary is a person who holds a legal or ethical relationship of trust with one or more parties. A

© 2019, 2020, 2021 NALA, Inc. All rights reserved.

principal or beneficiary is the person to whom a duty is owed.

Directors in a corporation, in fulfilling their managerial responsibilities, are charged with certain fiduciary duties. Primary of those are the Duty of Care and Duty of Loyalty.

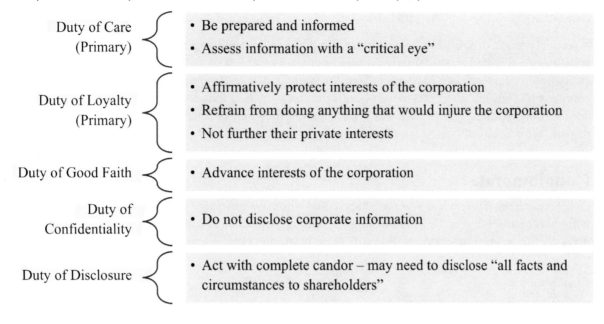

Duty of Care (Primary)	• Be prepared and informed • Assess information with a "critical eye"
Duty of Loyalty (Primary)	• Affirmatively protect interests of the corporation • Refrain from doing anything that would injure the corporation • Not further their private interests
Duty of Good Faith	• Advance interests of the corporation
Duty of Confidentiality	• Do not disclose corporate information
Duty of Disclosure	• Act with complete candor – may need to disclose "all facts and circumstances to shareholders"

BUSINESS JUDGMENT RULE

Besides Duty of Care and Duty of Loyalty, directors and officers of a corporation also need to be aware of the business judgment rule. Unless it can be proven otherwise, a court will presume that in making a business decision, directors and officers of a corporation acted: in an informed basis, in good faith, and in the honest belief that the actions taken were in the best interest of the corporation. Under this rule, courts will generally refrain from questioning the directors' and officers' judgment so long as their judgment can be attributed to some rational corporate purpose. This rule is designed to protect directors and officers of a corporation from making a decision that turns out badly. In the event a business decision of the directors and/or officers is challenged and taken to court, and the court determines that the director(s) did not act within the business judgment rule (they breached one or more of their fiduciary duties), a court may judge in favor of a plaintiff. It is imperative that directors and officers always uphold their fiduciary duties to the corporation.

COMMERCIAL TRANSACTIONS

Mergers and acquisitions (M&A) are transactions in which the ownership of companies, other business organizations, or their operating units are transferred or consolidated with other entities. Directors and management of a corporation typically view an M&A as a strategic management opportunity for a corporation. M&A can allow enterprises to grow or downsize and change the nature of their business or competitive position.

Mergers

There are many types of mergers that can occur between business entities.

A horizontal merger occurs when two or more businesses that offer similar or compatible products or services in the same market combine under a single entity. The driving force for this type of merger is typically not financial, but a desire to obtain a larger market share. In a horizontal merger, one company usually acquires a competitor. An example of a horizontal merger would be the merger of Hewlett Packard and Lexmark's printer divisions.

A vertical merger occurs when two or more companies who produce compatible products or services for a specific finished product merge with each other. The object of this type of merger is to create an entity that is more efficient in its operation. An example of a vertical merger would be the merger of a company that makes auto parts merging with the company that makes the automobile. The companies do not compete directly with each other, but together they may be able to streamline their business, thus providing potential efficiencies in manufacturing and sales.

Conglomerate

Conglomerate mergers occur when entities merge who have unrelated business activities. These occur within companies that really have nothing in common. Companies could enter this type of merger to diversify funds, start new revenue lines, increase branding, etc.

Example:

> General Electric over the years has acquired various types of businesses including radios, televisions, lighting, office appliance, and health care equipment. Through various conglomerate mergers, GE is now one of the biggest conglomerate companies trading on the stock exchange.

Consolidation

A consolidation or amalgamation is the merger and acquisition of many smaller companies into a few much larger ones.

NON-MERGERS

Joint Ventures

Joint ventures are business agreements in which the parties agree to develop, for a finite time, a new entity and new assets by contributing equity. They exercise control over the enterprise and consequently share revenues, expenses, and assets.

Dissolution

Once an entity no longer does business or no longer holds any assets, the entity will file the necessary documentation with the appropriate governmental agencies to dissolve. The documentation includes filings with the respective state authorities where the entity is formed and/or qualified to do business. In addition, the respective state and/or local government tax authorities, along with the IRS, will also need to be notified that the entity has dissolved.

© 2019, 2020, 2021 NALA, Inc. All rights reserved.

In some instances, if an entity does not file the required annual reports with a state government authority, the state may take the steps to administratively dissolve or automatically dissolve an entity. In most cases, if this happens, an entity can file the missing annual reports, pay the required fees and penalties, and the state will reinstate them back into good standing.

ACQUISITIONS

When a business is being sold, there are typically two methods that can be used to accomplish the sale. The seller will either sell the assets of the business or the ownership interest in the business (i.e., the shares of stock of a corporation, the membership interest of an LLC, or the partnership interest in a partnership). There are advantages and disadvantages to each type of method of sale.

Asset Sale

An acquisition of assets (by a buyer) or the sale of assets (of the seller) occurs when one business entity purchases all or substantially all the assets of another business. In this type of transaction, the buyer is purchasing just the assets and is not purchasing an ownership interest in the business.

There are various reasons that a buyer may favor an asset purchase over an ownership interest purchase.

- The buyer purchases only those assets that they want to purchase. A buyer is not required to purchase all the assets of a business. In this way, a buyer can pick and choose those assets that are beneficial for their business.

- A buyer's exposure to unknown liabilities is limited, so the buyer will not need to spend as much time and resources on completing and reviewing due diligence information on the business. The liabilities of a business entity are owned by the business entity and are typically not transferred with the assets on a sale of assets.

- Since the liabilities of a business are owned by the business, a buyer can dictate what liabilities, if any, they are willing to assume.

- A buyer can also purchase the goodwill of the company and can amortize the value of the goodwill over 15 years for tax purposes.

  ▫ According to Investopedia,[1] goodwill is defined as "an intangible asset that arises when one company purchases another for a premium value. The value of a company's brand name, solid customer base, good customer relations, good employee relations, and any patents or proprietary technology represent goodwill." In other words, the goodwill value of the company is based on its reputation and corporate image. A company's name can be part of its goodwill. If a company is doing well and has good brand recognition, then there may be a high value on its goodwill – so much so that in many cases the value of the goodwill of a company may be worth more than the physical assets of the company.

- A buyer can determine which employees, if any, they want to employ without impacting the buyer's current unemployment rates.

As with advantages, there are also various disadvantages that must be considered if contemplating an asset sale:

- The buyer needs to review the contracts of the selling business. Contracts are the lifeblood of

---

1 Investopedia, LLC (website https://www.investopedia.com/terms/g/goodwill.asp)

© 2019, 2020, 2021 NALA, Inc. All rights reserved.

a business. The buyer may want to continue some of the current contracts of the seller because of certain pricing terms, or the services being provided are crucial to the purchase of the assets. Typically, the terms of the contract will need to be renegotiated with the third party or assigned over to the buyer. The reassignment of the contract to the buyer or approval of the third-party vendor to allow the buyer to continue the terms of the current contract can be time-consuming and possibly expensive. The goodwill of the seller may have allowed the seller to obtain a favorable price structure under their contracts with their vendors that the buyer may not be able to obtain itself, after the purchase is completed.

- The tax liability for a seller in an asset sale can be higher than in a stock sale. Therefore, the seller may require a higher selling price in order to off-set their potential tax liability.

- Depending on the type of assets being purchased, the buyer may need to pay transfer taxes on the assets. An example of this would be the sale of real estate and the payment of transfer taxes to a county register of deeds.

- Depending on the type of asset being purchased, the asset(s) may need to be retitled into the name of the buyer.

- Finally, if it is determined that there are any liens on the assets being purchased, and the buyer is purchasing the assets free and clear of any liens, then the buyer will need to work with the seller to obtain the release of liens on such assets.

Ownership Sale

An acquisition of an ownership interest (by a buyer) or the sale of an ownership interest (of the seller) occurs when one business entity purchases the ownership interest of another business. The sale typically will occur between the owners of the business as the seller(s) (it could be all the owners or some of the owners) and the buyer. The buyer can either be an individual or another business entity.

There are various reasons that a buyer may favor the purchase of ownership interests in a business instead of purchasing its assets.

- The process of purchasing the ownership interests in a business is typically less complicated than purchasing assets.

- Since the assets of the company remain with the company, the buyer does not have to deal with the cost or time it takes to retitle assets.

- Since the contracts of the company remain with the company, the buyer will typically not have to renegotiate contracts. However, all contracts should be reviewed to ensure that no contract will be voided in the event of a change of control of the business.

- There may be tax advantages to the buyer as they may be able to avoid paying transfer taxes.

As with advantages, there are also various disadvantages that must be considered if contemplating an asset sale:

- It is imperative that the buyer do a complete and thorough due diligence review of all aspects of the business since the buyer will inherit the complete business. The review should include but not be limited to financials, tax returns, liabilities, assets, liens, contracts, employment liabilities, pension plans, etc.

- A buyer's exposure to liabilities is not restricted to just those that occur after they purchase the

 © 2019, 2020, 2021 NALA, Inc. All rights reserved.

ownership interest in the business. The liabilities of a business entity continue with the business.

- Although the goodwill of the company stays with the company, in an ownership purchase the value of the goodwill is not tax deductible to the buyer.

ANTITRUST ISSUES

Commerce in the United States is based on the belief that free trade and open markets will provide consumers with better products, services, and prices. An open market system also promotes innovation and provides consumers with more choices. Due to the importance of free trade in the United States, several antitrust acts have been put into place to protect the free trade and open markets that are vital to U.S. commerce. The purpose of antitrust laws is to prohibit practices that prohibit or restrain free trade. There are three major Federal antitrust laws in the United States. They are:

1. The Sherman Antitrust Act,
2. The Clayton Act, and
3. The Federal Trade Commission Act.

Sherman Antitrust Act of 1890

The Sherman Antitrust Act of 1890 (Sherman Act) was the first of the Federal antitrust acts passed into legislation in the U.S. This Act was an attempt by Congress to regulate competition among businesses in the U.S. The Sherman Act outlaws the restraint of trade and prohibits monopolies in business. Prior to the establishment of the Sherman Act, commerce in the U.S. was becoming controlled by a few who were interfering with trade and reducing competition in business.

Penalties under the Sherman Act can be severe and costly. Civil as well as criminal penalties can be imposed and are prosecuted through the U.S. Department of Justice (DOJ).

Clayton Antitrust Act of 1914

The Clayton Antitrust Act of 1914 (Clayton Act) is an amendment to the Sherman Act. The Clayton Act was enacted to address certain issues that were either not clear or were not addressed in the Sherman Act. The Clayton Act focuses on topics such as price discrimination, price fixing, and unfair business practices such as anti-competitive mergers. To clarify vague language of the Sherman Act, the Clayton Act clarified the legality of labor unions and their rights to peaceful strikes, picketing, and boycotts under Federal law.

The Clayton Act is enforced by the Federal Trade Commission (FTC) and the Antitrust Division of the Department of Justice (DOJ).

In 1976, The Hart-Scott-Rodino Antitrust Improvements Act (HSR Act) was enacted as a set of amendments to the Clayton Act. Under the HSR Act, parties are not able to enter into certain types of mergers, acquisitions, or transfer of securities or assets until a detailed filing is made with the FTC and DOJ prior to the transaction, and approval is obtained from both agencies to proceed with the transaction. The FTC and DOJ are charged with reviewing the information provided in the filing to determine that the transaction will not adversely affect commerce in the United States as defined under the antitrust laws. There are certain threshold levels and types of transactions that are required to make an HSR filing with the FTC and the DOJ. Whether or not a filing is required under the HSR Act is determined by looking at:

1. the Commerce Test,

2. the size of the transaction test based on the year of the transaction (threshold levels change annually), and

3. the size of person test. Failure to file under the HSR Act can result in large fines and penalties to all entities involved with the transaction.

Additional information on the HSR Act and the current requirements to do an HSR filing can be found by going to www.ftc.gov.

Federal Trade Commission Act of 1914

The Federal Trade Commission (FTC) was formed as a result of the Clayton Antitrust Act. The mission of the FTC is to enforce the rules of the competitive marketplace – to protect consumers and promote competition. The FTC enforces the various antitrust laws so that consumers will be protected from anticompetitive mergers and business practices. One can find additional information about the FTC and what they do to protect the free and open market places of the U.S. by going to go www.ftc.gov.

© 2019, 2020, 2021 NALA, Inc. All rights reserved.

CHAPTER 4: PRACTICE QUESTIONS

1. **Which of the following is not found in a general partnership?**

   A. Limited partner

   B. General partner

   C. Federal Employer Identification Number

   D. Written partnership agreement

2. **Which is not a reason that the court would use to pierce the corporate veil of a business:**

   A. Not following corporate formalities (i.e., holding annual shareholder and director meetings)

   B. Not timely filing tax returns

   C. Owners commingling corporate funds with personal funds

   D. Entity inadequately capitalized

3. **If a court pierces the corporate veil, then shareholders:**

   A. Must resign any officer position they hold

   B. Are personally liable for debts of the corporation

   C. Must sell their stock in the corporation

   D. May be fined

4. **Shareholder Agreements do not allow a corporation to dispense with:**

   A. The Board of Directors

   B. Discretion or power of the Directors

   C. The election of officers

   D. Annual meetings of the Directors

5. **To go public, a corporation must offer shares through:**

   A. A local stock exchange

   B. A GASBY 500 offering

   C. An initial public offering

   D. A Sarbanes-Oxley offering

6. **An S corporation is federally taxed as a/an:**

   A. Association

   B. Partnership

   C. Small business corporation

   D. Corporation

7. **Once formed, all nonprofit corporations are tax exempt.**

   A. True

   B. False

8. **A nonprofit corporation that is tax exempt must annually file with the IRS which of the following IRS tax form:**

   A. 1120

   B. 2553

   C. 8832

   D. 990

9. **An unincorporated entity with two or more persons is called:**

   A. Limited liability company

   B. Limited partnership

   C. Nonprofit corporation

   D. General partnership

10. **Which of the following are considered primary fiduciary duty?**

    A. Duty of care and duty of loyalty

    B. Duty of care and duty of confidentiality

    C. Duty of disclosure and duty of confidentiality

    D. Duty of disclosure and duty of good faith

11. **The Sarbanes-Oxley Act was enacted as a result of various major corporate and accounting scandals of larger corporations in the 1990s.**

    A. True

    B. False

© 2019, 2020, 2021 NALA, Inc. All rights reserved.

12. **Under the business judgment rule, a court will presume that in making a business decision, directors and officers of a corporation acted:**

    A. In an informed basis, in good faith, and in the honest belief that the actions taken were in the best interest of the corporation

    B. In an informed basis and in a manner that benefits the officers and directors

    C. Only for the benefit of the shareholders of the corporation

    D. There is no such thing as a business judgment rule

13. **The business judgment rule is designed to protect directors and officers from making decisions for the corporation when they were ill-informed.**

    A. True

    B. False

14. **The Hart-Scott-Rodino Act is:**

    A. A business corporation act enacted in Delaware

    B. Enacted by Congress to enforce the business judgment rule

    C. Is a set of amendments to the Clayton Antitrust Act

    D. Requires all sellers of a business to make a filing with the Department of Justice

15. **The first Federal antitrust act enacted in the U.S. is called the:**

    A. Clayton Antitrust Act

    B. Federal Trade Commission Act

    C. Hart-Scott-Rodino Antitrust Improvements Act

    D. Sherman Antitrust Act

16. **Goodwill of a company is defined as:**

    A. The value of a company's brand name

    B. The reputation of the company

    C. The amount of assets of a company

    D. The value of a company's brand name and the reputation of the company

17. **The sale of assets of a business always results in the change of owners of a business.**

    A. True

    B. False

© 2019, 2020, 2021 NALA, Inc. All rights reserved.

18. **A horizontal merger occurs when:**

    A.   Two businesses merge to offer different products or services

    B.   Two businesses form a third corporation in order to diversify product lines

    C.   Two businesses merge to offer similar or compatible products or services in the same market

    D.   Two businesses merge to offer new products in the market

19. **A vertical merger occurs when:**

    A.   Two businesses merge to offer different products or services

    B.   Two businesses form a third corporation in order to diversify product lines

    C.   Two businesses merge to offer new products in market

    D.   Two businesses merge who produce compatible products or services for a specific finished product

20. **Which of the following is not a type of merger?**

    A.   Vertical

    B.   Horizontal

    C.   Consolidation

    D.   Dissolution

21. **Which of the following is the default tax rule under the check-the-box regulations for a single member limited liability company?**

    A.   Single member LLC is taxed as a partnership

    B.   Single member LLC is taxed as a sole proprietorship

    C.   Single member LLC is taxed as a corporation

    D.   Single member LLC is taxed as an S corporation

22. **Which of the following is the default tax rule under the check-the-box regulations for a multi member limited liability company?**

    A.   Multiple member LLC is taxed as a partnership

    B.   Multiple member LLC is taxed as an association

    C.   Multiple member LLC is taxed as a corporation

    D.   Multiple member LLC is taxed as an S corporation

© 2019, 2020, 2021 NALA, Inc. All rights reserved.

23. The owners in an LLC are called:

A. Members

B. Managers

C. Shareholders

D. Partners

24. Under the Model Business Corporation Act, which of the following is the responsibility of the shareholders of a corporation:

A. Elect the Officers of the Corporation

B. Elect the Directors of the Corporation

C. Appoint the Registered Agent of the Corporation

D. Authorize the bank account of the Corporation

25. Under the Model Business Corporation Act, the officers elected must include which of the following:

A. President, Vice President, Secretary, and Treasurer

B. Chairman of the Board, Secretary, and Treasurer

C. Chairman of the Board, President, Secretary, and Treasurer

D. President, Secretary, and Treasurer

Suggested Reference Materials

- Uniform Partnership Act (UPA) and Revised Uniform Partnership Act (RUPA), National Conference of Commissioners on Uniform State Laws (NCCUSL)

- Uniform Limited Partnership Act (ULPA) and Revised Uniform Limited Partnership Act (RULPA), NCCUSL

- Doing Business Outside Your State: The CSC Guide, Corporation Service Company

- What Constitutes Doing Business, CT Corporation

- Model Business Corporation Act (MBCA), Committee on Corporate Laws of the Section of Business Law of the American Bar Association

- Uniform Limited Liability Company Act (ULLCA) and Revised Uniform Limited Liability Company Act (RULLCA), NCCUSL

- Internal Revenue Code (I.R.C.), (26 USC)

- Sherman Antitrust Act of 1890 (26 Stat. 209, 15 USC §§ 1-7)

- Clayton Antitrust Act of 1914 (15 USC §§ 12-27, 29 USC §§ 52-53)

- Federal Trade Commission Act of 1914 (15 USC §§41-58 as amended)

- Hart-Scott-Rodino Antitrust Improvements Act of 1976 (15 USC §18A)

- *Guide to Antitrust Laws*, Federal Trade Commission, https://www.ftc.gov/tips-advice/competition-guidance/guide-antitrust-laws

© 2019, 2020, 2021 NALA, Inc. All rights reserved.

Criminal Law & Procedure

Written by Penelope Long-Leahy, ACP

"If he who breaks the law is not punished, he who obeys it is cheated. This, and this alone, is why lawbreakers ought to be punished: to authenticate as good, and to encourage as useful, law-abiding behavior. The aim of criminal law cannot be correction or deterrence; it can only be the maintenance of the legal order."

- Thomas Szasz

© 2019, 2020, 2021 NALA, Inc. All rights reserved.

This chapter covers the substantive criminal law, which is the behavior or conduct that creates a crime, and criminal procedure, which are the rules which regulate how criminal cases are processed.

WHAT IS A CRIME?

A crime is any act which violates a public law put into place by local, state, and/or federal governments. This is different from a civil wrong (a tort), which is an action against an individual that requires compensation or restitution.

Criminal law is the prosecution by a government of an individual who has been accused of committing a crime. In criminal law, a suit is brought by a prosecutor working for the state in which the crime was committed. When a person is accused and convicted of a crime, the individual may be incarcerated, fined, or both. There are two primary crime classifications: felonies, which are serious such as rape and murder, and misdemeanors, which are less serious offenses such as petty theft. The prosecutor must establish proof for each element of each charged offense beyond a reasonable doubt.

In this chapter, we will explore the elements and classification of crimes, the constitutional amendments applicable to criminal law, and the complex practice of criminal procedure.

JURISDICTION

Criminal law jurisdiction determines which court has the right and power to govern a particular type of crime and/or where it was committed.

Federal Jurisdiction

In general, federal courts have exclusive jurisdiction over federal offenses, and state courts have exclusive jurisdiction over state offenses. However, some kinds of conduct qualify as both state and federal offenses.

Federal criminal jurisdiction commonly arises where:

- The crime occurred on land owned or controlled by the federal government (such as national parks and military bases).

- The offense took place on a ship flying the American flag, even if it occurred in foreign waters.

- The conduct occurred within the individual states when the power to regulate the conduct or activity was expressly granted by the Constitution such as taxation, federal officials, interstate commerce, and criminal activity that crossed state lines (i.e., kidnapping or drug trafficking).

Federal courts also may have jurisdiction over crimes occurring in foreign countries if the defendant intended an effect to occur inside the United States (examples include cybercrimes and terrorist attacks). But, depending on the foreign country, the federal government may have difficulty bringing the offender to court.

Federal jurisdiction also may extend to offenses occurring on Native American reservations. Federal jurisdiction would depend on the seriousness of the crime and agreements between the relevant tribe and other governments.

 © 2019, 2020, 2021 NALA, Inc. All rights reserved.

State Jurisdiction

Most crimes that occur within a state's borders, or within three miles of its coastline, are prosecuted in state court. Unlike the federal government, each state has inherent power to regulate its internal affairs to protect or to promote public health, safety, welfare, or morals (police power). However, if a crime occurs on land that is federally owned but rests entirely within one state's borders, it typically is a federal offense.

State law usually specifies which courts have jurisdiction over which types of cases. In many states, adult felonies and misdemeanors are divided between different courts. Most states also have juvenile courts, which have exclusive jurisdiction over crimes committed by minors. Juveniles can, however, be tried as adults in some circumstances, as discussed later in this chapter.

The names for the kinds of state courts vary from state to state. Courts of general jurisdiction usually are called "superior" or "circuit" courts. "Municipal court" is a common kind of limited jurisdiction court.

Concurrent Jurisdiction

Concurrent jurisdiction exists where more than one court can claim power to decide a case. For example, more than one state might have jurisdiction where the crime begins in one state and continues into another. Or a crime might occur partly on federal land and partly on non-federal land, giving the state and the federal government jurisdiction.

Often, the first court to exercise jurisdiction over the defendant keeps the case to itself, if only temporarily. That state's jurisdiction will be exclusive; any other courts claiming jurisdiction must wait until the case is over or the first court releases its jurisdiction. Simply filing a charge is not enough to obtain jurisdiction. The government must get the defendant to court (procedurally it usually does so by arrest and arraignment).

Some state laws and constitutions address concurrent jurisdiction, but others do not. In most cases, the first-in-time rule applies. When there are competing claims to jurisdiction, the prosecuting attorneys usually get together and try to reach an agreement about who will go first.

SOURCES OF CRIMINAL LAW

Criminal law defines crimes; sets the procedures for arrests, searches and seizures, and interrogations; establishes the rules for trials; and specifies the punishments for offenders. But from where did criminal law originate?

Common Law

During the 12th century in England, common law came into existence. Judges created common law by ruling that certain actions were crimes against the state. These crimes were subject to punishment and defined offenses such as murder, rape, arson, mayhem, robbery, larceny, and burglary. Over time, the British judges' rulings produced a book of unwritten laws and customs. The American colonists adopted the common law to define and enforce crimes for which there was no available statute. This law formed the basis of the legal system in the American colonies.

With common law came the law of precedent, or *stare decisis*. Once a court made its decision, that decision was binding on other courts in later cases presented with the same legal problem. *Stare decisis* literally means to "let the decision or precedent stand." This principle continues to guide courts in

---

© 2019, 2020, 2021 NALA, Inc. All rights reserved.

making decisions and to ensure fairness in the judicial process.

Although federal crimes are defined exclusively by statute, Congress still recognizes common law crimes in the District of Columbia.

The Constitution

Article VI of the United States Constitution asserts that:

> This Constitution, and the laws of the United States which shall be made in pursuance thereof; and all treaties made, or which shall be made, under the authority of the United States, shall be the supreme law of the land; and the judges in every state shall be bound thereby, anything in the Constitution or laws of any State to the contrary notwithstanding.

If a law conflicts with the Constitution, the U.S. Supreme Court can strike it down as unconstitutional. Each state adheres to its own constitution and all local laws are subordinate.

Statutes and Ordinances

Criminal law is made up of laws passed by Congress and by state legislature, in addition to ordinances passed by municipalities. The federal government and each state have a statutory criminal code. Generally, laws defining crimes are statutory. Some overlap does exist between state and federal statutes. When there is overlap, the state and federal government decide who will take responsibility. The consequences for federal crimes are usually much more severe.

Thousands of federal statutes fall into numerous categories, including statutes governing gun control, child protection, fair sentencing, and controlled substances, to name a few. Generally, federal crimes apply to areas of national interest and affect more than one state. Federal agencies that enforce federal crimes include the Federal Bureau of Investigation (FBI), which is the primary federal law enforcement agency. Since 9/11, many other such agencies have been created.

Administrative Rules with Criminal Penalties

U.S. governmental agencies and commissions make rules that are semi-legislative or semi-judicial in character. These rules are considered a branch of public law and commonly called regulatory law. Decision-making in the daily activities of various federal and state agencies is governed by administrative rules. Examples of administrative agencies that make such rules are the Federal Trade Commission (FTC), Internal Revenue Service (IRS), and Environmental Protection Agency (EPA). In addition to formulating rules, these agencies investigate violations and impose sanctions. Administrative agency rules relate to a variety of crimes, including securities fraud, income tax evasion, selling contaminated food, and dumping toxic waste.

Appellate Court Decisions

When the appellate courts decide a legal issue, the doctrine of precedence (*stare decisis*) mandates that future cases must follow that decision. This means that the holding in an appellate court case has the force of law. These decisions are referred to as case law. The entire criminal justice community depends on the appellate courts, especially the Supreme Court, to evaluate and clarify both statutory laws and government practices against the requirements of the Constitution. Such law results from appellate court

© 2019, 2020, 2021 NALA, Inc. All rights reserved.

interpretations of statutory law or from court decisions where rules have not yet been codified in statutes.

Constitutional Limitations

The U.S. Constitution limits the powers of federal and state governments. These limitations include the prohibition of ex post facto laws, and the requirements for statutory clarity, equal protection, freedom of speech, and privacy. *Black's Law Dictionary* defines ex post facto law as a law passed after the occurrence of a fact or commission of an act, which retrospectively changes the legal consequences or relations of such fact or deed.

Ex post facto laws seek to punish the commission of a crime that occurred before the law took effect. In other words, if a law is not in place to prohibit an act at the time the act is committed, then the act cannot be considered criminal, nor be punished, even if legislation is later passed that criminalizes the act in question.

Void for vagueness doctrine requires that a criminal statute define a crime with sufficient definiteness so that ordinary people can understand what conduct is prohibited, and the statute must not encourage arbitrary and discriminatory enforcement.

A bill of attainder is a legislative act, directed against a designated person, pronouncing the person guilty of an alleged crime (usually treason) without trial or conviction. Bills of attainder are prohibited by the U.S. Constitution.

ACCEPTED METHODS OF INTERPRETATION OF CRIMINAL LAW

Plain Meaning Rule

When the statute language is plain and clear, the court must interpret it as written, even if the court does not agree with the interpretation. The plain meaning rule means that the statute is to be interpreted according to the ordinary meaning of the language unless the result would be cruel or absurd. This rule requires the following: words are given their ordinary meaning; technical terms are given their technical meaning; and local and cultural terms are recognized as applicable. The plain meaning rule prevents courts from taking sides in legislative or political issues.

Strict Construction

Strict construction interpretation of criminal statutes is based on a literal or technical understanding of the words used. The strict construction principle complements the rule of lenity, which holds that ambiguity in a criminal statute should be resolved in favor of the defendant. An ambiguous statute is one that is capable of two or more equally reasonable interpretations.

Effect of Repeal

Under common law and absent a saving clause, the repeal of a statute operates to bar prosecution of earlier violations, provided the prosecution has not yet commenced at the time of the repeal. However, the repeal of a criminal statute cannot be used to free a person who has already been prosecuted and convicted under the repealed statute. A saving clause is a restriction in a repealing act, which is intended

© 2019, 2020, 2021 NALA, Inc. All rights reserved.

to save rights, pending proceedings, penalties, etc., from the eradication which would result from an unrestricted repeal.

The new legal consequences may take effect on the date of the new law, or they may apply backwards to the time of the original decision. The United States Supreme Court has been aware of, and sensitive to, the significance of retroactivity. Throughout the years, the Court considered common retroactivity issues involving legislatures, courts, and administrative agencies. In recent years (post-1997), the Court revised its thinking about the nature and legal effect of retroactivity, particularly legislative retroactivity. Lower court cases also seem to confirm that judicial review of retroactive lawmaking has undergone a change in recent years. This developing body of law from the Supreme Court and lower courts has, in the past decade, basically reconstructed the jurisprudence of retroactivity.

An example of this legal conundrum is the Fair Sentencing Act (FSA), which was signed by President Barack Obama in 2010. In a 2012 case reviewed and decided in the Supreme Court, two defendants committed offenses of crack cocaine distribution before, but were sentenced after, the FSA's enactment. Both argued they should be sentenced in accordance with the FSA's lower penalties. The district courts disagreed, and the Seventh Circuit upheld both sentences. The circuits were split 3-1-1 on the issue. In the Court's 2012 decision, Justice Stephen Breyer wrote the majority opinion for the Court, reversing the Seventh Circuit, holding that the defendants should have been sentenced under the new 2010 guidelines.

The FSA law, passed by Congress in 2010, reduced the prison sentences that judges may impose on individuals who are convicted of crimes involving cocaine in the form of "crack." "Crack" is the most common form of the drug when cocaine is distributed in street-level crime. Congress did not specify whether the more lenient sentences were available only to individuals whose "crack" crimes were committed after the law went into effect, or also covered those whose crimes occurred before the law was passed, but before sentencing. The Supreme Court ruled that the 2010 law should be interpreted to mean that the lower sentences were available to all who were sentenced after the law went into effect, no matter when their crimes were committed. The Court split 5 to 4 on the issue. See *Dorsey v. United States, 567 U.S. 260 (2012)*.

CONSTITUTIONAL AMENDMENTS APPLICABLE TO CRIMINAL LAW

Fourth Amendment

The Fourth Amendment to the U.S. Constitution protects personal privacy and every citizen's right to freedom from unreasonable government intrusion into their persons, homes, businesses, and property, whether through police stops, arrests, or searches of homes and businesses.

Legislators and the courts have put legal safeguards in place to limit law enforcement interference with Fourth Amendment rights, and to ensure proper procedural enforcement.

In criminal law, Fourth Amendment "search and seizure" protections extend to the following actions by law enforcement:

- Physical apprehension or "seizure" of a person, by way of a stop or arrest.

- Searches of places and items in which an individual has a reasonable expectation of privacy, including, for example, his or her person, clothing, purse, luggage, vehicle, residence, hotel room, and place of business.

 © 2019, 2020, 2021 NALA, Inc. All rights reserved.

The Fourth Amendment provides security to citizens during searches and detention. It also prevents unlawfully seized items from being used as evidence in criminal cases. The degree of protection available in an individual case depends on the nature of the detention or arrest, the type of place searched, and the circumstances under which the search occurs.

The legal standards derived from the Fourth Amendment provide constitutional protection to individuals in the following situations, among others:

- A person walking down the street is stopped for police questioning.

- A police officer searches the trunk of a person's vehicle during a stop for a minor infraction.

- An individual is arrested.

- Police officers enter a person's house to place the individual under arrest.

- Police officers enter an individual's house or apartment to search for evidence of crime.

- Police officers enter a corporation's place of business to search for evidence of crime.

- Police officers confiscate an individual's vehicle or personal property and place it under police control.

In most circumstances a police officer may not search or seize an individual or the individual's property unless the officer has:

- A valid search warrant

- A valid arrest warrant

- Probable cause that an individual has committed a crime

The "probable cause" provision comes from the Fourth Amendment of the U.S. Constitution and refers to the requirement in criminal law that police have adequate reason (facts and evidence) to arrest someone, conduct a search, or seize property relating to an alleged crime.

The warrant must be granted by a judge before law enforcement personnel can enter the suspect's property in search of evidence. This Amendment has both a positive and negative impact on the law. For citizens, it is positive because it protects their privacy and prevents police from arbitrarily searching through and taking property. From the perspective of law enforcement, it can be a negative because it could potentially give a criminal the opportunity to remove or destroy evidence before a warrant can be obtained.

Although too numerous to go over in this chapter, there are many potential scenarios implicating the Fourth Amendment, and law enforcement's legal obligation to protect Fourth Amendment rights.

Fifth Amendment

The Fifth Amendment provides that an individual cannot be prosecuted or punished without due process. Due process is the right to be served with notice, to be heard, and to defend oneself. This Amendment ensures that law enforcement, prosecuting attorneys, and courts follow criminal procedure. This procedure prevents people from being unjustly taken from their homes and punished without a trial or being tried and convicted without applicable constitutional protections.

Another right afforded under the Fifth Amendment is the right to remain silent, so that a person does not fall victim to self-incrimination. Upon arrest, a person must be made aware of his Fifth Amendment right to protect themselves from self-incrimination, which is included in the *Miranda* Warning (*Miranda* will be discussed later in this chapter). In a criminal trial, if a defendant is tried and found innocent, the Fifth Amendment prohibits the courts from trying that person again for the same crime. This is known as double jeopardy.

Sixth Amendment

The Sixth Amendment provides that a defendant has the right to a trial that is judged by a jury of the individual's peers in the state and district where the crime was committed. There are exceptions to these conditions in situations where the crime occurred in multiple states or at sea. In these instances, the location of the trial must be decided by government officials.

During this trial, the defendant also has the right to know the nature of the charges, have legal representation, and to face any witnesses for the prosecution. A defendant may self-represent if the defendant is mentally competent. The Sixth Amendment also grants a defendant the right to a public and speedy trial to minimize the time spent incarcerated before a conclusion in the case is reached.

Eighth Amendment

Rights under the Eighth Amendment mostly apply to the punishment phase of the criminal justice system, but these rights can also apply if an individual is injured at the hands of government officials. The Eighth Amendment right would attach if such an injury occurred during a detention or an arrest, or while in prison or other governmental custody. Individuals have the right to seek damages and other remedies for violations of their Eighth Amendment rights by filing civil rights cases. In addition to physical injuries, there are also situations when inaction through "deliberate indifference" of a government official can violate the Eighth Amendment. The failure to provide needed medical care to an individual in custody, for example, can constitute cruel and unusual punishment where it results in harm to that person. In these types of cases, usually brought by prisoners, a claim must show that:

- The offender was aware of some danger or risk of harm.

- The offender chose not to take any steps to remedy the problem.

- This resulted in harm to the plaintiff.

The Eighth Amendment is a crucial constraint on the government's ability to cause cruel and unusual punishment, whether physically, as mentioned above, or economically through an excessive bail or fine. The interpretation of cruel and unusual punishment has changed over the years. The Supreme Court has described cruel and unusual punishments as those which are "repugnant to the conscience of mankind."

In 1972, the Supreme Court placed a ban on the death penalty throughout the United States, due to concerns with the various methods of application, only to have the penalty reinstated in 1977. This five-year reprieve reversed the death penalties of the infamous Manson family murderers. There are also certain forms of the death penalty, such as the electric chair or gas chamber, which have been found to constitute cruel and unusual punishment, even though they had been used for several years and were not deemed repugnant at the time. Excessive prison sentences can also be challenged under the cruel and unusual punishment clause.

 © 2019, 2020, 2021 NALA, Inc. All rights reserved.

14th Amendment

"Our Constitution is color-blind, and neither knows nor tolerates classes among citizens." - Justice John Marshall Harlan

The 14th Amendment was formally and legally approved on July 9, 1868. It contributes greatly to the civil rights of all Americans. First, it made anyone born in the United States legal citizens, including former slaves. Prior to this Amendment, African Americans were not considered citizens of the United States; they were viewed as property. The 14th Amendment also made it illegal for any state to deny a person equal protection under the law. Additionally, this Amendment states that people have a constitutional right to life, liberty, and property that cannot be denied by the government. The 14th Amendment also provides the right to due process. This means that a person's legal rights must be respected when accused of a crime.

There is a difference between the right to due process in the Fifth and 14th Amendments. The Fifth Amendment says to the federal government that no one shall be "deprived of life, liberty or property without due process of law." The 14th Amendment, ratified in 1868, uses the same eleven words, called the Due Process Clause, to describe a legal obligation of all states.

CURRENT CONSTITUTIONAL LAW QUESTIONS AND CASES RELEVANT TO CRIMINAL LAW/PROCEDURE

Fourth Amendment

Police Tactics: The nation first became aware of the police chokehold maneuver after the death of Eric Garner in 2014. The extensive use of that tactic came into further public view after the 2020 police killing of George Floyd in Minnesota. The police officers involved in the Garner and Floyd cases faced criminal prosecution for these deaths.

In many states, police officers have specific immunities for their conduct pursuant to state statutes. The U.S. Supreme Court case *Tennessee v. Garner*, 471 U.S. 1 (1985), specifically addressed the Fourth Amendment, holding that a police officer could only use deadly force (like a chokehold) if deadly force is being used "to prevent the escape of a fleeing suspect," and "only if the officer has a good-faith belief that the suspect poses a significant threat of death or serious injury to the officer or others."

The Floyd and Garner cases surely will bring further Fourth Amendment questions.

Strip Searches: Another recent Fourth Amendment-related situation raises the question of whether some types of strip searches violate a person's constitutional rights, such as those routinely performed by TSA agents at airports in the United States.

Some case law holds that complete nudity is required to be constituted as a strip search. Other cases hold that a strip search can be illegal without the person being totally naked. There are many cases that address the degree of the search itself and how invasive it is on the person being searched. This can vary on the type of crime suspected and the urgency to perform the search to preserve potential evidence against the person. Most are based upon violations of the Fourth Amendment when asserted against a governmental agency or a person acting on behalf of the government. Other claims are brought under an invasion of privacy theory.

Constitutional Protection For Faces In A Crowd: The 2021 U.S. Capitol insurgency brought interesting

---

© 2019, 2020, 2021 NALA, Inc. All rights reserved.

Fourth Amendment questions. Is unlimited law enforcement use of facial recognition software to surveillance footage an unreasonable search and a violation of constitutional rights for people in a peaceful crowd? Should an officer need to demonstrate probable cause that the investigated face on camera is a criminal in order to receive permission to identify a face in a crowd with artificial intelligence? Some believe that police should be required to secure a warrant before running facial recognition software on a public crowd and should be protective of First and Fourth Amendment rights. In *Carpenter v. United States*, the Court held that government access to detailed location data obtained from Carpenter's cell phone provided a "near perfect surveillance," and recognized that the Fourth Amendment must protect such sensitive information. It added that old-world legal rules do not automatically apply in the digital age. According to the ACLU, "[This] decision stands as one of the most consequential rulings regarding privacy in the digital age, providing a roadmap for lower courts to protect many other kinds of sensitive data from warrantless government intrusion… in the digital age, it is virtually impossible to avoid leaving a trail of highly sensitive data..." The Court in the Carpenter case understood that courts have an essential role in digital age privacy protections.

Fifth Amendment

Smartphones: Is unlocking a smartphone protected under the Fifth Amendment? The following case interprets the law in Indiana, but the depth of the analysis into the Fifth Amendment federal case law probably will mean that this case will be cited in other jurisdictions that will have to contend with this issue in their own cases.

In *Seo v. State*, the defendant, Katelin Seo, was being investigated by local authorities for harassment and stalking. Police believed that she was using multiple texting and "Voice over Internet Protocol" (VoIP) on her smartphone to conceal her identity when texting an individual. During their investigation, detectives obtained two search warrants: the first to permit a forensic download of her smartphone contents, and the second to compel her to unlock her phone.

The Indiana court relied on the Fifth Amendment provision that protects a person from "being compelled to be a witness against himself," in its decision. This had further been elaborated upon by the U.S. Supreme Court in *Estelle v. Smith*, 451 U.S. 454, 662 (1981). The Court in the *Smith* case found a fundamental principle of this protection to be that "the State produces evidence against an individual through the independent labor of its officers, not by the simple, cruel expedient of forcing from his own lips." The Indiana Supreme Court held that compelling Seo to unlock her phone was tantamount to requiring her to "assist in the prosecution of her own criminal case."

This most definitely will be an issue in future cases, and this thorough review of Fifth Amendment application to electronic devices will be at the center in the analysis of those cases (*Seo v. State,* No. 18S-CR-595, __ N.E.3d __ [Ind., Jun. 23, 2020]).

Sixth Amendment

State Jury Verdicts for Serious Crimes Must Be Unanimous:

In 48 states and federal court, a single juror's vote to acquit is enough to prevent a conviction. But two states, Louisiana and Oregon, punish defendants based on 10-2 verdicts. For example, in *Ramos v. Louisiana*, petitioner Evangelisto Ramos was convicted of second-degree murder in a Louisiana court by a 10-2 jury verdict. Instead of the mistrial which would have occurred almost anywhere else, Ramos was sentenced to life without parole. A few years later, Louisiana voted for a constitutional amendment which eliminated non-unanimous jury verdicts. However, the amendment was not retroactive.

 © 2019, 2020, 2021 NALA, Inc. All rights reserved.

Subsequently, Ramos challenged his conviction. The Supreme Court agreed and held that the Sixth Amendment requires a unanimous jury verdict to convict for a serious offense, even in state courts. This decision opens the door for defendants convicted by divided juries to obtain new trials. The possible impact of *Ramos v. Louisiana* extends beyond the bounds of criminal procedure, as the judges' passionate debate over when and whether to overturn precedent took the spotlight and illuminated profound divisions within the Court (*Ramos v. Louisiana*, 2016–1199 (La. App. 4 Cir. 11/2/17), 231 So. 3d 44, reversed).

Essential Elements of a Crime

Any crime has four basic elements that must be proven before someone can be charged: *actus reus,* mens rea, causation, or social harm.

Actus Reus: physical or guilty act or unlawful omission.

For criminal liability to exist, the government must prove that the accused performed a physical act that caused social harm with the intent to bring about the harm. Alternatively, the defendant may be found criminally liable if the defendant failed to act when the defendant had a duty to act if:

- The defendant had a legal duty to act.

- It was reasonably possible for the defendant to perform the duty or to obtain the assistance from others to perform it.

A legal duty to act is in place when:

- A statute requires action (such as filing an accident report).

- The defendant contracts for the duty (such as a lifeguard).

- The relationship created the duty (parents have a duty to protect their children).

- The defendant voluntarily assumes the duty (good Samaritan who fails to satisfy reasonable standards of care).

- The defendant creates the dangerous situation (such as someone falling asleep while smoking a cigarette).

- Act is defined here as bodily movement. The act must be voluntary (a conscious exercise of will).

Mens Rea: mental or guilty state; the intent of the defendant at the time of the crime. The exact act or mental state that is required is usually defined in statutes. Bad thoughts alone cannot constitute a crime. However, speech may be an act that can create liability, such as perjury. Intent is required to distinguish between an inadvertent act and an act performed with a "guilty mind."

Intent may be specific, general, or transferred.
- **Specific**: Some crimes are defined to require a specific intent to accompany the actual crime, such as first-degree murder, which would require premeditation. Other specific intent crimes include intent to commit assault, attempt (intent to complete a crime), and larceny (intent to permanently deprive a person of the person's property).

- **General**: General intent can be inferred when the accused knowingly commits the crime and is aware of its prohibited result. In other words, all crimes are general intent crimes unless they are specific or strict liability crimes.

- **Transferred Intent**: Occurs when there is "collateral damage" in a crime. For example, there is a shoot-out and the defendant shot and killed an innocent bystander that he did not intend to shoot. Under transferred intent, the defendant would be found guilty of the bystander's murder.

- **Strict Liability**: Some acts produce outcomes that are punishable regardless of state of mind (for example, statutory rape). In most states, having sex with a minor is a crime even if the defendant did not know the sexual partner was (or reasonably thought that the partner was not) a minor. Selling alcohol to a minor is a strict liability crime in some states: a conviction is likely even if the seller honestly thought the buyer was of legal age and tried to confirm as much.

Causation: Defendant's act must be a proximate cause of the resulting harm; the act committed caused the end harm.

Social Harm: A harmful result caused, both factually and proximately, by the defendant's act. The harm generally is going to be a result of the act that was committed, such as hitting someone or stealing.

MODEL PENAL CODE (MPC)

The MPC does not distinguish between specific intent and general intent crimes. MPC proposes four separate states of mind for which criminal liability may be imposed:

- **Purposefully** – defendant consciously desires conduct to cause a particular result

- **Knowingly** – defendant is aware that conduct is almost certain to cause a particular result

- **Recklessly** – defendant is aware that conduct poses a risk that might cause a particular result

- **Negligently** – defendant should be aware that conduct poses a risk that might cause a particular result

The risks associated with the negligent and reckless MPC definitions must be substantial and unjustifiable. The MPC also assigns a specific state of mind to each element of a crime. For example, the crime of rape requires that the act of sexual intercourse be purposeful, but the element of the victim's non-consent may require only negligence. In the latter situation, if a defendant tells a jury that he believed the victim could have (but did not) expressed willingness, and the jury found his belief unreasonable, his acts would be construed as negligent. A defendant can be convicted whenever the asserted belief in consent is unreasonable. A few U.S. states impose a strict liability; if the jury finds non-consent, an honest belief to the contrary, no matter how reasonable, is no defense.

Under MPC, any intoxication is a defense if it negates mens rea of the crime. However, if it is a crime of recklessness, a defendant's intoxication is immaterial and unawareness of the risk due to voluntary intoxication will not negate mens rea.

CONCURRENCE OF *ACTUS REUS* AND MENS REA

Under the concurrence theory, a retroactive or retrospective application of one of the criminal elements cannot be used to prove guilt. In other words, the act and state of mind must occur in unison.

For example, the accused accidentally runs over a pedestrian while driving. Aware that he hit someone, he rushes from the car and finds that the victim is his hated enemy. Once the accused identifies the victim, he happily professes his joy at having caused the injury. The conventional rule is that no crime

---

 © 2019, 2020, 2021 NALA, Inc. All rights reserved.

has been committed. The *actus reus* is complete, and no rule of ratification applies in the criminal law. To be convicted, the accused must have formed the mens rea either before or during the commission of the *actus reus*.

CLASSIFICATION OF CRIMES

- *Malum in se* (wrong in itself):

    □ A crime that is inherently evil.

    □ Rape, murder, and larceny are *malum in se*.

    □ Crimes of moral turpitude are often *malum in se*.

- *Malum prohibitum*:

    □ A crime that is wrong because the legislature says it is wrong.

    □ Traffic violations and failure to comply with the Federal Drug Labeling Act are examples of malum prohibitum crimes.

- Treason is an attempt to overthrow the government or to betray the government in favor of a foreign power. A person can be convicted of treason only by the testimony of two witnesses or by confession in open court (Article III, Section 3, U.S. Constitution).

- Capital crime is a crime for which the penalty may be death. Many jurisdictions do not have a separate classification for capital crime because these crimes are classified as felonies.

- Felony is a crime for which the maximum penalty may be death. The minimum punishment may be imprisonment for one or more years. However, an accused may be sentenced to a prison term of less than one year upon conviction. Common law felonies included murder, rape, manslaughter, robbery, sodomy, larceny, arson, mayhem, and burglary. It is easier to remember these nine common law felonies by using the mnemonic: MR. & MRS. LAMB.

- Misdemeanor is a crime for which the maximum penalty may be imprisonment for less than one year or statutory violations for which the punishment may be a fine.

CRIMES AGAINST A PERSON

Homicide

Common law murder is the unlawful killing of a human being with malice aforethought. Malice afterthought is interpreted to exist if the actor possesses one of the four following states of mind:

- Intent to kill.

- Intent to inflict great bodily harm.

- An extreme recklessness and disregard for human life (also known as a "depraved heart"). Example: Shooting into a moving train or playing Russian roulette.

- Intent to commit an inherently dangerous felony. Example: Intentional use of a deadly weapon created an inference of intent to kill. The deadly weapon rule includes situations such as a person driving a car through a crowded park, or a person firing a bullet into a room full of people.

Common law voluntary manslaughter is the unlawful killing of a person without malice during a sudden heat of passion due to reasonable provocation. This is known as a "passion killing."

Elements of this homicide are:

- Sudden and intense passion in the mind of an ordinary person, causing oneself to lose self-control.

- Provocation caused by victim. (i.e., Finding spouse in bed with another person.)

- No time for a reasonable person to cool off.

- Defendant did not cool off.

- Mere words are generally insufficient provocation.

- Some jurisdictions allow exceptions to the "mere words" limitation for provoking words that suddenly reveal information sufficient to provoke heat of passion.

- Some jurisdictions have eliminated all exceptions to the "mere words" general rule.

Common law involuntary manslaughter is death caused by criminal negligence (driving under the influence of alcohol) or death caused by an unlawful act (brandishing a weapon and the person at whom the weapon is pointed dies of a heart attack at the sight of the gun).

Misdemeanor manslaughter rule: this rule treats an unintended killing during a misdemeanor as a manslaughter; legal fiction converts mens rea from the underlying misdemeanor to the requisite mens rea for manslaughter.

"Year and a day rule" is an old common law requirement that the death of the victim must occur within one year and one day from the infliction of the injury. There was no prosecution for homicide if death occurred after this time. This was the case even if it were proven that "but for" the defendant's actions, the victim would not have died. Most jurisdictions no longer follow the year and a day rule.

Today, statutes divide murder into degrees. A murder is first degree in the following situations:

- Unlawful premeditated and deliberate killing

  - A murder is premeditated when the defendant reflected on the killing, even if only briefly

  - The deliberation must be done with cool reflection

  - There is no set time requirement for premeditation and deliberation

- Killing is committed in a certain manner articulated by legislature (such as lying-in wait, poison, etc.)

A first-degree felony murder is a death/killing that occurs during the commission or attempted commission of certain felonies enumerated by statute, such as arson, kidnapping, robbery, burglary, and rape. The defendant must be found guilty of the underlying felony.

Second-degree murder, or involuntary manslaughter, is intentional killing without premeditation and deliberation. Involuntary manslaughter are killings, such as a passion killing or killing that occurs while committing a felony, other than those listed above. Many states have added motor vehicular homicide as a type of involuntary manslaughter.

 © 2019, 2020, 2021 NALA, Inc. All rights reserved.

Rape and Sexual Assault

Common law rape is forced sexual intercourse by a male on a female who is not his wife. Sexual intercourse must have been achieved:

- Without the woman's consent, by use of force

- By deception or fraud

- While the woman was asleep or unconscious

- If the female is not competent to consent

Statutory rape previously was intercourse by a male with an underage female who is not his wife. Even if the minor consents, the defendant is guilty of statutory rape because minors do not have capacity to give consent. Modern statutory rape laws protect underage victims, both male and female, and neither consent nor mistake is a defense in most jurisdictions.

Modern statutes define rape and sexual assault as nonconsensual sex. Sex is broadly defined to include more than intercourse. A marital exception is either partially or completely abolished in most states. Rape is now considered gender neutral. Thus, either a man or a woman can commit rape or be raped. The modern focus of law is on sexual autonomy, not chastity.

Incest is a statutory offense – typically a felony – wherein marriage or a sexual act (intercourse or a deviate sexual conduct) occurs between people who are closely related. Most states restrict the crime to blood relatives, but there are some jurisdictions that include some non-blood relatives (such as stepfamily or adoptive family).

Obscenity offenses include crimes such as the sale, publication, or display of material that appeals to a salacious sexual audience and involves patently offensive sexual conduct. Such material lacks literary, artistic, political, or scientific value. The private possession in the home of obscene materials that do not depict children cannot be prohibited. Private possession of pornography in the home is not itself a crime. However, children are not able to consent to participation in the production of pornography. Most states ban possession of materials depicting children engaged in sexual activity even where real children are not used as models. The justification for this is a belief that such pornography will incite consumers to commit real world violence against children.

Assault

Assault (also known as attempted battery) is an intentional attempt, using violence or force, to injure or harm another person. Some jurisdictions require the attempt to be coupled with a present ability to succeed. For example, an unloaded gun cannot succeed. There must be a reasonable fear in the victim's mind of imminent bodily harm. Spoken words are not enough. Simple assault is usually a misdemeanor.

Aggravated assault is the intent to create a more serious crime such as assault with intent to commit murder or rape. Aggravated assault is punished more severely than simple assault (typically a felony).

Battery

Battery is an unlawful (without consent) touching, which may or may not involve an application of force or result in bodily injury. Battery simply can be an offensive touching. In some jurisdictions, criminal negligence is enough, and a battery does not need to be intentional. The touching does not have to be direct. If the touching is applied by means of another force or by a substance put into action by the defendant, it is sufficient. For example, causing a victim to ingest poison or causing a dog to attack a victim.

Cybercrime Against People

These crimes include cyber harassment and stalking, distribution of child pornography, credit card fraud, human trafficking, spoofing, identity theft, and online libel or slander.

CRIMES RELATING TO PROPERTY

Theft or Larceny

The MPC and many states have consolidated numerous crimes involving the deprivation of another's property into one crime: theft. The specifics vary from state to state but combine all forms of larceny, embezzlement, false pretenses, bad checks, receiving stolen property, and extortion (blackmail). Robbery and forgery are treated as separate and more serious offenses.

Arson

Under common law, arson was defined as the malicious burning of the dwelling house of another. Modern statutes include purposeful burning of a structure, or land, that endangers other people or property.

Burglary

Burglary, under old common law, was the breaking and entering of the dwelling house of another, at nighttime, with the intent to commit a felony therein. Burglary has been expanded to include entering any structure with the intent to commit a felony or theft offense inside. For example, if a person enters a pharmacy with the intent to submit a forged prescription (felony), the act would be considered burglary. Modern statutes eliminated the nighttime element.

Larceny

Larceny is the trespassory taking and carrying away of the personal property of another with intent to permanently deprive the individual of that property. This includes finding and keeping lost property with the knowledge or means of discovering ownership. Larceny is a crime against possession. Modern statutes have expanded larceny to include written documents that embody intangible rights. The following cannot be the subjects of larceny: real estate, its fixtures, services, or intangibles. Gas and electric are considered tangible goods and can be the subject of larceny.

Larceny by Trick

This offense occurs when the defendant obtains possession of property by intentionally making a false statement to the victim.

 © 2019, 2020, 2021 NALA, Inc. All rights reserved.

Embezzlement

Embezzlement occurs when a defendant fraudulently or unlawfully converts an owner's entrusted property for the defendant's own use. A person is given access to someone else's property or money for the purposes of managing, monitoring, and/or using the assets for the owner's best interests, but then covertly misappropriates the assets for personal gain. The property owner gave access to the defendant based on trust and confidence in the relationship. The difference between larceny and embezzlement is that larceny requires the taking (asportation) with the intent to permanently deprive, while embezzlement requires intentional conversion with the intent to defraud.

False Pretenses

Under common law, false pretenses is defined as obtaining title by fraud (sale or trade transaction). The victim must have been deceived by, or acted in reliance upon, a misrepresentation. The offense of false pretenses consists of the following elements:

- Obtaining title to property of another

- By an intentional (or knowing) false statement of past or present fact

- With intent to defraud the other

Robbery

Robbery essentially is an aggravated form of larceny. In other words, robbery is larceny by force or threats of force. Robbery is the taking of personal property of another by force or intimidation, with the intent to permanently deprive the other person of the property. Robbery is a felony in all jurisdictions.

Forgery

Forgery is creating a false document or altering an existing document with intent to defraud.

Cybercrime Against Property

Some online crimes occur against property, such as a computer or server. These crimes include DDoS hacking (a distributed denial-of-service attack is a cyberattack on a server, service, website, or network that floods it with internet traffic), hacking, virus transmission, cyber and typo squatting, computer, computer vandalism, copyright infringement, and IPR violations (IPR is unauthorized use, duplication, or sale of materials or products that are legally regarded as protected intellectual property).

Cybercrime Against Government

Cybercrimes against the government include hacking, accessing confidential information, cyber warfare, cyber terrorism, and pirated software.

© 2019, 2020, 2021 NALA, Inc. All rights reserved.

Inchoate Crimes

Conspiracy

Conspiracy is an agreement between two or more persons to commit a crime at some time in the future. Some jurisdictions require at least one overt act to have been undertaken in furtherance of that agreement, to constitute an offense.

- **Wharton's Rule**: Need one more person than required to commit conspiracy of crime (i.e., adultery requires two people; conspiracy to commit adultery requires three people).

- **Husband & Wife Rule**: Under common law, a husband and wife were considered one person, and because conspiracy requires two or more persons, they could not conspire to commit a crime. As other laws concerning the relationship between husband and wife evolved, so have the laws of conspiracy. Today, a wife may legally act independently of her husband, so the two may commit conspiracy.

- **Two or More Rule**: The two or more rule requires that for a conspiracy to exist, two or more persons must be involved. Courts have taken various positions on this rule. If, for example, there are only two alleged conspirators, and one is acquitted, the other may not be convicted because there would only be one party to the conspiracy.

Agreement with Protected Class

If parties agree to commit a crime against persons in a protected class, persons within that class cannot be guilty of the criminal conspiracy based on an agreement with the person in the protected class.

Example:

> A, a woman, and B, a man, agreed on a scheme in which A would be transported over state lines for purposes of prostitution. Is B guilty of criminal conspiracy? No. The act of transporting women over state lines for immoral purposes violates a statute (The Mann Act – see below) that was designed to protect women; thus, A could not be guilty of a violation of the Act and cannot be guilty of conspiracy to violate the Act. Therefore, B cannot be guilty of criminal conspiracy because there were not two guilty parties to the agreement.

The Mann Act

The Mann Act, named after Congressman James Robert Mann of Illinois, in its original form made it a felony to engage in interstate or foreign commerce transport of "any woman or girl for the purpose of prostitution or debauchery, or for any other immoral purpose." Its primary stated intent was to address prostitution, immorality, and human trafficking, particularly where trafficking was for the purposes of prostitution. This was one of several acts of protective legislation aimed at moral reform during the Progressive Era. In practice, its ambiguous language about "immorality" has resulted in its being used to criminalize even consensual sexual behavior between adults. It was amended by Congress in 1978, and again in 1986, to apply to transport for prostitution purposes or illegal sexual acts.

 © 2019, 2020, 2021 NALA, Inc. All rights reserved.

RICO

Passed in 1970, the Racketeer Influenced and Corrupt Organizations Act (RICO) is a federal law directed toward conspiracy and fraud, designed to combat organized crime in the United States. It allows prosecution and civil penalties for racketeering activity performed as part of an ongoing criminal enterprise. Such activity includes illegal gambling, bribery, kidnapping, murder, money laundering, counterfeiting, embezzlement, drug trafficking, slavery, and other objectionable business practices.

Attempt

Attempt is defined as an overt act coupled with specific intent to commit a crime. The crime of attempt has two elements:

- A criminal intent

- A criminal act

Attempted offenses occur when an individual has a specific intent to commit a crime and takes direct action toward completion of the crime. Typically, an individual will have failed to complete the crime, but this is not necessarily required. For example, an attempted murder, where the perpetrator must have the intent to kill someone, then tries to kill, but fails to do so (perhaps just injuring the person).

Solicitation

Solicitation exists when a defendant solicits, or seeks to engage, another to commit a crime, not the subsequent commission of a crime. Therefore, a defendant can be convicted of soliciting, even though the person solicited refuses, and the solicited crime is never perpetrated, if the intent that that crime be committed is present.

Under the common law, inviting, hiring, requesting, commanding, or encouraging another to commit a felony or a serious misdemeanor can constitute the act required for a solicitation. A request to commit an attempted crime does not constitute a solicitation.

Example:

> If Traci asks Jim to steal some makeup for her, and Jim thinks that he is stealing, while Traci knows that the makeup is free, Traci is not guilty of solicitation, although Jim would be guilty of attempted theft. Further, a request for the other person to aid the actor in committing a crime does not constitute a solicitation. Using the Jim and Traci example, if Traci asks Jim if he will be a lookout while she steals some makeup, she is not guilty of solicitation under the common law.

Model Penal Code §5.02(1) defines solicitation as requesting, commanding, or encouraging another person to commit, attempt to commit, or be an accomplice to any crime. The MPC broadens the act requirement of solicitation by including requests to commit misdemeanors and requests to attempt and aid in the commission of criminal offenses. In the examples above, Traci would be guilty of solicitation in both instances under the MPC.

CRIMES INVOLVING JUDICIAL PROCEDURE

- **Perjury**: The voluntary (knowingly) violation of an oath or vow either by swearing to what is untrue or by omission to do what has been promised under oath. Truth is a complete defense to a charge of perjury.

- **Subornation of Perjury**: When a defendant convinces someone else to commit perjury. The defendant who commits subornation of perjury is treated the same as the perjurer for the purposes of sentencing.

- **Bribery**: Bribery refers to the offering, giving, soliciting, or receiving of any item of value as a means of influencing the actions of an individual holding a public or legal duty. This action constitutes a crime and both the offeror, and the recipient, can be criminally charged.

DEFENSES AGAINST THE CRIME

Justification

Justification is a defense when the defendant who committed the crime claims they did no wrong because committing the crime advanced some social interest or vindicated a right so important that it outweighs the wrongfulness of the crime. Therefore, the crime committed is not appropriate for criminal punishment.

Self-Defense, Defense of Property, and Prevention of Crimes

- **Non-deadly force**: A person may use such force as reasonably appears necessary to prevent the imminent use of unlawful force on that person, short of deadly force. There is no duty to retreat before using non-deadly force.

- **Deadly force**: May be used only in self-defense, when it reasonably appears necessary to prevent immediate death or significant injury, or to prevent the commission of a serious felony involving risk to human life. Use of deadly force for self-defense is allowed if the threat is imminent, a response is necessary, and deadly force is proportionate to the threat. The reasonable belief standard is applied to the use of self-defense. Thus, even if the belief in the threat is inaccurate, provided the belief is reasonable, the defense of self-defense still is valid to insulate one from criminal liability. Deadly force may only be used against an attacker who has initiated the aggression using unlawful force. The law recognizes a difference between defense of self and defense of property. Generally, it is not appropriate to use deadly force to defend objects unless a person is also in immediate danger.

- **Battered woman syndrome and reasonable belief**: During active confrontation, one can consider past incidents of violence to determine whether the current threat is deadly or non-deadly. Battered woman syndrome evidence generally is not allowed in nonconfrontational cases where there was no current or active threat of violence at the time deadly force was used. For example, battered woman syndrome will not protect a wife who kills her batterer while he is sleeping because there is no active threat at that moment.

  © 2019, 2020, 2021 NALA, Inc. All rights reserved.

Duty to Retreat Rule

In common law, one must retreat rather than use deadly force unless the attacker is in the individual's own home or business (Castle Doctrine, discussed later). Some jurisdictions have adopted the rule that there is no duty to retreat even if it can be done safely. Increasingly, more jurisdictions are abandoning the duty to retreat requirement and instead are following a new legal trend to allow victims to "stand your ground," even in instances where retreat could be done safely. In "stand your ground" jurisdictions, this right is extended beyond one's home, car, or business, and permits individuals to use deadly force in public with no obligation to retreat. If deadly force is used correctly within the confines of the "stand your ground" statute, it is a defense to the criminal charge. Some "stand your ground" jurisdictions, such as Florida's, specifically state that a person being attacked or threatened, even in a public place, "has the right to stand his or her ground" and meet force with force. This defense played a part in the 2013 Florida prosecution of George Zimmerman, accused of second-degree murder of the unarmed teenager Trayvon Martin. As many as 32 states have adopted some version of the "stand your ground" defense, while other states have retained traditional self-defense statutes that strictly limit the right of self-defense or defense of another to certain actions in certain circumstances.

Right of Aggressor to Use Self-Defense

Generally, the one who starts a fight has no right to use self-defense as a defense, but an aggressor can retain the right to use self-defense if:

- The aggressor removes himself or herself from the fight (withdrawal).

- The victim of minor aggression begins to use deadly force and the aggressor reasonably fears for life (sudden escalation).

- Future threats do not work. If the defendant is threatened with a future attack, the appropriate response is to inform law enforcement, so that they can incapacitate the threatening individual by arrest or prosecution.

Defense of Others

A defendant has the right to use force in defense of another person if the defendant believes the victim had the legal right to use force in the victim's own defense. No special relationship between the victim and the defendant is necessary, but the right to use force in defense of others is bolstered if the person defended is a family member or employee. Pursuant to the retreat rule, the defendant need not retreat unless it is known that the defendant can secure the complete safety of the victim.

Defense of Habitation (The Castle Doctrine)

Originated in common law, the Castle Doctrine permitted an occupant of a dwelling to use self-defense – including deadly force if necessary – within the home against an intruder who intends to commit a felony inside, or to cause harm to an occupant inside the dwelling. Today, a person is justified in using deadly force in defense of the person's home in only two situations:

- When the entry of the home is made in a violent manner and the occupant reasonably believes that the use of force is necessary to protect the occupant or another in the home

- When the occupant reasonably believes that force is necessary to prevent entry into the home by one who intends to commit a felony in the home

Defense of Property

In most jurisdictions, only non-deadly force may be used to defend one's property (in the person's possession) from unlawful interference. Deadly force is only permitted if the other person (other than the victim) allowed use of force. For example, in self-defense of a home invasion with a gun, the use of force must reasonably appear imminent. Few jurisdictions allow the use of deadly force to defend property.

Necessity (Lesser of Two Evils Defense)

Otherwise, criminal conduct is justifiable if, because of pressure from natural forces, the defendant reasonably believed that the defendant's conduct was necessary to avoid harm of self or society. For example, a person trespasses on private property for the purpose of finding the only available phone to call the fire department to report a rapidly spreading fire.

The test used to determine necessity is objective. Causing the death of another person to protect property never is justified. Accordingly, the necessity defense is not available if the defendant is at fault in creating the situation that requires the defendant to choose between the two evils (balance of evils test). For example, if the person in the example above started the rapidly spreading fire, the necessity defense would not apply.

Duress

As opposed to the pressure from natural forces for the necessity defense, duress involves a human threat. This threat must be of death or serious bodily harm to a defendant or family member, must be immediate (defendant cannot have had time to think about it), and the defendant must be free from guilt.

Example:

> A duress defense could arise where a defendant is told that if he does not commit a certain crime, his wife will be killed. However, the excuse of duress may extend to those other than members of the immediate family. Acts committed under duress are excusable rather than justifiable.

Mistake

The mistake defense is any mistaken belief other than a mistake of law. Examples include erroneous beliefs about the meaning of some term or about the identity of some person. In criminal law, a mistake of fact can usually operate as a defense so long as it is reasonable. With crimes that require specific intent, even an unreasonable mistake of fact might work as a defense.

Example:

> Jim picks up the wrong umbrella from a restaurant's coat room, believing it is his own. Jim would not be guilty of larceny because he believed the umbrella was his own. The mistake must be the type of mistake that any reasonable person would have made under the same circumstances.

 © 2019, 2020, 2021 NALA, Inc. All rights reserved.

Other Defenses

Entrapment consists of a two-prong test:

- Criminal design must have originated with law enforcement (a defendant cannot be entrapped by a private citizen).

- The defendant was not predisposed to commit the crime.

Consent of the victim generally is not a defense. However, if it negates an element of the crime, it is a complete defense. For example, proof that a victim consented to sexual intercourse is a complete defense to a charge of forcible rape. Proof that the victim of statutory rape consented is not a defense (due to lack of capacity as discussed previously in this chapter).

CRIMINAL CAPACITY DEFENSES

Infancy

Infancy, descended from British common law, attempts to disprove liability for a crime by reason of the defendant's age. Under the assumption that minors are incapable of forming criminal intent in the same manner as adults, the common law infancy defense traditionally bars the prosecution of children under the age of 7 for crimes and presumptively precludes the prosecution of children aged 7 to 14 years under the adult criminal law system. However, contemporary statutes in criminal law hold that children in the latter age group are eligible for prosecution through the juvenile justice system.

Insanity

In 1964, the American Law Institute (ALI) began to reevaluate the insanity defense while advocating a new MPC. What emerged from the ALI's reevaluation was a compromise between the limited M'Naghten Rule and the broad Durham Rule. The Durham Rule provides that a criminal defendant cannot be convicted of a crime if the act was the result of a mental disease or defect at the time of the crime (irresistible impulse test). This rule has been referred to as the "product defect" rule but does not require a medical diagnosis of mental illness. Federal courts and all but one state court rejected it for being too broad.

The M'Naghten Rule relies on whether a criminal defendant knew the nature of the crime or understood right from wrong at the time it was committed. The defendant must meet one of the two distinct criteria. Some courts differ as to whether the wrong in question refers to moral or legal wrong, or both. Some states have eliminated the first part of the test in which a defendant is ruled legally insane for not fully understanding what the defendant has done. The ALI test provided that a person was not responsible for criminal conduct if, at the time of the act, the person lacked "substantial capacity" to appreciate the conduct or to conform the conduct to the rule of law. The ALI test allowed for both cognitive and volitional insanity. It required only a lack of substantial capacity, less than complete impairment. The ALI insanity defense was adopted by more than half the states, and all but one federal circuit.

In 1981, another sensational crime led to more restrictions on the insanity defense. John W. Hinckley Jr. attempted to assassinate President Ronald Reagan. Hinckley was prosecuted and acquitted of all charges by reason of insanity, and the resulting public protest prompted Congress to enact legislation on the issue. In 1984, Congress passed the Insanity Defense Reform Act (Insanity Act, 18 U.S.C.A. § 17 [1988]) to abolish the irresistible-impulse test from federal courts. President Reagan had called for a total revocation of mental illness as a defense to criminal charges, but his administration backed down from this position after intense lobbying by various professional organizations and associations.

The Insanity Act placed the burden on the defendant to prove insanity. Before the Insanity Act, federal prosecutors carried the burden of proving the defendant's sanity beyond a reasonable doubt.

Most states joined Congress in reassessing the insanity defense after Hinckley's acquittal. The legislatures of these states modified and limited the insanity defense in numerous and a variety of ways. Some states shifted the burden of proof, and some limited the applicability of the defense in the same manner as Congress. A few states eradicated the defense entirely. Chief Justice William H. Rehnquist, of the U.S. Supreme Court, opined in a dissent that it is "highly doubtful that due process requires a State to make available an insanity defense to a criminal defendant" (*Ake v. Oklahoma*, 470 U.S. 68, 105 S. Ct. 1087, 84 L. Ed. 2d 53 [1985]).

Incompetency

The test for competency is to determine if the defendant is mentally aware of the nature of the charges against the defendant, and whether the defendant can assist the attorney in the defense. If not, the defendant cannot be tried, convicted, or punished. A notice and a hearing are required to make this determination. A ruling of incompetence delays criminal proceedings until the defendant regains competence.

Execution of the mentally insane is barred by the Eighth Amendment and state statutes (See *Ford v. Wainwright*, 477 U.S. 399 [1986]).

Diminished Capacity

Diminished capacity is defined by the defendant's state of mind as required for a specific crime. This defense differs from the insanity defense because it recognizes different degrees and can be used to mitigate culpability and reduce charges (e.g., murder to manslaughter).

Intoxication

Intoxication can be voluntary or involuntary, and caused by ingesting substances such as alcohol, illegal drugs, and medicines.

- **Voluntary intoxication**: Not a defense to a general intent crime. Common law rejects voluntary intoxication as an excuse or justification for the crime of homicide. It also is not a defense to crimes involving negligence, recklessness, or strict liability. A defense of voluntary intoxication to specific intent crimes provides that the intoxication prevents the defendant from formulating the requisite intent and thus can be used to reduce charges (e.g., bump first-degree murder down to second-degree murder).

- **Involuntary intoxication**: The taking of an intoxicating substance without knowledge of its nature, under duress, or under medical advice. Most jurisdictions apply the insanity test to the involuntary intoxication defense to determine the level of intoxication. Thus, a valid defense exists if, due to involuntary intoxication, the defendant was temporarily insane under the adopted standard for insanity in the particular jurisdiction: M'Naghten, Durham, or ALI.

 © 2019, 2020, 2021 NALA, Inc. All rights reserved.

PURPOSES OF PUNISHMENT

Punishment has five recognized purposes: deterrence, incapacitation, rehabilitation, retribution, and restitution.

Reformation and Rehabilitation

- Reforming criminals by way of developing skills in prison to transform them into productive citizens

- There are serious differences of opinion as to relative importance

Restraint and Incapacitation

- Imprisonment to protect society from harm

- Contra-argument suggesting restraint without reformation will not restrain but postpone criminal conduct

Deterrence

- **Individual deterrence**: Punishment to deter the individual defendant from committing future crimes [three strikes statute affirmed, *Ewing v. California*, 538 U.S. 11 (2003).; see also *Lockyer v. Andrade*, 538 U.S. 63 (2003)]

- **General deterrence**: Punishment to deter others from engaging in similar crimes due to fear of receiving similar punishment

Retribution

Punishment for revenge. "Make the punishment fit the crime."

Restitution

Restitution is not a punishment or an alternative to fines or sanctions. It is a debt owed to the victim of the crime. Restitution is ordered to compensate victims for damages (expenses) that are the direct result of the crime.

UNAUTHORIZED PRACTICE OF LAW (UPL): DEFINITION

In most states, high courts have claimed that courts have the authority to define and regulate UPL as well as the practice of law. In addition, almost all states' legislatures have implemented statutes that prohibit UPL, sometimes making UPL a criminal misdemeanor. Each state sets its own standards regarding UPL. That authority, derived from constitutional requirements of separation of powers between the judicial, executive, and legislative branches, has enabled courts to punish UPL as contempt of court.

The state definitions of paralegal UPL differ slightly, but they encompass essentially the same types of activities:

- **Holding oneself out as an attorney**: Practicing law includes representing to the public (by the paralegal) that the paralegal is an attorney.

- **Representing others**: With some exceptions, only attorneys can represent a client in a deposition, courtroom, formal arbitration, or mediation hearing. It also is UPL to negotiate on behalf of a client if the negotiation involves legal rights or responsibilities.

- **Preparing documents**: The act of selecting the type of legal document a person should prepare or the act of providing information to fill in blanks in a legal document is considered providing legal advice. Some states allow licensed legal document preparers to prepare forms, though the preparer must have a license or certification to do so in the jurisdiction. However, a legal document preparer or paralegal cannot select the appropriate legal document/form.

- **Legal advice**: It is considered UPL for a paralegal or other nonlawyer to advise someone regarding what legal actions to take pertaining to that individual's unique situation.

- **Limited practice**: Legal assistants, paralegals, legal technicians, or others may assist clients with legal needs and prepare legal documents under the supervision of an attorney. Some states also allow paralegals to represent clients in administrative or regulatory proceedings.

UPL Enforcement

State bar associations and prosecutors may seek the following remedies against nonlawyers for violation of UPL laws:

- Injunction
- Criminal prosecution
- Criminal contempt

Injunctions are the most common method employed to punish an accused and to prevent that individual from further UPL. The injunctive actions are supposed to be brought by the state's attorney general to protect the public interest.

Criminal prosecutions against UPL are rare, but it depends on the state, the severity of the UPL behavior, and its outcome.

A party may move for direct contempt against a paralegal appearing in a court proceeding on behalf of a client, or an interested party may initiate an action for indirect contempt for UPL that occurs outside the courtroom. Contempt also may be imposed against a nonlawyer who fails to comply with an injunction forbidding the UPL activity. A contempt charge may result in fines, imprisonment, or both.

CRIMINAL PROCEDURE

Introduction: Anatomy of a Criminal Case

Processing a criminal case involves many steps. Criminal procedure is the term used to describe those steps. Although every jurisdiction (state and federal) has its own procedural rules, the Certified Paralegal

© 2019, 2020, 2021 NALA, Inc. All rights reserved.

(CP) Exam, with its nationwide reach, focuses primarily on federal rules of procedure. In this chapter we will delve into this process more specifically, but to begin, we will take a cursory look at the major steps:

- **Investigation of a crime by the police**. The purpose of a criminal investigation is to gather evidence to identify a suspect and support an arrest. An investigation may require a search, an exploratory inspection of a person or property. Probable cause is the standard of proof required for a search. Probable cause means there are facts or apparent facts indicating that evidence of criminality can be found in a specific place.

- **Arrest of a suspect by the police**. An arrest involves taking a person into custody to hold that suspect until his first court appearance. Probable cause is the legal requirement for an arrest. It means that there is a reasonable link between a perpetrator and the crime.

- **Prosecution of a criminal defendant by a district or U.S. attorney**. When deciding whether to charge a person with a crime, prosecutors weigh many factors, including the seriousness of the offense and the strength of the evidence.

- **Indictment by a grand jury or the filing of an information by a prosecutor.** Under the Federal Rules of Criminal Procedure, an indictment is required when prosecuting a capital offense. A prosecutor has the option to file an indictment or an information in cases involving crimes punishable by imprisonment. In about half the states and the federal system, a grand jury decides whether to bring charges, in the form of an indictment. The grand jury convenes in a closed hearing during which only the prosecutor presents evidence. The defendant has no right to be present at grand jury proceedings or to be represented by a defense attorney before the grand jury. The standard for indicting a person for a crime is probable cause. In the remaining states, a prosecutor files a charging document called an information. A preliminary (probable cause) hearing is held to determine if there is enough evidence to warrant a trial. The defendant and attorney can be present at this hearing to dispute the charges.

- **Arraignment by a judge**. Before the trial, the defendant appears in court and enters a plea. The most common pleas are guilty and not guilty.

- **Pretrial detention and/or bail**. Detention refers to a period of temporary custody prior to trial. Bail is an amount of money paid by a defendant to ensure they will show up for a trial, if released pretrial.

- **Plea bargaining between the defense attorney and the prosecutor**. Usually, in plea bargaining, the defendant agrees to plead guilty to one or more charges in exchange for a charge reduction or sentence reduction.

- **Trial/adjudication of guilt by a judge or jury, with a prosecutor and a defense attorney participating**. A trial is held before a judge or jury. The standard of evidence for a criminal conviction is guilt beyond a reasonable doubt—less than 100 percent certainty but more than high probability. If there is doubt based on reason, the accused is entitled to be acquitted.

- **Sentencing by a judge**. If the accused is found guilty, a judge sentences the defendant. Possible sentences include a fine, probation, a period of incarceration in a correctional institution (such as jail or prison), or some combination of supervision in the community and incarceration.

- **Appeals filed by attorneys in appellate courts and then ruled on by appellate judges**. If an appellate court reverses a case, the case returns to trial court for retrial. With a reversal, the original trial becomes moot (that is, it is as though it never happened). Following a reversal, a prosecutor decides whether to refile or drop the charges. Even if a prosecutor drops the charges, the defendant

© 2019, 2020, 2021 NALA, Inc. All rights reserved.

can still be prosecuted later if the statute of limitations for the crime the defendant is accused of committing has not run out. The statute of limitations imposes time limits on the government to try a case.

- **Punishment and/or rehabilitation administered by local, state, or federal correctional authorities**. Most inmates do not serve the complete term and are released before the expiration of their maximum sentences. Release may be obtained by serving the maximum sentence mandated by a court or through early release, such as by parole or pardon.

CONSTITUTIONAL RESTRAINTS

Prosecutorial rules in criminal cases at the federal level are adopted from the United States Constitution, the United States Code, and the Federal Rules of Criminal Procedure. The Selective Incorporation Doctrine requires state courts to apply nearly all the guarantees of the Bill of Rights in state criminal trials. For example, the rights under the Fourth, Fifth, Sixth, and Eighth Amendments are binding on states under the due process provision of the 14th Amendment. However, the right to indictment by grand jury for capital crimes is not binding on states.

COMPLAINT AND ARREST WARRANT

Prior to any arrest, police must have probable cause to believe that a crime has been committed and the suspect being arrested has committed that crime. If there is sufficient evidence, the prosecutor will file a complaint. The complaint or one or more affidavits filed with the complaint must establish probable cause to believe that an offense has been committed and that the suspect/defendant committed it. If so, the judge must issue an arrest warrant to the officer authorized to execute it. At the request of an attorney for the government, the judge must issue a summons, instead of a warrant, to a person authorized to serve it. A judge may issue more than one warrant or summons on the same complaint. If an individual defendant fails to appear in response to a summons, a judge may, and upon request of an attorney for the government, issue a warrant. If an organizational defendant fails to appear in response to a summons, a judge may take any action authorized by United States law.

Felony or misdemeanor arrests conducted in a suspect's home usually require a valid arrest warrant. However, if there are exigent circumstances and the crime is serious, no warrant is necessary (e.g., destruction of evidence, hot pursuit). Felony or misdemeanor arrests made in a public place can be with or without a warrant. Misdemeanor arrests without a warrant can only be for offenses committed in the officer's presence.

An arrest warrant must:

- Contain the defendant's name or, if it is unknown, a name or description by which the defendant can be identified with reasonable certainty.

- Describe the offense charged in the complaint.

- Command that the defendant be arrested and brought without unnecessary delay before a magistrate judge or, if none is reasonably available, before a state or local judicial officer.

- Be signed by a judge.

A summons must be in the same form as a warrant except that it must require the defendant to appear

 © 2019, 2020, 2021 NALA, Inc. All rights reserved.

before a magistrate judge at a stated time and place.

A warrant is executed by arresting the defendant. Upon arrest, an officer possessing the original or a duplicate original warrant must show it to the defendant. If the officer does not possess the warrant, the officer must inform the defendant of the warrant's existence and of the offense charged and, at the defendant's request, must show the original or a duplicate original warrant to the defendant as soon as possible.

A summons is served on an individual defendant by:

- Delivering a copy to the defendant personally.

- Leaving a copy at the defendant's residence or usual place of abode with a person of suitable age and discretion residing at that location, and by mailing a copy to the defendant's last known address.

MIRANDA V. ARIZONA, 384 U.S. 436 (1966)

In *Miranda v. Arizona*, the Fifth Amendment privilege against self-incrimination became the basis of ruling on the admissibility of a confession. Pursuant to the *Miranda* case, a suspect in custody cannot be interrogated without first being informed:

- They have the right to remain silent.

- Anything they say can and will be used against them in court.

- They have the right to have an attorney present.

- If they cannot afford an attorney, one will be appointed if they desire.

The phrasing of the warnings can vary if the words reasonably convey the suspect's rights, and the suspect understands. Anyone accused of a crime and in police custody must be given the *Miranda* warning. *Miranda* rights may be waived, but if so, the prosecutor must prove that the suspect did so voluntarily, knowingly, and intelligently.

SEARCH & SEIZURE

As discussed earlier in this chapter, the search-and-seizure rights accorded by the Fourth Amendment concern privacy. The Fourth Amendment protects against unreasonable searches and seizures by state or federal law enforcement authorities.

Law enforcement may disregard privacy rights and conduct a search of a suspect, the suspect's home, barn, car, boat, office, personal or business documents, bank account records, trash barrel, or whatever, if:

- The law enforcement personnel have probable cause to believe they can find evidence that the suspect committed a crime, and a judge issues a warrant.

- The circumstances justify the search without a warrant first being issued.

The Fourth Amendment applies to a search only if a person has a legitimate expectation of privacy in the place or thing searched. If not, the Amendment offers no protection because there are, by definition, no privacy issues. Courts generally use a two-part test to determine whether, at the time of the search, a defendant had a legitimate expectation of privacy in the place or things searched:

- Did the person expect some degree of privacy?

- Was the person's expectation objectively reasonable (an expectation that society would recognize)?

Examples:

A person who uses a public restroom expects not to be spied upon (the person has an expectation of privacy), and most people, including judges, would consider that expectation to be objectively reasonable. Therefore, the installation of a hidden video camera by the police in a public restroom would be considered a "search" and would be subject to the Fourth Amendment's requirement of reasonableness.

On the other hand, if an officer stops a car and notices a bag of cocaine on the passenger seat, there has been no search under the Fourth Amendment. That is because, even if the driver considered the passenger seat to be a private place, society is not willing to extend privacy protections to that location. In other words, there is no objectively reasonable expectation of privacy with respect to the drugs because the bag was in the officer's plain view (**Plain View Rule**).

In one U.S. Supreme Court case, the court held that a bus passenger had a legitimate expectation of privacy in an opaque carry-on bag positioned in a luggage rack above the passenger's head. The Court held that the physical probing by the police of the bag's exterior for evidence of contraband constituted a search subject to Fourth Amendment limitations (*Bond v. U.S.*, 529 U.S. 334 [2000]).

The Fourth Amendment does not apply to searches carried out by non-governmental employees (such as private security guards) who are not acting on the government's behalf. If a court rules that an unreasonable search occurred, any evidence seized as a result cannot be used as direct evidence against the defendant in a criminal prosecution. This principle, established by the U.S. Supreme Court in 1961, has come to be known as the **Exclusionary Rule**.

Not only is evidence that is the product of an illegal search inadmissible in court, but so is additional evidence that was derived from the initial evidence. This principle is known as the **Fruit of the Poisonous Tree Doctrine**. The "tree" is the evidence that the police illegally seized in the first place; the "fruit" is the second-generation product of the illegally seized evidence. Both tree and fruit typically are inadmissible at trial.

Border Searches

Searches made at the United States border offer no Fourth Amendment protection. These searches require no warrant and no probable cause, not even the showing of some degree of suspicion that accompanies even investigatory stops. Customs officials have the flexibility to inspect incoming individuals and their belongings and to halt incoming contraband without having to inform a magistrate before the search. Border searches usually fall into two categories:

- **Routine**: usually conducted at border and consist of only a limited intrusion.

- **Non-routine**: usually conducted on a reasonable suspicion and vary in techniques and intrusiveness. Motor vehicles may be searched at the border, even to the extent of removing,

© 2019, 2020, 2021 NALA, Inc. All rights reserved.

disassembling, and reassembling the fuel tank.

POLICE REPORTS

When a person has been arrested and accused of a crime, a police report can be a significant source of information about the circumstances surrounding the arrest. But, by definition, police reports are hearsay: an out-of-court statement, used to prove the truth of the matter asserted (i.e., to prove the truth of what is stated in the report).

Hearsay evidence is generally inadmissible in court. However, there are some exceptions to the hearsay rule which could allow a police report into evidence.

Hearsay Exceptions

Although evidence rules vary by state, there are generally numerous exceptions to the hearsay rule that allow police reports to be used as evidence in court. These include:

- **Business records**. Records that are made in the normal course of "business" which include the records made by government agents such as police officers are generally admissible in court.

- **Refreshed recollection**. Witnesses may also be allowed to use a written document to refresh their memory when testifying in court.

- **Past recollection recorded**. When a witness is unable to accurately recall an event, a writing that was made at a time when the memory of the event was fresh may be introduced as evidence.

Police Video Cameras

Most police departments have a body-worn camera policy which requires that they be activated to record all contacts with citizens, while in the performance of official duties. The cameras are to stay activated until the event is completed to ensure the integrity of the recording.

These policies do not extend to any location where individuals have a reasonable expectation of privacy, such as a restroom or locker room.

Video from the cameras is downloaded at the end of each officer's shift and preserved on a server. Video not related to criminal cases is generally kept for six months. Video involving arrests and circumstances where criminal charges are filed is passed along to the prosecutor's office and kept until the case is over.

What is pertinent and allowed as evidence for a trial is determined by rules of evidence and a judge's interpretation. Body-cam evidence is available to both the prosecution and the defense.

The rules governing its admissibility are no different than any other photographic or video exhibits. Clearly, it must be relevant to the issues before the court, and it must be properly maintained to avoid any risk of tampering.

Before such evidence can be used in an attorney's closing statement, it must first be admitted as an exhibit through a witness, most often the officer who was wearing it. The general conclusion of law enforcement personnel is that this kind of real time evidence is helpful to jurors in many cases and, at times, can even determine a verdict.

Subpoenas

Pursuant to the Federal Rules of Criminal Procedure, a subpoena must state the court's name and the title of the proceeding, include the seal of the court, and command the witness to attend and testify at the time and place the subpoena specifies. The clerk must issue a blank subpoena, signed and sealed, to the party requesting it, and that party must fill in the blanks before the subpoena is served.

If a defendant cannot afford to pay witness fees to witnesses the defendant subpoenaed, must file an *ex parte* application stating such. Upon filing the application, the court must order that a subpoena be issued for a named witness if the witness's presence is necessary for an adequate defense. If the court orders a subpoena to be issued, the process costs and witness fees will be paid in the same manner as those paid for witnesses for government subpoenas.

A subpoena may order the witness to produce any books, papers, documents, data, or other objects the subpoena designates. The court may direct the witness to produce the designated items in court before trial or before they are to be offered in evidence. When the items arrive, the court may permit the parties and their attorneys to inspect all or part of them.

On motion made promptly, the court may quash or modify the subpoena if compliance would be unreasonable or oppressive.

After a complaint, indictment, or information is filed, a subpoena requiring the production of personal or confidential information about a victim may be served on a third party only by court order. Before entering the order and unless there are exceptional circumstances, the court must require giving notice to the victim so that the victim can move to quash or modify the subpoena or otherwise object.

A marshal, a deputy marshal, or any nonparty who is at least 18 years old may serve a subpoena. The server must deliver a copy of the subpoena to the witness and must tender to the witness one day's witness-attendance fee and the legal mileage allowance. The server need not tender the attendance fee or mileage allowance when the United States, a federal officer, or a federal agency, has requested the subpoena.

A subpoena requiring a witness to attend a hearing or trial may be served at any place within the United States. If the witness is in a foreign country, 28 U.S.C. §1783 governs the subpoena's service.

A court order to take a deposition authorizes the clerk in the district where the deposition is to be taken to issue a subpoena for any witness named or described in the order. After considering the convenience of the witness and the parties, the court may order – and the subpoena may require – the witness to appear anywhere the court designates.

The court (other than a magistrate judge) may hold in contempt a witness who, without adequate excuse, disobeys a subpoena issued by a federal court in that district. A magistrate judge may hold in contempt a witness who, without adequate excuse, disobeys a subpoena issued by that magistrate judge as provided in 28 U.S.C. §636(e). No party may subpoena a statement of a witness or of a prospective witness (Rule 26.2).

CONFESSIONS

Involuntary Confessions

Involuntary confessions violate due process and cannot be used for any purpose. As discussed previously

---

© 2019, 2020, 2021 NALA, Inc. All rights reserved.

in this chapter, suspects cannot be forced to incriminate themselves pursuant to the Fifth Amendment. And the 14th Amendment prohibits coercive questioning by police officers. Thus, confessions that are coerced, or involuntary, are not admissible against defendants in criminal cases, even though they may be true.

The legal standard for an involuntary confession is whether law enforcement officers used tactics that undermined the suspect's ability to exercise free will. This is a high standard and a difficult one for a defendant to meet. The classic case of an involuntary confession is a police officer questioning a suspect who is in pain after suffering serious injuries; the officer continues the interrogation despite the defendant's request for an attorney.

In determining whether the suspect was coerced, courts consider all the circumstances surrounding the interrogation. They review the following factors:

- The location of the questioning (the police station is usually considered more intimidating)

- The time of the questioning (middle of the night)

- The length of the interrogation (36-hour, nonstop interrogation deemed "inherently coercive" *Ashcraft v. Tennessee*, 322 U.S. 143 [1944])

- Whether officers gave *Miranda* warnings

- Whether police honored the suspect's requests for a lawyer or to remain silent

- Whether the defendant was allowed contact with family members or an attorney

- Who initiated the conversation (a defendant who freely interacts with police will have a harder time proving coercion)

- The defendant's age or immaturity

- The defendant's health or physical state

- The defendant's experience with the criminal justice system

PRETRIAL PROCEDURE

Right to Counsel

As discussed earlier in this chapter, the Sixth Amendment provides the defendant right to counsel. The 14th Amendment applies the Sixth Amendment right to the states, and the Sixth Amendment rights protect the defendant in all critical pretrial stages, once formal charges/proceedings have begun (such as lineups, arraignment, indictment, information, and preliminary hearings). The stages at which right to counsel applies are:

1. Custodial police interrogation

2. Post-indictment interrogation (whether custodial or not)

3. Preliminary hearing to determine probable cause to prosecute

4. Arraignment

5. Post-charge physical lineups

6. Guilty plea and sentencing

7. Felony trial

8. Misdemeanor trial when imprisonment is imposed

9. Appeals as a matter of right

Conversely, there are stages at which right to counsel does not apply:

1. Blood sampling

2. Taking handwriting samples

3. Pre-charge or investigative lineups

4. Photo identifications

5. Initial hearings to determine probable cause to detain

6. Discretionary appeals

7. Parole and probation revocation proceeding

8. Post-conviction proceedings (e.g., habeas corpus)

Bail

At the initial appearance, the prosecutor will move for detention if the government wants to detain the defendant. Bail in federal court is controlled by the Bail Reform Act (18 USC §3141, et seq.).

In presumption cases (offenses such as drug dealing, child sex offenses – including child pornography – and bank robbery), the government gets an automatic three (court) days to prepare for a bail hearing (18 USC §3142 (f)(1), (2)). In the bail hearing, the government may try to prove that the defendant is a flight risk (or a danger to the community). The defense also may ask for up to five days to prepare for the bail hearing.

United States Pretrial Services Officers provide pretrial services interviews for defendants seeking bail. From these interviews, the Pretrial Services Officer prepares for the court, short life backgrounds and criminal histories regarding defendants.

Magistrate judges decide whether there are any conditions of bond to reasonably assure the defendant is not a flight risk and/or is not a danger to the community. Bonds (unsecured bonds) in federal court generally do not require posting money or property. Typical conditions under which a defendant may be released on own recognizance (ROR) at the bail hearing include reporting to United States Pretrial Services, drug testing, and travel restrictions.

Initial Appearance — Arraignment

Pursuant to Federal Rules of Criminal Procedure 5.1., the defendant is entitled to a preliminary hearing or arraignment within 10 days of the initial appearance for in-custody defendants, and within 20 days of initial appearance for defendants who are not in custody.

 © 2019, 2020, 2021 NALA, Inc. All rights reserved.

An indictment, which contains the federal charges faced by the defendant, is reviewed by a grand jury. If there is sufficient evidence to bring about the charges, the grand jury signs off on (or "returns") the indictment. Additional indictments brought later in the case are called "superseding indictments."

There is no preliminary hearing in grand jury proceedings. Only a defendant charged with a federal felony may be tried pursuant to a grand jury indictment.

The arraignment is held before the district court judge who will preside over the case. A district court judge, or "Article III" judge, is appointed by the President, confirmed by the Senate, and serves for life. The district court judge will preside over the rest of the case, for the later trial or plea hearing, and for sentencing if necessary. The Sixth Amendment right to a speedy trial attaches once the defendant has been arrested and charged.

Pretrial Motions

There are numerous pretrial motions possible in a federal case. Pursuant to Federal Rules of Criminal Procedure 12, these can include motions to dismiss charges or suppress evidence, constitutional challenges, motions for a bill of particulars, motions to strike, motions in limine, and severance motions. A bill of particulars (BOP) motion is a detailed, formal, written statement of the prosecution's charges against the defendant. The defense files this motion for BOP as a formal request to the court for more detailed information.

The most typical pretrial motion is a suppression motion. In these types of motions, the defense moves to suppress evidence, or to prevent the government from using it at trial. These motions can include suppression of evidence, like a gun or drugs seized in a search, or statements, like a defendant's confession.

The defendant's motion outlines the facts and law in support of the claim for relief. The prosecutor usually has about 10 days to respond to that motion, and the defense has a right to a final reply. Subsequently, the magistrate hears arguments on the motion and takes witness testimony if needed. This is called an evidentiary hearing to resolve any disputed facts.

Plea

In most federal cases, the defendant pleads guilty and does not go to trial. A defendant can plead guilty "straight up," or without a plea agreement, or can strike a deal with the prosecutor and have a written contract (a plea agreement – discussed later in this chapter) drafted with the terms of the plea.

A defendant has a right to be informed of every plea offer made by the government. The defense attorney will also explain the terms of the plea agreement, will discuss a defendant's sentencing exposure at trial or through the proposed plea, and will review the good and bad evidence that awaits a defendant at trial. However, it is the defendant's decision alone on whether to take a plea offer from the prosecutor.

Competency

A defendant's mental condition at the time of trial determines whether the defendant is fit to stand trial. Insanity relates to the defendant's mental condition at the time of the crime. Incompetency is a bar to trial, not a defense.

The conviction of a defendant while mentally incompetent violates due process. See *Pate v. Robinson*, 383 U.S. 375, 378 (1966). Pursuant to 18 U.S.C. §4241(a), the court must order a competency hearing if there is reasonable cause to believe that the defendant may presently be suffering from a mental disease or defect rendering the defendant mentally incompetent to the extent that the defendant is unable to understand the nature and consequences of the proceedings or to assist properly in the defendant's defense (18 U.S.C. §4241(a)). The defendant, attorney for the government, or the court may move for a hearing *sua sponte* (*Id*).

> Before the date of the hearing, the court may order the defendant to be examined by a psychiatrist or psychologist. Pursuant to the provisions of Fed. R. Crim. P. §4247, the psychiatric or psychological report must be filed with the court. Section 4247(d) provides that, in this hearing, the defendant shall be represented by counsel, shall have the opportunity to testify, to present evidence, to subpoena witnesses on his or her behalf, and to confront and cross-examine witnesses who appear at the hearing. The court must determine whether the defendant is able to consult with, and assist, his lawyer with a reasonable degree of rational understanding and whether he rationally and factually understands the nature of the proceedings against him (*Dusky v. United States*, 362 U.S. 402 (1960)).

TRIAL

Federal trials that involve appointed counsel typically last up to a week. Pursuant to the Sixth Amendment, the defendant is entitled to trial by an impartial jury of the state and district in which the crime was committed. The defendant has the right to testify or not, and if the defendant does not testify, the jury cannot hold that against the defendant. The defendant also has the right to cross-examine government witnesses and can use the subpoena power of the court to secure evidence or witnesses for trial.

Burden of Proof

The government bears the burden of proving the defendant guilty beyond a reasonable doubt as to every element of a charge. Beyond a reasonable doubt means that no other logical explanation can be derived from the facts except that the defendant committed the crime, thereby overcoming the presumption that a person is innocent until proven guilty. The defendant will be found guilty of a particular offense only if a jury of 12 is unanimous as to every element of that charge. A "not guilty" verdict will end the case.

PLEA BARGAINING

Attorneys for both parties (government and defendant) may discuss and reach a plea bargain. The court does not participate in plea bargaining discussions. If a defendant pleads guilty or accepts conviction but does not accept guilt (*nolo contendere* plea), either to a lesser charge or related offense, the plea bargain agreement must specify that the government will:

- Not bring, or move to dismiss, other charges

- Recommend or agree not to oppose the defendant's request that the sentence or sentencing range is appropriate or that a particular provision of the Sentencing Guidelines applies or not (this type of recommendation does not bind the court)

- Agree that the defendant's sentence or sentencing range is the appropriate disposition of the case, or that a particular provision of the Sentencing Guidelines applies or not (this type of

© 2019, 2020, 2021 NALA, Inc. All rights reserved.

recommendation does bind the court once the court accepts the plea bargain agreement)

The parties must disclose the plea agreement in open court, unless the court for good cause allows the parties to disclose the agreement in chambers or in private (*in camera*). The court may accept or reject the plea arrangement or defer a decision until a pre-sentence report is reviewed. In addition, the court must advise the defendant that the defendant has no right to withdraw the plea if the court does not follow the request or recommendation. If the court does accept the plea, the agreed disposition will be included in the judgment. If the court rejects the plea, the court must inform the parties. The court also must advise the defendant personally that if the plea is not withdrawn, the court may dispose of the case less favorably toward the defendant than the plea agreement contemplated.

The defendant may withdraw a guilty or *nolo contendere* plea before the court accepts the plea, for any or no reason, or after the court accepts the plea but before a sentence is imposed. The guilty or *nolo contendere* plea can be withdrawn under the circumstances above if the court rejects a plea bargain agreement or if the defendant can show a fair and just reason for requesting the withdrawal. After the court imposes a sentence, the defendant may not withdraw the guilty or *nolo contendere* plea. The defendant's only recourse at that point is direct appeal or collateral attack (e.g., habeas corpus petition).

The court may admit pleas, plea discussions, and related statements as evidence:

- In any proceeding during which another statement was made during the same plea or plea discussions had been introduced, if in fairness the statements should be considered together; or

- In a criminal perjury or false statement proceeding, if the defendant made the statement under oath, on the record, with counsel present.

Sentencing

Federal Rules of Criminal Procedure §32 provides that sentencing take place about 75 days after a defendant is convicted, by either pleading guilty to a charge or by being found guilty after a trial, if the defendant is in custody, or about 90 days later if the defendant is not in custody. Continued bond is allowed for less serious convictions, but a defendant convicted of more serious offenses likely will remain in custody after trial.

At some point after the conviction, a Probation Officer will interview the defendant. Defense counsel may be present at this interview. The Probation Officer will prepare a draft pre-sentence report (PSR) after reviewing notes from the interview, as well as information submitted by the defendant and the government.

Before sentencing, the draft PSR is provided to defense counsel and the government. The parties are given 10 days to make factual or legal objections to the report. The objective is to resolve as many factual or legal errors as possible before the PSR is provided to the judge. Accordingly, the court does not receive a copy of this draft report.

The final PSR is provided to the judge before sentencing. This final report calculates Federal Sentencing Guidelines, as well as describes the defendant's background and the offense. It also lists any unresolved objections.

The parties must submit sentencing memoranda to the court arguing for their proposed sentences.

At the sentencing hearing, the district court judge must resolve any remaining objections to the PSR, make factual findings, and must consider the factors of the key sentencing statute, 18 USC §3553(a). Among the factors that the court must consider are the Federal Sentencing Guidelines. In addition to a custodial sentence, the court will decide how much restitution is owed, and whether a criminal fine is appropriate.

Before imposing the sentence, the court must permit the defendant to speak, or "allocute." Allocution is a procedure during sentencing by which a convicted person is given opportunity to address a judge (See Fed. R. Crim. Pro. 32(i)(4)). The defendant's counsel will provide advice on what to say at this point in the sentencing hearing. A federal sentence can range from probation to months or years in federal prison. If a sentence of imprisonment is imposed, the district judge also will impose a term of supervised release, whereby a defendant must abide by the law while under post-release supervision or risk additional punishment.

APPEALS AND PETITIONS FOR WRITS OF CERTIORARI

If the defendant did not waive the right to appeal in a plea agreement, the defense may appeal both the conviction and the sentence imposed. Unless the defendant has private counsel, the public defender will continue to represent the defendant, for free, during the appeal. There is a very short period during which the defense must state its intention to appeal ("notice" of appeal), so defense counsel should discuss this with the defendant immediately after sentencing.

Federal Rule of Appellate Procedure (Fed. R. App. P.) §4(b)

A defendant's notice of appeal must be filed in the district court within 14 days after the entry of either the judgment or order appealed from, or the filing of the government's notice of appeal. If a defendant makes a timely motion in the district court under the Federal Rules of Criminal Procedure of a type specified in Fed. R. App. P. 4(b)(3), the notice of appeal from a judgment of conviction must be filed within 14 days after the entry of the order disposing of the last such motion, or within 14 days after the entry of the judgment of conviction, whichever period ends later. The notice must be received and filed in District Court no later than the last day of the appeal period – no additional days are provided for mailing.

If the defendant does not win the appeal in the United States Court of Appeals, a petition can be filed for writ of certiorari (discussed further below) with the Supreme Court of the United States. Ordinarily, the public defender would continue to represent the defendant during the petition for certiorari and, if the writ is granted, during the briefing and oral argument in the Supreme Court.

SUPERVISED RELEASE AND VIOLATIONS

Almost every federal offense carries with it a term of supervised release. Supervised release is like probation: a defendant must report to the Probation Office, submit to drug testing, and abide by the law and standard conditions of supervised release.

There are many ways to violate supervised release, including not submitting monthly reports, having a positive drug test, or being arrested for new criminal conduct.

When a Probation Officer files supervised release charges, they are contained in a charging document called a "Petition." If the defendant cannot afford an attorney, the public defender will be appointed for these revocation proceedings.

The defendant has fewer rights in revocation proceedings than when facing substantive federal charges. For example, at a revocation hearing there is no jury. The government need only prove the charges by a preponderance, instead of beyond a reasonable doubt. Also, hearsay is admissible, so a Probation Officer can simply repeat the allegations of other witnesses in the hearing.

 © 2019, 2020, 2021 NALA, Inc. All rights reserved.

WRITS OF CERTIORARI

A petition for a writ of certiorari is a document which a losing party files with the Supreme Court asking the Supreme Court to review the decision of a lower court. It includes a list of the parties, a statement of the facts of the case, the legal questions presented for review, and arguments as to why the Court should grant the writ.

The actual writ of certiorari is the decision by the Supreme Court to hear an appeal from a lower court.

Example:

> If the defendant is dissatisfied with the ruling of the Court of Appeals, the defendant can request the Supreme Court to review the decision of the Court of Appeals. The Supreme Court can, but almost always refuses, to take the case. In fact, the Court receives thousands of petitions per year, and denies all but about one hundred. If the Court accepts the case, it grants a writ of certiorari.

"Review on writ of certiorari is not a matter of right, but a judicial discretion. A petition for writ of certiorari will be granted only for compelling reasons" (Rule 10, Rules of the U.S. Supreme Court).

HABEAS CORPUS PROCEEDINGS

Federal habeas corpus statutes are found at 28 U.S.C. §§ 2241-2255. The writ of habeas corpus, or the "great writ of liberty," is a writ or order directing the government to "produce the body" to the court so that the court can rule on the legality of the detention. The purpose of the writ is to free the prisoner from unlawful restraint. To initiate a habeas corpus proceeding, a prisoner files a civil petition against the government that holds the prisoner in its custody. Provided and protected by the United States Constitution, the writ is available to both federal and state prisoners in custody in violation of the laws of the United States.

Because this is a civil proceeding, the petitioner (prisoner) has the burden of proof by a preponderance to show that the prisoner's detention is unlawful. In addition, the Sixth Amendment right to counsel does not extend to habeas corpus proceedings.

PUNISHMENT

Sentencing and punishment for federal crimes fall under federal jurisdiction. Penalties for federal charges typically carry harsher sentences than state criminal charges. The Sentencing Guidelines determine sentences primarily on two factors:

1. The conduct associated with the offense (which produces the offense level)

2. The defendant's criminal history

There are 43 offense levels and six criminal history categories. Each category is associated with a range of criminal history points.

Example:

A defendant with zero or one criminal history points would be in Criminal History Category One, whereas a defendant with 13 or more criminal history points would be in Criminal History Category Four. There are four sentencing zones: A, B, C, and D.

In determining length and severity of punishment, the court takes, among others, the following occurrences regarding the defendant's crime in consideration:

- If a death occurred
- There was physical injury
- There was severe psychological injury
- Abduction or unlawful restraint
- Property damage or loss
- Weapons or dangerous instrumentalities used
- Disruption of governmental function
- Extreme conduct
- Criminal purpose
- Victim's conduct

PRISONER'S RIGHTS

Although prisoners do not have full constitutional rights, they are protected by the Eighth Amendment's prohibition of cruel and unusual punishment. Inmates have rights to adequate medical care, the freedom to practice their religion, and the right to access the courts and counsel.

DOUBLE JEOPARDY

The Fifth Amendment provides that no person shall "be subject for the same offense to be twice put in jeopardy of life or limb." In other words, the government cannot prosecute someone more than once for the same crime. Double jeopardy applies to criminal cases only, not civil or administrative proceedings. For example, a defendant convicted of a crime is not immune from a civil lawsuit for damages from the victim of the crime.

JUVENILE PROCEEDINGS

Juveniles do not have the same constitutional rights as adults. For example, juvenile proceedings are heard by judges only because juveniles do not have the right to a jury trial. They also do not have the right to bail or to a public trial.

 © 2019, 2020, 2021 NALA, Inc. All rights reserved.

Juveniles do have some extra protections in the juvenile court system that they likely would not otherwise receive in the adult criminal court. Their records are sealed and when the juvenile turns 18, the records are usually expunged (erased) if the juvenile has met certain conditions. The juvenile also has rights to notice of the juvenile's delinquent acts before the hearing, the right to prerelease if the delinquent acts are not violent, and the right to a free public defender if necessary.

Once the case is adjudicated, the judge decides whether the juvenile is guilty or not, and what the sentence should be. Judges must follow certain guidelines when sentencing and must act in the best interest of the child. The objective of the sentence is not to punish, but hopefully to rehabilitate the juvenile so that the individual can become a productive adult.

There are situations wherein a juvenile commits a serious crime and is determined not to be an appropriate candidate for juvenile court. Under these circumstances, the case may be transferred to an adult court for trial on criminal charges. For example, a case would be transferred if a 17-year-old individual committed a capital crime such as first-degree murder.

VOCABULARY FOR CRIMINAL LAW & PROCEDURE

For the criminal law and procedure chapter of the CP Exam, the paralegal should recognize and understand the following terms:

Acquittal	Concurrent sentence	Forgery
Aggravated assault	Conviction	Fraud
Appeal	Count	General intent
Assault	Court-appointed attorney	Habeas Corpus
Arraignment	Crime	Inculpatory evidence
Arrest warrant	Crime against the person	Indictment
Arson	Crime against property	Infraction
Actus Reas	Criminal negligence	Jurisdiction
Bail / Bail Reform Act	Custody	Larceny
Bail bond	Defendant	*Malum in se*
Battery	Double Jeopardy	*Malum Prohibitum*
Burden of proof	Due Process	Manslaughter
Burglary	Elements of a crime	Mitigation
Capital offense	Embezzlement	Mens Rea
Common Law	Entrapment	*Miranda* Rights
Complaint	Evidence	Murder
Exclusionary Rule	Extradition	*Nolo Contendere*
Exculpatory evidence	Felony	Pardon
Expungement	Forcible rape	Parole
Perjury	Recidivism	Standard of proof
Plea	Robbery	Statute
Plea bargain	Search warrant	Statutory rape
Precedent	Selective Incorporation Doctrine	Specific intent
Probable cause	Sentence	Transferred intent
Probation	Sentencing guidelines	Strict liability
Prosecution	Specific intent	*Sua sponte*
Rape	Plea bargain	Venue
Reasonable doubt	Precedent	Verdict
Recklessness	Probable cause	Warrant

© 2019, 2020, 2021 NALA, Inc. All rights reserved.

CHAPTER 5: PRACTICE QUESTIONS

1. Which of the following is not a common law felony?

   A. Treason
   B. Larceny
   C. Murder
   D. Sodomy

2. Unreasonable search and seizure and right to a speedy trial are rights provided by the Eighth and Fifth Amendments.

   A. True
   B. False

3. In the following scenario, Paul's confession can be used against him. Police officers beat and threaten Paul until he confesses to robbing a local jewelry store. Paul also tells the officers where he hid the stolen jewelry. The officers locate the jewelry to use as evidence against Paul.

   A. True
   B. False

4. An arrest must meet the requirements of which Amendment:

   A. Fifth Amendment
   B. Eighth Amendment
   C. Sixth Amendment
   D. Fourth Amendment

5. Passion killing is an example of first-degree murder.

   A. True
   B. False

6. An example of an inchoate crime is:

   A. Robbery
   B. Forgery
   C. Conspiracy
   D. Larceny

7. Gwendolyn points a gun at Mike and threatens to kill him if he does not steal his neighbor's car. If Mike complies and is caught, he may use the following defense:

    A. Entrapment

    B. Necessity

    C. Duress

    D. Self-defense

8. The Exclusionary Rule is one of the remedies for violations of a defendant's Fourth Amendment rights.

    A. True

    B. False

9. Fruit of the Poisonous Tree evidence is admissible in court.

    A. True

    B. False

10. Border searches are an exemption to the 14th Amendment clause of the U.S. Constitution.

    A. True

    B. False

11. Pursuant to federal appellate procedure, a defendant must file a notice of appeal within how many days after the entry of either the judgment or order from which the defendant appealed?

    A. 7 days

    B. 14 days

    C. 21 days

    D. 30 days

© 2019, 2020, 2021 NALA, Inc. All rights reserved.

12. **In which of the following situations is the defendant likely to be found guilty of the crime charged?**

    A.   Defendant obtains permission to borrow Owner's motorcycle for the weekend by falsely promising to return it (he does not intend to do so). Three days later, he changes his mind and returns the motorcycle. Defendant is charged with larceny by trick.

    B.   Without the permission of Owner, Defendant takes Owner's motorcycle with the intention of driving it 100 miles to a casino and back. Defendant is charged with larceny.

    C.   With permission and promising to return it by 10:00 p.m., Defendant borrows Owner's motorcycle. Later that evening, Defendant decides to keep the motorcycle until the next morning and does so. Defendant is charged with embezzlement.

    D.   Defendant obtains permission to borrow Owner's motorcycle for the weekend by misrepresenting his identity and by falsely claiming that he has a license to drive a motorcycle. He returns the motorcycle the following Monday. Defendant is charged with obtaining property by false pretenses.

13. **Ambiguity in a criminal statute should be resolved in favor of the defendant.**

    A.   True

    B.   False

14. **Statutory rape is a strict liability crime.**

    A.   True

    B.   False

15. **A person can be convicted of treason only by the testimony of _____ or by confession in open court.**

    A.   Four witnesses

    B.   Two witnesses

    C.   Three witnesses

    D.   Five witnesses

RESOURCES

- Cornell Law School Legal Information Institute, https://www.law.cornell.edu/rules/frcrmp/

- Supreme Court of the United States Blog, http://www.scotusblog.com

- Singer and La Fond, *Criminal Law Examples and Explanations*, Sixth Edition, Wolters Kluwers Law & Business Publishing Company

- Reid, *Criminal Law: The Essentials*, Third Edition, Oxford University Press

- Gifts, *Barron's Law Dictionary,* Third Edition, Barron's Educational Series

- Koerselman, *CLA Review Manual*, Second Edition, West Publishing

- *The National Law Review*, https://www.natlawreview.com/type-law/constitutional-law

© 2019, 2020, 2021 NALA, Inc. All rights reserved.

Estate Planning and Probate

Written by Lori Young, MPS

"In this world nothing can be said to be certain, except death and taxes."

- Benjamin Franklin

© 2019, 2020, 2021 NALA, Inc. All rights reserved.

OVERVIEW

To plan, or not to plan, that is the question. This chapter covers estate planning and probate, including the stages of what occurs during the estate planning and probate processes. This section discusses how estate planning affects individuals during their lifetimes in the event of incapacity, upon death, and how property transfers to beneficiaries or heirs.

The information in this chapter will negate some common myths and validate the facts:

- **Myth**: Wills and living wills are the same thing.

- **Fact**: Wills and living wills are not the same thing.

- **Myth**: If one does not prepare a will, the government will take the assets.

- **Fact**: If one does not prepare a will, the estate will go to the surviving relatives per the laws of intestate succession. An estate escheats to the state if there are no surviving blood relatives or next of kin, which is a rare occasion.

- **Myth**: To avoid probate, prepare a will.

- **Fact**: Preparing a will does not necessarily avoid probate.

- **Myth**: A durable power of attorney continues to be operative upon the death of the principal.

- **Fact**: A durable power of attorney becomes inoperative upon the death of the principal.

- **Myth**: Revocable living trusts avoid taxes.

- **Fact**: Revocable living trusts do not avoid income or estate taxes. A revocable living trust is a legal entity created to hold the grantor's assets and is subject to taxes.

ESTATE PLANNING

Estate planning occurs during a person's lifetime. It is the preparation of legal documents setting forth one's wishes how to manage one's personal and financial affairs prior to death or in the event of incapacity. These legal documents may consist of a will, trust, power of attorney, living will, or advance health care directive. Without estate planning, one will rely on the laws of the state to determine who manages and controls the personal and financial affairs upon incapacity or death.

Estate Administration

Estate administration occurs after death. An estate consists of all the property owned by a person at the time of death. Estate administration is the process of collecting the decedent's property, paying the decedent's debts, and distributing the remainder of the decedent's property to the beneficiaries or the heirs at law.

 © 2019, 2020, 2021 NALA, Inc. All rights reserved.

Types of Property and Ownership

It is important to understand the two main classifications of property and the various types of ownership of one's estate. There are two main classifications of property, real and personal. Whether the property is real or personal, it is essential to determine the ownership of the property. The individual must have actual title to the property in order to dispose of it by gift, will, or through a trust. There are several methods by which individuals may take title to property, and each method is significant when it comes to estate planning and estate administration. Briefly, the methods of title and its effect on ownership will be discussed. The Real Estate and Property chapter covers the title of ownership in detail.

Real Property

Real property is land or anything permanently affixed or built on the land such as buildings, apartment complexes, houses, or garages. Real property includes anything permanently affixed to those buildings such as fixtures.

Personal Property

Personal property is distinguishable from real property. Personal property is moveable, not permanently affixed to the land. Personal property includes items such as vehicles, furniture, furnishings, jewelry, art, stocks, or cash. Personal property is personal possessions, also known as chattel.

Ownership

Joint tenancy is a form of ownership by two or more parties having an equal share and right to the property. Upon the death of one of the parties, that decedent's share will transfer to the remaining joint tenants through operation of law and avoid probate administration. Assume two parties hold title to real property as joint tenants, each owning one-half interest. If one of the parties dies, the decedent's one-half interest transfers to the surviving joint tenant, now owning 100 percent of the property. Assume three parties hold title to property as joint tenants, each owning one-third interest of the property. If one of the parties dies, and there are two surviving joint tenants remaining, then each will own one-half of the property since there are two survivors of the joint tenancy property. Joint tenancy is right by survivorship and does not pass to beneficiaries or heirs through a will, trust, or intestate succession.

Tenancy in common is another form of ownership by two or more parties. However, it differs from joint tenancy in that there is no right of survivorship, and the ownership by the parties is a separate transferable interest. Assume there are two parties who hold title to property as tenants in common. One party dies. That decedent's interest in the property does not transfer to the tenant in common through survivorship. That decedent's interest transfers through testate or intestate procedures, meaning the surviving tenant in common will now be a co-owner with the decedent's beneficiaries or heirs.

Another method of ownership is tenancy by the entirety, recognized by tenancy by the entirety states. This type of ownership is similar to joint tenancy except tenancy by the entirety is only for legally married persons. Upon the death of one spouse, the property automatically passes to the surviving spouse. Tenancy by the entirety is not available for community property states.

Community property states recognize community property as a form of ownership only for legally married persons. There are nine community property states: Arizona, California, Idaho, Louisiana, Nevada, New Mexico, Texas, Washington, and Wisconsin. This type of ownership applies to property acquired during marriage, and each spouse owns an undivided one-half interest in the property. Upon the death of one spouse, the surviving spouse will retain the one-half acquired during marriage and the deceased spouse's one-half interest will pass by will or state law. Community property with right of survivorship is another type of ownership recognized by six states: Alaska, Arizona, California, Idaho, Nevada, and Wisconsin. Both tenancy by the entirety and community property with right of survivorship automatically transfer ownership of the decedent's one-half interest to the surviving spouse. With these types of ownership, the individuals have the right to transfer title to the property upon death.

A life estate is another form of ownership; however, the holder of the life estate does not hold title in a manner to transfer the property. The holder of the life estate has permission to use the property during the holder's life. Upon the death of the life estate holder, the property will transfer in accordance with the person's estate plan who had created the life estate. Assume two parties marry and this is a second marriage for both. The husband owns 100 percent of the real property, the residence, as a widower. He wants to provide for his second wife if he should predecease her; however, he wants his two children from his first marriage to inherit the property. The husband creates a life estate for his second wife to live at the property until her death, and upon her death, the property will pass to the predeceased husband's children.

While most of the forms of ownership discussed pertain to real property, there are types of ownership that transfer personal property to a designated beneficiary or beneficiaries to avoid probate such as bank or investment accounts. An account holder who includes a payable on death clause, or POD, transfers title of a bank or investment account directly to the named beneficiary or beneficiaries upon the account holder's death. The beneficiary only needs to present a death certificate to the financial institution to have the funds transferred, avoiding probate. Another type of ownership for a bank account is a Totten Trust, which is not really a true trust. A Totten Trust is a bank account in the holder's name "in trust for" someone else. Upon the death of the account holder, the funds pass to the person named on the account as the beneficiary. The named person on the account presents a death certificate to the financial institution to complete the transfer of funds. Like payable on death accounts, Totten Trusts avoid probate.

Now that there is an understanding of real and personal property, and the various types of ownership, we will discuss estate planning and the different legal documents individuals may use to express their wishes when unable to communicate due to incapacity or death.

WILLS AND TYPES OF WILLS

A Last Will and Testament, a "will" for simplicity, is a legal document expressing one's final wishes as to what should occur with one's property and debts upon death. A person who makes or creates a valid will is known as a testator. The will explains and clarifies the disposition of the decedent's estate, meaning who will inherit the estate and when. The most common will is a formal will, usually prepared by an attorney. This is a document prepared on a computer or typed and is properly signed by the testator before witnesses.

A statutory will is an informal will not recognized by all states. A statutory will is a pre-printed standardized form that includes the state's statutory provisions of a will. The testator completes the simple statutory will by filling in the blanks and properly executing the document before witnesses. There are advantages due to its simplicity and ease in completing; however, there are disadvantages as to the simplicity in that it may not fulfill all of the testator's needs.

A holographic will is an informal will. It is a will handwritten by the testator in the testator's own handwriting, not typed or computer generated. Not all states permit holographic wills. If a testator elects

© 2019, 2020, 2021 NALA, Inc. All rights reserved.

to prepare a holographic will, one must follow the state requirements to avoid a will contest.

A nuncupative, another type of informal will, is an oral will. It is a set of instructions expressed orally by the testator. The majority of states do not permit nuncupative wills, but this type of will is worth mentioning as there are a few states that do permit an oral will under limited circumstances according to statute.

A pour-over will is a formal Last Will and Testament regularly used in conjunction with a living trust. Under the terms of a pour-over will, the property that passes through the will upon death is transferred, or poured over, into the trust. A pour-over will must contain a clause or provision allowing property not previously titled in the trustee's name of a living trust to transfer to the current trustee of the living trust. A discussion on this issue will take place later in this chapter.

Testamentary Capacity

In order for a testator to create a will, the testator must have testamentary capacity. Testamentary capacity has the components of age and mental ability with intent. For most states, the legal age for a testator to make and execute a will is 18 years of age. In addition to being an adult, the testator must have the mental ability to know the natural objects of the testator's bounty (the nearest relatives), know the nature and extent of testator's property, and the purpose of creating a will freely and voluntarily. Having testamentary capacity is probably one of the most important statutory requirements needed to execute a will.

Provisions

When constructing a will, there are general provisions to consider. The opening clause identifies the following: testator's name; domicile; testamentary capacity, including being over the age of 18; and the testator's intent of this being the Last Will and Testament. Within the opening clause, the testator may indicate family status, such as single or married, and name immediate family members. At the testator's option, the testator may make specific or general testamentary gifts, giving or leaving property to a named individual or individuals. If the testator leaves specific real property, the gift of real property is a devise, and the recipient is a devisee. If the testator leaves personal property, the gift of personal property is a bequest, and the recipient is a beneficiary. If the testator leaves money, the gift of money is a legacy, and the recipient is a legatee. However, beneficiary is a catch-all term for inheriting specific gifts disposed of by a will. If there is a specific provision in the will, the specific gift or gifts must be satisfied prior to the general disposition of the residual estate.

A residuary clause is necessary for a testator to make wishes known how to dispose of the residue of the testator's estate or the remaining property of the estate. The residuary clause disposes the residue of an estate to the entitled beneficiaries as outlined in the will. For example: *I hereby give, devise, and bequeath all the rest, residue, and remainder of my estate, whether real, personal, and mixed, to* _____. If a beneficiary is unable to accept a specific gift or the residuary estate because of death, likely, an anti-lapse provision will provide for the deceased beneficiary's issue to inherit the specific gift or residual estate. If there is not an anti-lapse provision, the specific gift or residual estate will pass to the heirs-at-law in accordance with the state's statute.

The clause for appointment of a personal representative and the clauses setting forth the rights and duties of the personal representative are important. The generic term for a personal representative named in a will is executor. The testator names a primary executor, as well as alternate executors, to carry out the terms of the will. If the primary executor is unable to serve, the first alternate executor named in the will

© 2019, 2020, 2021 NALA, Inc. All rights reserved.

is next in line to serve and so forth. If the will fails to appoint a personal representative, the court will appoint a person deemed suitable. The executor is the person tasked with the duties and responsibilities in paying the decedent's last expenses and distributing the estate in accordance with the clauses of rights and duties. Further, an executor must post a bond with the probate court unless it is waived. The bond is for the protection of creditors and beneficiaries upon the negligence or malfeasance of the executor.

A guardianship clause provides the testator the ability to nominate a guardian of a minor child or children. This clause takes effect if the minor child or children have no surviving parents to care for them. The guardian will serve as guardian of the person and estate of the minor child, caring for the child and managing the inheritance until the minor attains the age of majority.

Another option for the testator to implement in a will is a testamentary trust clause for a beneficiary. This is a trust created through the probate process after the death of the testator where a specific gift or residual estate benefits a person for a specific time. A trustee is tasked with managing the trust estate for the beneficiary in accordance with the provisions of the trust set forth in the will, such as until the beneficiary attains the age of 25 years, graduates from a university, or gets married. The testamentary trust terminates after the trustee satisfies the terms of the testamentary trust and distributes the assets outright to the beneficiary.

The execution of the will is of utmost importance. Without the proper execution of the will, the will is invalid. The testimonium clause is the last section in the will before the testator's signature. For example: *"In witness whereof, I have hereunto set my hand this ___ day of _____, 20__."* The testator declares this is the Last Will and Testament before the witnesses and signs the will in the presence of at least two witnesses in most states (or three witnesses in a few states).

The attestation clause appears after the testator's signature and is a statement signed by the witnesses. The adult witnesses attest the following: they saw the testator sign the will; the testator is of sound mind; and the testator signed the will without being under duress, menace, fraud, misrepresentation, or undue influence. The witnesses sign the will in the presence of each other and the testator. The testator now has a valid will setting forth the wishes of how to distribute one's assets upon death.

Separate from the will, but attached, may be an affidavit signed by the witnesses before a notary affirming the following: under penalty of perjury that they, the witnesses, observed the testator sign the will, and the testator stated it was the testator's will. This is a self-proving will. The attached affidavit serves as a substitute for live testimony of the attesting witnesses in court if the validity of the will is not contested.

Codicil

If the testator later desires to make changes to the existing will, an amendment known as a codicil can be prepared instead of preparing a new will. A codicil can amend, change, or delete provisions of an existing will and incorporate the other terms of the will by reference into the codicil. A codicil has the same formalities as a will, including the execution by the testator before witnesses attesting to the document, making a codicil a valid document accompanying a will.

Contest or Challenges to a Will

If a will or codicil is challenged as to its validity, a will contest occurs. Persons who have standing may bring an action before the courts to challenge the validity of the will or contest a will. Common grounds to contest a will include:

- Testamentary capacity – testator lacked capacity at the time of signing the will not knowing the

 © 2019, 2020, 2021 NALA, Inc. All rights reserved.

nature and extent of the property or the natural bounty of the estate.

- Proper execution – execution did not conform to the statutory requirements or a holographic will was not entirely written by the testator's own handwriting.

- Forgery of testator's signature – the signature is not the testator's and may require an analysis by a handwriting expert.

- Induced by duress or fraud – testator did not act freely on their own free will to execute a will.

- Induced by undue influence – testator was convinced by a person in a close position to execute a will.

TRUSTS

Now that there is an understanding of the different types of ownership of property and the various types of wills, this portion of the chapter will discuss the following: the two basic types of trusts, revocable and irrevocable; another type of ownership – property held in a trust; and the parties involved in a trust. The person who creates a trust is known as a trustor, grantor, or settlor. The terms are interchangeable. The person who manages the trust is the trustee, and the person who benefits from the trust is a beneficiary. These three fundamental parties are the players in a revocable trust or irrevocable trust. The main difference between a revocable trust and an irrevocable trust is that a trustor may amend or revoke a revocable trust; however, a trustor may not amend or revoke an irrevocable trust.

Revocable – Living Trust

The most common revocable trust is the inter vivos trust or living trust. A person creates a living trust while alive, defining the operative guidelines, transferring assets to the trust, and providing provisions how to distribute the trust assets upon death while avoiding probate. Recall, the person who creates the trust is the trustor, grantor, or settlor. The person who manages the trust is the trustee. Think of a living trust like a business, a separate legal entity. A business has an owner and a manager. A living trust has an owner (trustor, grantor, or settlor) and a manager (the trustee). Like a business that has inventory, the trust must contain inventory or property. This is where another type of ownership occurs. The trustor transfers real or personal property to the trustee of the trust.

Example:

> Richard Young creates the "Richard Young Living Trust" and then transfers the title of his real property from his individual name to the trustee of the trust. The conveyance document reflects the transfer from Richard Young, a single man, to Richard Young, Trustee of the Richard Young Living Trust. The trustee of the living trust now has title to the property. Richard is the owner and the manager of the property in the trust. Richard may continue to transfer other real property or personal property into the trust by taking the necessary steps to change the title of his assets from an individual to himself as trustee of the trust. If Richard fails to transfer ownership of property to the trustee of the living trust, then the trust has no assets. If Richard dies, and there are no assets in the trust, there is nothing to distribute in accordance with the distribution provisions. The pour-over will is a remedy to get the assets transferred to the trust after death; however, the pour-over will requires a probate proceeding in order to complete the transfer of the assets to the successor trustee of the living trust.

One of the purposes in creating a living trust is to avoid a probate proceeding and the time and expense associated with a probate. A properly funded and managed living trust avoids probate. While the trustor is alive, the trustor has control over the assets. The trustor and trustee are not always the same person. For instance, upon incapacity of a trustor, a successor trustee can take over the trust and manage the trust property for the incapacitated trustor, without requiring court action. If the incapacitated trustor dies, the successor trustee continues to manage the trust estate; however, upon the death of the trustor, the living trust becomes irrevocable (more on this later).

The successor trustee of a revocable trust or irrevocable trust, or any trustee of a trust, has a fiduciary duty and responsibility to abide by the trust's provisions, and its powers granted to the trustee. The trustee entrusted with the fiduciary duty maintains a standard of care higher than ordinary care. The trustee may not delegate trust duties to another individual and must perform the duties personally for the benefit of a trust and the beneficiary. The trustee is responsible for collecting and managing the assets held in trust and preparing tax filings for the trust. A valid trust has a named beneficiary or beneficiaries. Each beneficiary receives the share as a separate interest, not as a joint tenant or tenant in common.

Upon the death of the trustor, the trustee accounts to the beneficiaries and distributes the trust assets in accordance with the provisions of the trust. The trustee must pay special attention to the wording of the distribution provisions, particularly if there are clauses that describe how to distribute the estate, such as "by right of representation," "*per stirpes*," or "per capita."

Right of representation, also known as per stirpes, refers to the lineal descendants of the person creating the trust (or will). This provision means the person wishes the estate to be divided equally among one generation of beneficiaries, most often the children, and if one of the children predeceases the creator of the trust (or will), then to that child's descendants.

 © 2019, 2020, 2021 NALA, Inc. All rights reserved.

Example of Right of Representation (also known as *Per Stirpes*):

John leaves his estate in equal shares to his three children, Joanne, Jill, and James, by right of representation or per stirpes. James predeceased his father leaving two children, Jacob and Joshua. Upon John's death, the estate is distributed into three equal shares: 1/3 to Joanne; 1/3 to Jill; and 1/3 to the descendants of James, who are Jacob and Joshua.

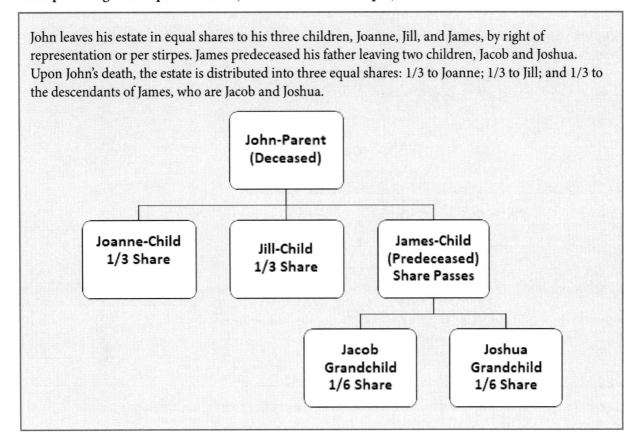

Per capita refers to the head count or total number of individuals in a class or generation who receive an equal share.

Example of Per Capita:

John leaves his estate in equal shares to his three children, Joanne, Jill, and James, per capita. James predeceased his father. Upon John's death, the estate is distributed into two equal shares, 1/2 to Joanne and 1/2 to Jill. Because James predeceased his father, his share does not pass to his descendants but rather to the individuals of the same class or generation as James.

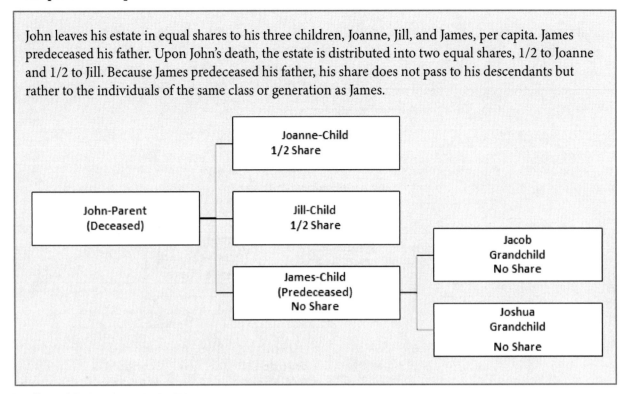

Right of representation or *per stirpes* is used more commonly than per capita for estate planning purposes. It is the trustee's duty to adhere to the distribution provisions.

If a trustee breaches the duties of a trust, there are grounds for beneficiaries to remove the trustee. Common grounds to remove a trustee may include:

- Breach of trust – trustee violates a fiduciary obligation.

- Refusal to account to beneficiaries – trustee fails to provide proper accountings.

- Failure to act as trustee – trustee takes no action in performing duties.

- Hostile or lack of cooperation among co-trustees – trustee impairs the administration of the trust estate.

- Shows favoritism to one beneficiary – trustee must treat all beneficiaries equally according to the terms of the trust.

A living trust may not exist in perpetuity, as this would contradict the "rule against perpetuities." The rule against perpetuities means that all interests in a trust must vest within 21 years after the death of the lives in being, plus the period of gestation. Other ways a living trust terminates is through a revocation by the trustor or through full distribution of the trust assets after the death of the trustor.

An amendment to a living trust is comparable to a codicil to a will. A trustor who creates a living trust has the power to amend, revoke, or restate a living trust. However, if the trust is irrevocable, the trustor does not have such a power.

 © 2019, 2020, 2021 NALA, Inc. All rights reserved.

Irrevocable Trusts

If a trustor creates and funds an irrevocable trust while alive, the trustor gives up the right of ownership and management of the property, and the right to change the provisions of the trust and the beneficiary. The beneficiary of an irrevocable trust may grant permission to make changes. However, the assets in the irrevocable trust are no longer under control of the trustor, and no longer a part of the trustor's estate. The irrevocable trust is a separate taxable entity. The most common reasons to create an irrevocable trust are to:

- Minimize estate taxes – the assets are not a part of the trustor's estate upon death.

- Apply for government benefits – the trustor may need to apply for Medicaid benefits due to long-term care, and Medicaid imposes income and asset limitations.

- Shelter assets and income from creditors – depending upon state law, a trustor may wish to protect assets from creditors. This does not include deliberate hiding of assets or attempting to defraud a creditor's claim.

There are common types of irrevocable trusts that a trustor may choose to create. The first is a Charitable Remainder Trust. The purpose of this type of trust is to allow the trustor, a donor, to transfer a highly appreciated asset to a trustee of a Charitable Remainder Trust. The trustee sells the asset paying no capital gains taxes, reinvests the asset, and generates income. The generated income can serve as an income stream or retirement benefit for the donor. Upon the death of the donor, the named charity benefits with the remainder of the assets.

A Credit Shelter Trust, also known as a Bypass Trust or A-B Trust, is another type of irrevocable trust and available to married couples. The primary purpose of this type of trust is to maximize the use of federal exemptions from estate taxes by both parties. An A-B Trust takes effect when the first spouse dies. Upon the death of the first spouse, the trust assets split into two separate trusts: one-half to the A Trust or Survivor's Trust, and one-half to the B Trust or Bypass Trust. The A Trust or Survivor's Trust continues as a revocable trust. However, the B Trust or Bypass Trust continues as an irrevocable trust providing the surviving spouse with a life interest in all of the income generated by the B Trust. Upon the death of the surviving spouse, the remaining assets of the B Trust pass to the persons indicated in the trust.

A Life Insurance Trust, albeit irrevocable, is a trust funded by a life insurance policy with the main goal to avoid federal estate taxes for a taxable estate. The trustor creates the Life Insurance Trust naming someone other than trustor as the trustee. The trustor provides the funds to the trustee to purchase a life insurance policy. The trustor is the insured, but not the owner of the policy. The Life Insurance Trust is the owner and the named beneficiary of the life insurance policy.

Typically, the life insurance trust contains a Crummey provision, allowing the trustor to make gifts to the irrevocable trust. The trustor continues to provide funds to the trustee to pay the annual insurance premiums, making annual gifts to the irrevocable trust throughout the trustor's lifetime of the trust. When a gift is made to the trust, the trust beneficiaries are entitled to receive a written notification, known as a Crummey notice. The notification states the beneficiaries have the power for a specified amount of time, usually 30 days, to withdraw some or all of the gift made to the trust. The gift to the trust with the Crummey provision qualifies for the annual gift tax exclusion. Upon the death of the insured, the trustee invests the insurance proceeds, administers the trust, and distributes the trust to the beneficiaries.

OTHER ESTATE PLANNING DOCUMENTS

In addition to wills and trusts, there are other powerful estate planning documents. A power of attorney document authorizes another to act on one's behalf to transact financial or business affairs. A HIPAA authorization permits a personal representative access to health care records. An end-of-life document authorizes another to make medical decisions or life support treatment on one's behalf.

Power of Attorney

Although there are different types of financial powers of attorney, the most common is the durable power of attorney. The principal, or creator, creates a durable power of attorney by naming an agent to act on the principal's behalf as an "attorney-in-fact" and gives the agent broad powers. The durable power of attorney takes effect immediately upon execution while the principal is cognizant and continues even if the principal becomes incapacitated. Unlike the durable power of attorney, a springing power of attorney does not take effect immediately. The springing power of attorney springs into action or takes effect only upon certain conditions occurring and the principal lacking capacity. A limited power of attorney authorizes an agent a specific power clearly defined. The limited power of attorney is restrictive. Power of attorney documents require the signature of the principal before a notary and depending upon state requirements, a witness may be required.

HIPAA Authorization

A HIPAA authorization complements the estate plan. HIPAA stands for Health Insurance Portability and Accountability Act of 1996 (HIPAA). This release authorization permits a personal representative to have various rights to access the individual's protected health care records and treatment information. The authorization allows the personal representative the ability to communicate with health care professionals and health insurance companies. The HIPAA authorization takes immediate effect upon the individual signing the HIPAA authorization, and the HIPAA authorization remains effective after death. The HIPAA Privacy Rule protects an individual's health information for 50 years following the individual's death.

End-of-Life Document

Although each state has specific requirements for end-of-life documents, this is an overview of a living will and advance health care directive. A living will is different from a Last Will and Testament. A living will is an end-of-life document a person creates to express desires and preferences of medical and life support decisions. The living will takes effect when there is a terminal illness or the person is no longer able to communicate wishes. The designated agent makes the decisions in accordance with the provisions of the living will. A living will is a type of advance directive.

An advance health care directive is another type of end-of-life document. This document is similar to the living will but has more options. In addition to the person expressing desires and preferences of medical and life support decisions, options include donation of organs and designation of a primary physician. The advance health care directive is similar to a power of attorney as it takes effect immediately without the person having to be terminally ill or incapacitated.

When an individual dies, the power of attorney, living will, and advance health care directive terminate. The documents are no longer in force and they become inoperable upon death. However, the Last Will and Testament or living trust documents are in force. The decedent's estate commences with

---

     © 2019, 2020, 2021 NALA, Inc. All rights reserved.

administration through a probate or non-probate process.

PROBATE

Probate is the legal process through a court proceeding overseeing the distribution of a decedent's estate to the beneficiaries or heirs-at-law and payment to creditors. If the decedent dies with a valid will, an executor will administer the estate. If the decedent dies without a will, an administrator administers the estate. Nevertheless, the court oversees the actions of the executor or administrator. However, if a decedent dies with a small estate, a summary probate or simplified probate may be available. Each state provides for its own summary probate procedure and has its own requirements as to what qualifies as a small estate. For purposes of this chapter, the focus is on probate administration, the process of collecting assets, paying debts, and distributing a person's property after death.

Laws of Intestate Succession

If a person dies intestate, meaning without a valid will, the laws of intestate succession determine who inherits the estate and in what proportion. In essence, the state makes a will for the decedent. Generally, the decedent's assets pass to the closest blood relatives or next of kin, except when there is a legal spouse (a legal spouse is the closest relative). One of the easiest ways to determine the heirs is to draw a generational family tree. Another way is to refer to a table of consanguinity (relation by blood) and diagram the degrees of relationship. There are other considerations in locating heirs:

- Adopted children are considered blood relatives under most statutes;

- Persons related by marriage, known as affinity, are not blood relatives; and

- Persons related by half-blood are blood relatives if the person is related by blood to the decedent.

Administration of Non-Trust Assets

The next process is to determine which assets of the decedent will eventually pass to the beneficiaries or heirs after payment of any creditors through the probate process. Now is a good time to recall how assets may avoid probate:

- Assets with a designated beneficiary, in trust for, or a payable on death clause will pass directly to the beneficiary or beneficiaries.

- Assets titled in joint tenancy will pass to the surviving joint tenant or surviving joint tenants. Assets titled in the name of a trustee of a trust will pass to the successor trustee for distribution to a beneficiary or beneficiaries in accordance with the trust provisions.

The assets that are in the decedent's separate name will have to go through the probate process for the eventual distribution to the heirs or beneficiaries. The decedent is not alive and therefore cannot transfer title of assets after death, nor can an agent act as attorney-in-fact under a power of attorney.

Petition for Probate

The probate process begins with the filing of a petition for probate with the appropriate court. Appendix A contains a sample Petition for Probate. The probate matter is set for hearing and the persons who have an interest in the estate receive proper notice if not waived. The petition requests the court to appoint a personal representative to administer the estate and issue Letters Testamentary to an executor if the decedent died testate (with a valid will) or Letters of Administration to an administrator if the decedent died intestate (without a valid will). The court may require an executor or administrator to post a bond in an amount that is close to the value of the decedent's estate prior to issuing the Letters. A bond protects the decedent's estate if a personal representative is incompetent, fraudulent, or commits unethical behavior. However, a will may waive a bond, or the beneficiaries entitled to a decedent's estate may waive a bond.

Letters of Appointment

Once the court approves the Petition for Probate and determines if a bond is necessary, the court will issue the "Letters." The Letters Testamentary or Letters of Administration is an official court document authorizing the executor, administrator general, or specific powers to administer the estate. The term "Letters" is not to be confused with the definition of a written correspondence to communicate with another. The court form, "Letters," in the probate arena has a different meaning. The court form, "Letters," authorizes the executor or administrator to take control of the decedent's estate. Appendix B contains a sample of Letters.

The personal representative, a catch-all term for executor or administrator, has fiduciary responsibilities in administering the estate. A fiduciary is held to a higher standard when managing assets. The personal representative in a fiduciary capacity takes the following actions in administering a decedent's estate:

- Applies for a federal taxpayer identification number for the estate. Uses this number for new estate accounts instead of the decedent's Social Security number.

- Gathers and collects the decedent's assets, including the opening of any safe deposit box and collection of the contents.

- Establishes an ancillary probate if the decedent held title to real property outside of the domiciliary state by filing another petition for probate in that particular state. For example, if Nina Baker is a resident of California and dies, the proper jurisdiction to file the petition for probate is California; however, if Nina Baker also owned real property in Arizona, then Arizona is the proper jurisdiction for that particular real property. An ancillary probate has the same procedures as filing the initial petition for probate with the related hearing and forms.

- Opens an estate checking account. Takes title in the name of the personal representative of the decedent's estate. For example: "Robert Brown, Executor of the Estate of David Brown."

- Maintains accurate records throughout the administration.

- Notifies any creditors of the estate through publication or other proper notice to allow creditors the proper timeframe to file a claim against the estate according to statute. Determines the validity of the creditor's claim and pays if warranted.

- Inventories the decedent's assets and obtains appropriate date-of-death values or appraisals of each asset.

- Prepares and files the decedent's final federal and state personal income tax returns if applicable. The time period covers January 1st, the year the decedent died, through the date of death.

- Prepares a detailed accounting of the activity during the estate administration, including income, expenses, gains, and losses. Files the accounting with the court and provides a copy to the persons who have an interest in the estate.

 © 2019, 2020, 2021 NALA, Inc. All rights reserved.

- Distributes the decedent's estate pursuant to the terms of the will, or if intestate, pursuant to the law of intestate succession, and obtains receipts on distribution from each beneficiary.

- Prepares and files federal and state fiduciary income tax returns as applicable. The time period covers the date of death through the closing of the estate. Prepares and files federal estate tax return if applicable.

- Terminates the bond and obtains a discharge relieving the personal representative from any further duties in administering the estate.

Escheatment

If a decedent dies with no heirs, meaning no living blood relatives, the decedent's estate will escheat to the state. In other words, if there are no children, parents, grandparents, aunts, uncles, or cousins, the decedent's estate reverts to the government of the state where the decedent resided. A court-appointed personal representative will administer the decedent's estate through the probate procedures discussed above, and upon closing of the probate, distribute the balance of the estate to the state.

Estate Tax Issues

Unfortunately, taxes do not disappear upon death. If a decedent owes taxes at the time of death, the taxes are still due and owing. A primary responsibility of the personal representative is the preparation and filing of the decedent's last income tax return from the end of the last calendar tax year until the date of death. The personal representative will use IRS Form 1040 to report the final income taxes and mark the box "final." After a death, there are various tax forms and deadlines that pertain to a decedent's estate.

TYPES OF TAX FORMS

IRS Form 1041

Similar to IRS Form 1040, the form an individual uses to report income tax, Form 1041, U.S. Income Tax Return for Estates and Trusts, is the form a personal representative uses to report income for a decedent's estate or trust. Form 1041 is used if the estate generates more than $600 in annual gross income such as rental income, dividends, or interest on an estate account. If the estate has no income-producing assets or the annual gross income is less than $600, the personal representative is not required to file Form 1041. Form 1041 is sometimes referred to as a fiduciary income tax return since the personal representative acts in a fiduciary capacity. The deadline to file Form 1041 can vary. If the personal representative elects a calendar year, the deadline is April 15th. If the personal representative elects a fiscal year, the deadline is the 15th day of the fourth month following the close of the tax year. For example, the personal representative elects a fiscal year end of June 30th. The deadline to file Form 1041 is October 15th, which is the 15th day of the fourth month after the close of the tax year. The personal representative must also file a Notice of Fiduciary Relationship with the IRS and attach a copy of the Letters.

IRS Form 706

IRS Form 706, U.S. Estate (and Generation-Skipping Transfer) Tax Return, is for very large estates when the value of the decedent's estate meets or exceeds the threshold for paying federal estate taxes. For instance, a large estate is $11.7 million for year 2021, and the exemption amount will rise with inflation each year through 2025. At the end of 2025, the current tax exemption is set to expire and revert back to 2017 with a cumulative inflation adjustment. (Note: the amounts are subject to change each year and it is necessary to check the current IRS codes.) Currently, there is a very small percentage of personal representatives who must file Form 706 on behalf of a decedent. The deadline to file Form 706 and pay the estimated taxes is nine months from the date of death unless there is an extension granted. IRS Form 706 is complex and contains many schedules relating to assets, deductions, and credits. The personal representative may seek the assistance of a certified public accountant.

IRS Form 709

IRS Form 709, U.S. Gift (and Generation-Skipping Transfer) Tax Return, is for the use by an individual to report taxable gifts and it also allocates the lifetime use of a taxpayer's generation-skipping transfer tax exemption. If a taxpayer makes a gift to a person in excess of the tax year's annual gift tax exclusion ($15,000 for year 2021), the taxpayer files Form 709. (Note: the amount is subject to change each year and it is necessary to check the current IRS codes.) Some gifts are exempt from being reported, such as gifts to spouses who are U.S. citizens, educational institutions for a student's tuition or expenses, medical bills paid directly to a care provider or medical facility on behalf of another, and gifts to charitable or political organizations. The deadline to file Form 709 is April 15th following the year in which the taxable gift was made.

IRS Form SS-4

Aside from reporting income taxes, estate taxes, and gifts, there is another form that is common with estate administration, IRS Form SS-4, Application for Taxpayer Identification Number. The personal representative uses this form to apply for a taxpayer identification number for the decedent's estate or trust. As an estate is its own entity, the personal representative uses the new taxpayer identification number instead of the decedent's Social Security number when transacting business during the estate administration and when filing fiduciary or estate tax returns.

SUMMARY

In summary, estate planning allows one to express decisions in writing as to health care decisions and financial matters entrusting another party to manage a person's affairs during life or after death. Estate administration allows one to manage and settle an estate with or without estate planning documents. To plan, or not to plan, is no longer a question.

 © 2019, 2020, 2021 NALA, Inc. All rights reserved.

APPENDIX A

ATTORNEY OR PARTY WITHOUT ATTORNEY:	STATE BAR NO.:	FOR COURT USE ONLY
NAME:		
FIRM NAME:		
STREET ADDRESS:		
CITY: STATE: ZIP CODE:		
TELEPHONE NO.: FAX NO.:		
E-MAIL ADDRESS:		
ATTORNEY FOR (name):		

SUPERIOR COURT OF CALIFORNIA, COUNTY OF
STREET ADDRESS:
MAILING ADDRESS:
CITY AND ZIP CODE:
BRANCH NAME:

ESTATE OF (name):
DECEDENT

PETITION FOR ☐ Probate of ☐ Lost Will and for Letters Testamentary
☐ Probate of ☐ Lost Will and for Letters of Administration with Will Annexed
☐ Letters of Administration
☐ Letters of Special Administration ☐ with general powers
☐ Authorization to Administer Under the Independent Administration of Estates Act ☐ with limited authority

CASE NUMBER:

HEARING DATE AND TIME: DEPT.:

1. Publication will be in (specify name of newspaper):
   a. ☐ Publication requested.
   b. ☐ Publication to be arranged.
2. Petitioner (name each):

   requests that
   a. ☐ decedent's will and codicils, if any, be admitted to probate.
   b. (name): be appointed
      (1) ☐ executor
      (2) ☐ administrator with will annexed
      (3) ☐ administrator
      (4) ☐ special administrator ☐ with general powers
      and Letters issue upon qualification.
   c. ☐ full ☐ limited authority be granted to administer under the Independent Administration of Estates Act.
   d. (1) ☐ bond not be required for the reasons stated in item 3e.
      (2) ☐ $ bond be fixed. The bond will be furnished by an admitted surety insurer or as otherwise provided by law. (Specify reasons in Attachment 2 if the amount is different from the maximum required by Prob. Code, § 8482.)
      (3) ☐ $ in deposits in a blocked account be allowed. Receipts will be filed. (Specify institution and location):

3. a. Decedent died on (date): at (place):
      (1) ☐ a resident of the county named above.
      (2) ☐ a nonresident of California and left an estate in the county named above located at (specify location permitting publication in the newspaper named in item 1):

   b. ☐ Decedent was a citizen of a country other than the United States (specify country): .
   c. Street address, city, and county of decedent's residence at time of death (specify):

Page 1 of 4

Form Adopted for Mandatory Use
Judicial Council of California
DE-111 [Rev. July 1, 2017]

PETITION FOR PROBATE
(Probate—Decedents Estates)

Probate Code, §§ 8002, 10450;
www.courts.ca.gov

© 2019, 2020, 2021 NALA, Inc. All rights reserved.

ESTATE OF (name):	CASE NUMBER:
DECEDENT	

3. d. Character and estimated value of the property of the estate (complete in all cases):

    (1) Personal property: $ _____

    (2) Annual gross income from

        (a) real property: $ _____

        (b) personal property: $ _____

    (3) **Subtotal** (add (1) and (2)): $ _____

    (4) Gross fair market value of real property: $ _____

    (5) (Less) Encumbrances: ($ _____)

    (6) Net value of real property: $ _____

    (7) **Total** (add (3) and (6)): $ _____

  e. (1) ☐ Will waives bond. ☐ Special administrator is the named executor, and the will waives bond.

    (2) ☐ All beneficiaries are adults and have waived bond, and the will does not require a bond. (Affix waiver as Attachment 3e(2).)

    (3) ☐ All heirs at law are adults and have waived bond. (Affix waiver as Attachment 3e(3).)

    (4) ☐ Sole personal representative is a corporate fiduciary or an exempt government agency.

  f. (1) ☐ Decedent died intestate.

    (2) ☐ Copy of decedent's will dated: _____ ☐ codicil dated _____ (specify for each): _____

    are affixed as Attachment 3f(2). (Include typed copies of handwritten documents and English translations of foreign-language documents.)

        ☐ The will and all codicils are self-proving (Prob. Code, § 8220).

    (3) ☐ The original of the will and/or codicil identified above has been lost. (Affix a copy of the lost will or codicil or a written statement of the testamentary words or their substance in Attachment 3f(3), and state reasons in that attachment why the presumption in Prob. Code, § 6124 does not apply.)

  g. Appointment of personal representative (check all applicable boxes):

    (1) Appointment of executor or administrator with will annexed:

        (a) ☐ Proposed executor is named as executor in the will and consents to act.

        (b) ☐ No executor is named in the will.

        (c) ☐ Proposed personal representative is a nominee of a person entitled to Letters. (Affix nomination as Attachment 3g(1)(c).)

        (d) ☐ Other named executors will not act because of ☐ death ☐ declination ☐ other reasons (specify): _____

            ☐ Continued in Attachment 3g(1)(d).

    (2) Appointment of administrator:

        (a) ☐ Petitioner is a person entitled to Letters. (If necessary, explain priority in Attachment 3g(2)(a).)

        (b) ☐ Petitioner is a nominee of a person entitled to Letters. (Affix nomination as Attachment 3g(2)(b).)

        (c) ☐ Petitioner is related to the decedent as (specify): _____

    (3) ☐ Appointment of special administrator requested. (Specify grounds and requested powers in Attachment 3g(3).)

    (4) ☐ Proposed personal representative would be a successor personal representative.

  h. Proposed personal representative is a

    (1) ☐ resident of California.

    (2) ☐ nonresident of California (specify permanent address): _____

    (3) ☐ resident of the United States.

    (4) ☐ nonresident of the United States.

DE-111 [Rev. July 1, 2017]

PETITION FOR PROBATE
(Probate—Decedents Estates)

Page 2 of 4

© 2019, 2020, 2021 NALA, Inc. All rights reserved.

ESTATE OF *(name)*:	CASE NUMBER:
DECEDENT	

4. ☐ Decedent's will does not preclude administration of this estate under the Independent Administration of Estates Act.

5. a. Decedent was survived by *(check items (1) or (2), and (3) or (4), and (5) or (6), and (7) or (8))*

    (1) ☐ spouse.

    (2) ☐ no spouse as follows:

       (a) ☐ divorced or never married.

       (b) ☐ spouse deceased.

    (3) ☐ registered domestic partner.

    (4) ☐ no registered domestic partner. *(See Fam. Code, § 297.5(c); Prob. Code, §§ 37(b), 6401(c), and 6402.)*

    (5) ☐ child as follows:

       (a) ☐ natural or adopted.

       (b) ☐ natural adopted by a third party.

    (6) ☐ no child.

    (7) ☐ issue of a predeceased child.

    (8) ☐ no issue of a predeceased child.

  b. Decedent ☐ was ☐ was not survived by a stepchild or foster child or children who would have been adopted by decedent but for a legal barrier. *(See Prob. Code, § 6454.)*

6. *(Complete if decedent was survived by (1) a spouse or registered domestic partner but no issue (only a or b apply), or (2) no spouse, registered domestic partner, or issue. (Check the first box that applies):*

  a. ☐ Decedent was survived by a parent or parents who are listed in item 8.

  b. ☐ Decedent was survived by issue of deceased parents, all of whom are listed in item 8.

  c. ☐ Decedent was survived by a grandparent or grandparents who are listed in item 8.

  d. ☐ Decedent was survived by issue of grandparents, all of whom are listed in item 8.

  e. ☐ Decedent was survived by issue of a predeceased spouse, all of whom are listed in item 8.

  f. ☐ Decedent was survived by next of kin, all of whom are listed in item 8.

  g. ☐ Decedent was survived by parents of a predeceased spouse or issue of those parents, if both are predeceased, all of whom are listed in item 8.

  h. ☐ Decedent was survived by no known next of kin.

7. *(Complete only if no spouse or issue survived decedent.)*

  a. ☐ Decedent had no predeceased spouse.

  b. ☐ Decedent had a predeceased spouse who

    (1) ☐ died not more than 15 years before decedent and who owned an interest in real property that passed to decedent,

    (2) ☐ died not more than five years before decedent and who owned personal property valued at $10,000 or more that passed to decedent. *(If you checked (1) or (2), check only the first box that applies):*

       (a) ☐ Decedent was survived by issue of a predeceased spouse, all of whom are listed in item 8.

       (b) ☐ Decedent was survived by a parent or parents of the predeceased spouse who are listed in item 8.

       (c) ☐ Decedent was survived by issue of a parent of the predeceased spouse, all of whom are listed in item 8.

       (d) ☐ Decedent was survived by next of kin of the decedent, all of whom are listed in item 8.

       (e) ☐ Decedent was survived by next of kin of the predeceased spouse, all of whom are listed in item 8.

    (3) ☐ neither (1) nor (2) apply.

8. Listed on the next page are the names, relationships to decedent, ages, and addresses, so far as known to or reasonably ascertainable by petitioner, of (1) all persons mentioned in decedent's will or any codicil, whether living or deceased; (2) all persons named or checked in items 2, 5, 6, and 7; and (3) all beneficiaries of a trust named in decedent's will or any codicil in which the trustee and personal representative are the same person.

PETITION FOR PROBATE
(Probate—Decedents Estates)

© 2019, 2020, 2021 NALA, Inc. All rights reserved.

ESTATE OF *(name)*:		CASE NUMBER:
	DECEDENT	

8.

Name and relationship to decedent	Age	Address

☐ Continued on Attachment 8.

9. Number of pages attached: [   ]

Date: [   ]

_____   ▶ _____
(TYPE OR PRINT NAME OF ATTORNEY)   (SIGNATURE OF ATTORNEY) *

* (Signatures of all petitioners are also required. All petitioners must sign, but the petition may be verified by any one of them (Prob. Code, §§ 1020, 1021; Cal. Rules of Court, rule 7.103).)

I declare under penalty of perjury under the laws of the State of California that the foregoing is true and correct.

Date: [   ]

_____   ▶ _____
(TYPE OR PRINT NAME OF PETITIONER)   (SIGNATURE OF PETITIONER)

_____   ▶ _____
(TYPE OR PRINT NAME OF PETITIONER)   (SIGNATURE OF PETITIONER)

☐ Signatures of additional petitioners follow last attachment.

DE-111 [Rev. July 1, 2017]

PETITION FOR PROBATE
(Probate—Decedents Estates

Page 4 of 4

© 2019, 2020, 2021 NALA, Inc. All rights reserved.

DE-150

ATTORNEY OR PARTY WITHOUT ATTORNEY *(Name, state bar number, and address)*:	TELEPHONE AND FAX NOS.:	FOR COURT USE ONLY

ATTORNEY FOR *(Name)*:

SUPERIOR COURT OF CALIFORNIA, COUNTY OF

STREET ADDRESS:

MAILING ADDRESS:

CITY AND ZIP CODE:

BRANCH NAME:

ESTATE OF *(Name)*:

DECEDENT

LETTERS

☐ TESTAMENTARY	☐ OF ADMINISTRATION	CASE NUMBER:
☐ OF ADMINISTRATION WITH WILL ANNEXED	☐ SPECIAL ADMINISTRATION	

LETTERS

1. ☐ The last will of the decedent named above having been proved, the court appoints *(name)*:

   a. ☐ executor.
   b. ☐ administrator with will annexed.

2. ☐ The court appoints *(name)*:

   a. ☐ administrator of the decedent's estate.
   b. ☐ special administrator of decedent's estate
      (1) ☐ with the special powers specified in the *Order for Probate.*
      (2) ☐ with the powers of a general administrator.
      (3) ☐ letters will expire on *(date)*:

3. ☐ The personal representative is authorized to administer the estate under the Independent Administration of Estates Act ☐ **with full authority**
☐ **with limited authority** (no authority, without court supervision, to (1) sell or exchange real property or (2) grant an option to purchase real property or (3) borrow money with the loan secured by an encumbrance upon real property).

4. ☐ The personal representative is not authorized to take possession of money or any other property without a specific court order.

WITNESS, clerk of the court, with seal of the court affixed.

(SEAL)	Date:
	Clerk, by
	_____
	(DEPUTY)

AFFIRMATION

1. ☐ PUBLIC ADMINISTRATOR: No affirmation required (Prob. Code, § 7621(c)).

2. ☐ INDIVIDUAL: **I solemnly affirm** that I will perform the duties of personal representative according to law.

3. ☐ INSTITUTIONAL FIDUCIARY *(name)*:

I solemnly affirm that the institution will perform the duties of personal representative according to law. I make this affirmation for myself as an individual and on behalf of the institution as an officer. *(Name and title)*:

4. Executed on *(date)*:
at *(place)*: , California.

▶ _____
(SIGNATURE)

CERTIFICATION

I certify that this document is a correct copy of the original on file in my office and the letters issued by the personal representative appointed above have not been revoked, annulled, or set aside, and are still in full force and effect.

(SEAL)	Date:
	Clerk, by
	_____
	(DEPUTY)

Form Approved by the
Judicial Council of California
DE-150 [Rev. January 1, 1998]
Mandatory Form [1/1/2000]

LETTERS
(Probate)

Probate Code, §§ 1001, 8403,
8405, 8544, 8545;
Code of Civil Procedure, § 2015.6

Westlaw Doc & Form Builder*

© 2019, 2020, 2021 NALA, Inc. All rights reserved.

CHAPTER 6: PRACTICE QUESTIONS

1. Jerry Smith, a single man, dies intestate at the age of 29. Jerry has a sister, Anne Smith. Anne meets with an attorney to administer Jerry's estate. Anne will receive Jerry's interest in the real property without going through probate. Which of the following best describes how Jerry Smith held title?

    A.   Jerry Smith and Anne Smith, as tenants in common

    B.   Jerry Smith and Anne Smith, as joint tenants

    C.   Jerry Smith and Anne Smith, as tenancy in partnership

    D.   Jerry Smith, a single man

2. A person's wishes with respect to their health care can be included in the following documents except:

    A.   Living will

    B.   Do-not-resuscitate directive

    C.   Statutory will

    D.   Advance directive

3. If a person dies without a valid will, what happens to the person's property?

    A.   The property passes in accordance to the intestate statute of the decedent's state of domicile.

    B.   The property escheats to the state where the decedent was domiciled.

    C.   The property passes according to the wishes of the decedent's spouse or next of kin.

    D.   The property passes to the decedent's children, or to the decedents next of kin if decedent has no children.

4. Sally wants to make sure that if she becomes incapacitated, the doctors do not use artificial means to keep her alive. She wants them to "pull the plug" on her if she is in a permanent vegetative state. What estate planning document should Sally create to make her wishes known?

    A.   An advance health care directive

    B.   A durable power of attorney

    C.   A trust

    D.   A will

© 2019, 2020, 2021 NALA, Inc. All rights reserved.

5. Marsha Molina's father, Kevin Molina, recently passed away and left a sizable estate. Kevin Molina was a widower, and at the time of his death he lived with Betty Nichols, a caregiver that took care of his needs on a daily basis. Mr. Molina's will was changed about two years ago when Betty Nichols took him to the law office for this purpose. In the new will, Kevin Molina left his entire estate to Betty Nichols. Marsha feels that Betty Nichols coerced her father into changing his will and leaving his sizable estate to her. Which of the following facts best supports Marsha's beliefs?

   A. Betty Nichols was with Kevin Molina every day and had access to him and his business interests.

   B. Betty Nichols did not like Marsha Molina because she did not visit her father often enough.

   C. Betty Nichols took Kevin Molina to his doctors' appointments and ran his errands for him; she threatened to quit if he did not change his will and leave his estate to her.

   D. Betty Nichols did the laundry and cooking and told Kevin Molina when meals would be served.

6. The deadline to file IRS Form 706 to report estate and/or Generation-Skipping Tax is due:

   A. 9 months after the date of the decedent's death

   B. 12 months after the date of the decedent's death

   C. 18 months after the date of the decedent's death

   D. 6 months after the date of the decedent's death

7. Andrew created a will. In his will, Andrew devised his summer cottage that he owns out-right to Chelsea, his friend of 20 years, for her life, and then to his granddaughter, Allison. Chelsea has a:

   A. Tenancy in common with Allison

   B. Life estate

   C. Joint tenancy with Allison

   D. Trust estate

8. A trustee has certain duties to perform in order to carry out the wishes of the trustor. A trustee may perform the following duties except:

   A. Delegate the performance of trust duties

   B. Maintain accurate records and accounts

   C. Take possession of the trust property and to make it profitable

   D. Preserve, protect, and defend the corpus of the trust

9. **What does it mean to die intestate?**

    A. Die with a valid will

    B. Die with a contested will

    C. Die without a valid will

    D. Die with no living issue

10. **HIPAA is an acronym for a U.S. law designed to provide privacy standards to protect patients' medical records and other health information provided to health plans, doctors, hospitals, and other health care providers. HIPAA stands for:**

    A. Health Insurance Portability and Accountability Act

    B. Health Insurance Private and Accountability Act

    C. Health Insurance Protection and Accountability Act

    D. Health Insurance and Public Accountability Act

11. **A Charitable Remainder Trust (CRT) is used to reduce income and capital gains taxes while increasing the settlor's immediate cash flow. Some of the benefits for the settlor of this type of trust include:**

    A. A lifetime of income from the CRT assets during the settlor's life or a specified number of years

    B. An income for the settlor which is free of taxes

    C. The CRT trust never ends and continues to perform charitable acts for the beneficiaries without the need for the settlor to be involved

    D. Neither settlor nor the CRT will have to file tax returns for the first 10 years after the trust has been established

Real Estate
and Property

Written by Eva M. Merrell, MBA, ACP

© 2019, 2020, 2021 NALA, Inc. All rights reserved.

Property laws regulate how property owners, lenders, and other parties own, possess, and use both real and personal property. These laws reflect society's values and its attempts to balance the competing interests of individual owners against the interests of lenders, neighboring owners, and the community at large. Many concepts in property law have been in effect for centuries and remain remarkably unchanged, while others have evolved substantially as social mores and technology have progressed.

Upon completion of this chapter, readers will be able to:

- Identify the types of property and the sources of law through which they are regulated.

- Describe the concept of a bundle of rights and how it applies to the various types of property ownership.

- Differentiate freehold estates, the forms of concurrent ownership, and other ownership interests.

- Contrast freehold estates against nonfreehold estates and other interests.

- Understand the duties and rights held by landlords and tenants.

- Describe servitudes and other limitations on property rights and explain the role of private restrictions and distinguish them from public restrictions.

- Compare and contrast the methods of voluntarily conveying freehold estates, nonfreehold estates, and other interests in property against the processes by which such interests may be taken involuntarily by public or private parties.

- Explain the due diligence process and its role in assessing the legal, physical, and economic status of property and explain the reports to be obtained and reviewed during the due diligence stage of property transactions.

- Describe the most typical documents used to convey estates and to provide notice of interests in property.

- Identify statutory requirements for the preparation and recording of such documents.

PROPERTY RIGHTS AND OWNERSHIP

In property law, objects fall into two general categories: real property and personal property. Real property consists of land and the rights pertaining to land. Also included in the category of real property are improvements and appurtenances such as buildings, fences, and trees. All property not considered real property is designated personal property and is sometimes referred to as chattel. This includes cars and other vehicles, personal belongings such as clothing and furniture, and anything else that is tangible and unattached to real property. Personal property also includes intangible rights such as trademarks and other intellectual property or information stored electronically.

Fixtures are items of personal property that have been attached to real property. For example, shelving units stored in a warehouse awaiting sale and delivery would be considered personal property. Once those shelving units have been affixed to real property, such as in a retail store, they are referred to as fixtures and treated as real property. The distinction between real property and personal property is essential for security and ownership purposes. For instance, when a retail store owner installs shelving units in a rented space, the landlord could argue that the shelving is considered a fixture affixed to real property and, therefore, the landlord's property. The tenant could argue that the shelving units are not permanently affixed to the real property and remain personal property to be removed when the lease

 © 2019, 2020, 2021 NALA, Inc. All rights reserved.

expires. Any lender secured by the landlord's real property or the tenant's personal property would also have an interest in determining the status of such property. As a result, leases, mortgages, and other real estate documentation should be clear as to how such property will be treated.

Many basic concepts in property law originated in feudal Europe, with kings granting estates and other rights to reward favored subjects or to inspire allegiance. From those beginnings, common law regarding real property grew as an attempt to limit or modify these feudal traditions. This heritage of feudal interests and common law was brought to the United States and has been modified by statutory law and case law. Although it is not necessary for paralegals to understand all the details of this long and deeply rooted history, it is helpful to recognize that many contemporary real estate concepts arose from those early sources. As a result, certain concepts which may seem strange to us today may be better understood if we comprehend the role those ideas played in their first incarnation hundreds of years ago.

Bundle of Rights

One of the oldest concepts in real property law is that of a bundle of rights or, as it is sometimes referred to metaphorically, a bundle of sticks. The rights to possess, lease, mortgage, convey, use and enjoy, and exclude others are all contained within the bundle of rights. Although an individual owner may have any or all these rights with respect to their real property, this does not mean that they have absolute control over such property. Because of this, it can be said that an owner does not own real property as much as they possess certain rights in the real property. An owner may choose to retain all their rights in the real property or to grant other parties some of these rights, or they may have some of those rights taken from them against their wishes, all while still continuing to own an estate in the real property. Other parties, such as governing bodies, public utility companies, or neighboring property owners, often have rights in such real property. The following is a discussion of the rights contained within the bundle of rights and examples of the limitations imposed upon those rights.

The right to possess real property includes the owner's rights to control, occupy, and have custody of the property. A real property owner has the right to possess their property, but that right is limited by the police power of the state. For instance, the local building code enforcement authority may terminate the owner's right to occupy the property if the property falls into disrepair to the point where it must be condemned for health reasons.

Generally, an owner has the right to lease or permit another party to possess their property pursuant to an oral or written lease. However, zoning regulations affecting property in a single-family residential zoning district often prevent an owner from dividing up their residence and leasing it as apartments to multiple families. Building codes may regulate leasing by requiring leased residential apartments to meet stringent construction and safety standards. In addition, the Statute of Frauds requires certain leases to be in writing to effectively convey an interest in the real property.

When an owner mortgages their property, they are pledging the property as collateral or security for the repayment of a loan. The owner's right to mortgage their property is limited by state statutes governing the type of mortgage lien that may be granted. Some states require such liens to be in the form of a mortgage while others require a deed of trust, which contains provisions that favor the lender more than those contained in a mortgage. In addition, the federal government regulates many banks and other lenders, including the practices used by those lenders in making loans secured by real property. This is especially true of loans secured by residential property that meet certain lending criteria.

To convey real property means to transfer title to that property to another party by deed, will, or other written instrument. A real property owner has the right to convey whatever interest the owner has in the property to another party, although that right may be limited. For example, a court may require co-

© 2019, 2020, 2021 NALA, Inc. All rights reserved.

owners to convey their interests in property as a result of a partition suit. Zoning regulations may require parcels of real property in a particular zoning district to be larger than a specified size. As a practical result, an owner would probably not be able to sell a parcel of property if that parcel does not meet the minimum size requirements because the buyer would not be permitted to build upon the lot. Such a conveyance may also be prohibited if the owner's remaining property would not meet such lot size requirements.

An owner's rights to their real property include the right to use and enjoy the property. However, like the rights discussed above, that right is not unlimited. For example, the use of property in residential neighborhoods for commercial purposes may be prohibited by city zoning regulations. In addition, state statutes and local regulations govern the use of property for the sale or consumption of alcohol or tobacco products.

In general, a real property owner has the right to exclude or remove another party from their property. In fact, an owner has a responsibility to eject an interloper from their property if they want to prevent such party from obtaining rights in the property through adverse possession. However, even the right of ejection may be regulated or limited by the exercise of the government's police power. For instance, each state adopts its own regulations controlling how and when an owner or occupant may use lethal force against a trespasser. In case of a fire, earthquake, or other crisis, an owner's right to eject trespassers would not permit them to prevent emergency workers from entering onto their property to perform life-saving work.

Freehold Estates

From as far back as feudal times, parties receiving an ownership interest in real property held what is known as a freehold estate. Such possession of a freehold estate is referred to as seisin. Freehold estates are alienable, meaning they can be sold or inherited. They have an indefinite duration, meaning that the ending date of such estate is not known.

The owners of freehold estates during feudal periods could grant tenants limited rights to use or possess such property. Such possessory interest in real property was a nonfreehold estate which will be discussed later in this chapter. This system of granting freehold and nonfreehold estates in real property provided a way to regulate the ownership and use of real estate and to organize society. Many of these early concepts of real property law are still in use today.

The following table illustrates the relationships between certain present interests and their corresponding future interests. Those relationships are discussed in the following pages.

© 2019, 2020, 2021 NALA, Inc. All rights reserved.

Freehold Estates	
Present Interests	**Future Interests**
Fee Simple	
Fee Simple Absolute	N/A
Fee Simple Determinable	Possibility of Reverter
Fee Simple Subject to Condition Subsequent	Right of Reentry/Power of Termination
Fee Simple Subject to Executory Limitation	Executory Interests
Fee Tail	Reversion
Life Estate	Remainder

Present Interests

As the name implies, a present interest in real property means that the owner has current rights in their estate, including seisin and possession, unless the owner has granted a tenant a right of possession. The freehold fee simple, fee tail, and life estates all constitute present interests in real property. Any party conveying a freehold estate, or any other interest in real property, is known as a grantor. Any party receiving such an estate or interest is known as a grantee.

The most common freehold estate in use today is the fee simple absolute estate. This estate contains all the rights that can possibly relate to land or the bundle of rights. As noted above, those rights are not absolute and may be limited. The fee simple absolute estate may be conveyed to a third-party grantee or inherited by any heir of the owner. It has no ascertainable termination date, meaning that it is unknown when the owner will convey the property to another party or die, leaving the estate to be inherited.

A defeasible estate is a fee simple estate subject to a condition wherein the estate can be terminated upon the occurrence of certain events. The fee simple determinable, fee simple subject to condition subsequent, and fee simple subject to executory limitation are methods of creating such a defeasible estate. A fee simple determinable estate is created when the conveyance is made "as long as" or "until such time as." An example would be the grant of a conservation deed to a governmental agency "as long as" the property is used for conservation purposes. In the event the property is put to another use, it automatically reverts to the grantor or the grantor's heirs. An interest in property is said to revert when it is transferred back to the original grantor (or the grantor's heirs or successors, if the grantor is no longer living or in existence). A fee simple estate subject to condition subsequent is similar to a fee simple determinable, but the reversion to the grantor (or the grantor's heirs or successors, if the grantor is no longer living or in existence) is subject to such party's election rather than automatic. A fee simple determinable estate or an estate subject to condition subsequent may provide that the real property be transferred to a third party rather than reverting to the grantor (or the grantor's heirs or successors, if the grantor is no longer living or in existence) in the event the grantee (or the grantee's heirs or successors, if the grantee is no longer living or in existence) violates the conditions. In such a case, the grantor's estate is known as fee simple subject to executory limitation.

The fee tail estate and the life estate could also be created as a defeasible estate. The fee tail estate was essentially the same as the fee simple absolute estate, but it could only be inherited by the grantee's children, grandchildren, and further descendants, also known as issue. If the grantee died without having children, the estate would revert to the grantor (or the grantor's heirs, if the grantor is no longer living). A fee tail could be further limited to specific issue, such as to the direct issue of the grantee and his wife or to male heirs only. These strict limitations could be used in feudal times to ensure that real property and wealth remained in the hands of favored families, thereby ensuring future support of the grantor in wars or politics. Such practices continued for generations even after feudal systems broke down. Their effects on more recent society can be seen in the writings of authors such as Jane Austen and Anthony Trollope and in the television series *Downton Abbey*. In such stories, the family estate has been entailed away from the daughters of the current owner to the nearest male heir under a fee tail male, with potentially disastrous results for the daughters. The fee tail estate is not permitted in most jurisdictions and is rarely, if ever, seen today.

A life estate is a fee simple estate granted to a grantee to possess during that party's lifetime. Following the grantee's death, the property would again be owned in fee simple absolute by the grantor (or the grantor's heirs or successors, if the grantor is no longer living or in existence) or transferred to another party designated by the grantor. A life estate granted for the life of another, also known as a life estate pur autre vie, is held by the grantee during the lifetime of the other named party. For instance, a nephew may be granted a life estate during the life of his special needs uncle to ensure that the uncle has a home and guardian during his lifetime. When the uncle dies, the estate would revert to the grantor (or the grantor's heirs or successors, if the grantor is no longer living or in existence) and the nephew would no longer have rights to the property. Life estates are rarely used in modern times. Instead, trusts are typically used to accomplish similar results.

Future Interests

The holder of a present interest in a freehold estate has lawful seisin and possession. The holder of a future estate also has an interest in real property but will not take possession or ownership until the occurrence of a future event. It is helpful to think of these future interests as being the flip side of the defeasible estates and life estates discussed above.

The possibility of reverter is the interest retained by the grantor in a fee simple determinable estate. For instance, the grantor conveying a conservation deed to a governmental agency "as long as" the property is used for conservation purposes would hold the possibility of reverter in the estate owned by such agency.

A power of termination, also known as a right of reentry, arises when an estate is conveyed subject to a condition subsequent. If Main Street Church conveys an estate "to General Retail, Inc., but if the property is used for the sale of alcohol, grantor may reenter and terminate the estate," Main Street Church holds the power of termination and right of reentry. If the property is subsequently used for the sale of alcohol, the grantor (or its successors, if it is no longer in existence) may elect to terminate the estate granted to General Retail, Inc., and take ownership and possession of the real property.

An executory interest is held by the third party named in a deed conveying a fee simple estate subject to an executory limitation. An example would be the grant of a conservation deed to a governmental agency "as long as" the property is used for conservation purposes, otherwise to the National Wildlife Federation. In such a case, the National Wildlife Federation would have an executory interest.

Reversion is the interest in real property retained by a grantor of a life estate. If a grantor conveyed a life estate to their aunt Mary, the grantor would have a reversionary interest in the real property during Mary's lifetime. Following Mary's death, the grantor (or the grantor's heirs, if the grantor is no longer living) would hold a fee simple absolute estate in the property.

 © 2019, 2020, 2021 NALA, Inc. All rights reserved.

A remainder is a similar interest of a third party in a life estate. For instance, if a grantor conveyed a life estate to "my daughter Mary, with the remainder to my son John," John would have a remainder interest in the real property during Mary's lifetime. Following Mary's death, John would have a fee simple absolute estate in the property.

Concurrent Ownership

Any present freehold estate may be held by more than one owner. Those owners' interests are referred to as concurrent. The following table sets forth the types of concurrent ownership and some of their basic characteristics.

Unities	Joint Tenancy, Right of Survivorship	Tenancy in Common	Tenancy by the Entirety
Possession	Undivided	Undivided	Undivided
Time	Must take at same time	May take at different times	Married couple must take at same time
Title	Must take by same conveyance	May take by different conveyances	Married couple must take by same conveyance
Interest	Equal	May be unequal	Equal
Right of Survivorship	Yes	No	Yes
Right to Sell Interest	Yes, but new owner is tenant in common	Yes	No
Use	Disfavored under law	Modern default tenancy if not specified	Applies only to married couple

A joint tenancy with right of survivorship, sometimes shortened to joint tenancy, may arise when two or more grantees are conveyed equal interests in real property, at the same time, and through the same grant. The right of survivorship means that if one joint tenant dies, the remaining joint tenants inherit that joint tenant's estate equally. A joint tenant may convey their interest in real property to one or more third parties, but the grantees will take their interests as tenants in common since they do not meet the requirements for taking at the same time and in the same conveyance as the original joint tenants. The requirements for tenants in common are much less strenuous. Tenants in common may take at different times through different conveyances, and they may have unequal interests in the property. There is no right of survivorship among tenants in common, meaning that if a tenant in common dies, their interest will be inherited by their heirs rather than by their co-owners. In modern times, most jurisdictions favor the tenant in common form of ownership over joint tenancy or prohibit joint tenancy entirely. In those jurisdictions where joint tenancy is permitted, an affirmative statement is required to create such a form of ownership.

The following scenario provides an illustration of the differences between a joint tenancy and tenancy in common.

Example:

> Emma and her business partners Martin and José buy a farm as joint tenants, with each being granted a 1/3 interest in the farm via one deed. Each of them has an undivided right to use the entire property, rather than the property being divided into three physical sections. If Emma dies during the period of joint tenancy among the three co-owners, Martin and José (the surviving joint tenants) would inherit Emma's interest equally.
>
> If, however, Martin had sold 1/2 of his interest in the farm to Ann and 1/2 of his interest to Barbara prior to Emma's death, Ann's and Barbara's interests would be as tenants in common because they did not take an equal interest at the same time and through the same conveyance as Emma and José. Later upon Emma's death, José, as the sole surviving joint tenant, would inherit Emma's entire 1/3 interest. At that point, José, Ann, and Barbara would be tenants in common, with José having a 2/3 interest in the farm, Ann having a 1/6 interest, and Barbara having a 1/6 interest.

Tenancy by the entirety is a form of joint tenancy with the additional requirement that the co-owners be a married couple. Traditionally, under tenancy by entirety, the married couple is treated as a single entity. The result of this is that, in some jurisdictions, a creditor may not be able to foreclose on property owned by the couple if only one of couple is the borrower.

Example:

> Chris and Jody own their home as tenants by the entirety. Chris obtains a second mortgage on the house for repairs and then defaults on the loan. Chris's lender may not be able to foreclose on its mortgage because Chris as an individual was not able to properly grant a lien on the real property owned by Chris and Jody as tenants by the entirety.

Tenancy by the entirety is no longer permitted in some jurisdictions, including those adhering to the community property form of ownership. As a result, the tenancy by the entirety form of ownership does not provide the protection from creditors it did previously.

Other forms of ownership by multiple parties include:

- **Community Property**. A small number of states have adopted statutes establishing the community property form of ownership for married couples rather than adhering to the common law form of tenancy by the entirety. This form of ownership for both real property and personal property provides that property acquired during marriage, with certain exceptions, is owned in equal shares by each spouse.

- **Planned Communities**. Houses and condominiums located within planned communities may be owned as fee simple and may be granted in the forms of concurrent ownership discussed above. Common areas such as lobbies and elevators in condominium buildings, or swimming pools in subdivisions, may be owned by all the residents as co-owners. Alternatively, they may be owned by a condominium or neighborhood association of which the residents are members by virtue of their ownership of a home in the condominium development or the subdivision. Multi-family housing may include party walls owned and maintained jointly by neighbors.

- **Cooperatives**. Cooperatives are established when a corporation owns a multi-unit residential

 © 2019, 2020, 2021 NALA, Inc. All rights reserved.

building. Each resident purchases shares in the corporation and obtains possession of a unit through a lease of such unit from the corporation. Common areas are governed and maintained by agreement among the shareholders.

- **Time Shares**. Time shares, commonly used for vacation property, may be in the form of a lease. Other time shares take the form of ownership wherein the owner has an interest in a particular unit for a certain time period. Owners may also hold a remainder interest for the rest of the year shared with other co-owners and concurrent ownership of common areas.

Other Ownership Interests

In addition to the freehold estates and general interests held by owners of real property, there are other, more specific rights and interests that owners may have in real property such as water rights, oil, gas, and mineral rights, and rights to subsurface and lateral support, and airspace rights. Historically, an owner of real property was assumed to own the property from the surface to the sky and from the surface to the center of earth. This would include ownership of water, gas, oil, and minerals under the surface and rights to the airspace above the surface, in addition to the land and water located on the surface. However, these subsurface and air rights can be severed by private agreement or limited by public policy.

Regulation of water rights affects the ways in which real property owners use flowing waters, such as rivers and streams, as well as lakes, underground water, and surface water. Riparian rights are held by owners of property located adjacent to streams, and littoral rights are held by owners of property located adjacent to lakes. The rights of both types of owners are the same and may be referred to in general as riparian. In the United States, riparian rights vary between eastern and western states. In western states, riparian rights are based on a system of prior appropriation, meaning that ownership of water rights is established by priority of claim based on the purpose of use. In eastern states, riparian rights were historically governed by the natural flow doctrine which held that a downstream owner is entitled to the natural flow of water passing by their property, with the result that upstream owners were prohibited from significantly altering the flow of water. In most eastern states, this theory has been replaced by the reasonable use doctrine which holds that a downstream owner's rights are subject to the reasonable use of water by upstream owners.

Subsurface water, also referred to as ground water, is categorized as streaming or percolating. Streaming ground water refers to water in a defined underground channel. Percolating refers to water located within the soil layers, such as that located in an aquifer. The absolute ownership rule with respect to ground water holds that an overlying owner owns the water below the surface of their land absolutely. This rule only applies where water is plentiful. Other states regulate the use of ground water using the principle of reasonable use. In many western states, rights to ground water are governed by the same prior appropriation rules as riparian rights.

The third category of water rights relates to the discharge of excess surface waters. The natural servitude rule relating to surface waters holds that each owner has the right to have water flow away from the owner's land and onto neighboring lands naturally, as well as the duty to allow the water to flow naturally onto the owner's land from neighboring lands. The common enemy doctrine permits owners to take any necessary steps to remove water or prevent it from entering their land. The natural servitude and common enemy doctrines may be limited by principles of reasonableness. Similarly, the reasonable use rule permits owners to control the flow of surface waters in a manner which does not unreasonably interfere with neighboring properties.

Water rights vary greatly, with each state adopting one or more versions of the doctrines outlined above with respect to the flowing, underground, and surface waters within that state. These rights are

---

© 2019, 2020, 2021 NALA, Inc. All rights reserved.

administered by a variety of water commissions, engineers, departments, agencies, and courts. In arid states and during times of drought, water regulations can become more extensive and strictly enforced than in places and times where and when water is plentiful.

Originally, oil, gas, and mineral rights are owned by the owner of the land beneath which they are located. The owner may sell or lease its interest in oil, gas, and minerals located beneath the surface of their property to a third party. That party may access the oil, gas, and minerals from the surface of the land or below the surface through neighboring properties. Once such sale or lease has been made, the interest is considered severed from the fee simple estate of the surface. As a result, the applicable oil, gas, and/or mineral estates will be conveyed separately from the surface estate from that point forward. When buying or selling real property in states where oil, gas, and mineral deposits are common, it is important to examine how the rights of the owner or lessee of such rights may affect the rights of the owner of the surface.

Surface property owners have the right to support from the soil beneath the property. This means that any party extracting water, oil, gas, or minerals from below the surface must provide for the subsurface support of the land above such resources. In addition, the owner of any property has the right to the lateral support of the owner's property from the neighboring properties and a responsibility to refrain from interfering with the physical support of neighboring properties. This means that one owner may not excavate property in a manner that deprives the adjoining property of such lateral support. In addition to statutory rights, neighboring real property owners sometimes enter into agreements to provide support for each other's property, such as when large buildings are erected in close proximity to each other.

The historic assumption that real property owners own the property from the surface to the sky has been modified over time as technology has developed. For instance, the air rights of owners of property located near airports are limited to accommodate the flight paths of airplanes taking off from or landing at the airport. An owner's right to construct buildings of certain heights can also be limited by zoning regulations. In addition, real property owners can sell or burden all or a portion of their air rights. For instance, they may agree to refrain from constructing a building in their airspace that would block the sunlight from a neighboring property owner, or they may sell the right to construct a portion of a neighboring building within the airspace over their existing building.

Nonfreehold Estates

Nonfreehold estates are estates of possession but not ownership or seisin. Nonfreehold estates are also known as leasehold estates or, more commonly, leases.

A tenancy for a term, also referred to as a tenancy for years, has a fixed term and ends automatically without notice and may not be shortened or extended without the mutual agreement of the parties. The term of a tenancy for a term must be specified, although it may be for a period shorter than a year. A lease for a term in excess of one year must be in writing pursuant to the Statute of Frauds. Many states limit leases to a maximum term such as 50 or 99 years.

Like the tenancy for a term, the periodic tenancy has a fixed term, but that term is automatically renewed unless steps are taken to terminate it. Periodic tenancies can be created when explicitly provided in a lease but can also be created by implication when the parties have made no formal agreement. This can occur when a tenant occupies the property pursuant to an invalid lease and pays rent, or when a tenant remains in possession after a lease term expires and continues to pay rent. The term under a periodic tenancy may be any length, such as week to week. The operative date for this type of tenancy is determined by the date when rent must be paid. For instance, if rent is due on the first of each month, a month-to-month tenancy is created. Whether or not rent is paid, the tenancy automatically renews on

---

 © 2019, 2020, 2021 NALA, Inc. All rights reserved.

such operative date.

A tenancy at will occurs when a tenant lawfully comes into possession without a valid agreement regarding the payment of rent or the term. This may happen when a tenant takes possession before an agreement is reached or when a lease for a period in excess of one year violates the Statute of Frauds because it has not been set forth in writing. A tenancy at will is terminated by notice given by either party or by the death of either party.

A tenancy at sufferance is not really a tenancy. Rather, it is the status of a tenant that has held over after the expiration of its tenancy against a landlord which has not yet acted to evict.

Landlord and Tenant Rights and Duties

A lease is a contract between the landlord and the tenant. Although the covenants under most contracts are dependent, historically the covenants under a lease were independent. Because of this, short of actual eviction, a landlord's breach did not release the tenant from the payment of rent, and a tenant's failure to pay rent did not permit the landlord to evict the tenant. The independent nature of these covenants stems from the fact that a lease conveys an estate in land in addition to being an agreement between the landlord and the tenant. The effect was that the tenant continued to hold its estate even if it did not pay rent, and the tenant had an obligation to continue to pay rent even when the property was uninhabitable. In each case, the wronged party had to enforce its rights in court while continuing to meet its own obligations. Today, landlords can usually evict tenants for failure to pay rent, and tenants may have various remedies to a landlord's failure to meet its lease obligations.

The most basic duty of a landlord is to provide the tenant with possession of the leased premises and the right to enjoy the premises without interference, which is also referred to as the right of quiet enjoyment. In addition, in modern times, it has been held that leases include an implied warranty of habitability, meaning that the landlord has the duty to provide a premises that is physically habitable.

The most basic duty of a tenant is to pay the landlord the amount of rent agreed upon by these parties for the agreed upon period of time. This obligation to pay rent will remain in effect during that period of time unless it is terminated by actual or constructive eviction. Eviction means the expulsion of a tenant by legal process or by force. Constructive eviction occurs when a landlord's action or failure to act substantially interferes with a tenant's right to enjoy the premises or constitutes a breach of the warranty of habitability. Examples include situations where a landlord's intentional failure to provide utilities to the premises or to repair physical conditions renders the premises uninhabitable and causes the tenant to quit the premises. The typical remedies in the case of constructive eviction are the termination of the lease and payment of damages. Other remedies such as rent reduction may be available. Conversely, the landlord's remedies for a tenant's failure to pay rent include terminating the lease, recovering rent and other fees, and being reimbursed for damages.

In addition to these basic rights and duties, leases can contain many other provisions, such as requirements that the landlord maintain the premises and that the tenant refrain from committing waste. These rights and duties are sometimes dictated by state statutes, especially with respect to residential leases, or are agreed upon between the parties and set forth in the lease. Further information about these additional provisions is provided in the section titled "Documents Transferring Interests and Related Documents – Lease" later in this chapter.

© 2019, 2020, 2021 NALA, Inc. All rights reserved.

SERVITUDES AND OTHER LIMITATIONS ON PROPERTY RIGHTS

Servitudes are burdens on the ownership of real property which exist for the benefit of a party other than the owner. A servitude is a limitation on the use of the property by the owner, while also being an interest in such property possessed by another party. Easements, licenses, and profits are servitudes. The rights of real property owners can also be burdened by covenants and public restrictions. Most servitudes are said to run with the land. This means that they will continue to be enforceable against the property after the property has been conveyed to another owner.

Easements

An easement is the nonpossessory right of one party to use property owned by another for a particular purpose. Common easements are those permitting utility companies the right to install lines, pipes, or other hardware in or under the land of an owner or easements granting one property owner the right to drive across the driveway of a neighbor. An easement can be granted by a property owner or taken under powers of eminent domain, such as when a city takes a right-of-way upon which to construct a road.

Real property law includes many terms unique to the area of easements, including the following:

- **Affirmative Easement versus Negative Easement**. An affirmative easement grants the owner of the dominant estate the right to do something which would otherwise not be permitted. An example would be a water company's easement permitting it to install and maintain a water line under the land of a homeowner. A negative easement prohibits the owner of the servient estate from engaging in activities they would otherwise be permitted to do. For instance, a negative easement would be created when the owner of East Parcel grants the owner of West Parcel an easement providing that no trees will be planted on or improvements erected within a 10-foot strip of land along the western boundary line of East Parcel.

- **Appurtenant Easement versus Gross Easement (or Easement in Gross)**. An appurtenant easement benefits a particular parcel of land while a gross easement benefits a particular party. For example, the owner of East Parcel may grant an appurtenant easement permitting the owner or tenant of the adjoining West Parcel the right to drive across a private road located on East Parcel. The owner of East Parcel may grant a gross easement to the electric provider permitting such company to erect electric poles across East Parcel.

- **Dedication and Acceptance**. A dedication is a type of easement which arises when an owner grants the public the right to use property for a roadway or other purposes. This often occurs when a real estate developer is subdividing property. An acceptance is the action taken by the applicable governmental agency when it agrees to receive the benefit of the dedication and to maintain the roadway.

- **Dominant Estate versus Servient Estate**. The dominant estate benefits from an easement and the servient estate is burdened by the easement. In the example of a gross easement above, the owner of East Parcel holds the servient estate while the electric company holds the dominant estate.

- **Easement by Necessity**. A court may determine that an easement is necessary in certain circumstances involving the conveyance of real property. For example, if the owner of Accessible Acres sells a portion of its property to a new owner and that parcel (Landlocked Acres) has no access to a public roadway, a court may determine that an easement across Accessible Acres is necessary in order to provide the owner of Landlocked Acres access to a public roadway and may

 © 2019, 2020, 2021 NALA, Inc. All rights reserved.

grant such an easement.

- **Easement by Reservation**. An easement by reservation occurs when an owner conveys property to another party and reserves or retains an easement for themselves or another. For instance, the owner of Lakeview Acres may convey a portion of his property to a buyer but reserve the right to walk across the conveyed property to access an adjoining lake.

- **Express Easement**. Most easements are express easements in that they are created by written instrument such as an easement agreement or a right-of-way dedication.

- **Implied Easement** (or Easement by Implication). An implied easement arises when a court determines that an easement is implied by a conveyance although it was not explicitly stated. For example, if the owner of Private Drive Acres sells a portion of their property to a third party but fails to include an easement granting the new owner an easement to drive on an existing driveway that runs from the new parcel over Private Drive Acres to reach the public roadway, a court may find that such an easement was implied.

- **Prescriptive Easement (or Easement by Prescription)**. A prescriptive easement arises through the use of the real property of another as an easement without the permission of the servient estate owner throughout the applicable required period of time. The same elements which must be met for a finding of adverse possession must be met for a prescriptive easement. See the section titled "Transactions – Methods of Transferring Interests in Property" later in this chapter. If the owner of West Acres openly uses a driveway crossing East Acres without the owner's permission for the prescribed period of time, and otherwise meets the requirements for adverse possession in that state, a court could find that West Acres is benefitted by a prescriptive easement across East Acres for such purpose.

Profits

A profit is an easement permitting the holder to both enter upon the property of the servient estate and remove something from the property, such as timber. Permitting another party to enter upon your land to hunt or fish would also be a profit. A profit may benefit a certain tract of land, in which case the profit would run with the land, or a particular person, in which case it could be revoked by the grantor or would terminate upon the grantee's death.

Licenses

A license is not an interest in property but is a right to enter into the land of another in a manner which would otherwise be a trespass. For example, the owner of Forest Hills may grant a license permitting their neighbor to hike through the woods located on their property. Licenses can be revoked at any time by the grantor and terminate with the death of the holder or by the sale of the property by the grantor. However, licenses cannot be transferred to another party.

Covenants

Simply put, a covenant is an agreement or promise. Like easements, covenants affecting real property run with the land. Real property covenants are agreements to engage in certain acts, such as paying dues to maintain a private street in a subdivision, or to refrain from engaging in certain acts, such as storing boats in one's driveway. These are known as affirmative covenants and negative covenants, respectively. Negative covenants are also referred to as restrictions. Although they are generally understood as agreements, covenants can be imposed unilaterally by a grantor executing a deed or a real estate developer recording covenants for a subdivision or condominium development. The grantee of property burdened by such covenants is held to have agreed to abide by the covenants by its acceptance of the conveyance of the property.

Many developers adopt covenants when they subdivide property to be sold for the construction of residential homes, condominiums, or commercial subdivisions. The documents establishing the covenants are often called declarations of covenants, conditions, and restrictions (CCRs). Covenants and restrictions can also be included in deeds. Covenants contained in CCRs recorded against subdivisions and condominiums may be enforced by the neighborhood or condominium association or other body set forth in the CCRs, such as a board of trustees. The grantor of a deed which contains covenants, and the owners of properties which benefit from the covenants, may enforce such covenants.

In older subdivisions, the restrictions are often relatively simple and may be limited to restrictions, such as those prohibiting commercial uses in a residential neighborhood or parking boats or recreational vehicles in driveways. These older restrictions sometimes contained restrictive covenants banning minorities from owning or living upon the real property conveyed by the deed. Those discriminatory restrictions have been found to be unenforceable because they violate the equal protection clause of the 14th Amendment. The other restrictions contained in these deeds, such as prohibitions against operating a business on the property, are still enforceable.

Some critics have condemned CCRs as being discriminatory or imposing monotonous uniformity on suburbia. Supporters, however, encourage the use of conditions and restrictions as a method of maintaining safe, aesthetically pleasing neighborhoods with high economic values. The following are some of the most typical covenants and restrictions found in modern CCRs. Similar covenants and restrictions can be found in condominium declarations or CCRs relating to business developments.

- Establishment of homeowners' association to enforce CCRs

- Method of setting assessments and collecting delinquent assessments

- Grants of easements to the association or cross-easements among owners

- Roadway dedications and grants of easements to utility providers

- Restrictions prohibiting certain uses of property in a subdivision, such as commercial or industrial uses

- Restrictions against parking in certain areas of the subdivision

- Architectural requirements for items such as:

  □ Fences and outbuildings

  □ Size of lot and size of houses and garages

  □ Building materials and colors

- Architectural review process

- Affirmative covenants requiring maintenance of property

- Rules for use of common ground and common areas such as clubhouses or swimming pools

© 2019, 2020, 2021 NALA, Inc. All rights reserved.

Public Restrictions

While deed restrictions and CCRs are enforced privately, other restrictions on the use or ownership of property are enforced under the police power of government. Police power refers to the role of the government to act to promote the safety, health, and welfare of its citizens even at the detriment of individual freedom or property rights. Some examples of the use of police power with respect to real property are set forth in the section titled "Property Rights and Ownership – Bundle of Rights."

Land use regulations are another example of the use of police power to regulate the use of real property. These regulations can be used to promote community safety, preserve property values, manage growth, preserve neighborhood character and aesthetics, and provide for traffic safety. To do this, local governments may establish planning and zoning commissions and departments. These authorities are charged with enforcing zoning regulations restricting the use of property and establishing requirements for the physical characteristics of property, regulations for the subdivision of real property, and building codes. Cities or counties are often divided into zoning districts in which certain uses are permitted by right, permitted upon the satisfaction of certain conditions, or prohibited. Within each type of district, there can be various requirements such as minimum lot sizes, building setback requirements, and parking requirements. Buildings and improvements within each district may be subject to various building codes designed to promote the safety of residents residing in and businesses located in those districts. Some of the commonly used terms relating to planning and zoning are set forth below.

- **Building Code.** Building codes comprise the regulations adopted by a city or county that require buildings and improvements to be constructed to certain electrical, plumbing, fire and safety, and other standards.

- **Building Permit.** Building permits are authorizations granted to owners and/or builders upon the submission and review of building plans meeting the requirements of building codes. These permits allow the building to be constructed or altered in accordance with the approved building plans.

- **Comprehensive or Master Plan.** Plans adopted by local governments that provide guidance for the development and growth of the community. If both a comprehensive plan and a zoning ordinance are adopted by local government, the zoning ordinance usually must be in accordance with the comprehensive plan.

- **Conditional Use Permit.** Conditional use permits, or approvals with similar names, are authorizations permitting the use of property within a zoning district for a purpose for which certain conditions are required. For instance, gas stations may be permitted within a residential district when they meet requirements for the flow of traffic into and around the station, fences between the station and neighboring homes, and lighting in parking areas.

- **Nonconforming Use.** A nonconforming use arises when a property is developed before a zoning ordinance is adopted and the property is used in a manner not permitted in the adopted zoning district. Such nonconforming use is typically grandfathered and, therefore, permitted for as long as the building exists and is used consistently.

- **Permitted Use.** A permitted use is a use for which a property is permitted by right, without conditions. For instance, a single-family home would typically be a permitted use in a residential district.

- **Planning Commission.** A planning commission, or similarly titled authority, is an entity established by the local government and charged with enforcing the planning and zoning

© 2019, 2020, 2021 NALA, Inc. All rights reserved.

regulations of that jurisdiction.

- **Variance**. A variance is an exception made to permit an owner to use their property in a manner which is not normally permitted in a zoning district. This occurs when the use or area requirements in a zoning ordinance create a hardship for a property owner due to the specific nature of their property. An example would be an oddly shaped lot which make adhering to building set back lines a hardship or physically impossible.

- **Zoning District**. Zoning districts are the areas into which the jurisdiction is divided under the zoning ordinance for purposes of establishing the uses permitted within such areas and the regulations affecting the property within that district.

- **Zoning Map**. A zoning map is the drawing of the various zoning districts of a city or county adopted by the governing body of that jurisdiction.

- **Zoning Ordinance**. A zoning ordinance or code is the legislation adopted by the local government which adopts the zoning map and establishes the restrictions and requirements for zoning in that jurisdiction.

Governments can also limit the rights of real property owners through the use of eminent domain. Eminent domain is the power of governments or other authorized entities to take private property for a public use or a public purpose. Eminent domain is discussed in further detail in the section titled "Transactions – Methods of Transferring Interests in Property."

TRANSACTIONS – METHODS OF TRANSFERRING INTERESTS IN PROPERTY

The most typical method of transferring a freehold or nonfreehold estate in real property, or other interest such as an easement, is through voluntary sale or lease. Property can also be transferred to a devisee or beneficiary by will, to an heir pursuant to intestate statutes upon the death of a property owner, to a grantee by gift, or to a government or other organization through a dedication. The instruments used for these processes include purchase contracts, deeds, easements, plats, and leases. See the section titled "Transactions – Documents Transferring Interests and Related Documents" later in this chapter.

Partition

Co-owners may voluntarily partition, or divide, their property in any manner and at such time as they mutually agree, if permitted by zoning regulations. Partition proceedings occur when there is a dispute among co-owners as to whether the property is to be conveyed or held. In such a case, one or more co-owners can petition a court to partition the property. A partition in kind occurs when the court divides the property into what it determines to be parcels of equal value and grants each co-owner a parcel. Alternatively, if the court determines that it is not possible to divide the property equitably, it can order a forced sale of the property and distribute the proceeds of the sale among the co-owners.

Quiet Title Action

A quiet title action occurs when there is a dispute as to which party is the owner of a property. In a quiet title action, the plaintiff requests that the court declare that they have title to the property and that no

© 2019, 2020, 2021 NALA, Inc. All rights reserved.

other party holds an interest in the property. This may happen when there is a cloud on title, meaning there is an error in a deed in the chain of title, or there is a claim of adverse possession. Chains of title are discussed under the section titled "Transactions – Due Diligence, Title Review" later in this chapter.

Adverse Possession

Adverse possession occurs when an owner fails to eject a trespasser for a period of time longer than the statute of limitations in the state in which the property is located. If the claimant's possession (or use in the case of a prescriptive easement) of the property in dispute also meets all the other elements required by the state, the claimant will gain title to the property. For example, a claim of adverse possession could arise when a party erects a fence across a portion of a neighboring property without permission, and the owner fails to eject the trespasser before the statute of limitations expires. Although each state adopts its own elements required for the establishment of an adverse possession claim, the following are elements common to many states:

- **Statute of Limitations**. The claim must be for a period of time longer than the statute of limitations for ejectment of trespassers on real property in the state.

- **Open and Notorious**. The property must be possessed in an open way that would be obvious to an owner of record who pays reasonable attention to the owner's property.

- **Hostile and Under Claim of Right**. The possession must be without the permission of the record owner, and the possessor must be under the belief that they have a right to possess the property in question.

- **Exclusive**. The claimant must possess the property exclusively just as they would if they were the owner of record. If, for instance, most of the residents of a neighborhood use a path running through the back yard of one owner to the neighborhood common ground, no one neighbor could claim possession of the pathway for themselves.

- **Continuous and Uninterrupted**. The possession must be continuous for the intended use of the property for the period of time required by the statute of limitations. For instance, if the property subject to the adverse possession claim is agricultural, continuous possession would occur if it were used during each planting season for the required number of years. The disused time during the fallow seasons would not be considered an interruption to the possession since this is the typical method of possessing and using agriculture property.

Additionally, some states permit the adverse possession claimants to count any time their predecessor owner possessed the claimed property toward the required period of possession. This practice is called tacking.

Example:

> If Joel built a fence onto the property of Robert and used the enclosed portion of Robert's property for three years before selling the property to Rachel, Rachel could tack Joel's three years of possession onto her own to meet the required period of possession.

Some states lower the required period of possession for claimants with color of title, meaning that their claim includes a deed or other evidence of purported ownership. Other states add additional requirements for a claim of adverse possession, such as the payment of taxes on the disputed property.

Upon completion of the required period of possession, and the satisfaction of the other requirements for a claim of adverse possession or prescriptive easement, the claimant can file a quiet title action requesting that the court determine that they are the owner of the disputed property or holder of a prescriptive easement.

Eminent Domain

Eminent domain is the power of the government or other authorized party, such as a utility company, to take private property through the process of condemnation for a public use or, in some cases, for a public purpose. For instance, a city could take private property to use as a public park or school. Alternatively, a city could use its power of eminent domain to take property within a blighted area and sell it to a private party constructing a privately-owned, mixed-use development which will benefit the public. The Fifth Amendment of the United States Constitution prohibits the taking of private property by the government through its power of eminent domain without just compensation.

The interest taken under eminent domain may be a fee simple estate or a temporary or permanent easement. The property taken may be personal or real. For instance, a county may take permanent ownership of a parcel of land for the construction of a highway or a dam. In times of war or emergency, the federal government may commandeer personal property such as ships or other vehicles on a temporary basis. A utility company may take an easement interest across an owner's real property for the construction of power lines. All of these would be permitted uses of the power of eminent domain so long as the private property owner is justly compensated. If the condemning party and the owner cannot mutually agree upon what constitutes just compensation, the condemning party will apply to the court to make such a determination.

Inverse Condemnation

Inverse condemnation occurs when a government takes or damages private property without paying compensation. In such a situation, the owner may sue the government in order to be compensated. An example would be when a government builds a dam that causes periodic flooding of a farmer's field so that the field can no longer be used for agriculture.

Foreclosure

Mortgages and deeds of trust secure the lenders of money used for purchasing or improving real property or for other purposes. State statutes determine whether deeds of trust, mortgages, or both may be used within each state and specify the process for foreclosing thereon. When the borrower fails to make required loan payments or to otherwise fulfill requirements under the loan, the lender may foreclose. Foreclosure is a process by which the lien holder forces the sale of real property. The proceeds of the sale are then used to pay the principal of, and interest and fees due on, the loan.

The parties to a mortgage are the borrower, referred to as a mortgagor, and the lender, referred to as the mortgagee, although the lender does not typically sign the mortgage. Depending on the jurisdiction, the mortgagor grants ownership of the real property or a lien upon the real property to the lender under the mortgage. Upon payment in full of the loan, the lender is required to release the mortgage or the lien upon the real property, as applicable, resulting in the borrower's unencumbered ownership of the property. If the borrower defaults on the loan, the lender must engage in a court proceeding to extinguish the borrower's interest in the property and to exercise the lender's rights under the mortgage. This process is known as judicial foreclosure. Once the court authorizes the sale of the property, the sheriff

© 2019, 2020, 2021 NALA, Inc. All rights reserved.

or other appointed party conducts the sale, and the proceeds are paid on the outstanding balance of the secured loan.

Under a deed of trust, the borrower grants ownership of the real property to a trustee who holds the property on behalf of the lender. As is the case with a mortgage, the lender is required to release the deed of trust upon payment in full of the loan. Upon a default under the loan, the trustee may foreclose on the property directly, without engaging in the litigation required for a judicial sale. Instead, the trustee must follow the sale provisions contained within the deed of trust and applicable state statutes. This process, known as non-judicial foreclosure or power of sale, is much less onerous and time-consuming than the judicial process.

Until either type of sale has occurred, the borrower has the right to pay the full balance of the loan and all collection costs to redeem the property and avoid the sale. Some states allow certain borrowers such a right of redemption for a prescribed period of time after the sale as well. Depending on the terms of the mortgage or deed of trust and state law, the lender may be required to pay any sale proceeds in excess of the loan amount to the borrower or may be able to obtain a deficiency judgment against the borrower for any outstanding loan balance after the sale proceeds are applied. Regardless of whether the lender holds a mortgage or a deed of trust, and regardless of the particular statutory requirements of the applicable state, the foreclosure process includes numerous deadlines and conditions which the lender must satisfy prior to foreclosing on the secured property.

TRANSACTIONS – DUE DILIGENCE

Taken literally, the words due diligence mean the proper amount and type of steadfast inquiry. More broadly, due diligence can be defined as the process of obtaining the information relevant to evaluate and effectuate a transaction, such as the sale of real property or personal property like stock or membership interests in an existing company.

When problems are discovered during the due diligence process, the parties must determine if those issues are significant enough that the transaction should be abandoned or if they can be resolved so that the deal can move forward. The due diligence process also provides information that assists the parties in understanding what the real outcomes of the transaction will be. In a real estate purchase, for example, due diligence will provide the buyer with a clear understanding of the value and characteristics of the real property being purchased and will assist the lender in determining whether the property will provide adequate security for the loan.

Title Review

A due diligence review of the title to real property involves numerous terms unique to this area of the law, including the following:

- **Chain of Title**. A chain of title is the record of all the deeds and other instruments that conveyed an interest in a property from one prior owner to another prior owner and, ultimately, to the current owner.

- **Encumbrance**. An encumbrance against title is an interest in real property held by a third party. For example, an easement granted to a utility company or a declaration of covenants, conditions, and restrictions would be an encumbrance.

- **Endorsement**. Endorsements are additions to the title policy which provide supplemental coverage not contained in the standard policy. For instance, a purchaser who plans to use the real property to build a factory may request an endorsement ensuring that the property is zoned for industrial use.

- **Exception**. An exception is any item which the title company will exclude from the coverage it provides under the title policy. Exceptions can include encroachments, encumbrances, clouds on title, liens, mortgages, Uniform Commercial Code (UCC) financing statements, litigation involving the property, and other instruments or interests affecting the rights of the property owner.

- **Gap**. A gap is the period of time between the date when a title search is last run or updated and the date a title policy is issued.

- **Legal Description**. A legal description is a written narrative which identifies real property and is used in documents such as title commitments and policies, deeds, mortgages, and other instruments affecting real property.

- **Marketability of Title**. Title to a particular piece of real property is said to be marketable if the current owner has a valid estate in the property which they may convey to a purchaser with no claim by a third party to ownership of such property.

- **Pro Forma Policy**. A pro forma policy sets forth all the information and exceptions that will be contained in the final policy upon satisfaction of all requirements and closing on the transaction, with blanks for the recording information for all documents to be recorded in connection with the deal such as the mortgage. Pro forma polices also contain the form of the title policy and all endorsements to be issued.

- **Requirements**. Requirements are the conditions set forth in a title commitment which must be met in order for the title company to issue the policy. Any requirement which is not satisfied prior to closing will result in the title company refusing to issue a policy or, more commonly, the requirement becoming an exception to the policy. For instance, if the seller fails to remove a mechanic's lien recorded against the property, it will become an exception to the purchaser's and lender's policies.

- **Title Abstract**. A title abstract provides a complete history of the property, including all instruments recorded against the property such as deeds, mortgages, releases of mortgages, and easements.

- **Title Commitment**. A title commitment is a written assurance of a title company that it will issue a title policy to a proposed insured upon the satisfaction of specified requirements and conditions and subject to specified exceptions.

- **Title Opinion**. A title opinion contains the written conclusions of a licensed attorney as to the marketability of title of the subject property based on the information set forth in the title abstract for such property.

- **Title Plant**. A title plant is a database which contains all the recorded real property records of the county served by the title plant as well as other related documents such as probate, divorce, and tax records.

- **Title Report**. A title report or letter report is a statement issued by a title company as to basic facts concerning real property, such as the name of the current owner, the legal description of the property, and a list of the encumbrances affecting the property. A title report is not a commitment to issue a title policy or a full title abstract.

- **Vesting Deed**. Vesting deeds are the deed or deeds that previously conveyed real property to the

© 2019, 2020, 2021 NALA, Inc. All rights reserved.

current owner.

The purpose of title review is to determine whether or not the seller has the right to convey marketable title to the purchaser or whether the borrower can provide a lender with a valid lien against the real property. Historically, chains of title, title abstracts, and title opinions were used to provide information regarding the marketability of title. Although title abstracts and opinions provided some assurance of the status of title, they did not guarantee the marketability of title or the validity of a lien. However, a title insurance policy insures the status of title as of the date and time that the deed or mortgage is recorded. Subsequent title defects are not covered, and coverage is not transferred to subsequent owners or lenders.

An owner's policy of title insurance guarantees that the property is owned by the owner, subject to the exceptions described in the title policy. A loan policy of title insurance ensures that the mortgage or deed of trust is a valid lien on the title and that the lender holds a first lien position with respect to the property as of the date of the policy, subject to the exceptions contained in the policy. If the title is ever questioned, the title company is required to defend the title covered under the policy, and, if it is found invalid, the title company must pay the value of the property up to the policy limit.

In most jurisdictions other than Iowa, where title insurance is provided through a state sponsored nonprofit agency and attorneys provide title opinions, title insurance policies are issued by private title insurance companies. Title insurers own or pay for access to title plants from which they obtain title abstracts, prepare title reports and commitments, and issue title policies. After obtaining and reviewing the title abstract for the subject real property, the title company's examiner prepares a title report for a customer who requests information only or a title commitment for a customer who intends to purchase a title policy.

The introductory section of title commitments provides a variety of basic identifying information regarding the property. The effective date of a commitment is the date through which the title record has been examined by the title company. Title commitments also include the proposed amount of the policy and the name of the current owner. The type of estate possessed by the current owner is also listed. Usually this will be a fee simple estate unless the title company has been requested to review a leasehold estate. Title commitments also identify the name of the proposed insured and the type of policy to be issued, such as an owner's policy or a loan policy. The title commitment will indicate which form of policy will be issued, usually the latest version of the American Land Title Association (ALTA) policy form. Policies issued for property in California can be issued as ALTA policies or California Land Title Association (CLTA) policies. The introductory section of the commitment will also contain the legal description of the property. This can be the legal description contained in the vesting deed of the current owner or a new legal description prepared for a buyer purchasing a portion of the current owner's property.

The requirements section of a title commitment lists the information and documents which must be provided and the tasks which must be accomplished in order for the title company to issue the title policy. If a requirement is not met, the title company will not issue the policy, or the unsatisfied item will become an exception to coverage under the policy.

Most commitments contain standard requirements such as payment of the full value for the subject property. This is required because recording statutes protect only bona fide purchasers for value. Title companies will require the recording of the deed in the case of the issuance of an owner's policy or the recording of a mortgage or deed of trust in the case of the issuance of a loan policy. They may require that the parties to the transaction deliver powers of attorney or authorizing documents to the title company that provide evidence that the parties have the power to enter into the transaction. There may also be requirements which are unique to the county or state in which the property is located, such as statutory

© 2019, 2020, 2021 NALA, Inc. All rights reserved.

requirements with respect to the method of payment of funds to the title company.

The standard requirements may also include the requirement that the title company be notified if there has been any recent construction on the property or if any loan proceeds will be used for construction purposes. In these cases, the title company may require affidavits, indemnities, or lien waivers for construction. The title company, the purchaser, and the lender may need to enter into a disbursement agreement in the case of funds being loaned for the purpose of construction. Failure to satisfy these requirements will invalidate any mechanic's lien coverage provided by the policy.

Special requirements are requirements which are unique to the property, including the removal of any particular mortgages, UCC financing statements, or tax liens affecting the subject property. Special requirements can also include documents required by the title company in order to issue specific endorsements. An example of this would be the requirement that organizational documents be provided so that a non-imputation endorsement will list the appropriate parties. In addition, many title companies include information regarding the property, such as pending litigation or overdue real property taxes, in the requirements section of the commitment.

A title commitment also contains a section on exceptions to title for the property. Exceptions are the defects in title or encumbrances affecting the property that the title company plans to except from coverage under the title policy. The title policy guarantees that the title company has made an accurate search of the real property records. If title defects or encumbrances that should have been disclosed by the title company are discovered after the policy is issued, the title company will be liable for any damages to the insured resulting from such items. Because of this, the title company includes exceptions to the coverage it will provide for any title defect or encumbrance of record or otherwise known at the time of issuance of the policy. Just as title commitments contain standard requirements and specific requirements, title commitments contain standard exceptions and exceptions unique to the subject property.

Standard exceptions often include defects, liens, and encumbrances or other matters which appear in the public records subsequent to the effective date of the title commitment, but prior to the date the insured will acquire an interest in the property. This period is referred to as the gap. This exception will be removed by the title company once a final update of the title search is done at closing. Any instruments which were recorded during the gap will be added as exceptions to the policy. The title company may also require the seller to execute a gap indemnification covering the title company for any such recordings.

Other standard exceptions include, but are not limited to, any rights of parties in possession of the property, any unrecorded easements, shortages in area, or encroachments that a survey would disclose, any unfiled mechanic's liens, and any assessments and taxes for the current tax year and subsequent tax years.

Title commitments will also list any agreements or instruments affecting and recorded against the property as special exceptions. These can include easements, party wall or parking agreements, instruments which convey mineral, oil and gas, or water rights independently from the interests of the current owner of the property, and covenants, conditions, and restrictions. Subdivision plats often contain lot lines, easements, and building set back requirements that are included as exceptions. The title commitment will except recorded leases or unrecorded leases if the title company is made aware of them. Finally, the title exceptions will include any other defects that may affect the marketability of title, such as improper recording of a deed in the chain of title or scrivener's errors in legal descriptions.

In transactions involving commercial property or high value residential property, the proposed insured often requests a pro forma title policy following the review of the title commitment. The pro forma policy shows the proposed insured what the final policy will look like, assuming all the requirements

---

                                              © 2019, 2020, 2021 NALA, Inc. All rights reserved.

are satisfied, and no new instruments are recorded during the gap. The pro forma will include the forms of the endorsements requested by the insured. Common endorsements include zoning endorsements, comprehensive endorsements, and leasehold owner's endorsements issued for tenants wishing to insure their leasehold interest in the property. Endorsements can be issued in the ALTA or CLTA formats, depending on which policy is being issued and what is requested. Additionally, some states have unique endorsements approved by the state, such as certain oil, gas, and mineral rights endorsements issued in Texas.

Following the closing of the transaction and recording of the deed, mortgage, and other documents, the final title policy will be issued in either the form set forth in the commitment, with the requirements removed or changed to exceptions, or in the form of the pro forma policy. In either case, all recording information for the transaction will be inserted and all requested endorsements issued.

Survey

Along with the title work, a survey is one of the most essential elements of a due diligence review for real property. There are numerous types of surveys. Boundary surveys are simple surveys depicting the property lines, the location of improvements on the property, and other basic information. These types of surveys often state that they are not to be used for the construction of improvements, but they may satisfy the requirements of residential property lenders. Topographical surveys depict the elevations of the property and can be useful for planning construction on the property. As-built surveys depict improvements constructed on real property and are often used during or following the construction process. The most comprehensive type of survey used in connection with the purchase or mortgaging of commercial or high value residential property is an ALTA survey.

ALTA surveys must adhere to the minimum standard requirements established by the American Land Title Association and the National Society of Professional Surveyors (ALTA/NSPS) whose standards can be found on their websites. The latest ALTA/NSPS minimum survey standards became effective as of February 23, 2021. Surveys meeting these standards, commonly referred to as ALTA surveys, can also include what are referred to as Table A items. Table A items include information or services such as the listing of the property address on the survey, placement of monuments on each corner of the property, or calculation of the gross land area of the property. When a title company is asked to remove the standard survey exceptions and issue a survey endorsement ensuring that the property covered by the title policy is the same as that shown in the survey, it will usually require the issuance of an ALTA survey.

ALTA surveys are based on the information contained in the title commitment. The title commitment and survey should complement each other, with each containing the same information for items such as the owner of the property, the easements and other instruments affecting title, and the legal description. When the property being conveyed or used as collateral for a loan is the same as the property owned by the current owner, the legal description for the title commitment and survey will be taken from the vesting deed. The legal description contained in the vesting deed is sometimes referred to as the "record legal description." In situations where only a portion of seller's property is being conveyed or other boundary changes are being made, the survey will contain a new legal description for the new parcel of property. This new legal description is sometimes referred to as the "survey legal description." In these cases, the title commitment should be revised to include the survey legal description.

In addition, because of advances in the technology used by contemporary surveyors, current survey legal descriptions are often more precise than record legal descriptions, even when no changes are being made to the parcel described in the vesting deed. When this happens, the surveyor may certify that the record legal description and the survey legal description both describe the same property and/or the new deed conveying the property may contain both descriptions. The title company may then issue the title policy with the more accurate survey legal description based on the survey's certification and/or the deed containing both descriptions.

Because the purpose of the legal description is to identify real property so that it cannot be confused with any other property in the world, it is essential that the correct legal description be used in the title commitment, the survey, the deed, and all other documents affecting the property. Legal descriptions generally fall within two categories: a map or plat description, or a metes and bounds description.

A map or plat description is a simple description referencing a map or plat recorded for the subdivision or condominium in which the property is located. This type of description usually includes the lot or parcel number of the property, the subdivision block in which the property is located, the county and state in which the property is located, and the recording information for the subdivision or condominium map or plat. An example of a map description relating to property within a subdivision would be "Lots 121 and 122 of Oakwood Subdivision in Block 987 of the City of St. Louis, Missouri, recorded in Plat Book 158, Page 967 in the City of St. Louis, Missouri, Recorder's Office." An example of a plat description for a condominium unit would be "Unit 212 of Westgate Condominium, Phase 2, according to the plat thereof recorded in Plat Book 385, Page 1287 in the Jefferson County, Missouri, Recorder's Office."

A metes and bounds description is a more detailed description identifying the property by a series of distances and directions, known as calls, and other identifying information such as roads abutting the property. In the 30 states which were the subject of the U.S. Government Survey (also referred to as the public land survey system or rectangular system), metes and bounds descriptions also contain references to the applicable townships, sections, ranges, and meridians used in the government's initial surveys of such states. In those states, land was divided into north-south lines called principal meridians and east-west lines called principal base lines to form rectangles. Between the principal meridians are range lines, set six miles apart, and between the principal base lines are township lines, set six miles apart. Each six-mile by six-mile square created by this system is known as a township that is divided into 36 square mile sections. Each section can then be further divided into half sections, quarter sections, and so on. Each section corner is marked with a monument, where possible. Because of the curvature of the earth and irregularities in surveying methods, townships and sections are not exact squares in reality. However, many metes and bounds descriptions use references to section corners or township identification as a part of locating the subject property within the general area. An example of such a metes and bounds description is as follows:

> The following described real property situated in Your County, Your State: Beginning at a point on the north side of Main Street in Your Town, where Jones lands and lands of Smith join; thence North 14 degrees East 208 feet; thence North 1 degrees East a distance of 74 feet, thence North 82 degrees East a distance of 132 feet; thence in a northern direction along Thompson land a distance of 121.5 feet to the point of beginning of the lands herein conveyed; thence North 82 degrees East a distance of 61 feet; thence North 1 degrees 30 minutes West to a stone for a corner; thence in a southern direction a distance of 479.0 feet to the point of beginning; the lands herein being triangular in shape and being part of Section 26, Township 43 N, Range 10 West.

All metes and bounds descriptions should begin at a fixed point (referred to as the point of beginning), trace the boundaries of the property clockwise or counterclockwise, and end at the point of beginning. Any metes and bounds description that does this is said to close and effectively identifies the property. Some metes and bounds descriptions describe a property line that contains a break (also called a gap) or does not return to the place of beginning. Any metes and bounds description that does this fails to close

 © 2019, 2020, 2021 NALA, Inc. All rights reserved.

and, therefore, does not effectively identify the property. Such a description creates a cloud on title.

In addition to the boundary lines described in the legal description, ALTA surveys depict all recorded exceptions which appear on the title commitment that affect the property. This will include utility easements, parking or driveway easements, party wall agreements, portions of the property affected by restrictions, and portions of the property affected by oil, gas, or mineral rights owned by others.

Also depicted on an ALTA survey are any encroachments onto the subject property from adjoining properties or encroachments from the subject property onto neighboring properties or rights-of-way. Examples of common encroachments are portions of fences or driveways which cross property lines. Following review of the survey by the title company, the title commitment will be updated so that it lists as exceptions any encroachments or other problematic features depicted on the survey.

ALTA surveys also depict all existing improvements such as buildings, fences, and parking lots. Sidewalks and roadways, including the roadways providing access to the property, will also be depicted. The survey should confirm that the property is not landlocked, meaning that access to the property is provided by public roadways or private agreement with adjoining landowners.

The drawing and the surveyor's notes contained in an ALTA survey can also include the optional Table A items described at the beginning of this section. The survey will include a surveyor's certification made to the title company, the purchaser, and/or the lender, as applicable.

Additional Due Diligence Reports

An appraisal provides a certification of the economic value of real or personal property. Appraisals are used by investors to confirm the value of their investment in the property or by lenders to confirm that property to be used as collateral has adequate value to secure the loan, to confirm the loan to value ratio, or to establish the amount of the mortgage. They can be prepared based on comparable sales, cost to replace, or income value. As-is appraisals provide the value of the property as of the date of the appraisal, and as-constructed appraisals provide the expected value of a property assuming all planned construction is completed. As-stabilized appraisals provide the prospective value of a property after construction has been completed and the property is occupied and generating income.

A Phase I environmental report is often obtained by the purchaser or lender in order to determine whether any environmental issues affect the property. Phase I reports contain an executive summary of the report, which summarizes the engineer's investigative techniques and findings and identifies the property. Phase I reports also contain extensive records which show the work performed by the engineer. If environmental problems are found, the Phase I report may suggest that a Phase II environmental report be prepared to further investigate the problematic condition. In such a case, the Phase II report would contain an executive summary which describes the investigative work done and the engineer's recommendations as to remediation or removal of the environmental condition, as well as all the supporting documentation.

Zoning authorities in the city or county in which real property is located usually will provide a verification of the zoning of a property in the form of a zoning certification or letter. The purchaser or lender in a real estate transaction may want a zoning letter that verifies that the property can be used for the purpose for which it is being purchased and/or that there are no zoning or building code violations on the property. Zoning reports can be obtained from surveyors or other vendors. These contain the types of information typically contained in a zoning letter and are often obtained when a zoning letter is not available or adequate. If a zoning endorsement is going to be issued in connection with a title policy, the title company will require a zoning certification, letter, or report.

A flood certificate or letter is a certification from an insurance broker, surveyor, or other vendor stating the flood zone designation of the property and whether flood insurance may be purchased in such location. A flood certification is typically required by lenders obtaining a collateral interest in real property.

Searches of state and local records regarding UCC financing statements are often obtained during the due diligence process in order to confirm the status of security interests in any real or personal property being purchased or used to secure financing. This may include items such as equipment located on the real property or intangibles, including accounts receivable or stocks. UCCs filed against the real property and fixtures located on the real property are known as fixture filings. Additionally, tax lien, pending litigation, and judgment searches may be run against property or parties such as a borrower, seller, or guarantor.

TRANSACTIONS – DOCUMENTS TRANSFERRING INTERESTS AND RELATED DOCUMENTS

There are a variety of documents which are used to convey estates and other interests in real and personal property. These documents must meet certain requirements to validly convey the interests intended and to provide notice of such interest to third parties.

Statute of Frauds

Each state has adopted its own version of the Statute of Frauds. At its simplest, the Statute of Frauds requires that certain types of contracts be made in writing, be signed by the parties, and contain sufficient content to evidence the contract. This includes purchase contracts for real property and certain personal property, deeds, leases longer than a year or other minimum period of time, easements, and mortgages or deeds of trust.

Recording

In addition to being in writing, documents conveying an interest in real property are usually recorded for the purpose of providing notice of the grantee's ownership or security interest in the freehold or leasehold estate or other interest in real property. Each state and some counties set their own requirements for recording such as a certain amount of blank space on the first page of a document and other formatting requirements, the payment of recording fees and transfer taxes, the inclusion of tax parcel identification numbers in legal descriptions, required parties' signatures, notarization, and/or witnessing thereof.

Instruments conveying an interest in real property which meet the applicable requirements of the state are effective upon execution, delivery, and acceptance, regardless of whether the instrument is recorded. Conversely, recording an invalid instrument does not create a valid claim in the property purportedly conveyed. Nevertheless, recording is a useful method of providing notice to third parties of a party's interest in real property. Each state has adopted statutes which dictate the priority of claims based on when the interest is purportedly conveyed and when notice is provided by recording. States that adopt pure race recording statutes grant priority to the first party to record regardless of whether they had notice of another party's claim, while pure notice statutes grant priority to the most recent claimant who had no notice of a prior conveyance. Race-notice statutes favor the party that has recorded first, so long as they have no notice of another party's claim. Notice may be considered constructive, meaning

© 2019, 2020, 2021 NALA, Inc. All rights reserved.

that parties are assumed to have notice of recorded instruments, or actual, meaning that the party has, in fact, received notice. Although many nuances exist among the states as to the required methods of conveying and providing notice of an interest in real property, parties can protect themselves against other claimants by performing adequate due diligence searches of real property records, executing and recording valid instruments of conveyance at the earliest opportunity, and obtaining title insurance insuring their interests in real property.

Purchase Agreement

One of the real property documents covered by the Statute of Frauds is the real estate purchase contract. All owners of the property must be parties to the contract in order for the entire ownership interest in the property and related interests, such as mineral rights, to be covered by the contract. For instance, if the property is owned by two tenants in common, but only one executes the contract, only that owner's interest in the property will be the subject of the contract. In addition, all purchasers should be identified in the contract, as well as any option for the purchaser to assign the contract to another party. Such options are typically seen in commercial property acquisitions where a purchaser plans to form a separate entity to hold the property. As with any contract, a real property purchase contract must include consideration, which is usually the exchange of ownership of the property for a specified purchase price. The purchase contract must also evidence the meeting of the minds of the parties thereto, meaning that the contract must contain a valid offer and acceptance of the terms of the agreement.

Other provisions are unique to real property purchase and sale contracts. For instance, the real property must be adequately identified in the contract through the use of the legal description of the property, address, tax identification number, or description of the acreage or square footage to be conveyed. Other provisions that may be contained in a purchase contract are agreements concerning the conveyance of appurtenant rights such as easements benefitting the property to be purchased, water rights, oil, gas, and mineral rights, and personal property related to the real property. Purchase contracts often contain provisions for the delivery of earnest money deposits and the pro-ration of property taxes, utilities, insurance, tenant security deposits, or other applicable financial considerations. They should also contain a schedule for due diligence tasks, such as title and survey reviews and the obtaining of financing, and provisions for the termination of the agreement if the results of these due diligence reviews are unsatisfactory to the purchaser. Finally, purchase contracts usually contain provisions for the delivery of funds, due diligence documents, and instruments of conveyance between the parties prior to or at closing. These are referred to as seller's and purchaser's deliverables.

Bill of Sale

A bill of sale is a document used to convey personal property. These are often seen in connection with the sale of real property. For instance, if a factory is being sold, a bill of sale may be executed by the seller in order to convey the factory equipment and machinery. Bills of sale can also be used to convey interests in other types of personal property, such as membership interests in limited liability companies.

Deed

Freehold estates in real property are typically conveyed by deed. In a deed, the seller or grantor makes certain covenants or warranties. Depending on the type of deed used and the statute adopted in the state in which the property is located, the deed may contain all or any of the following warranties:

- **Seisin.** The grantor warrants that it has legal ownership of the property.

© 2019, 2020, 2021 NALA, Inc. All rights reserved.

- **Right to Convey**. The grantor affirms that it has the power to convey the property.

- **Encumbrances**. The grantor declares that the property is free from encumbrances except as set forth in the deed.

- **Quiet Enjoyment**. The grantor covenants that the grantee shall have the right to quiet enjoyment of the property without interference from third parties.

- **Further Assurances**. The grantor promises to defend the title being conveyed and to execute any additional instruments necessary to perfect title in the grantee. This covenant is helpful when deeds in the chain of title have been recorded in inverse order or where there are errors in a deed such as a scrivener's error in a legal description.

The forms of deeds used in the state in which the real property is located may or may not explicitly set forth any or all of these covenants. However, state statutes provide that various types of deeds used in such state are deemed to include one or more of these covenants. For instance, general warranty deeds include all or most covenants with respect to the grantor's own acts and the acts of all predecessors in title. As a result, the general warranty deed provides the maximum protection for the purchaser. A special warranty deed limits such warranties to the acts of the seller only.

Many other types of deeds contain few or no covenants. A quit claim deed contains no warranties and is essentially a statement that the grantor transfers to the grantee whatever ownership interest they have in the property, if any. This type of deed is often used when a deed is between related parties or is being executed in order to clear a cloud on title. A tax deed is used to convey real property following a sale for tax delinquencies and contains no warranties as to the state of title. A sheriff's deed is used to convey title following foreclosure on a mortgage or a court ordered sale for a judgment. Similarly, a trustee's deed is used when a trustee sells real property pursuant to the power of sale provisions of a deed of trust. When real property is conveyed in probate by an estate representative following the owner's death, a personal representative's deed is used. A beneficiary deed can be used by an owner to designate who their property will be conveyed to upon their death. Depending on the statutes in the applicable state, a beneficiary deed may be revoked at any time prior to the grantor's death and, therefore, does not convey an interest in the property to the beneficiary while the grantor is alive.

In addition to applicable covenants, deeds must contain certain elements to effectively convey the estate being granted. A deed must contain the language of conveyance, or granting clause, used in the applicable state, such as "grant," "bargain," "sell," or other required language relating to the type of deed being used. The deed must evidence that consideration has been given for the conveyance because recording statutes only protect grantees of deeds which are given for value. Such consideration does not need to be monetary. The deed must contain the correct legal description in order for it to effectively convey the grantor's interest in that unique property. The deed should also identify the parties by their names, their status as married or single individuals or type of entity, and their states of residence or formation.

To effectively convey the real property, a deed must be signed by the grantor and be delivered to and accepted by the grantee. In most states, the recording of the deed is considered adequate evidence of acceptance, although some jurisdictions require the written acceptance of the purchaser for any conveyance. In addition, deeds are often executed by the grantee to evidence the grantee's acceptance of specific conditions contained in the deed, such as reversion clauses. The signatures on a deed are usually required to be notarized and, in some states, deeds must be witnessed. As noted previously, each state and local jurisdiction may also adopt its own requirements for recording documents such as deeds. Each of the applicable state and local requirements relating to the validity and recording of a deed must be satisfied in order to effectively convey the real property to the grantee and to provide notice of the

  © 2019, 2020, 2021 NALA, Inc. All rights reserved.

conveyance to the world.

Leases

At its simplest, a lease is an agreement between a property owner (as a lessor) and another party (as a lessee) pursuant to which the lessor grants the lessee possession and use of the leased property and the lessee covenants to pay rent and, in some cases, other expenses. Just as both real and personal property may be owned and conveyed, both real and personal property can be leased by a lessor to a lessee.

Under personal property leases, lessees can rent tangible personal property such as furniture, automobiles, trucks, and other vehicles (sometimes referred to as rolling stock), or intangible personal property such as trademarks. Equipment leases can be used as a method of either renting or purchasing property such as computers, medical equipment, or industrial technology. Operating leases are often utilized by companies that continually update or replace equipment, such as computers or copiers, and want to use such equipment without ownership. This type of lease allows the lessee to return the equipment at the end of the lease term so that they are free to lease or purchase more up-to-date equipment. A finance lease is a personal property lease in which the lessee purchases the personal property, such as equipment, furniture, or vehicles at the termination of the lease for a fixed amount. Under a finance lease, the lessee may be responsible for maintenance, taxes, and insurance, in addition to rental payments.

Real property leases can be entered into with respect to residential or commercial property. Under real property leases, landlords grant nonfreehold estates, such as a tenancy for a term, a periodic tenancy, or a tenancy at will, to tenants.

As the term implies, residential leases relate to residential property such as apartments or single-family homes. Residential leases are subject to regulations, that are designed to protect residential tenants, and that do not usually apply to commercial leases. Examples of this would be rent control ordinances, lead-based paint disclosure requirements, and the Fair Housing Act.

One category of commercial real property leases includes net, gross, or modified gross leases. In a net lease, the tenant pays a base rent for the commercial space, plus its pro-rata share of certain expenses associated with the operation, maintenance, and use of the property. These expenses can include real estate taxes, property insurance, and common area maintenance (CAM) charges. CAM charges may include costs of common area utilities and operating expenses such as janitorial services, property management fees, trash collection, landscaping, and any other commonly shared services. The tenant's pro-rata share is calculated by multiplying the total of such costs by the percentage of total building space leased by the tenant. For example, a tenant that leases 1,000 square feet of a 10,000-square-foot building would be expected to pay 10 percent of the building's expenses, which it has agreed to pay pursuant to a single, double, or triple net lease.

There are several types of net leases:

- **Single Net Lease.** In a single net lease, the tenant pays base rent plus its pro-rata share of the building's property tax. The landlord is responsible for all other building expenses.

- **Double Net Lease.** In a double net lease, the tenant is responsible for base rent plus its pro-rata share of the building's property taxes and property and/or liability insurance covering the entire property. The landlord pays all other building expenses.

- **Triple Net Lease.** In a triple net lease, the tenant pays base rent plus its pro-rata share of all three "nets," meaning property taxes, insurance, and CAM.

Under any type of net lease, the tenant also pays the costs associated with its premises, including janitorial services, utilities, and its own insurance and taxes. Costs for the tenant under a net lease can fluctuate from month to month and year to year as the applicable property taxes, insurance, and operating expenses increase or decrease.

Under a gross lease or, as it is sometimes called, a full-service lease, the tenant's rent is set at a fixed amount, although it may increase at an agreed upon rate over the term of the lease. The rent is all-inclusive, meaning that the landlord pays all expenses associated with the property, including taxes, insurance, and maintenance. Utilities and janitorial services for the tenant's premises may also be included in the rent.

Another type of commercial lease is known as a modified gross lease or a modified net lease. This type of lease is similar to a gross lease in that the rent is paid in a fixed amount. However, the modified gross lease payment includes any or all the "nets" agreed upon by the landlord and tenant. Utilities and janitorial services for the premises are typically excluded from the rent and paid directly by the tenant.

Under a ground lease, the tenant is permitted to construct improvements on the real property during the term of the lease. Afterwards, the tenant conveys ownership of the improvements to the landlord. These leases are usually long term, such as 50-99 years.

Other types of commercial leases provide for other forms of rent. Percentage leases require the tenant to pay a percentage of its sales revenue as rent in addition to, or as an alternative to, base rent payments and pro-rata expenses. These are often used for retail space, such as stores inside malls. Oil, gas, and mineral leases may provide for the payment of royalties, meaning a percentage of the profits arising from the sale of the oil, gas, or minerals extracted from the land, or fixed payments if there is a delay by the lessee in operations. All leases may contain default charges for late or insufficient rent payments and other rental provisions agreed to by the parties.

Like personal property, real property can be the subject of leasing for financial purposes. Such a lease can be between a landlord and a tenant that are related corporate entities. The business entities may enter into these types of leases in order to achieve income tax savings for the preferred entity, to provide for control of the real property by a specific affiliate, or to avoid internal corporate restrictions on the ownership of real property. These leases are sometimes referred to as lease/leaseback arrangements.

Additionally, real property can be the subject of financings structured to provide real property tax exemption. An example of this would be a manufacturer that conveys ownership of its factory to the county in which it is located and then leases the real property back from the county. During the period of time in which the county owns the factory, the real property, and often the personal property located thereon, is exempt from property taxes and related assessments.

Another type of real property financing lease involves a lease/leaseback arrangement between governmental or nonprofit entities for the purpose of issuing bonds. For instance, a city can lease its recreational complex to the city's industrial development authority, which then leases the complex back to the city. The industrial development authority issues bonds and loans the proceeds of the bonds to the city for a project such as improving the recreation center. As rent, the city makes payments to the industrial development authority equal to the principal and interest payments on the bonds. Typically, the bonds are tax-exempt, resulting in a lower interest rate for the city than it would have under a traditional loan.

In a capital lease, the landlord conveys a long-term lease to the tenant, which grants the tenant ownership for tax purposes while the landlord retains legal ownership. These are often used in financings where the parties want to separate the benefits of tax ownership from the benefits of legal ownership, such as in

© 2019, 2020, 2021 NALA, Inc. All rights reserved.

historic tax credit transactions.

As the above examples demonstrate, leases vary widely in terms of the property leased, the purpose of the lease, the length of term, and the payment of rent. Regardless of the type of lease and whether the property leasesd is real or personal, most leases should contain the following terms and information:

- Names and identifying information of the parties.

- Term of the lease and any renewal options, including the rent to be paid under such renewal options, and any options to purchase the property.

- Any security deposit requirements, the amount and type of rent, any default charges, and any other costs and terms of payment.

- Any requirements for insuring and maintaining leased property.

- Description of property being leased.

In addition, real property leases should contain the following:

- Legal description of leased property.

- Permitted or prohibited uses of the premises. These can be broad categories such as office or retail, or more specific uses, such as medical office space. In other cases, leases may contain use restrictions. For instance, leases in a retail development with a grocery store anchor may prohibit the sale of groceries by other tenants located within the development.

- Division of responsibility between landlord and tenant for liability to guests and other third parties.

- Requirement that tenant return the real property in same condition as received, prohibiting any waste, but permitting ordinary wear and tear.

- Option to lease additional space or purchase the property, including right of first refusal if landlord receives a purchase offer.

- Division of responsibility between landlord and tenant for maintenance, repairs, and tenant improvements.

- Insurance requirements, use of insurance proceeds in event of casualty, and division of compensation in event of condemnation of the property during the lease term.

- Provisions relating to tenant's subleasing, mortgaging, or assigning the property.

- Requirements that tenant provide landlord's lenders or potential purchasers of the property with either estoppel certificates that confirm certain facts involving the lease or subordination, non-disturbance, and attornment agreements that set forth the rights of the landlord, tenant, and landlord's lender in the event the landlord defaults on a loan secured by the property.

- Events that would constitute a default under the lease and the parties' remedies in such cases. This could include cure rights and *force majeure* provisions excusing certain defaults.

The parties to leases sometimes record a copy of the lease to provide notice of the tenant's interest in the property. More typically, a memorandum of the lease outlining only the basic information about the lease is recorded for this purpose.

© 2019, 2020, 2021 NALA, Inc. All rights reserved.

Security Interests and Liens

As noted before, mortgages and deeds of trust are required to be in writing. These instruments are recorded against real property to provide notice to third parties of the lender's interest in the property. Recording is also important with respect to these documents in order to establish the priority of multiple lenders who may have security interests in the property. Documents evidencing other security interests may or may not be recorded, depending on the agreements of the parties. For instance, promissory notes obligating a borrower to repay a debt to a lender are usually not recorded.

A security agreement grants the holder a collateral interest in personal property such as accounts receivable or equipment. Although these documents usually are not recorded, the collateral described in the agreement may be included in UCC financing statements filed against the borrower in its state of formation. Again, the purpose of doing this is to provide notice to third parties and establish priority. UCC fixture filings can also be recorded in the county where real property and the fixtures attached to the real property are located. Liens, including mechanic's liens, tax liens, and judgments, can also be filed or recorded against real or personal property by vendors, governments, and other third parties. These documents do not convey an interest but provide notice of those parties' financial claims against the real property. If an owner wishes to sell real property with mechanic's lien recorded against it or a vehicle with a lender's lien filed against the title, it must satisfy the lien holder in order to convey a clear title.

Borrowers often execute assignments of leases and rents, assignments of contracts, and assignments of various other interests in real property or personal property to lenders as collateral for loans. If the borrower defaults, the lender can use these agreements to step into the shoes of the borrower with respect to the property or agreements being assigned. For instance, when a lender forecloses on a mortgage of an apartment building, it can also exercise its rights under any assignment of lease or assignment of contracts which the borrower executed. This allows the lender or the buyer under the foreclosure to take the place of the borrower under the apartment leases and to manage and operate the building pursuant to any management or service contracts the borrower assigned.

Closing Statement

The closing or settlement statement is a schedule prepared for the purchase of real property which lists all the pro-rations and other adjustments made to the purchase price pursuant to the purchase contract. This is usually prepared by the title company, escrow agent, or counsel to one of the parties. For example, in the sale of an apartment building, the rent of the current tenants and real property taxes would be pro-rated between the portion of the year in which the seller owned the property and the period in which the purchaser will own the property. The amount credited to the seller would be added to the amount to be paid to the seller by the purchaser at closing. Settlement statements for commercial properties can be prepared in any format agreed upon by the parties. With respect to residential real property, the Real Estate Settlement Procedures Act requires lenders to prepare a Closing Disclosure form in a standard format. Other items which can be included in a settlement statement and charged to either the seller or purchaser include security deposits, earnest money deposits, funds required to satisfy existing loans or liens secured by the property, recording fees, title insurance fees, escrow agent and real estate agent fees, and attorney fees.

Other Closing Documents

The buyer and seller of property are often required to execute a variety of ancillary closing documents. The title company may require numerous affidavits such as an owner's affidavit containing representations as to issues such as recent construction on the property and whether there are parties in

---

 © 2019, 2020, 2021 NALA, Inc. All rights reserved.

possession of the property, a non-foreign person affidavit certifying that the seller is not a foreign entity for whom the buyer must withhold taxes on the sale of the property, or a survey affidavit affirming that there have been no construction or other specified activities with respect to the property since the date of the survey. Other documents may be required in order to record the deed, depending on the jurisdiction. For instance, some states or counties require the purchaser to provide transfer tax forms or certificates of value stating the amount of consideration for the property. These are used to determine the transfer tax due at conveyance or the property tax to be charged for the tax year in which the conveyance occurred.

CHAPTER 7: PRACTICE QUESTIONS

1. **What is the least commonly used type of freehold estate today?**

   A.   Fee simple estate

   B.   Life estate

   C.   Fee tail estate

   D.   Trust

2. **Which is an example of a nonfreehold estate?**

   A.   Life estate

   B.   Investment in a real estate investment trust

   C.   Membership in a real estate cooperative

   D.   Long-term ground lease

3. **Elizabeth is negotiating a lease for 1,000 square feet of office space. She plans to expand her premises after a few years of business into the neighboring 500-square-foot space. Which provision should Elizabeth request the landlord include in her lease?**

   A.   Option to lease

   B.   Renewal option

   C.   Option to purchase

   D.   Right of first refusal

4. **In which type of deed does the grantor provide warranties of title limited to those claiming under the grantor?**

   A.   Quit claim deed

   B.   Sheriff's deed

   C.   General warranty deed

   D.   Special warranty deed

5. **Hunter executes a general warranty deed conveying his farm to Ginger. Ginger later discovers a mortgage recorded against the real property. Which of the covenants included in the deed would be violated by the existence of the mortgage?**

   A.   Covenant of right to convey

   B.   Covenant against encumbrances

   C.   Covenant of warranty

   D.   Covenant of quiet enjoyment

 © 2019, 2020, 2021 NALA, Inc. All rights reserved.

6. Under which type of lease does a landlord charge an all-inclusive rental payment which covers all costs of renting the real property?

  A. Triple net lease

  B. Gross lease

  C. Modified gross lease

  D. Single net lease

7. Rachel is negotiating a lease for a music store she is opening in a retail center. She would prefer it if no other music store opens in the retail center which would compete with her business. Which provision should Rachel ask the landlord to include in the leases of other tenants in the center?

  A. Right of first refusal

  B. Option to lease

  C. Use restriction

  D. Termination clause

8. Charles, Tasha, and Donna are co-owners of a ranch. In which form of concurrent ownership would Tasha's interest be transferred to Charles and Donna upon her death?

  A. Joint tenancy with right of survivorship

  B. Tenancy by the entirety

  C. Tenancy in common

  D. Community property

9. Jane grants her neighbor, William, an easement permitting William to drive on Jane's private road. Which type of easement did Jane grant?

  A. Gross

  B. Appurtenant

  C. Easement in necessity

  D. Negative

10. Which of the following is not an element of adverse possession?

  A. Hostile

  B. Continuous

  C. Open

  D. Non-exclusive

11. **Which would not be listed on a title commitment?**

    A. Mortgage

    B. Easement

    C. Bundle of rights

    D. Tax lien

12. **Which of the following instruments conveys an interest in real property to a trustee for the benefit of a lender?**

    A. Trustee's deed

    B. Deed of trust

    C. Bill of sale

    D. Security agreement

© 2019, 2020, 2021 NALA, Inc. All rights reserved.

Torts

Written by Nancy L. Jordahl, ACP, FRP, FCP

© 2019, 2020, 2021 NALA, Inc. All rights reserved.

HISTORY OF TORT LAW IN THE UNITED STATES

Black's Law Dictionary defines a tort as a private or civil wrong or injury, other than a breach of contract, for which the court will provide a remedy in the form of an action for damages.

The word tort comes from either the Latin words *torquere* (to twist), *tortus* (twisted), or *tortum* (wrong) or the French word *tort* (wrong or fault). As discussed in the United States Legal System chapter, United States law is based primarily on the English common law system. The English common law system originally did not recognize a separate legal action in tort. Tort law gradually developed over time so that individuals could bring a claim against each other without resorting to violence or chaos. It is believed that the origins of tort law came from the Germanic system of fining people for wrongdoing. Current tort law is created through common law such as a slip and fall case and through statutory law such as a false imprisonment case.

Like contract law, tort law is a civil law as opposed to criminal law. Tort law and contract law are similar because they both involve breach of duties. Tort law differs from contract law because in contract law both parties enter an agreement knowingly, and each party consents to the contract. In tort law, the interaction between the parties is not based on consent. A tort occurs by one party creating some type of harm to the other party. The term tortfeasor refers to the person who commits the act that caused the harm.

A tort can be an intentional act or it can be a not intentional (negligent) act. A tort is a private wrong, as opposed to a criminal act, which is a public wrong. While the same event could create both a criminal case and a tort case, tort law differs from criminal law. To illustrate, a man causes an accident while driving his vehicle under the influence of alcohol. He would be charged criminally by the state for the crime of driving under the influence. He would be sued civilly by the owner of the vehicle that he hit for the damage done to the vehicle and any injuries the owner suffered. The party who initiates the case is different for criminal law (the State or the Federal government prosecutes the crime) versus civil law (the injured party files the lawsuit). Another important difference is that the burden of proof at trial varies between criminal law and civil law. The burden of proof in a criminal case is guilt of a defendant beyond a reasonable doubt. The burden of proof in a civil case is the preponderance of the evidence (more than 50 percent). But note the preponderance of evidence is based on the more convincing evidence, not the amount of evidence. Quality of evidence is more important than quantity of evidence. Finally, the results of a civil and criminal lawsuit are different. A plaintiff in a civil case is normally seeking monetary damages. A prosecutor in a criminal case is seeking punishment by jail/prison sentence, a fine, or probation.

ELEMENTS OF A TORT

The elements of a tort are:

- **The existence of a legal duty**. A legal duty is the responsibility to other people to act according to the law.

- **Breach of the duty.** Breach means to break or fail to observe.

- **A causal relation between the plaintiff's damage and the defendant's act**. A causal relation means the connection between the cause and effect.

- **Damage/injury.** Damage is a loss or harm that is the result of injury to a person, property, or reputation.

 © 2019, 2020, 2021 NALA, Inc. All rights reserved.

Think back to the drunk driver illustration above. The driver had a duty to obey the traffic laws, but the driver breached that duty and caused harm to the other driver. Keep in mind that in tort law the term "damages" is not the plural of "damage." Damage means the extent to which the plaintiff was harmed. The damage could be physical harm, property damage, monetary loss, or emotional distress. Damages means the award or compensation given to the plaintiff who was harmed.

CAUSATION

Causation is the cause and effect relationship between the act or omission and the damage alleged in a tort.

There are two types of legal causation:

- Actual cause/cause-in-fact
- Proximate cause/legal cause

Actual cause/cause-in-fact is less complicated and a factual concept. Actual cause is straightforward and easy to understand. A car runs into a bicycle. The actions of the driver of the car are the actual cause of the accident.

Proximate cause/legal cause is a more complicated and legal concept. Proximate cause is an event that is related enough to an injury that the court determines that the event was the cause of the injury. Proximate cause does not have to be the closest cause in time. Proximate cause may be the first thing that starts a sequence of events that ultimately ends up causing the damage. Proximate cause usually means that the injury must have been foreseeable or expected. A drunk driver runs into a bicycle. It is reasonably foreseeable that driving drunk will result in an accident.

Sine qua non is another causation term. The phrase derives from a Latin term meaning "without which it could not be." *Sine qua non* causation is an essential action, condition, or ingredient. It is commonly known as "but-for" causation. "But-for" that action, the result would not have occurred. Water is a *sine qua non* for swimming.

Intervening cause is an event that occurs after the tortfeasor's initial wrong act and before the damage to the plaintiff. The connection between the wrong act and the damage is broken by the intervening cause, and it may relieve the original tortfeasor from liability for the injury. A car runs into a bicycle. At the hospital, the doctor negligently treats the bicyclist and makes the injury worse. The doctor's negligence is an intervening cause.

A superseding cause is similar to the intervening cause but is an unforeseeable, abnormal, or unpredictable event. A car runs into a bicycle. While the bicyclist is laying on the side of the road tending to his injuries, a plane crashes nearby, and the bicyclist is hit by burning plane debris. The plane crash is a superseding cause.

INTENTIONAL TORTS

There are two broad categories of torts: intentional torts and negligent torts. An intentional tort is performed on purpose, while a negligent tort is not on purpose but caused by a lack of reasonable care.

It is important to keep in mind that intent is not the same as motive. Intent is a state of mind. Intent means the person wanted to cause the act. Motive is the reason why the person wanted to cause the act.

A dignitary tort is a type of intentional tort where the person experiences an indignity to reputation or honor. Not every jurisdiction refers to these types of tort as dignitary torts. Historically, dignitary torts were primarily assault, battery, and false imprisonment. As the law has progressed, other torts like defamation and intentional infliction of emotional distress are considered dignitary torts.

In common law torts (as opposed to criminal law), assault means one person acts with either general or specific intent to cause the reasonable apprehension of an immediate or harmful contact to another person. It is not a tort of negligence because there is intent involved. Battery means the person acts intentionally to harmfully or offensively contact another person or something closely associated with that person. Battery is different from assault because there is actual contact. The contact can be person to person, with or without a weapon or other object. Because assault and battery are considered intentional torts, they can serve as the basis for a civil lawsuit in addition to the basis for criminal charges. The difference between civil battery and criminal battery is that civil battery requires the element of damage/injury.

False imprisonment means confining another person in a bounded area. It is an intentional tort such as assault and battery, and similarly to assault and battery, it can be a tort and a crime depending if there is the element of damage/injury. A person can be confined in various ways: by physical barriers that leave no room for escape, overpowered by brute physical strength, or by fraud/deception.

Intentional infliction of emotional distress (IIED) is a tort claim for intentional, outrageous conduct that results in extreme emotional distress. In some jurisdictions, a physical manifestation of the mental injury is required to recover damages. IIED is also sometimes referred to as the tort of outrage. Many courts substitute the word mental for the word emotional. The most important element of a claim for IIED is determining what is extreme or outrageous conduct. Normal rudeness or obnoxious behavior is not enough to qualify as IIED. Yelling at a clerk at a store would not be an example of IIED. Sending a letter to a mother falsely claiming that her son had died would be an example of IIED.

Fraud is deliberate deception to secure unfair or unlawful gain or to deprive the other person of a legal right. Civil fraud requires that damage/injury has to have occurred. A civil fraud at the federal level can be brought through the False Claims Act. Congress enacted the False Claims Act (also known as the "Lincoln Law") during the Civil War to "aid in the effort to root out fraud against the government (and to encourage private individuals who are aware of fraud being perpetrated against the Government to bring such information forward." Abraham Lincoln requested the Act to prevent fraud against the federal government by suppliers to the Union Army. *Qui tam* lawsuits are a type of whistleblower lawsuit brought under the False Claims Act. A whistleblower is a person who exposes illegal or unethical activity. The False Claims Act law rewards and protects the whistleblower. Health care fraud, financial industry fraud, defense contractor fraud, and grant fraud cases are frequent targets of False Claims Act lawsuits.

Defamation is communicating false information about a person, group, or entity (such as a corporation) that harms reputation or standing in the community. It is a tort that allows a person, who is the target of a defamatory statement, to sue the person that made the statement. Defamation law can be divided into two areas: libel and slander. Libel is defamation by written or printed words, pictures, or any other broadcast form other than spoken words or gestures. Slander is defamation by spoken words or gestures.

Invasion of privacy allows a person to bring a lawsuit against someone who: (1) uses another person's name or likeness, such as using Tom Cruise's face on a billboard without his permission; (2) intrudes upon seclusion, solitude, or into private affairs, such as using electronic equipment to eavesdrop on a private conversation; (3) publicly discloses a private fact; or (4) false light. False light is similar to defamation but it is only a person's feelings or dignity that are damaged and not a person's reputation.

Malicious prosecution is the wrongful initiation of a civil or criminal case without probable cause and

© 2019, 2020, 2021 NALA, Inc. All rights reserved.

that causes damage. Malicious prosecution can happen when a person wants to harass another person, when a corporation is trying to intimidate a competitor, or when a police officer makes a false arrest.

Tortious interference is intentional interference with a contract causing economic harm. It happens when a person intentionally damages a contractual or other business relationship. The interference can be through unethical business practices, blackmail, inducement, or force. There are two types of victims in a tortious interference case: the person or entity damaged by the broken contract and the person who is forced to break the contract. Either victim can file a lawsuit if they are damaged.

PROPERTY TORTS

The most common property torts are trespass, nuisance, and conversion.

There are generally three types of trespass: to people, to chattel, and to land. Trespass to the person (assault, battery, false imprisonment) is discussed above with dignitary torts. Trespass to chattel is a tort where a party intentionally interferes with another party's lawful possession of a chattel. Chattel is an item of property other than real estate. The interference can be physical contact with the chattel, disposing of the chattel by taking or destroying it, or by barring the other party's access to the chattel. If a person took his neighbor's couch and the neighbor was not able to use the couch, it would be trespass to chattel. The third form of trespass is trespass to land. Trespass to land is committed when a person or the object of a person intentionally enters land of another person without a lawful excuse. Trespass to land is actionable per se. This means that the party whose land is entered may sue even if no actual harm is done. In some jurisdictions, this also applies to entry on public land that has restricted access.

Nuisance is interference with the right to use and enjoy land. A nuisance is something that is highly offensive and annoying like a pile of trash. There are both private nuisance and public nuisance. Private nuisance laws protect the individual landowner from things such as a neighbor's dangerous dog. Public nuisance laws protect the public at large from things such as air pollution.

Private or public nuisance is not the same as attractive nuisance. The attractive nuisance doctrine states that a landowner may be held liable for injuries to children trespassing on the land if the injury is caused by an object on the land that is likely to attract children. Attractive nuisance laws were created in the late 1800s after a child was injured playing on a railroad turntable that was not guarded or locked. The doctrine acknowledges that children can be attracted to items without knowing the risks involved. Common attractive nuisances are swimming pools, construction sites, discarded appliances, and trampolines.

Conversion is a tort where a person converts another property to their own use. Converts is a polite way to say steals. An example of conversion is when a person rents a steam cleaner to clean carpet and then fails to return the steam cleaner. Conversion is the civil version of the criminal act of larceny. Conversion is a more serious interference with personal property than trespass to chattel. According to the Restatement (Second) of Torts, the court may consider: (1) the extent and duration of the tort or trespass to chattel; (2) the tortfeasor's intent; (3) the tortfeasor's good faith; (4) the extent and duration of the interference; (5) the harm done to the property; and (6) the inconvenience and expense.

NEGLIGENT TORTS

A negligent tort has the same elements as an intentional tort: (1) duty; (2) breach of duty; (3) causation; and (4) damages. There is ordinary negligence (failure to exercise reasonable care), recklessness

---

© 2019, 2020, 2021 NALA, Inc. All rights reserved.

(knowing failure to exercise reasonable care), and gross negligence (extreme disregard of the need to exercise reasonable care). As Oliver Wendell Holmes. Jr. stated: "Even a dog distinguishes between being stumbled over and being kicked." Negligence would be a restaurant owner who mops a slippery floor and does not put up a "wet floor" sign. Recklessness would be having unprotected sex. Gross negligence would be a doctor amputating the wrong limb of a patient.

Civil negligence per se is a legal doctrine where an act is considered negligent because it violates a statute or regulation and causes harm to the defendant. Running a red light would be negligence per se.

Res ipsa loquitur in Latin means "the thing speaks for itself." The facts make it self-evident that something happened or not. In the tort realm, *res ipsa loquitur* can mean that just the occurrence of an accident implies that there was negligence. If a person is walking down the street and a piano falls from a building and hits the person on the head, there is no need for any additional explanation to show negligence.

Prima facie is a Latin term that means "at first sight." It means that there is enough evidence to support a case, but it does not mean the person filing the case will necessarily win the case. *Prima facie* does not prove the case, it just means the fact is presumed to be true until shown otherwise.

EXAMPLES OF VARIOUS NEGLIGENCE TORTS AND UNIQUE ISSUES

Personal injury is a very broad term that refers to a civil matter where one person causes another person harm by failing to take reasonable precautions or exercise a reasonable level of care. The harm is almost always unintentional. Personal injury is injury to a person and not to property. Motor vehicle accidents, slip and fall, and medical malpractice are all examples of personal injury.

People who cause car accidents commit a tort. In tort law, liability insurance is an important component of the process. Usually, the tortfeasor's insurance ends up paying the damages that are incurred. But, if the tortfeasor is uninsured or underinsured, the injured person will make a claim for coverage to their own insurance company pursuant to uninsured motorist (UM) or underinsured motorist (UIM) coverage rather than file a lawsuit.

Several states' legislatures have enacted "no fault" car insurance in which a person's own automobile insurer will pay certain damages (usually medical bills and lost wages) up to a set amount no matter who is at fault for the accident. Personal Injury Protection (PIP) coverage and claims are related to no fault insurance. Another no fault concept is medical payments to others (usually called Med Pay) which covers medical payments for passengers in the vehicle who are injured. Med Pay does not pay for lost wages or other damages in which PIP coverage will pay.

Federal Rule of Evidence 411 states that evidence that a person was or was not insured against liability is not admissible to prove whether the person acted negligently or otherwise wrongfully. But the court may admit this evidence for another purpose, such as proving a witness's bias or prejudice or proving agency, ownership, or control.

Medical/legal malpractice is a legal cause of action that occurs when a medical or legal professional deviates from standards in the profession and that deviation causes injury to a patient or client. Medical malpractice arises out of improper, unskilled, or negligent treatment of a patient by a physician, dentist, nurse, pharmacist, or other health care professional. A doctor who fails to diagnose a woman's breast cancer could be sued for medical malpractice. Legal malpractice is the term for negligence, breach of fiduciary duty, or breach of contract by an attorney who causes harm to a client. According to the

© 2019, 2020, 2021 NALA, Inc. All rights reserved.

American Bar Association's Profile of Legal Malpractice Claims, the most common forms of legal malpractice are failing to know or properly apply the law, conflicts of interest, failure to timely file documents, and failure to calendar/follow up.

The phrase "standard of care" in legal terms is the level at which an average person in the field would practice. The requirements depend on the circumstances. There is a higher standard of care for someone who is being paid rather than someone who is doing a favor. It is up to the trier of fact, usually the jury, to determine whether the standard of care has been breached. The standard of care concept is closely tied to the reasonable person concept. *Vaughan v. Menlove* (1837) 132 ER 490 (CP) is the English tort case that first introduced the concept of the reasonable person in law. The concept is described as whether the individual "proceed[ed] with such reasonable caution as a prudent man would have exercised under such circumstances." In that 1837 case, Mr. Menlove was warned several times that the stack of hay that he placed near Mr. Vaughan's cottage could catch on fire and burn the cottage. Mr. Menlove ignored the warning and the cottage burned. Today, most jurisdictions follow the reasonable man standard from Restatement (Second) of Torts section 283(b), which finds the reasonable person standard is an objective standard that provides a comparison between the defendant and the ideal person who is acting reasonably. Factors important in determining reasonableness sometimes include the defendant's profession, custom, age, whether the defendant violated a statute or law, and physical characteristics of the defendant. For example, a blind person is not held to the same standard of care as people who have eyesight.

Nursing homes can be held legally responsible for negligence, neglect, or abuse that causes harm to a patient or resident. Nursing homes are regulated by both federal and state laws. In 1987, Congress enacted laws that required nursing homes that participate in Medicare and Medicaid to comply with rules regarding quality of care. The Nursing Home Reform Act was a response to reports of widespread neglect and abuse in nursing homes. Nursing homes "must provide services and activities to attain or maintain the highest practicable physical, mental, and psychosocial well-being of each resident in accordance with a written plan of care," per Social Security Act §1919(c)(1) from www.ssa.gov.

Employment law is a very broad area of law that encompasses all aspects of the employer/employee relationship. It includes cases where an employer is held legally responsible for tortuous acts of an employee such as: (1) negligent hiring; (2) negligent retention; (3) negligent supervision; and (4) negligent training. Employees can also assert tort claims directly against their employers for many causes of action including discrimination, retaliation, pension issues, workplace safety, unemployment compensation, and harassment. Several federal laws apply to employment law: Americans with Disabilities Act (ADA) for discrimination; Fair Labor Standards Act (FLSA) regarding wages and overtime pay; the Immigration and Nationality Act (INA); the Occupational Safety and Health (OSH) Act; the Employment Retirement Income Security Act (ERISA) that regulates employers that offer pension plans to employees; and the Family and Medical Leave Act (FMLA), to name a few.

Workers' compensation is a form of insurance that provides wage replacement and medical benefits to employees who are injured in the course of their employment. Each state has its own workers' compensation laws, so the circumstances under which workers' compensation is available to workers, the amount of benefits that workers may receive, and the duration of the benefits paid to injured workers, vary by state. Workers' compensation statutes generally make the employer immune from any liability for negligence. In the majority of states, the jurisdiction for workers' compensation disputes have been transferred by statute from the trial courts to special administrative agencies. But a few states still allow the employee to initiate a lawsuit in a trial court against the employer. For example, in Ohio, workers' compensation appeals are allowed to go before a jury.

Wrongful death is a claim against a person who can be held liable for the death of another person. Under

© 2019, 2020, 2021 NALA, Inc. All rights reserved.

common law, a dead person cannot bring a suit. A wrongful death claim is brought by the personal representative of the estate of the person who died or by the survivors of the person who died. The definition of survivor and the relationship to the deceased varies by state and is defined by statute.

Product liability is the area of law to sue manufacturers, distributors, suppliers, retailers, and others who make products available to the public for the injuries those products cause. "Product" can mean many things: a medical device, a gate motor, or an automobile. A plaintiff must prove that the product was defective, and the defect made the product unreasonably dangerous. The claims are usually that the product was a manufacturer mistake (carelessness in putting the product together), defectively designed (Ford Pinto exploding when rear-ended), or the product failed to provide adequate warnings or instructions about how to properly use the product (tobacco companies failing to warn consumers about the dangers of smoking).

A concept related to motor vehicle products liability is the crashworthiness or "enhanced injury" doctrine, which is traced back to *Larsen v. General Motors Corporation*, 391 F.2d 495 (8th Cir. 1968). This legal theory states an automobile manufacturer may be liable either for injuries that a person sustains in an accident where a manufacturing mistake or design defect caused or enhanced the injuries, although they did not cause the accident itself. The doctrine places a duty on the automobile manufacturer to use reasonable care to prevent additional risk to vehicle occupants when the vehicle is in an accident. The types of automobile components in crashworthiness cases are things such as airbags, seatbelts, and windshields.

Premises liability is a type of personal injury case where the injury was caused by some type of unsafe or defective condition on someone's property. For premises liability to apply: (1) the defendant must possess the premises/land; (2) the plaintiff must be an invitee or a licensee; and (3) there must be negligence. An invitee is a person who is invited to the premises by the possessor as a member of the public for the purpose of business (shopper at a store). A licensee is a person who is invited to the premises by the possessor for a purpose other than financial gain (neighbor dropping by). An invitee and a licensee both have permission to be on the premises. A trespasser does not have permission to be on the premises. The Restatement (Second) of Torts defines a trespasser as "a person who enters or remains upon land in the possession of another without a privilege to do so created by the possessor's consent or otherwise." Slip and fall cases are the most common types of premises liability cases. Dog bite or inadequate security cases are other premises liability examples.

Even though dram shop laws apply to premises such as a bar serving alcohol to adults or minors, dram shop cases are not premises liability cases. Dram shop laws are associated with DUI accidents or other injuries caused by intoxicated adults or minors. Dram shop laws are created by statute and make the business liable to anyone injured by the drunken patron. Not all states have dram shop laws. Typically, dram shop laws apply to businesses and not to individuals. Social host liability is a similar concept to dram shop laws but applies against individuals. Social host liability is created by statute or case law and imposes liability on social hosts as a result of their serving alcohol to adults or minors.

Maritime law is also known as admiralty law. It is a group of laws, conventions, and treaties that govern private maritime businesses and other nautical matters such as shipping on the waters of the world. A maritime tort is an injury to a person or property where admiralty takes jurisdiction because the tort occurred in a maritime setting.

Negligent infliction of emotional distress (NIED) is a legal theory that is available in nearly all states but limited in many states. The concept behind NIED is that a person has a legal duty to use reasonable care to avoid causing emotional distress to another person. In some states, a person can sue for NIED without any corresponding physical injuries. However, most states require that the plaintiff's emotional

 © 2019, 2020, 2021 NALA, Inc. All rights reserved.

distress be so severe that it creates physical symptoms such as loss of appetite, lack of sleep, or anxiety. The California Supreme Court awarded NIED damages in the 1968 ruling in *Dillon v. Legg*, 68 Cal.2d 768. A car, driven by Legg, killed the child Dillon. Dillon's mother and sister sued for wrongful death and emotional distress. The trial court found that the sister was inside the zone of danger, but the mom was considered outside the zone of danger and so not eligible for emotional distress. The supreme court awarded damages to the mother for emotional distress and relied on the concept of foreseeability explained further below.

Several rules limit the liability of people against whom NIED claims are made. Most jurisdictions have abandoned the "impact rule" and it is only followed in a few states. It requires that something contact or impact the plaintiff as a result of the defendant's negligent act, even if the impact is minor. The "zone of danger" rule is followed in some states and requires that the plaintiff be close enough to the defendant's negligent act that the plaintiff was at immediate risk of physical harm. The "foreseeability" rule is followed by most states. A defendant must have been able to reasonably predict that their actions could result in the negative consequence experienced by the plaintiff. The difference between the foreseeability rule and the zone of danger or impact rules is that there is no requirement that the defendant's negligent conduct involves some form or risk of physical harm. The "bystander exception" is a type of negligent infliction of emotional distress case when a close family member witnesses or arrives immediately on the scene of an accident where another family member was injured or killed by the defendant's negligence. The bystander, who suffered no physical injury as a result of the defendant's negligence, may sue for NIED.

LIABILITY

Liability is legal responsibility for something. There are different types of legal liability that apply to torts. Primary liability is a direct obligation. Strict liability means the person is legally responsible for the things that go wrong, even if the person did not intend for the wrong to occur. A person is strictly liable no matter what the circumstances. Under the strict liability rule, a person must pay compensation for damages even if they are not at fault. The purpose of strict liability laws is to be "strict" and encourage safety and improved standards of prevention to offer the general public better protection from the risks involved in particular activities. Examples of strict liability are product liability or ownership of wild animals. Other examples are ultra-hazardous activities such as storing explosives or transporting toxic waste.

Secondary liability is where one party assumes the legal liability for the actions of another party. It is typically applied to copyright matters or intellectual property rights such as patent infringements. Secondary liability can be vicarious liability or contributory infringement.

Vicarious liability means one person is held liable for the torts of another person, even though that person did not commit the harmful act. An example of vicarious liability is when an employer is liable for the tort of an employee that is committed during the course of employment. This type of vicarious liability that applies to employment relationships is called *respondeat superior*, meaning "let the master answer."

Joint and several liability occurs when there are two or more persons liable for the same tort. They may be jointly liable, severally liable, or jointly and severally liable. If the two people have joint liability, then they are each liable up to the full amount of the obligation. If the two people have several liability, then they are each liable only for their respective obligation. Under joint and several liability, the plaintiff can recover all of the damages from any defendant regardless of the individual share of liability.

Contribution and indemnity are concepts that are closely related to joint and several liability. They are both ways in which a defendant can sue other parties to pay for some or all of the plaintiff's damages. In a contribution claim, the defendant asserts entitlement to contribution from a third party for the money damages. For example, a plaintiff sues a restaurant after they slip and fall in a restaurant. The defendant restaurant then can sue a third party such as the contractor that repaired the leaky roof. Indemnity is when one individual takes on the obligation to pay for any loss or damage that has been or might be occurred by another individual. The right to indemnity and the duty to indemnify usually arise out of a contract. For example, a car dealer and an automobile manufacturer get sued for breach of warranty. The car dealer may request that the manufacturer indemnify the dealer for the claims as a result of an indemnity clause in the contract between the manufacturer and the dealer.

DEFENSES TO NEGLIGENCE TORTS

Assumption of risk is a defense that completely bars or partially reduces a plaintiff's right to recovery against a negligent tortfeasor if the negligent tortfeasor can show the plaintiff voluntarily and knowingly assumed the risks inherent to the dangerous activity in which the plaintiff was participating at the time of injury. The injury to the plaintiff must be foreseeable. For example, a passenger knows the driver is drunk and then gets in the vehicle as a passenger. Another example is that if a person goes sky diving, that person will sign a Release, Waiver of Liability, and Assumption of Risk. A liability waiver is a form that releases a party from liability for any harm or damage that may happen. The person signing the form waives or gives up the right to hold the other party liable for harm or damage.

Comparative fault or contributory negligence are possible defenses to a negligence claim depending on which is followed in a particular jurisdiction. Comparative fault or contributory negligence apply when the plaintiff has, through the plaintiff's own negligence, contributed to the harm suffered by failing to act prudently. The defense is relevant to the determination of liability and damages by the fact finder (usually a jury) who must decide the percentage to which the plaintiff's negligence and the combined negligence of all the other parties or non-parties contributed to cause the plaintiff's damages. States that recognize pure contributory negligence prevent the plaintiff from the recovery of any damages if the plaintiff is even one percent at fault. States that recognize pure comparative fault allow the plaintiff to recover damages if they are even 99 percent at fault, although recovery is reduced by the plaintiff's percentage of fault. States that recognize modified comparative fault use the 50 percent bar rule (plaintiff is allowed to recover damages if the plaintiff is 49 percent or less at fault) or by the 51 percent bar rule (plaintiff is allowed to recover damages if the plaintiff is 50 percent or less at fault). The last clear chance doctrine is recognized in contributory negligence jurisdictions. Under this doctrine, a negligent plaintiff can still recover if the plaintiff proves the defendant had the last opportunity to avoid the accident. The plaintiff negligently puts themselves in danger, the plaintiff cannot avoid the danger or get away from the danger, the defendant is aware of the danger and had the opportunity to avoid the danger, or the defendant does not avoid the danger and as a result the plaintiff is hurt. Assume the plaintiff stops on a train track and the car stalls. If the oncoming train conductor, who sees the plaintiff's car from a mile away and is only going 10 miles per hour, fails to stop, the plaintiff may assert the conductor had the last clear chance to avoid the danger.

Recreational use statutes are defenses to premises liability claims. The statutes vary by state and by local municipality. Every state has a statute that encourages owners of privately-owned large acreage to provide and promote public recreational use of that land. The recreational use statutes give landowners some protection for liability for recreational users' personal injuries or property damage. There is an exception for the landowner's willful or malicious failure to warn against a dangerous condition, use, structure, or activity.

 © 2019, 2020, 2021 NALA, Inc. All rights reserved.

Act of God or "Force Majeure" is a legal term for events outside of human control (like a natural disaster) for which no one can be held responsible such as an earthquake, volcano, or flash flood. The act of God defense is an affirmative defense to liability for cleanup, damages, or penalties that are the result of the natural disaster.

Historically, citizens have not been able to sue their government, which is referred to as sovereign immunity. The theory is that a sovereign or state cannot commit a legal wrong and is immune from civil suit. Sovereign immunity/governmental immunity can be a defense to a tort. The principle is referred to as *rex non potest peccare*, meaning "the king can do no wrong." However, there are many circumstances where the government can be sued. The Federal Tort Claims Act (FTCA) is a 1946 federal statute that permits private parties to sue the United States in a federal court for most torts committed by persons acting on behalf of the United States. The FTCA constitutes a limited waiver of sovereign immunity, permitting citizens to pursue some tort claims against the government.

Statutes of limitations are federal or state laws that restrict the time within which a legal proceeding may be brought. The statutes were designed to prevent stale claims from arising after evidence has been lost, facts have become obscure, and witnesses have disappeared. The defense should be asserted as an affirmative defense to the complaint.

The discovery rule can affect when the statute of limitations begins to run. In some cases, an injury that caused a wrongful death was not apparent at first. Under the discovery rule, the statute of limitations will begin when the injury is discovered or reasonably should have been discovered. States do not apply the discovery rule uniformly. The type of injury and other circumstances can affect the application of the discovery rule.

Defenses to Intentional Torts

Consent is a defense for an intentional tort used by a defendant to negate responsibility for the tort. If a plaintiff consented to the defendant's actions, as long as that person is mentally competent and did not consent due to misrepresentation of the facts, there is no tort. Consent can be written, oral, or even implied by the plaintiff's actions. Consent can be revoked.

Self-defense and the defense of others are defenses to intentional torts. Defendants have a right to use physical force to defend themselves from bodily harm. It is commonly referred to as a justifiable defense. A defendant also has the right to defend another person from harm if they reasonably believe it is justified and the other person could have a legitimate claim for self-defense. The defendant claiming defense of others must physically witness the attack. The defense must be appropriate and proportionate. Self-defense or the defense of others cannot be used as an excuse for revenge.

In addition to self-defense or defense of others, intentional tort law allows a person to use physical force to protect land or chattel. Defense of property is similar to self-defense in that the defendant must be able to prove the property was in danger and they used appropriate force in its defense. The defendant must also show legal possession of the land or chattel.

There is also a necessity defense to an intentional tort. The intentional tort defense of necessity gives the state or an individual the right to take or use the property of another. It is usually a defense against the tort of trespass to chattel, trespass to land, or conversion. The defense applies to emergency situations where there is not another alternative to avoid harm, the defendant did not cause the threat of harm, and the ultimate damage caused was less than what would have happened. An example of a necessity defense would be breaking into an office building on the weekend when a tornado pops up, and there is no other shelter in the immediate area.

© 2019, 2020, 2021 NALA, Inc. All rights reserved.

Miscellaneous Protections

The **eggshell skull rule** (also referred to as the **thin skull rule**) is the opposite of a defense. The fragility of an injured person is not a valid defense to the seriousness of any injury to that person. It does not matter whether the plaintiff's constitution is like concrete or an eggshell, the tortfeasor is still responsible for the damage.

A covenant not to sue is a legal agreement in which the party seeking damages agrees not to sue the party that it has cause against. A covenant not to sue may last forever or may just postpone a lawsuit for a period of time. The covenant not to sue must be in writing.

Good Samaritan laws offer legal protection to people who give reasonable assistance to other people who are or who they believe to be injured, ill, in peril, or otherwise incapacitated. The protection is intended to reduce a bystander's hesitation to assist for fear of being sued.

REMEDIES AND DAMAGES AND OTHER RELATED TOPICS

Compensatory damages focus on the plaintiff's loss. It is a sum of money awarded by the court to compensate a person for the particular loss or injury suffered as a result of the tort. Compensatory damages provide the monetary amount necessary to replace what was lost and nothing more. An example of compensatory damages is past medical bills.

Compensatory damages can be further broken down to economic or special damages which are objective and unique to the plaintiff versus non-economic or general damages which are subjective, and any plaintiff could incur.

Economic or special damages are compensatory damages that the plaintiff receives as a result of money lost because of the accident such as past and future lost wages, loss of future earning capacity, repair and replacement of damaged property, and past and future medical expenses.

Non-economic or general damages would be for pain and suffering, inconvenience, physical impairment, loss of consortium, and mental anguish. Loss of consortium is also called loss of affection or loss of companionship. Loss of consortium refers to the deprivation that the family suffers due to the injuries caused to the plaintiff by the tortfeasor. The deprivation can be sexual relations, affection, or the ability to do household chores or take care of children. Damages caps are laws that limit the amount of non-economic damages that may be awarded for a case. Each state has its own damages cap. For example, California caps non-economic damages in medical malpractice cases at $250,000.00 per Civil Code 3333.2.

The purpose of punitive or exemplary damages is to punish and not to compensate. The damages are intended to reform or deter the defendant and others from engaging in the same conduct. Punitive damages awards are controversial and vary from state to state. Punitive damages have been awarded in cases against tobacco makers like Phillip Morris.

Liquidated damages are in contract cases and are agreed to by the parties at the time the contract is made. Damages that are uncertain may be referred to as unliquidated damages. Neither of these terms are commonly associated with tort law.

The general rule in the United States is each party pays its own attorney's fees. This is also called the "American Rule." Attorney's fees can be awarded to the prevailing party but the award is usually pursuant to a statute or to a contract. The Magnuson-Moss Warranty Act is a federal law that provides for attorney's fees to the prevailing party.

© 2019, 2020, 2021 NALA, Inc. All rights reserved.

Attorney's fees in tort cases are often based on a contingent fee agreement. The plaintiff's lawyer agrees to accept a percentage of the recovery paid to the plaintiff. If the client prevails, the lawyer's fee is subtracted from the money awarded to the client. If the client loses the claim, the lawyer does not get paid. The percentage is typically 33 percent to 40 percent. The client normally pays court filing fees and witness expense costs whether they win or lose. The contingency fee contract must be in writing and signed by the client and the lawyer.

Certain costs can be awarded to the prevailing party in a lawsuit under Federal Rule of Civil Procedure 54 Judgment; Costs. 28 U.S.C §1920 has the categories of costs that are taxable in federal court actions which include: fees of the clerk and marshal; fees for printed or electronically recorded transcripts necessarily obtained for use in the case; fees and disbursements for printing and witnesses; fees for copies; docket fees; and fees for court appointed experts. States usually also have a similar statute outlining taxable costs.

Subrogation is the substitution of one person or group by another in respect to a debt or insurance claim. Insurance companies can recover the amount paid for a loss by suing the party that created the loss. For example, a house gets flooded, the insurance company pays the claim for damages under a homeowner's insurance policy, and then sues the contractor that improperly installed the hot water heater that leaked and created the flood. A waiver of subrogation is a contractual provision/endorsement where the insured waives the right of the insurance provider to seek compensation for the loss from a negligent third party.

Replevin is also referred to as claim and delivery. It is a legal remedy for recovery of the personal property that was wrongfully or unlawfully taken from the party, and to obtain compensation for the loss of property. Trover is a legal remedy for recovery of damages for the wrongful or unlawful taking of personal property. It differs from replevin because the recovery is only for the value of whatever was wrongfully or unlawfully taken; it is not for the recovery of the actual property.

A rule related to recovery of damages is the collateral source rule. The doctrine prohibits admission into evidence at trial about any compensation the plaintiff has already received from a source other than the damages the plaintiff wants from the defendant. For example, evidence that the plaintiff's insurance company already paid the medical bills would not be admissible. Some states have tried to modify or get rid of the collateral source rule.

Once a settlement has been reached in a workers' compensation or personal injury liability matter, a Medicare Set Aside account may be required to be created for the plaintiff under certain circumstances. Under federal law, Medicare is always a "secondary payer" which means if there is any other insurance or recovery available, Medicare will not pay bills for the injury unless that other insurance or recovery is not available. If a plaintiff received settlement money from an insurance company to cover future medical treatments, Medicare wants to make sure the plaintiff spends that portion of the settlement money on medical treatment before the taxpayers start paying for the injury through Medicare.

A medical lien is the right of a health care provider to be paid from the settlement or the trial verdict proceeds the patient receives from a personal injury lawsuit. The amount recoverable by a medical lien is limited to the cost of the treatment or the cost of the service provided. The medical care provider can place a lien on the settlement by filing a lawsuit, or the health care provider can have a letter of protection (LOP) sent by a personal injury attorney representing an injured person. The letter of protection guarantees that the attorney will pay the health care provider for medical treatment when the lawsuit is settled or a verdict is awarded. If there is a contingency fee recovery, typically the attorney collects the amount owed in the contingency fee agreement first, then medical liens and other costs are paid, and the remaining money belongs to the plaintiff. For example, a slip and fall case settles for $10,000.00. The attorney receives 1/3 or $3,333.33. The plaintiff's doctor is paid $1,000.00 under a LOP, and then costs

© 2019, 2020, 2021 NALA, Inc. All rights reserved.

for filing fees, etc., of $600.00 are deducted. The plaintiff will receive the remaining $1,733.33 of the $10,000.00 settlement.

EVIDENCE/ADMISSIBILITY

Tort cases require evidence to prove or disprove a point or element in the case by the parties. There is almost no limit to what can serve as evidence. Some of the most common forms of evidence are discussed here. Admissible evidence is any document, testimony, or tangible evidence used in a court of law.

An important Federal Rule of Evidence that relates to torts is Rule 407, Subsequent Remedial Measures. When measures are taken that would have made an earlier injury or harm less likely to occur, evidence of the subsequent measures is not admissible to prove: (1) negligence; (2) culpable conduct; (3) defect in a product or its design; or (4) a need for a warning or instruction. The court may admit the evidence for another purpose such as impeachment.

Another important Federal Rule of Evidence related to tort law is Rule 409, Offers to Pay Medical and Similar Expenses. Evidence of furnishing, promising to pay, or offering to pay medical, hospital, or similar expenses resulting from an injury is not admissible to prove liability for the injury.

A police report is considered hearsay for use at trial. Federal Rule of Evidence 801(c) defines hearsay as a statement that: (1) the declarant does not make while testifying at the current trial or hearing; and (2) a party offers in evidence to prove the truth of the matter asserted in the statement. Hearsay is usually inadmissible evidence that is used to describe a statement or action of another person. Even though police reports cannot be used at trial they are still very valuable evidence in a tort case. The police report contains factual information about the incident including the weather, time, and location and provides names of witnesses. Federal Rule of Evidence outlines the exceptions to the rule against hearsay, such as excited utterance or a statement made for medical diagnosis or treatment.

Medical records can be obtained through a signed authorization or through a subpoena to the medical care provider. Each state has different standards for acquiring medical records used for legal purposes. The federal Health Insurance Portability and Accountability Act of 1996 (HIPAA) sets the standard for protecting sensitive patient data. The complete set of HIPAA regulations can be found at www.hhs.gov/hipaa. The stated "major goal of the Privacy Rule is to assure that individuals' health information is properly protected while allowing the flow of health information needed to provide and promote high quality health care and to protect the public's health and well-being. The Rule strikes a balance that permits important uses of information, while protecting the privacy of people who seek care and healing" (Summary of the HIPAA Privacy Rule).

The federal Freedom of Information Act (FOIA) provides the public the right to request access to records from federal agencies. A FOIA request can be made for any agency record. The request can also specify the format for receipt of the records (for example, printed or electronic form). The FOIA does not require agencies to create new records or to conduct research, analyze data, or answer questions when responding to requests. See www.foia.gov for more complete information.

School and employment records, like medical records, can be obtained through a signed authorization or through a subpoena. School records may include medical, legal, or mental health information that may be valuable to a tort claim. Employment records contain documents and materials related to the employee's health, sick day records, health insurance claims, and workers' compensation claims that could be helpful.

Depending on the type of tort involved, driving records and the criminal/litigation history of all parties

© 2019, 2020, 2021 NALA, Inc. All rights reserved.

(plaintiff, defendant, and witnesses) can be valuable evidence.

Mobile devices, including smartphones and tablets, contain data storing personal information that are becoming very valuable sources for evidence, including social media and email.

A fact or lay witness is an individual with personal knowledge of the events that pertain to the case. A lay witness may be the plaintiff, the defendant, or someone who saw the accident. Per Federal Rule of Evidence 701, a lay witness can testify about facts. Lay opinions are limited to opinions that are: (1) rationally based on the witness's perception; (2) helpful to clearly understand the witness's testimony or to determining a fact in issue; and (3) not based on scientific, technical, or other specialized knowledge.

Federal Rule of Evidence, Rule 702, defines an expert witness as a witness who is qualified as an expert by knowledge, skill, experience, training, or education. An expert witness is someone with special expertise about an element of the case. Expert witnesses can be classified in two ways: consulting experts and testifying experts. The consulting expert advises and educates both the attorney and client. In general, consulting experts do not testify. Testifying experts testify at deposition and at trial if the case does not settle before the expert is deposed or the case goes to trial. Tort cases frequently require expert testimony. The most common types of experts used in tort cases are: medical experts, car accident reconstruction specialists, life care planners, toxicologists, pain management specialists, accounting experts, securities experts, rehabilitation experts, and vocational experts.

Spoliation of evidence happens when a document, item, or information that is crucial for discovery in a case is destroyed or altered. Spoliation of evidence is prohibited by American Bar Association's Model Rules of Professional Conduct, Rule 37 of Federal Rules of Civil Procedure, and Title 18 United States Code. There are sanctions for spoliation like fines, dismissal of the case, or the right to file a separate tort action for spoliation. A typical spoliation sanction is a negative evidentiary inference, which means a court will consider the altered document or item with inference against the spoliator and in favor of the opposing party. The theory behind spoliation inference is that when a party has destroyed evidence, it shows that the party had a negative reason to avoid admitting the spoliated evidence, so the court will conclude that the evidence was not in the spoliator's favor.

SETTLEMENT NEGOTIATIONS, MEDIATION, AND TRIAL

Settlement negotiations, mediation, and trial are discussed in the civil litigation chapter of this book. However, there are some aspects of settlement negotiations, mediation, and trial that are unique to torts addressed here.

Demand letters give formal notice that a person is considering legal action. Most demand letters contain a demand for money or some other form of remedy. The demand letter usually begins the settlement negotiations process between the parties. Under Federal Rule of Evidence 408, settlement negotiations cannot usually be introduced as evidence at trial.

The majority of tort disputes never reach a trial verdict. Most tort cases are filed in state court according to http://www.uscourts.gov/about-federal-courts/court-role-and-structure/comparing-federal-state-courts. Most state courts require the parties complete mediation in personal injury and other tort cases before proceeding to trial. Mediation can be a valuable tool to settle a tort case before the expense and uncertainty of going to trial. Mediation is led by a neutral third party. The mediator's role is to help the parties reach a settlement that all can agree on.

"A day in the life" video is a collection of video clips of the activities of daily living of an injured plaintiff. The admissibility of the video at trial is typically up to the judge's discretion. If the video demonstrates

---

facts and does not contain artistic highlighting or obvious exaggerations, the video is more likely to be admitted. Day in the life videos can be very effective at mediation.

Tort law is trial law. The American Bar Association has a Tort Trial & Insurance Practice Section (TIPS) of 30,000 members made up of plaintiff, defense, insurance, and corporate attorneys. Most tort cases are jury trials. Even though most cases do not go to trial, every case needs to be prepared as if it is going to trial. Tort law can move slowly. Some tort cases take years or decades to resolve. Tort law is constantly evolving.

REFERENCE MATERIALS

- Federal Rules of Civil Procedure
- *Prosser and Keeton on Torts*, 5th Edition
- *Black's Law Dictionary*
- Restatement (Second) of Torts

 © 2019, 2020, 2021 NALA, Inc. All rights reserved.

12/15

CHAPTER 8: PRACTICE QUESTIONS

1. **Which of the following is not an element of a tort?**

   A. Duty

   B. Breach of duty

   C. Consideration

   D. Injury

2. **The burden of proof in a tort case is:**

   A. Beyond a reasonable doubt

   B. Preponderance of the evidence

   C. Clear and convincing

   D. Conclusive

3. **The eggshell skull rule is:**

   A. Used to explain why Humpty Dumpty fell off the wall.

   B. The plaintiff must be close enough to the defendant's negligent act that the plaintiff was at immediate risk of physical harm.

   C. A sovereign or state cannot commit a legal wrong and is immune from civil suit.

   D. The unexpected frailty of the injured person is not a valid defense to the seriousness of any injury that is caused to them.

4. **Four basic causes of action in _____ law are: (1) negligent hiring; (2) negligent retention; (3) negligent supervision; and (4) negligent training.**

   A. Employment

   B. Maritime

   C. Product liability

   D. Premises liability

5. **A person injured by a drunk driver that was over-served at a bar can sue pursuant to:**

   A. Criminal law

   B. Dram shop law

   C. Premises liability

   D. Social host liability

6. A close family member witnesses or arrives immediately on the scene of an accident where another family member was injured or killed by the defendant's negligence is called:

   A. The impact rule

   B. The zone of danger

   C. The foreseeability rule

   D. A bystander case

7. What type of liability occurs when there are two or more persons liable for the same tort?

   A. Primary liability

   B. Joint and several liability

   C. Strict liability

   D. Vicarious liability

8. Which type of evidence will not be allowed at a tort trial?

   A. Employment record

   B. Medical record

   C. Police report

   D. School record

9. Which of the following events could be the basis for a strict liability case:

   A. Dog bite

   B. Slip and fall

   C. Negligent hiring

   D. Medical malpractice

10. False imprisonment is:

   A. A negligence tort

   B. An intentional tort

   C. A strict liability tort

   D. A personal injury tort

11. Which of the following is a defense to a negligence tort?

   A. Consent

   B. Self-defense

   C. Necessity

   D. Comparative fault

 © 2019, 2020, 2021 NALA, Inc. All rights reserved.

12. **Running into a pedestrian because the driver is speeding is an example of:**

    A. Product liability

    B. The Lincoln Law

    C. Negligence per se

    D. Premises liability

13. **In a product liability case, the Plaintiff sues:**

    A. A manufacturer

    B. A doctor

    C. An employer

    D. A condominium association

14. **Which of the following elements is not necessary for a premises liability case to apply?**

    A. The defendant must possess the premises/land

    B. The plaintiff must be an invitee or licensee

    C. There must be recreational use

    D. There must be negligence

15. **The purpose of punitive damages is:**

    A. To compensate the plaintiff

    B. To deprive the plaintiff

    C. To encourage the defendant

    D. To deter the defendant

Professional and Ethical Liability

Written by Bobby T. Rimas, Associate Professor

"In civilized life, law floats in a sea of ethics."

- Earl Warren, 14th Chief Justice of the United States of America

© 2019, 2020, 2021 NALA, Inc. All rights reserved.

This chapter provides a comprehensive overview of professional and ethical liability issues that paralegals sometimes encounter in the professional arena as well as the general public. The chapter begins by emphasizing the importance of compliance with the ethical rules for paralegals and by listing various rules and guidelines which paralegals must abide by in their day-to-day responsibilities. Next, the chapter provides the National Association of Legal Assistants, Inc., (NALA) Model Standards and Guidelines for the Utilization of Paralegals and a list of several state regulations governing paralegals, followed by examples of conflicts of interest. Unauthorized practice of law and attorney-client protected communications follow along with the overall importance of communications within the legal team. The chapter then concludes with hypothetical scenarios where each paralegal must confront an ethical dilemma. Learning about the NALA Code of Ethics and Professional Responsibility and the American Bar Association (ABA) Model Rules of Professional Conduct is strongly recommended for full understanding of this chapter as well as for future success in the paralegal profession. Comprehension of the NALA Model Standards and Guidelines for the Utilization of Paralegals will also prove beneficial for your understanding of your ethical roles within the workplace. By the end of this chapter, you will comprehend the significance of ethics and professional liabilities and become familiar with the ethical rules and considerations so that you may adhere to them and remain compliant throughout your paralegal career.

ETHICAL RULES FOR PARALEGALS

First and foremost, all paralegals across the United States must adhere to their state regulations, ethical opinions, and state bar associations where applicable. Additionally, many states make it clear that the supervising attorneys of the paralegals are responsible for ensuring ethical conduct. For example, in Illinois, Article VIII of the Illinois Rules of Professional Conduct, Rule 5.3(b), indicates that supervising attorneys with direct authority over nonlawyers have an ethical obligation to ensure that the conduct of those persons is compatible with the obligations of the lawyer. Even though several states mandate that supervising attorneys are responsible for their staff's professional conduct, paralegals themselves must adhere to the highest ethical standards by ensuring they follow their state regulations, guidelines, bar associations, and paralegal association rules of ethical conduct.

On the national level, paralegals can refer to the NALA Code of Ethics and Professional Responsibility.

In 2020, the American Bar Association's "…policy making body, the House of Delegates, adopted the current definition of paralegal, as recommended by the Standing Committee on Paralegals. The current definition reads as follows:

> A paralegal is a person, qualified by education, training or work experience who is employed or retained by a lawyer, law office, corporation, governmental agency, or other entity and who performs specifically delegated substantive legal work for which a lawyer is responsible.

The current definition replaces the definition adopted by the House of Delegates in 1997. This updated definition removes the term 'legal assistant' in order to reflect terminology that more accurately represents the type of substantive work that paralegals perform."

As a reminder, the American Bar Association's Model Rules of Professional Conduct is strongly recommended for full understanding of this chapter as well as for future success in the paralegal profession.

© 2019, 2020, 2021 NALA, Inc. All rights reserved.

NALA CODE OF ETHICS AND PROFESSIONAL RESPONSIBILITY

Each NALA - The Paralegal Association (NALA) member agrees to follow the canons of the NALA Code of Ethics and Professional Responsibility. Violations of the Code may result in cancellation of membership. First adopted by the NALA membership in May of 1975, the Code of Ethics and Professional Responsibility is the foundation of ethical practices of paralegals in the legal community.

A paralegal must adhere strictly to the accepted standards of legal ethics and to the general principles of proper conduct. The performance of the duties of the paralegal shall be governed by specific canons as defined herein, so that justice will be served, and goals of the profession attained. (See Model Standards and Guidelines for Utilization of Paralegals, Section II.)

The canons of ethics set forth hereafter are adopted by NALA, as a general guide intended to aid paralegals and attorneys. The enumeration of these rules does not mean there are not others of equal importance although not specifically mentioned. Court rules, agency rules, and statutes must be taken into consideration when interpreting the canons.

Definition: A legal assistant or paralegal is a person qualified by education, training or work experience who is employed or retained by a lawyer, law office, corporation, governmental agency, or other entity who performs specifically delegated substantive legal work for which a lawyer is responsible. (Adopted by the ABA in 1997 and NALA in 2001).

The ABA adopted a revised definition in 2020, removing the term "legal assistant." NALA realizes that the terms legal assistant and paralegal are used in the United States. NALA recognizes and supports paralegals, regardless of title; however, as an organization, we primarily use the term paralegal.

- **Canon 1**
  A paralegal must not: (a) engage in, encourage, or contribute to any act which could constitute the unauthorized practice of law; (b) establish attorney-client relationships, set fees, give legal opinions or advice, or represent a client before a court or agency unless so authorized by that court or agency; and (c) engage in conduct or take any action which would assist or involve the attorney in a violation of professional ethics or give the appearance of professional impropriety.

- **Canon 2**
  A paralegal must not perform any of the duties that attorneys only may perform or take any actions that attorneys may not take.

- **Canon 3**
  A paralegal may perform any task which is properly delegated and supervised by an attorney, as long as the attorney is ultimately responsible to the client, maintains a direct relationship with the client, and assumes professional responsibility for the work product.

- **Canon 4**
  A paralegal must use discretion and professional judgment commensurate with knowledge and experience but must not render independent legal judgment in place of an attorney. The services of an attorney are essential to the public interest whenever such legal judgment is required.

- **Canon 5**

  A paralegal must disclose status as a paralegal at the outset of any professional relationship with a client, attorney, a court or administrative agency or personnel thereof, or a member of the general public. A paralegal must act prudently in determining the extent to which a client may be assisted without the presence of an attorney.

- **Canon 6**

  A paralegal must strive to maintain integrity and a high degree of competency through education and training with respect to professional responsibility, local rules and practice, and through continuing education in substantive areas of law to better assist the legal profession in fulfilling its duty to provide legal service.

- **Canon 7**

  A paralegal must protect the confidences of a client and must not violate any rule or statute now in effect or hereafter enacted controlling the doctrine of privileged communications between a client and an attorney.

- **Canon 8**

  A paralegal must disclose to an employer or prospective employer any pre-existing client or personal relationship that may conflict with the interests of the employer or prospective employer and/or their clients.

- **Canon 9**

  A paralegal must do all other things incidental, necessary, or expedient for the attainment of the ethics and responsibilities as defined by statute or rule of court.

- **Canon 10**

  A paralegal's conduct is guided by bar associations' codes of professional responsibility and rules of professional conduct.

NALA MODEL STANDARDS AND GUIDELINES FOR UTILIZATION OF PARALEGALS

Paralegals are a distinguishable group of persons who assist attorneys in the delivery of legal services. Through formal education, training, and experience, paralegals have knowledge and expertise regarding the legal system and substantive and procedural law which qualify them to do work of a legal nature under the supervision of an attorney.

Introduction

The purpose of this annotated version of NALA – The Paralegal Association (NALA)'s Model Standards and Guidelines for the Utilization of Paralegals (the Model) is to provide references to the existing case law and other authorities where the underlying issues have been considered. The authorities cited will serve as a basis upon which conduct of a paralegal may be analyzed as proper or improper.

The Model represents a statement of how the paralegal may function. The Model is not intended to be a comprehensive or exhaustive list of the proper duties of a paralegal. Rather, they are designed as guides to what may or may not be proper conduct for the paralegal. In formulating the Model, the reasoning and rules of law in many reported decisions of disciplinary cases and unauthorized practice of law cases have been analyzed and considered. In addition, the provisions of the American Bar Association's Model Rules

© 2019, 2020, 2021 NALA, Inc. All rights reserved.

of Professional Conduct, as well as the ethical promulgations of various state courts and bar associations, have been considered in the development of the Model.

This Model forms a sound basis for the paralegal and the supervising attorney to follow. This Model will serve as a comprehensive resource document and as a definitive, well-reasoned guide to those considering voluntary standards and guidelines for paralegals.

I. Preamble

Proper utilization of the services of paralegals contributes to the delivery of cost-effective, high-quality legal services. Paralegals and the legal profession should be assured that measures exist for identifying paralegals and their role in assisting attorneys in the delivery of legal services. Therefore, NALA, hereby adopts these Standards and Guidelines as an educational document for the benefit of paralegals and the legal profession.

The three most frequently raised questions concerning paralegals are: (1) How do you define a paralegal? (2) Who is qualified to be identified as a paralegal? and (3) What duties may a paralegal perform? The definition adopted by NALA answers the first question. The Model sets forth minimum education, training, and experience through standards which will assure that an individual utilizing the title "legal assistant" or "paralegal" has the qualifications to be held out to the legal community and the public in that capacity. The Model identifies those acts which the reported cases hold to be forbidden and give examples of services which the paralegal may perform under the supervision of a licensed attorney.

This Model constitutes a statement relating to services performed by paralegals, as defined herein, as approved by court decisions and other sources of authority. The purpose of the Model is not to place limitations or restrictions on the paralegal profession. Rather, the Model is intended to outline for the legal profession an acceptable course of conduct. Voluntary recognition and utilization of the Standards and Guidelines will benefit the entire legal profession and the public it serves.

II. History

NALA adopted this Model in 1984. At the same time, the following definition of a legal assistant was adopted:

> Legal assistants, also known as paralegals, are a distinguishable group of persons who assist attorneys in the delivery of legal services. Through formal education, training, and experience, legal assistants have knowledge and expertise regarding the legal system and substantive and procedural law which qualify them to do work of a legal nature under the supervision of an attorney.

Historically, there have been similar definitions adopted by various legal professional organizations. Recognizing the need for one clear definition, the NALA membership approved a resolution in July 2001 to adopt the paralegal definition of the American Bar Association. The ABA adopted a revised definition in 2020, removing the term "legal assistant." NALA realizes that the terms legal assistant and paralegal are used in the United States, including the authorities cited below. NALA recognizes and supports paralegals, regardless of title; however, as an organization, we primarily use the term paralegal. This definition continues to be used today.

© 2019, 2020, 2021 NALA, Inc. All rights reserved.

III. Definition

A paralegal is a person qualified by education, training, or work experience who is employed or retained by a lawyer, law office, corporation, governmental agency, or other entity who performs specifically delegated substantive legal work for which a lawyer is responsible (Adopted by the ABA in 1997 and by NALA in 2001).

Comment

This definition emphasizes the knowledge and expertise of paralegals in substantive and procedural law obtained through education and work experience. It further defines a paralegal as the professional working under the supervision of an attorney as distinguished from a nonlawyer who delivers services directly to the public without any intervention or review of work product by an attorney. Such unsupervised services, unless authorized by court or agency rules, constitute the unauthorized practice of law.

Statutes, court rules, case law, and bar association documents are additional sources for paralegal definitions. In applying the Standards and Guidelines, it is important to remember that they were developed to apply to the paralegal as defined herein. Lawyers should refrain from labeling those as paralegals who do not meet the criteria set forth in this definition and/or the definitions set forth by state rules, guidelines, or bar associations. Labeling secretaries and other administrative staff as paralegals is inaccurate.

For billing purposes, the services of a legal secretary are considered part of overhead costs and are not recoverable in fee awards. However, the courts have held that fees for paralegal services are recoverable, as long as they are not clerical functions, such as organizing files, copying documents, checking docket, updating files, checking court dates, and delivering papers. As established in *Missouri v. Jenkins* (491 U.S.274, 109 S.Ct. 2463, 2471, n.10 (1989)), tasks performed by legal assistants must be substantive in nature which, absent the legal assistant, the attorney would perform.

There are also case law and Supreme Court Rules addressing the issue of a disbarred attorney serving in the capacity of a paralegal.

IV. Standards

A paralegal should meet certain minimum qualifications. The following standards may be used to determine an individual's qualifications as a paralegal:

- Successful completion of the Certified Paralegal (CP) certifying examination of NALA;

- Graduation from an ABA approved program of study for paralegals;

- Graduation from a course of study for paralegals which is institutionally accredited but not ABA approved, and which requires not less than the equivalent of 60 semester hours of classroom study;

- Graduation from a course of study for paralegals, other than those set forth above, plus not less than six months of in-house training as a paralegal;

- A baccalaureate degree in any field, plus not less than six months in-house training as a paralegal;

- A minimum of three years of law-related experience under the supervision of an attorney, including at least six months of in-house training as a paralegal; or

---

 © 2019, 2020, 2021 NALA, Inc. All rights reserved.

- Two years of in-house training as a paralegal.

For purposes of this Model, "in-house training as a paralegal" means attorney education of the employee concerning paralegal duties. In addition to review and analysis of assignments, the paralegal should receive a reasonable amount of instruction directly related to the duties and obligations of the paralegal.

Comment

This Model sets forth minimum qualifications for a paralegal. These minimum qualifications, as adopted, recognize legal related work backgrounds and formal education backgrounds, both of which provide the paralegal with a broad base in exposure to and knowledge of the legal profession. This background is necessary to assure the public and the legal profession that the employee identified as a paralegal is qualified.

The Certified Paralegal (CP) Exam, established by NALA in 1976, is a voluntary nationwide certification program for paralegals. The CP designation is a statement to the legal profession and the public that the paralegal has met the high levels of knowledge and professionalism required by NALA's certification program. Continuing education requirements, which all Certified Paralegals must meet, assure that high standards are maintained. The CP designation has been recognized as a means of establishing the qualifications of a paralegal in Supreme Court Rules, state court, and bar association standards and utilization guidelines.

On April 30, 2014, The National Commission for Certifying Agencies (NCCA) granted accreditation to the NALA Certified Paralegal Program for demonstrating compliance with the NCCA Standards for the Accreditation of Certification Programs.

NCCA is the accrediting body of the Institute for Credentialing Excellence. The NCCA Standards were created to ensure certification programs adhere to modern standards of practice for the certification industry. The NALA Certified Paralegal program joins an elite group of more than 120 organizations representing over 270 certification programs that have received and maintained NCCA accreditation. The accreditation requires annual reports and renewal every five years to ensure standards.

Certification through NALA is available to all paralegals meeting the educational and experience requirements. Certified Paralegals may also pursue advanced certification in specialty practice areas through the ACP, Advanced Certified Paralegal, credentialing program. Paralegals may also pursue certification based on state laws and procedures in California, Florida, Louisiana, North Carolina, and Texas.

V. Guidelines

These guidelines relating to standards of performance and professional responsibility are intended to aid paralegals and attorneys. The ultimate responsibility rests with an attorney who employs paralegals to educate them with respect to the duties they are assigned and to supervise the manner in which such duties are accomplished.

Comment

In general, a paralegal is allowed to perform any task which is properly delegated and supervised by an attorney, as long as the attorney is ultimately responsible to the client and assumes complete professional responsibility for the work product.

ABA Model Rules of Professional Conduct, Rule 5.3 provides: With respect to a nonlawyer employed or retained by or associated with a lawyer:

- a partner in a law firm shall make reasonable efforts to ensure that the firm has in effect measures giving reasonable assurance that the person's conduct is compatible with the professional obligations of the lawyer;

- a lawyer having direct supervisory authority over the nonlawyer shall make reasonable efforts to ensure that the person's conduct is compatible with the professional obligations of the lawyer; and

- a lawyer shall be responsible for conduct of such a person that would be a violation of the Rules of Professional Conduct if engaged in by a lawyer if:

  □ the lawyer orders or, with the knowledge of the specific conduct, ratifies the conduct involved; or

  □ the lawyer is a partner in the law firm in which the person is employed, or has direct supervisory authority over the person, and knows of the conduct at a time when its consequences can be avoided or mitigated but fails to take reasonable remedial action.

There are many interesting and complex issues involving the use of paralegals. In any discussion of the proper role of a paralegal, attention must be directed to what constitutes the practice of law. Proper delegation to paralegals is further complicated and confused by the lack of an adequate definition of the practice of law.

Kentucky became the first state to adopt a Paralegal Code by Supreme Court Rule. This Code sets forth certain exclusions to the unauthorized practice of law:

> For purposes of this rule, the unauthorized practice of law shall not include any service rendered involving legal knowledge or advice, whether representation, counsel or advocacy, in or out of court, rendered in respect to the acts, duties, obligations, liabilities, or business relations of the one requiring services where:
>
> □ The client understands that the paralegal is not a lawyer;
>
> □ The lawyer supervises the paralegal in the performance of his or her duties; and
>
> □ The lawyer remains fully responsible for such representation including all actions taken or not taken in connection therewith by the paralegal to the same extent as if such representation had been furnished entirely by the lawyer and all such actions had been taken or not taken directly by the attorney (*Paralegal Code*, Ky.S.Ct.R3.700, Sub-Rule 2).

South Dakota Supreme Court Rule 97-25 Utilization Rule a(4) states: The attorney remains responsible for the services performed by the legal assistant to the same extent as though such services had been furnished entirely by the attorney and such actions were those of the attorney.

Guideline 1

Paralegals should:

- Disclose their status as paralegals at the outset of any professional relationship with a client, other attorneys, a court or administrative agency or personnel thereof, or members of the general public;

- Preserve the confidences and secrets of all clients; and

 © 2019, 2020, 2021 NALA, Inc. All rights reserved.

- Understand the attorney's Rules of Professional Responsibility and these Guidelines in order to avoid any action which would involve the attorney in a violation of the Rules or give the appearance of professional impropriety.

Comment

Routine early disclosure of the paralegal's status when dealing with persons outside the attorney's office is necessary to assure that there will be no misunderstanding as to the responsibilities and role of the paralegal. Disclosure may be made in any way that avoids confusion. If the person dealing with the paralegal already knows of the paralegal's status, further disclosure is unnecessary. If at any time in written or oral communication the paralegal becomes aware that the other person may believe the paralegal is an attorney, immediate disclosure should be made as to the paralegal's status.

The attorney should exercise care that the paralegal preserves and refrains from using any confidence or secrets of a client and should instruct the paralegal not to disclose or use any such confidences or secrets.

The paralegal must take any and all steps necessary to prevent conflicts of interest and fully disclose such conflicts to the supervising attorney. Failure to do so may jeopardize both the attorney's representation of the client and the case itself.

Guidelines for the Utilization of Legal Assistant Services adopted December 3, 1994, by the Washington State Bar Association Board of Governors states:

> Guideline 7: A lawyer shall take reasonable measures to prevent conflicts of interest resulting from a legal assistant's other employment or interest insofar as such other employment or interests would present a conflict of interest if it were that of the lawyer.

In Re Complex Asbestos Litigation (232 Cal. App. 3d 572 (Cal. 1991)), addresses the issue wherein a law firm was disqualified due to possession of attorney-client confidences by a legal assistant employee resulting from previous employment by opposing counsel.

In Oklahoma, in an order issued July 12, 2001, in the matter of *Mark A. Hayes, M.D. v. Central States Orthopedic Specialists, Inc.*, a Tulsa County District Court Judge disqualified a law firm from representation of a client on the basis that an ethical screen was an impermissible device to protect from disclosure confidences gained by a nonlawyer employee while employed by another law firm.

In applying the same rules that govern attorneys, the court found that the Rules of Professional Conduct pertaining to confidentiality apply to nonlawyers who leave firms with actual knowledge of material, confidential information, and a screening device is not an appropriate alternative to the imputed disqualification of an incoming legal assistant who has moved from one firm to another during ongoing litigation and has actual knowledge of material, confidential information. The decision was appealed, and the Oklahoma Supreme Court determined that, under certain circumstances, screening is an appropriate management tool for nonlawyer staff.

In 2004, the Nevada Supreme Court also addressed this issue at the urging of the state's paralegals. The Nevada Supreme Court granted a petition to rescind the Court's 1997 ruling in *Ciaffone v. District Court*. In this case, the court clarified the original ruling, stating "mere opportunity to access confidential information does not merit disqualification." The opinion stated instances in which screening may be appropriate and listed minimum screening requirements. The opinion also set forth guidelines that a district court may use to determine if screening has been or may be effective. These considerations are:

- Substantiality of the relationship between the former and current matters

---

- The time elapsed between the matters

- Size of the firm

- Number of individuals presumed to have confidential information

- Nature of their involvement in the former matter

- Timing and features of any measures taken to reduce the danger of disclosure

- Whether the old firm and the new firm represent adverse parties in the same proceeding rather than in different proceedings

The ultimate responsibility for compliance with approved standards of professional conduct rests with the supervising attorney. The burden rests upon the attorney who employs a paralegal to educate the latter with respect to the duties which may be assigned and then to supervise the manner in which the paralegal carries out such duties. However, this does not relieve the paralegal from an independent obligation to refrain from illegal conduct. Additionally, and notwithstanding that the Rules are not binding upon nonlawyers, the very nature of a paralegal's employment imposes an obligation not to engage in conduct which would involve the supervising attorney in a violation of the Rules.

Attorneys must make sufficient background investigation of the prior activities, character, and integrity of their paralegals. Further, attorneys must take all measures necessary to avoid and fully disclose conflicts of interest due to other employment or interests. Failure to do so may jeopardize both the attorney's representation of the client and the case itself.

Paralegal associations strive to maintain the high level of integrity and competence expected of the legal profession and, further, strive to uphold the high standards of ethics. NALA's Code of Ethics and Professional Responsibility states "A paralegal's conduct is guided by bar associations' codes of professional responsibility and rules of professional conduct."

On August 6, 2012, the American Bar Association approved revisions to the Model Rules of Professional Conduct, many of which specifically relate to technology. Changes include the Comment on Rule 1.1 Competence. The change to the Comment, now section 8 on Maintaining Competence, states:

> To maintain the requisite knowledge and skill, a lawyer should keep abreast of changes in the law and its practice, including the benefits and risks associated with relevant technology, engage in continuing study and education and comply with all continuing legal education requirements to which the lawyer is subject.

With the increasing reliance on technology and the movement of the courts toward electronic filing and eDiscovery, it is imperative that paralegals hold to the highest standards of professional and technological competence.

Guideline 2

Paralegals should not: establish attorney-client relationships; set legal fees; give legal opinions or advice; or represent a client before a court, unless authorized to do so by said court; nor engage in, encourage, or contribute to any act which could constitute the unauthorized practice law.

Comment

Case law, court rules, codes of ethics and professional responsibilities, as well as bar ethics opinions now

 © 2019, 2020, 2021 NALA, Inc. All rights reserved.

hold which acts can and cannot be performed by a paralegal. Generally, the determination of what acts constitute the unauthorized practice of law is made by state supreme courts.

Numerous cases exist relating to the unauthorized practice of law. Courts have gone so far as to prohibit the paralegal from preparation of divorce kits and assisting in preparation of bankruptcy forms and, more specifically, from providing basic information about procedures and requirements, deciding where information should be placed on forms, and responding to questions from debtors regarding the interpretation or definition of terms.

Cases have identified certain areas in which an attorney has a duty to act, but it is interesting to note that none of these cases state that it is improper for an attorney to have the initial work performed by the paralegal. This again points out the importance of adequate supervision by the employing attorney.

An attorney can be found to have aided in the unauthorized practice of law when delegating acts which cannot be performed by a paralegal.

Guideline 3

Paralegals may perform services for an attorney in the representation of a client, provided:

- The services performed by the paralegal do not require the exercise of independent professional legal judgment;

- The attorney maintains a direct relationship with the client and maintains control of all client matters;

- The attorney supervises the paralegal;

- The attorney remains professionally responsible for all work on behalf of the client, including any actions taken or not taken by the paralegal in connection therewith; and

- The services performed supplement, merge with, and become the attorney's work product.

Comment

Paralegals, whether employees or independent contractors, perform services for the attorney in the representation of a client. Attorneys should delegate work to paralegals commensurate with their knowledge and experience and provide appropriate instruction and supervision concerning the delegated work, as well as ethical acts of their employment. Ultimate responsibility for the work product of a paralegal rests with the attorney. However, a paralegal must use discretion and professional judgment and must not render independent legal judgment in place of an attorney.

The work product of a paralegal is subject to civil rules governing discovery of materials prepared in anticipation of litigation, whether the paralegal is viewed as an extension of the attorney or as another representative of the party itself (Fed.R.Civ.P. 26 (b) (3) and (5)).

Guideline 4

In the supervision of a paralegal, consideration should be given to:

- Designating work assignments that correspond to the paralegal's abilities, knowledge, training, and experience;

- Educating and training the paralegal with respect to professional responsibility, local rules and practices, and firm policies;

- Monitoring the work and professional conduct of the paralegal to ensure that the work is substantively correct and timely performed;

- Providing continuing education for the paralegal in substantive matters through courses, institutes, workshops, seminars, and in-house training; and

- Encouraging and supporting membership and active participation in professional organizations.

Comment

Attorneys are responsible for the actions of their employees in both malpractice and disciplinary proceedings. In the vast majority of cases, the courts have not censured attorneys for a particular act delegated to the paralegal, but rather, have been critical of and imposed sanctions against attorneys for failure to adequately supervise the paralegal. The attorney's responsibility for supervision of paralegals must be more than a willingness to accept responsibility and liability for the paralegals' work. Supervision of a paralegal must be offered in both the procedural and substantive legal areas. The attorney must delegate work based upon the education, knowledge, and abilities of the paralegal and must monitor the work product and conduct of the paralegal to ensure that the work performed is substantively correct and competently performed in a professional manner.

Michigan State Board of Commissioners has adopted Guidelines for the Utilization of Legal Assistants (April 23, 1993). These guidelines, in part, encourage employers to support legal assistant participation in continuing education programs to ensure that the legal assistant remains competent in the fields of practice in which the legal assistant is assigned.

The working relationship between the lawyer and the paralegal should extend to cooperative efforts on public service activities wherever possible. Participation in pro bono activities is encouraged in ABA Guideline 10.

Guideline 5

In the supervision, except as otherwise provided by statute, court rule or decision, administrative rule or regulation, or the attorney's rules of professional responsibility, and within the preceding parameters and proscriptions, a paralegal may perform any function delegated by an attorney, including, but not limited to, the following:

- Conduct client interviews and maintain general contact with the client after the establishment of the attorney-client relationship, so long as the client is aware of the status and function of the paralegal, and the client contact is under the supervision of the attorney;

- Locate and interview witnesses, so long as the witnesses are aware of the status and function of the paralegal;

- Conduct investigations and statistical and documentary research for review by the attorney;

- Conduct legal research for review by the attorney;

- Draft legal documents for review by the attorney;

- Draft correspondence and pleadings for review by and signature of the attorney;

 © 2019, 2020, 2021 NALA, Inc. All rights reserved.

- Summarize depositions, interrogatories, and testimony for review by the attorney;

- Attend executions of wills, real estate closings, depositions, court or administrative hearings, and trials with the attorney; and

- Author and sign letters providing the paralegal's status is clearly indicated and the correspondence does not contain independent legal opinions or legal advice.

Comment

The United States Supreme Court has recognized the variety of tasks being performed by paralegals and has noted that use of paralegals encourages cost-effective delivery of legal services (*Missouri v. Jenkins*, 491 U.S.274, 109 S.Ct. 2463, 2471, n.10 (1989)). In *Missouri v. Jenkins*, the Court further held that paralegal time should be included in compensation for attorney fee awards at the market rate of the relevant community to bill paralegal time. Courts have held that paralegal fees are not a part of the overall overhead of a law firm. Paralegal services are billed separately by attorneys and decrease litigation expenses. Tasks performed by paralegals must contain substantive legal work under the direction or supervision of an attorney, such that if the paralegal were not present, the work would be performed by the attorney.

In *Taylor v. Chubb* (874 P.2d 806 (Okla. 1994)), the Court ruled that attorney fees awarded should include fees for services performed by paralegals and, further, defined tasks which may be performed by the paralegal under the supervision of an attorney including, among others: interview clients; draft pleadings and other documents; carry on legal research, both conventional and computer aided; research public records; prepare discovery requests and responses; schedule depositions and prepare notices and subpoenas; summarize depositions and other discovery responses; coordinate and manage document production; locate and interview witnesses; organize pleadings, trial exhibits, and other documents; prepare witness and exhibit lists; prepare trial notebooks; prepare for the attendance of witnesses at trial; and assist lawyers at trials.

Except for the specific proscription contained in Guideline 1, the reported cases do not limit the duties which may be performed by a paralegal under the supervision of the attorney.

An attorney may not split legal fees with a paralegal, nor pay a paralegal for the referral of legal business. An attorney may compensate a paralegal based on the quantity and quality of the paralegal's work and value of that work to a law practice.

Conclusion

These Standards and Guidelines were developed from generally accepted practices. Each supervising attorney must be aware of the specific rules, decisions, and statutes applicable to paralegals within the paralegal's jurisdiction.

Addendum

For further information, the following cases may be helpful to you:

Duties

Taylor v. Chubb, 874 P.2d 806 (Okla. 1994); *McMackin v. McMackin*, 651 A.2d 778 (Del.Fam Ct 1993);

© 2019, 2020, 2021 NALA, Inc. All rights reserved.

Davis v. Mostyn Law Firm, P.C. (S.D. Tex., 2012)

Work Product

Fine v. Facet Aerospace Products Co., 133 F.R.D. 439 (S.D.N.Y. 1990)

Unauthorized Practice of Law

Akron Bar Assn. v. Green, 673 N.E.2d 1307 (Ohio 1997); *In Re Hessinger & Associates*, 192 B.R. 211 (N.D. Calif. 1996); *In the Matter of Bright*, 171 B.R. 799 (Bkrtcy. E.D. Mich); *Louisiana State Bar Assn v. Edwins*, 540 So.2d 294 (La. 1989); *Doe v. Condon*, 532 S.E.2d 879, 341 S.C. 22 (S.C., 2000)

Attorney/Client Privilege

In Re Complex Asbestos Litigation, 232 Cal. App. 3d 572 (Calif. 1991); *Makita Corp. v. U.S.*, 819 F.Supp. 1099 (CIT 1993)

Conflicts

In Re Complex Asbestos Litigation, 232 Cal. App. 3d 572 (Calif. 1991); *Makita Corp. v. U.S.*, 819 F.Supp. 1099 (CIT 1993); *Phoenix Founders, Inc., v. Marshall*, 887 S.W.2d 831 (Tex. 1994); *Smart Industries v. Superior Court*, 876 P.2d 1176 (Ariz. App. Div.1 1994)

Supervision

Matter of Martinez, 754 P.2d 842 (N.M. 1988); *State v. Barrett*, 483 P.2d 1106 (Kan. 1971); *Hayes v. Central States Orthopedic Specialists, Inc.*, 2002 OK 30, 51 P.3d 562; *Liebowitz v. Eighth Judicial District Court of Nevada*, Nev Sup Ct., No 39683, November 3, 2003, clarified in part and overrules in part *Ciaffone v. District Court*, 113 Nev 1165, 945. P2d 950 (1997)

Fee Awards

In Re Bicoastal Corp., 121 B.R. 653 (Bktrcy.M.D.Fla. 1990); *In Re Carter*, 101 B.R. 170 (Bkrtcy.D.S.D. 1989); *Taylor v. Chubb*, 874 P.2d 806 (Okla.1994); *Missouri v. Jenkins*, 491 U.S. 274, 109 S.Ct. 2463, 105 L.Ed.2d 229 (1989) 11 U.S.C.A.'330; *McMackin v. McMackin,* Del.Fam.Ct. 651 A.2d 778 (1993); *Miller v. Alamo*, 983 F.2d 856 (8th Cir. 1993); *Stewart v. Sullivan*, 810 F.Supp. 1102 (D.Hawaii 1993); *In Re Yankton College*, 101 B.R. 151 (Bkrtcy. D.S.D. 1989); *Stacey v. Stroud*, 845 F.Supp. 1135 (S.D.W.Va. 1993); *Missouri v. Jenkins Agyei*, 491 U.S. 274, 109 S.Ct. 2463, 105 L.Ed.2d 229 (1989); Upheld by the U.S. Supreme Court in *Richlin Sec. Serv. Co. v. Chertoff*, 128 S.Ct. 2007, 170 L.Ed.2d 960, 553 U.S. 571, 8 Cal. Daily Op. Serv. 6601, 22 Fla. L. Weekly Fed. S 279, 76 USLW 4360, 2008 Daily Journal D.A.R. 8004 (2008); *Nolen v. Colvin* (W.D. Okla., 2013) – Court utilizes NALA's wage report to affirm paralegals rate in the case

Court Appearances

Louisiana State Bar Assn v. Edwins, 540 So.2d 294 (La. 1989)

In addition to the above referenced cases, you may contact your state bar association for information

---

© 2019, 2020, 2021 NALA, Inc. All rights reserved.

regarding guidelines for the utilization of paralegals that may have been adopted by the bar, or ethical opinions concerning the utilization of paralegals.

State Regulations and Several Comparisons

California

In California, paralegals are required to attend more mandatory continuing legal ethics seminars on an annual basis than attorneys. Specifically, the State Bar of California mandates that attorneys complete 25 total hours of mandatory continuing legal education every three years, four hours of which must be in legal ethics. In comparison, paralegals in this state are also required to complete four hours of legal ethics, every two years.

California Business & Professions Code §6450

(d) Every two years, commencing January 1, 2007, any person who is working as a paralegal shall be required to certify completion of four hours of mandatory continuing legal education in legal ethics and four hours of mandatory continuing legal education in either general law or in an area of specialized law. All continuing legal education courses shall meet the requirements of Section 6070. Certification of these continuing education requirements shall be made with the paralegal's supervising attorney. The paralegal shall be responsible for keeping a record of the certifications.

Furthermore, according to California Business & Professions Code §6452, (a) It is unlawful for a person to identify themselves as a paralegal on any advertisement, letterhead, business card, or sign, or elsewhere unless they have met the qualifications of subdivision (c) of Section 6450 and performs all services under the direction and supervision of an attorney who is an active member of the State Bar of California or an attorney practicing law in the federal courts of this state who is responsible for all of the services performed by the paralegal. The business card of a paralegal shall include the name of the law firm where they are employed or a statement that they are employed by, or contracting with, a licensed attorney.

(b) An attorney who uses the services of a paralegal is liable for any harm caused as the result of the paralegal's negligence, misconduct, or violation of this chapter.

California Business & Professions Code §6453

A paralegal is subject to the same duty as an attorney specified in subdivision (e) of Section 6068 to maintain inviolate the confidentiality, and at every peril to themselves to preserve the attorney-client privilege, of a consumer for whom the paralegal has provided any of the services described in subdivision (a) of Section 6450.

North Carolina

In North Carolina, the North Carolina State Bar – Paralegal Certification website page indicates the following:

> [The] State Bar's paralegal certification program promotes proper utilization of paralegals and helps to ensure that legal services are professionally and ethically offered to the public. Paralegals, like lawyers, should be held to the highest ethical and professional

standards. The State Bar regulates the activities of paralegals indirectly through each lawyer's professional duty to supervise employees and contractors to whom legal work is delegated. The Rules of Professional Conduct establish the standards for the supervision of nonlawyer assistants, including paralegals. The statutes on unauthorized practice of law in Chapter 84 of the North Carolina General Statutes, Rules 5.3 and 5.5 of the Rules of Professional Conduct, and the formal ethics opinions interpreting those rules determine the extent to which law-related tasks may properly be performed by paralegals.

Texas

Texas was the first state bar association in the United States to create a "Paralegal Division." On the Texas State Bar website, the "Code of Ethics and Professional Responsibility" can be found with the following canons which are meant to be a guide:

- **Canon 1**
  A paralegal shall not engage in the practice of law as defined by statutes or court decisions, including but not limited to accepting cases or clients, setting fees, giving legal advice or appearing in a representative capacity in court or before an administrative or regulatory agency (unless otherwise authorized by statute, court or agency rules); the paralegal shall assist in preventing the unauthorized practice of law.

- **Canon 2**
  A paralegal shall not perform any of the duties that attorneys only may perform or do things which attorneys themselves may not do.

- **Canon 3**
  A paralegal shall exercise care in using independent professional judgment and in determining the extent to which a client may be assisted without the presence of any attorney, and shall not act in matters involving professional legal judgment.

- **Canon 4**
  A paralegal shall preserve and protect the confidences and secrets of a client.

- **Canon 5**
  A paralegal shall not solicit legal business on behalf of an attorney.

- **Canon 6**
  A paralegal shall not engage in performing paralegal functions other than under the direct supervision of an attorney and shall not advertise or contract with members of the general public for the performance of paralegal functions.

- **Canon 7**
  A paralegal shall avoid, if at all possible, any interest or association which constitutes a conflict of interest pertaining to a client matter and shall inform the supervising attorney of the existence of any possible conflict.

- **Canon 8**
  A paralegal shall maintain a high standard of ethical conduct and shall contribute to the integrity of the paralegal profession.

- **Canon 9**
  A paralegal shall maintain a high degree of competency to better assist the legal profession in

 © 2019, 2020, 2021 NALA, Inc. All rights reserved.

fulfilling its duty to provide quality legal services to the public.

- **Canon 10**
  A paralegal shall do all other things incidental, necessary or expedient to enhance professional responsibility and the participation of paralegals in the administration of justice and public service in cooperation with the legal profession. Adopted March 27, 1982, Amended June 26, 2005 - Paralegal Division, State Bar of Texas

Florida

In Florida, according to the Florida Bar, a Registered Paralegal must follow its Code of Ethics and Responsibility as follows:

20-7. Code of Ethics and Responsibility Rule 20-7.1

Generally, a Florida Registered Paralegal shall adhere to the following Code of Ethics and Responsibility:

- **Disclosure**. A Florida Registered Paralegal shall disclose his or her status as a Florida Registered Paralegal at the outset of any professional relationship with a client, lawyers, a court or administrative agency or personnel thereof, and members of the general public. Use of the initials FRP meets the disclosure requirement only if the title paralegal also appears. For example, J. Doe, FRP, Paralegal. Use of the word "paralegal" alone also complies.

- **Confidentiality and Privilege**. A Florida Registered Paralegal shall preserve the confidences and secrets of all clients. A Florida Registered Paralegal must protect the confidences of a client, and it shall be unethical for a Florida Registered Paralegal to violate any statute or rule now in effect or hereafter to be enacted controlling privileged communications.

- **Appearance of Impropriety or Unethical Conduct**. A Florida Registered Paralegal should understand the attorney's Rules of Professional Conduct and this code in order to avoid any action that would involve the attorney in a violation of the rules or give the appearance of professional impropriety. It is the obligation of the Florida Registered Paralegal to avoid conduct that would cause the lawyer to be unethical or even appear to be unethical, and loyalty to the lawyer is incumbent upon the Florida Registered Paralegal.

- **Prohibited Conduct**. A Florida Registered Paralegal should not:

  - establish attorney-client relationships, accept cases, set legal fees, give legal opinions or advice, or represent a client before a court or other tribunal, unless authorized to do so by the court or tribunal;

  - engage in, encourage, or contribute to any act that could constitute the unlicensed practice of law;

  - engage in the practice of law;

  - perform any of the duties that attorneys only may perform nor do things that attorneys themselves may not do.

© 2019, 2020, 2021 NALA, Inc. All rights reserved.

New York

Engagement letters set forth by attorneys defines the terms of the relationship between the clients and the law firm. According to the New York State Bar Association's Committee on Professional Ethics, the hourly rates of paralegals are usually set forth within the engagement letters, and points out the following:

Because New York State does not require paralegals to be certified, the term "paralegal" does not imply certification. Consequently, it is not deceptive for a lawyer to use the title "paralegal" to describe a layperson who assists the lawyer with substantive legal work for which bar admission is not necessary but who is not a graduate of a paralegal program or certified by any certifying body. Nor is it improper to charge for the time of such paralegal in accordance with the lawyer's engagement letter.

The only requirement in the Rules pertaining to the work of paralegals is that an employing law firm must ensure that the work of nonlawyers who work for the firm is "adequately supervised, as appropriate." Rule 5.3(a). The degree of supervision required is that which is "reasonable under the circumstances, taking into account such factors as the experience of the person whose work is being supervised, the amount of work involved and the likelihood that ethical problems might arise in the course of working on the matter." Id. See also N.Y. State 393 (1975) (degree of responsibility that may be entrusted to individual legal assistants may vary according to their education and experience).

Source: Ethics Opinion 1079 - New York State Bar Association (nysba.org)

CONFLICTS OF INTEREST

A conflict of interest is a situation where the consideration of one party is to the detriment of another. In today's legal landscape, paralegals are faced with conflicts of interest with the clients they work with, their co-workers, supervisors, and more. Regardless of any situation that paralegals may find themselves in, it is imperative that conflicts of interest be avoided.

A paralegal can avoid a conflict of interest by asking the law firm for a list of legal cases that the firm is handling. The paralegal should review that list to identify the clients they may recognize from their previous paralegal positions at other law firms or corporations. If there is a potential conflict, the paralegal must ask for a waiver from one party or be recused from working on the case in question to protect both clients' interests and the paralegal's law firm. Many sometimes wonder why and how working for prior law firms or corporations that represent opposing clients can cause harm. If the paralegal works for two clients with opposing interests, they may have information that could be detrimental to one or the other. This is the case even if the paralegal no longer works for one of those clients and can jeopardize the entire case. For example, the Georgia case, *Hodge v. Urfa-Sexton*, LP, 295 Ga. 136 (2014), provides a scenario in which the Hodge law firm employed a paralegal who worked at another law office that was suing one of the new law firm's clients. The paralegal and the law firm did not reveal the conflict of interest until several months later. The former law office where the paralegal was employed filed a motion to disqualify the law firm which months earlier had hired the paralegal. Had the paralegal and law firm addressed the conflict of interest earlier, the results of the scenario might have been very different.

An ethical wall is a screening mechanism that protects a client from a conflict of interest. Specifically, the ethical wall is utilized by asking attorneys and paralegals regarding any conflicts that may arise from the law firm's client list (such as when a lawyer or paralegal had previously worked for another firm for the

---

 © 2019, 2020, 2021 NALA, Inc. All rights reserved.

same case). When this occurs, all attorneys and paralegals who will be screened from the matter should be informed that they are screened from such conflict of interest matters and the reasons for the screen. Usually, law firms and companies distribute the notice in writing. This could be in the form of an email and demonstrates that the firm is exercising its ethical obligations. It is important for a firm to have proof it notified all affected and potentially disqualified persons of the screen as soon as possible, and that they received a notification that reflects specific instructions (such as disqualified persons would be blocked to access certain files, etc.) and requiring and retaining written acknowledgment of the notice of a screen.

Paralegals must keep in mind that according to the American Bar Association, Rule 1.7, conflict of interest, current clients:

- Except as provided in paragraph (b), a lawyer shall not represent a client if the representation involves a concurrent conflict of interest. A concurrent conflict of interest exists if:

    ▫ The representation of one client will be directly adverse to another client; or

    ▫ There is a significant risk that the representation of one or more clients will be materially limited by the lawyer's responsibilities to another client, a former client, or by a third person or by a personal interest of the lawyer.

It should also be noted that lawyers cannot:

- Enter into business ownership transactions with a client unless the terms are fair; the client has a chance to seek independent legal advice, and the client consents;

- Assume representation when the opposing party is represented by counsel who is related to the lawyer, unless the client knows of the relationship and consents to the representation;

- Acquire proprietary interest in litigation being handled for a client except by reasonable contingency fee contract for lawful attorney's lien to secure fees or expenses; and

- Advise or assist a client to engage in conduct that the lawyer knows to be fraudulent or criminal.

UNAUTHORIZED PRACTICE OF LAW (UPL)

Unauthorized Practice of Law (UPL) definitions vary from state to state, so paralegals must become familiar as to what the definition of UPL is in their own state. Most states, with the exception of California, require law school graduation as a prerequisite to sit for the bar examinations. In general terms, the practice of law is any act that involves the giving of legal advice to clients, drafting legal documents for clients, and representing clients in legal negotiations and court proceedings such as lawsuits. Attorneys can also commit UPL if they have been disbarred or suspended from practice, and yet still practice law.

In general, paralegals cannot:

- Provide direct legal advice to clients;

- Represent a client in court;

- Accept cases;

- Set fees;

- Negotiate legal matters on behalf of clients;

© 2019, 2020, 2021 NALA, Inc. All rights reserved.

- Represent clients in court settings;

- Tell clients directly which legal forms to use; and

- Contract with, or be employed by, a natural person other than an attorney to perform paralegal services.

Beyond such limitations listed above, paralegals can perform many legal tasks on behalf of the law firm clients as long as three criteria are met:

- The paralegal's work is properly supervised by a licensed attorney;

- The supervising attorney maintains a direct relationship with a client; and

- The supervising attorney assumes full professional responsibility for the work product.

A paralegal's NALA membership and CP designation may be permanently revoked if it has been found that they have violated a UPL statute.

One of the best ways to not appear to be involved with the unauthorized practice of law is to make it known that one is a paralegal. A paralegal's business cards, letterhead, and email signatures should clearly state that one is a legal assistant or paralegal. During meetings with clients, if the attorney has not already introduced the paralegal by title, the paralegal should introduce themselves as a paralegal.

COMMUNICATIONS

Communications, whether verbal or written, with the paralegal's attorney, fellow law firm employees, clients, and opposing party can be critical to one's cases, one's success at the firm, and the paralegal's employment. Along with communication comes attorney-client privilege, which is defined as a client's right to refuse to disclose and prevent any other person from disclosing confidential communications between the client and attorney. According to the American Bar Association, "[T]he attorney-client privilege and the ethical obligation of client confidentiality extend to the paralegal and all nonlawyers working with the lawyer. As a practical matter, lawyers must implement policies to protect client information, and to train their paralegals about the importance of client confidentiality."

One of the biggest complaints that attorneys encounter is the lack of communication with clients. Often, paralegals will come across clients' requests inquiring about the status of their cases. Paralegals can assist their attorneys in this area by exercising due diligence – communicating (reminding) the attorney that a client has repeatedly called the office to find out the status of the case. With the attorney's permission and oversight, the paralegal can convey the case status to clients, thereby mitigating the client's anxiety to obtain such information – and reducing the chances that the client would reach out to the state bar association to file a complaint.

Because many law firm and corporate employees communicate via email, many times paralegals will email attorneys' work-product. Work-product refers to the writings, notes, memoranda, reports on conversations with the client or witness, research, and confidential materials that reflect an attorney's or paralegal's impressions, conclusions, opinions, or legal research, and suggested legal strategies or theories. Work-product materials are confidential and are not required to be submitted in answer to discovery requests or subpoenas.

For many reasons, the paralegal should type in the "Subject" line of the email (or on the top of the email): "ATTORNEY WORK-PRODUCT." The work-product doctrine protects materials prepared in

© 2019, 2020, 2021 NALA, Inc. All rights reserved.

anticipation of litigation from discovery by opposing counsel. It is also known as the work-product rule, the work-product immunity, and the work-product exception. It is sometimes mistakenly called work-product "privilege." The work-product doctrine is more inclusive than the attorney-client privilege. Where the attorney-client privilege only applies to communications between the attorney and the client, the work-product doctrine includes materials prepared by persons other than the attorney, such as paralegals. Attorney work-product are the products that paralegals can create for the attorney that are confidential, such as those referenced in the above paragraph.

Communications with a paralegal's legal team is very significant for a number of reasons. A paralegal should be proactive with their communications with all members of the legal team to not just receive specific directions for their multiple projects, but to also learn about law updates and which legal procedures and practices are being implemented and utilized in the law firm. Some legal practices and procedures can require increasing one's technology skills within the legal field, especially since technology has grown exponentially more important and complex. As a paralegal, it is important to keep abreast with the laws as well as current and upcoming legal practices and technology trends within the legal field.

CASES

- *Missouri vs. Jenkins*, 491 U.S. 274, 109 S. Ct. 2463, 105L. Ed.2d 229 (1989): The United States Supreme Court declared that a legal fee may include a charge for legal assistant services at market rates rather than actual cost to attorneys.

- *American Petroleum Institute vs. United States*, 52F. 3d 1113 (Fed.Cir. 1996): This case's award of paralegal fees was found to be reasonable and appropriate as a component of attorneys' fees, however, the court reduced such fees when it found them to be unreasonable.

- *Hodge v. Urfa-Sexton*, LP, 295 Ga. 136 (2014): provides a scenario in which the Hodge law firm employed a paralegal who worked at another law office that was suing one of the new law firm's clients.

ETHICAL ISSUES – SCENARIOS AND DISCUSSION

Example:

Samantha works at a law firm that has many well-known clients. After a long and stressful day at the office, Samantha comes home and tells her husband about some of the interesting details of a case that involve a high-profile client. Is Samantha breaking attorney-client privilege?

Proposed Answer/Solution:
Yes, privileged information should not be discussed with anybody outside the law firm, not even your spouse.

Example:

Jonathan, a paralegal, overhears friends discussing a divorce. Jonathan immediately promotes the family law firm where he works and gives out his business cards, so that his friend can possibly retain the attorney for whom he works. Is Jonathan violating any rule?

Proposed Answer/Solution:
Please be sure to check with your state bar association regarding marketing practices for attorneys and law firms. Several bar associations have specific requirements as to which employees may or may not provide marketing and client development materials.

Example:

Ana begins employment as a paralegal at a new law firm. During Ana's first day, she realizes that one of the clients who has been assigned to her and her attorney was a client she worked for at another law firm. What should Ana do?

Proposed Answer/Solution:
Immediately disclose this information to the supervising attorney(s) as this may cause ethical issues and may jeopardize the case.

Example:

Randy, a paralegal, notices that the workload of his legal team is extremely heavy, and that sometimes clients leave voicemail messages and send emails indicating how frustrated they are because the attorney working on their cases does not return their calls. Randy understands through several communications with clients that their main concerns are knowing the status of their cases. How can Randy assist the attorney with such matters?

Proposed Answer/Solution:
Randy should speak with the supervising attorney to possibly identify what is the status of the client's case. With the permission of the supervising attorney, Randy can email the client the case status as long as he copies the supervising attorney. Paralegals should know that some of the reasons clients report their attorneys to the state bar include lack of communication and not knowing the current status of their cases.

 © 2019, 2020, 2021 NALA, Inc. All rights reserved.

Example:

> A paralegal working for a major law firm is asked to introduce himself to a prospective client as an associate attorney of the firm. Is this an ethical violation, and what, if anything, would this cause if the prospective client retains them?
>
> **Proposed Answer/Solution:**
> Yes, this is an ethical and professional violation. Individuals who have posed as attorneys when they are not (and those who knowingly assisted in such situations) can be charged with a criminal offense and can face jail time.

Example:

> A paralegal graduate is looking for employment. During the interview, the office manager tells the paralegal that he wants to have the paralegal set up a desk in the office and help the agents and their clients process legal forms, for which the paralegal will charge the agents and clients directly. The paralegal will be responsible for preparing motions to compel, oppositions, and replies. The office manager assures the paralegal that all the documents are on forms in the office database. Should the paralegal take the job? Why or why not?
>
> **Proposed Answer/Solution:**
> No, the paralegal should not take the job. The law firm should charge the clients directly, not the paralegal. On a related note, many state bar associations do not allow "fee-splitting" between attorneys and paralegals but may allow fee-splitting between attorneys.

Example:

> Upon an attorney winning a case for her client, a check soon arrives from the opposing party for a settlement in connection with the case. The paralegal later notices that the attorney uses some of the settlement monies for a variety of expenses such as office utility bills and office supplies. What ethical issues are involved with these expenditures? What factors are involved in determining the ethical or unethical nature of this act?
>
> **Proposed Answer/Solution:**
> In this situation, the attorney may be liable for comingling of funds, which is an ethical and professional violation. Paralegals should make themselves familiar with the state bar rules to understand such scenarios.

Example:

> A paralegal's supervising attorney wants to give a paralegal compensation for hard work. The supervising attorney tells the paralegal that they will be given 20 percent of the fee received from the case. Should the paralegal accept this offer? Why or why not?
>
> **Proposed Answer/Solution:**
> No, the paralegal should not accept this offer. Many state bar associations do not allow "fee-splitting" between attorneys and paralegals but may allow fee-splitting between attorneys. The paralegal should indicate that they should be paid for all hours worked.

Example:

> A paralegal, Jason, has over 17 years' experience in employment law. His friend, Susan, who has known Jason as a good friend for over 20 years, felt comfortable to ask Jason a legal question relating to employment law. She believes she may have a claim against her employer. Should Jason answer Susan's legal question?
>
> **Proposed Answer/Solution:**
> No, since answering such a question may be construed as giving legal advice, which can equate to the unauthorized practice of law (UPL) by a paralegal. UPL goes against the NALA Code of Ethics and Professional Responsibility and state bar associations' rules of conduct. In Florida, Texas, and California, paralegals who are involved with the unauthorized practice of law may face fines and/or imprisonment.

 © 2019, 2020, 2021 NALA, Inc. All rights reserved.

CHAPTER 9: PRACTICE QUESTIONS

1. **What is one example of a conflict of interest?**

   A. Working for the same law firm where a paralegal's co-workers were once employed

   B. Disclosing details of a high-profile case to one's neighbors

   C. Being employed as a contract paralegal for numerous law firms

   D. Working or knowing about a case where one's prior law firm represented the opposing party

2. **What is one of most common complaints about attorneys?**

   A. They have too many clients to oversee each case individually

   B. At times, they fail to communicate with the client regarding the status of their case

   C. At times, they are rude to the staff

   D. Most are accused of commingling client and general funds

3. **How can a paralegal assist an attorney with communicating with the clients of the law firm?**

   A. Remind the attorney that clients are calling several times for case status

   B. With the permission and oversight of the attorney, call the clients to discuss case status

   C. Write the details of the clients' request for case status

   D. All the above

4. **What is an example of unauthorized practice of law?**

   A. An attorney giving legal advice to prospective clients

   B. An attorney giving legal forms to a client

   C. A paralegal giving a legal opinion to a friend

   D. A paralegal giving legal forms to a client

5. **What is an ethical wall?**

   A. An ethical wall is a screening mechanism that protects a client from a conflict of interest

   B. An ethical wall is a screening mechanism that protects the public from a conflict of interest

   C. An ethical wall is a screening mechanism that protects the courts from a conflict of interest

   D. An ethical wall is a screening mechanism that protects the client from slander

6. **What can happen to a law firm if it is discovered that the attorney or law firm did not properly identify and disclose a conflict of interest?**

    A. The law firm can be disqualified

    B. The case would be transferred to another court jurisdiction

    C. The case would be expedited

    D. The case would be given to another judge

7. **The Georgia case, *Hodge v. Urfa-Sexton,* LP, 295 Ga. 136 (2014), provides a scenario where a:**

    A. Case was adjudicated faster

    B. Conflict of interest was discovered at a later time and eventually caused the law firm to be disqualified

    C. Conflict of interest was discovered at a later time and eventually caused the case to be transferred to another jurisdiction

    D. Conflict of interest was discovered at a later time and eventually caused the case to be given to another judge

8. **Can an attorney be guilty of unauthorized practice of law?**

    A. No

    B. Yes, only if the legal advice is not their area of legal expertise

    C. Yes, if the state bar association has suspended or disbarred their membership

    D. Yes, if the state bar association indicated that the attorney has had prior complaints

9. **What is a conflict of interest?**

    A. A conflict of interest is a situation when the consideration of one party is the same as the other

    B. A conflict of interest is a situation when the consideration of one party is realized

    C. A conflict of interest is a situation when the consideration of one party is ignored

    D. A conflict of interest is a situation when the consideration of one party is to the detriment of another

10. **What is one way that a paralegal can ensure their ethical compliance in their own state?**

    A. Adhere to the local paralegal association's ethical guidelines

    B. Adhere to the local bar association's ethical guidelines

    C. Know about the state's laws or statutes concerning paralegal requirements

    D. Know about the local state bar association's ethical guidelines

    E. Locate and understand the state laws or statutes concerning paralegal ethical requirements. If none, then refer to the state bar association's ethical guidelines.

© 2019, 2020, 2021 NALA, Inc. All rights reserved.

11. **When emailing legal research results, notes, and memoranda, the paralegal should use the term, "ATTORNEY WORK-PRODUCT" in the email "Subject" line because:**

A. The work-product doctrine protects materials prepared in anticipation of litigation from discovery by opposing counsel

B. The work-product doctrine is more exclusive than the attorney-client privilege

C. Where the attorney-client privilege only applies to communications between the attorney and the client, the work-product doctrine includes materials prepared only by the attorney

D. Attorney work-product are the products that paralegals can create for the attorney that are not confidential

12. **A paralegal should be proactive with their communications with all members of the legal team to:**

A. Know about the legal procedures and practices that are being implemented and utilized in the law firm

B. Only understand specific directions for their multiple projects

C. Learn about law updates and which legal procedures and practices are being implemented and utilized in the law firm

D. Know about law updates that are being implemented and utilized in the law firm

© 2019, 2020, 2021 NALA, Inc. All rights reserved.

SKILLS EXAM
—CHAPTERS—

Grammar

Written by Elizabeth W. Marchioni

© 2019, 2020, 2021 NALA, Inc. All rights reserved.

After reading this chapter the paralegal should be able to:

- Apply the correct rules of grammar to legal writing.

- Write more clearly, precisely, and effectively in the legal setting.

- Evaluate and edit legal writing when proofreading the paralegal's own work or the work of others.

- Differentiate between grammar conventions that apply to formal legal writing versus less formal means of communication.

The importance of correct grammar in legal writing cannot be stressed enough. Correct grammatical construction strongly impacts how people understand and misunderstand communication, particularly written communication. For example, the use of the correct article (the, a/an) will affect the interpretation of legal documents such as contracts, wills, and deeds. The proper use of the article may potentially change the outcome of a legal case. The following two sentences illustrate this point:

1. **John Bradford will sell *a* black car to Jose Perez for $8,000.00.**

2. **John Bradford will sell *the* black car to Jose Perez for $8,000.00.**

In the first sentence, John has contracted to sell Jose what seems to be one of several black cars that John owns. The sentence does not clarify which of the black cars John must sell to Jose. In the second sentence it appears that John has contracted to sell a particular car, the only black car that he owns, to Jose. While neither sentence is precise enough for an agreement of sale, the second sentence is clearly more definitive.

Although the rules of grammar and punctuation fluctuate and change over time, the legal field is conservative and slow to adopt such changes. Legal writing is formal writing which differs from more informal spoken English and more informal types of writing such as text messages, email, and even professional writings such as newspaper or magazine articles. The "old rules" still apply in the law. For example, it is important to avoid being too informal by using language in the vernacular which is everyday language, including slang and the way we generally talk to people. On the other hand, it also important to avoid jargon and "legalese" in modern legal writing. This chapter is intended to provide the paralegal with some of the more important, basic rules of grammar and to address certain common mistakes in legal writing. However, the chapter does not cover the entire spectrum of rules and application of grammar. The reader is encouraged to consult additional sources such as those listed at the end of the chapter.

While many people use the words grammar and punctuation interchangeably, they do have different meanings. Grammar refers to the structure of a language such as the order of words in a sentence, while punctuation refers to the marks and symbols used to clarify the meaning of those words. This chapter of the manual will focus on grammar, and there is a separate chapter that will focus on punctuation.

THE PARTS OF SPEECH

All words can be classified into eight or nine (some authorities use 10) parts of speech which are: nouns, pronouns, verbs, adjectives, articles, adverbs, conjunctions, prepositions, and interjections. Some authorities consider articles as a form of an adjective and will list eight parts of speech, but this chapter treats articles as a separate part of speech due to their importance in legal writing.

© 2019, 2020, 2021 NALA, Inc. All rights reserved.

Nouns

Nouns refer to persons, places, things, ideas, and events, and are often the easiest part of speech to identify in a sentence. Proper nouns refer to specific persons, places, or things and should always begin with a capital letter. Common nouns refer to general items and should only be capitalized if they are the first words in a sentence.

- **The case was filed in the *Delaware Chancery Court*.**

- **The case was filed in the *state court*.**

Nouns may also be classified as singular nouns or plural nouns. A singular noun names one person, place, or thing (juror) while a plural noun names more than one (jurors). Nouns can be the subject of a sentence or the object of a sentence. When a noun is the subject of a sentence, the sentence says something about that noun, and the subject is performing some type of action. When a noun is the object of the sentence, the noun is the person or thing that is acted upon by the subject of the sentence. In the following example, the proper noun, John, is the subject of the sentence, and the general noun, court, is the object of the sentence.

- ***John* filed his complaint with the *court*.**

Pronouns

Pronouns are words that take the place of nouns in a sentence, and, just like nouns, pronouns may be the subject or object of a sentence. Personal pronouns such as I, he, she, it, we, and they take the place of the subject of a sentence, while other personal pronouns such as me, him, her, us, and them, take the place of the object of the sentence. The noun that the pronoun refers to (takes the place of) is called the antecedent of the pronoun.

In addition to personal pronouns, there are relative pronouns such as who, which, that, and what. These pronouns are often used to introduce additional information into a sentence. Other categories of pronouns include indefinite pronouns such as some, anybody, and everyone; reflexive pronouns such as myself, yourself, and themselves; and possessive pronouns such as mine, yours, hers, and theirs.

- ***John* signed the contract. *He* will receive $50,000 for the boat. (subjective pronoun)**

- **The *judge who* decided the case was appointed to the bench last year. (relative pronoun)**

- ***John himself* signed the deed yesterday. (reflexive pronoun)**

Verbs

Verbs are the word or words in a sentence that express action, feeling, or a state of being. Verbs have multiple tenses based on time such as past, present, and future tenses.

- **The paralegal *filed* the complaint yesterday.**

- **The attorney *will file* the complaint tomorrow.**

- **The client *is* angry.**

Verbs must always agree in number with the subject of the sentence, and this point is discussed in the section below on subject-verb agreement.

Adjectives

Adjectives are used to describe, modify, or give more information about nouns and pronouns. They tell the reader something about a thing or a person.

- The *large* tract of land will be subdivided into smaller lots.

- The contract was *complex.*

- The *two* paralegals worked quickly to finish the questions.

Articles

Articles are used with nouns, and many authorities consider them a subclass of adjectives. The articles in English are "the" and "a/an", and their purpose is to determine whether the noun is specific or general.

- After *a* long day in court, *an* attorney may still have work to do.

- After *the* long day in court, *the* attorney still had work to do.

The first example is a general statement that may refer to any attorney on any given day in court, while the second example refers to a particular attorney who had a particularly long day in court.

Adverbs

Adverbs are used to describe or modify verbs, adjectives, and other adverbs. They usually tell the reader about how something is done, and often (although not always) end in "ly."

- The lawyer argued *vehemently* that the contract was breached.

- The paralegal researched the issue *very thoroughly.*

While adverbs can and do serve a purpose, many authorities discourage the use of adverbs in legal writing because adverbs tend to clutter up the writing and may weaken the points being made. In the above example, for instance, is it necessary to know that the lawyer argued vehemently or that the paralegal's research was very thorough? In fact, *The Elements of Style* advises the writer to "write with nouns and verbs, not with adjectives and adverbs." (p. 71)

Conjunctions

A conjunction is a word that connects other words or phrases (groups of words) and often shows how the words are related. Examples of conjunctions are "and," "but," and "or."

- John read the case, *but* he did not find any useful information.

- Sara *and* Joe are going to the courthouse tomorrow.

- *When* John goes to the courthouse, he will meet Sara there.

Prepositions

Prepositions are words that indicate location or some other relationship between words, phrases, or clauses. Prepositions are located within a prepositional phrase and usually come before a noun or

---

    © 2019, 2020, 2021 NALA, Inc. All rights reserved.

pronoun to describe its relationship to another word or part of a sentence.

- **Dante is working *at* home today.**
- **The accident took place *on* a divided highway.**

Interjections

Interjections are words in sentences that are used to convey emotion or surprise, or to catch the reader's attention. Interjections can be stand-alone sentences, or they can be part of a longer sentence. Interjections are often followed by an exclamation point (stand-alone sentence), but they can also be followed by a comma (as part of a longer sentence).

- **Wow! Did you see how fast that car was going?**
- **Hey, do you think you can help me with my research?**

While interjections may play an important role in creative writing or in informal writing, such as a text message or possibly an email to a friend, they are rarely used in formal, legal writing. With very few exceptions, paralegals should not use interjections in their legal writing including communications with clients. One punctuation mark to avoid using is the exclamation point.

COMMON TROUBLE AREAS

Subject-Verb Agreement

A verb must agree in number with the subject of the sentence. If the subject of the sentence is singular (the statute), the verb must also be singular (requires), and if the subject of the sentence is plural (the statutes), the verb must also be plural (require).

- *He is* **going to the courthouse in the morning.**
- *They are* **going to the courthouse in the morning.**

In simple sentences with one subject and one verb, subject-verb agreement is not usually a problem. However, issues arise when the sentence contains more than one subject or more than one verb, when indefinite pronouns are used, when the subject is a collective noun, or when there are words between the subject and the verb. Issues can also arise when the subject follows the verb in a sentence.

Subjects Joined by "and," "or," or "nor"

Subjects joined by "and" take a plural verb.

- **The attorney and the client *have* to be at the courthouse tomorrow.**

However, the writer must be careful when phrases such as "in addition to" or "along with" are inserted into the sentence between the subject and the verb because the subject still remains singular in these cases.

- **The attorney, in addition to the clients, *has* to be at the courthouse tomorrow.**

The rule becomes a bit more complicated when subjects are joined by "or" or "nor." If two singular subjects are joined by one of these conjunctions, the verb should be singular.

- **The witness or the plaintiff *knows* the truth of the matter.**
- **Neither the defendant nor the plaintiff *was* present.**

However, if the subject contains a singular and plural word, the verb should agree with the subject closest to the verb.

- **Either the plaintiff or the defendants *are* going to be upset.**
- **Either the defendants or the plaintiff *is* going to be upset.**

Collective Nouns

A collective noun refers to a group of individuals or things such as a jury, team, family, or herd. A collective noun usually takes a singular verb because the group is acting as a single unit.

- **The jury *has* reached a verdict.**
- **The team *is* prepared for the game.**

However, if the members of the group are acting individually, plural verbs should be used.

- **The jury *are* allowed to go home each night.**
- **The board *are* voting on the proposal today.**

In this example, each member of the jury is going to separate homes, and each board member will cast a separate vote. However, this sentence construction sounds very awkward. While it is technically correct, a better way is to use the plural form of the noun.

- **The jurors *are* allowed to go home each night.**
- **The board members *are* voting on the proposal today.**

Intervening Words

Words that are placed between a subject and a verb can cause confusion with subject-verb agreement. If the subject is singular, it takes the singular verb regardless of whether or not the intervening words are singular or plural.

- **The *client*, as well as his two daughters, *wants* to settle the case.**
- **The *deadline* to file the complaint, the cover sheet, and the exhibits, *is* tomorrow.**
- **One of the jurors *is* biased.**

Indefinite Pronouns

Indefinite pronouns do not refer to a specific person, place, or thing. Some typical indefinite pronouns are: anybody, someone, each, neither, all, few, some, and something. Most indefinite pronouns are either singular or plural, but some can be either singular or plural depending on the context of the sentence. The following chart lists some commonly used indefinite pronouns.

 © 2019, 2020, 2021 NALA, Inc. All rights reserved.

Pronoun	Verb	Example
anyone/anybody	singular	Anyone is allowed to speak.
everyone/everybody	singular	Everyone is responsible for the mess.
each	singular	Each of the jury voted to acquit.
either/neither	singular	Either of the partners is responsible.
nobody/no one	singular	Nobody is required to sign the agreement.
something	singular	Something is wrong with the deed.
both, few, many, several, others	plural	Few of the jurors are ready to vote.
all, any, none, some	singular or plural depending upon context	All of the property is distributed. All have arrived.

When the Subject Follows the Verb

A sentence structure in which the subject comes first followed by the verb is the most common. In some sentences, however, the order is reversed and the subject will follow the verb. This construction may cause confusion in subject-verb agreement.

- **In the courtroom there *are* several *jurors*. (The subject of this sentence is actually jurors not courtroom.)**

- **There *are* several *beneficiaries* under the will.**

- **There *is* one *beneficiary* under the will.**

Noun-Pronoun Agreement

Pronouns take the place of nouns and are used so that writing does not become stilted and cumbersome. Like subject-verb agreement, noun-pronoun agreement can pose challenges to writers. The incorrect use of pronouns can confuse readers such as when the antecedent is not clear or when the noun and pronoun disagree in number. Additionally, the use of gendered pronouns can make writing appear sexist and even offensive.

Antecedents

The noun to which the pronoun refers is called the antecedent of the pronoun, and a pronoun should always refer to a specific antecedent in legal writing. Indefinite pronouns such as everyone, all, or none, also commonly function as antecedents of pronouns. If an antecedent cannot be clearly identified, the pronoun should be replaced with a noun. In the following example, it is not clear who she is, so the pronoun should be replaced with a noun.

- ***She* argued that the defendant was negligent.**

- ***The attorney* argued that the defendant was negligent.**

Pronouns can cause confusion in a sentence when there are multiple nouns of the same type, and it is not clear which antecedent the pronoun is referring to in the sentence. The reader may struggle to understand the sentence in these cases.

© 2019, 2020, 2021 NALA, Inc. All rights reserved.

- *James* and *Carlos* worked on the client's file together until *he* left for the day.

- *American trials* differ from *European trials* because *they* are more adversarial than inquisitorial in nature.

In the first sentence it is not clear which man left for the day, and in the second sentence it is not clear whether American trials or European trials are more adversarial. The sentences should be corrected as follows:

- *James* and *Carlos* worked on the client's file together until *James* left for the day.

- *American trials* differ from *European trials* because *American trials* are more adversarial than inquisitorial in nature.

Agreement in Number

A pronoun must agree in number with its antecedent. If the antecedent is singular, the pronoun must be singular; if the antecedent is plural, the pronoun must be plural.

- The *jurors* were not permitted to discuss what *they* heard during the trial.

- *Thomas* was not permitted to discuss what *he* heard during the trial.

If there are two or more antecedents joined by "and," the pronoun must be plural.

- *Angel, Matthew,* and *Tyler* have made *their* arguments before the court.

If two or more antecedents are joined by "or" or "nor," the pronoun must agree in number with the antecedent closest to the pronoun.

- Neither Matthew nor the *others* have made *their* arguments before the court yet.

- Neither the *others* nor Matthew has made *his* argument before the court yet.

Although the second sentence is grammatically correct, it sounds awkward, so the first sentence construction is a better choice stylistically. When the antecedent is a collective noun such as jury, group, team, or board, then a singular form of the pronoun is used.

- The *jury* made *its* decision.

- The *board* would not discuss *its* decision with the reporter.

Agreement and Gender

Gender in grammar refers to whether a noun or pronoun is masculine, feminine, or neutral. In English, most nouns and pronouns are neutral (child, adult, people, I, me, you, their) unless they clearly refer to something that is masculine (boy, man, he, him, his) or something that is feminine (girl, woman, she, her, hers). While most nouns and all indefinite pronouns are gender neutral, the singular pronouns used to replace them can be masculine (he/his) or feminine (she/hers). For instance, in the sentence "An attorney should file his brief on time," the subject of the sentence "the attorney," is gender neutral, but the pronoun is masculine. Indefinite pronouns (all, anyone, each, either, etc.) pose a particular problem such as "Each person should take his seat now." In the past, the practice was generally to use the male gendered personal pronoun (he/his) which was said to include males and females alike. The exception would be if the antecedent was clearly female such as princess, or if the antecedent was presumed to be

 © 2019, 2020, 2021 NALA, Inc. All rights reserved.

female such as nurse. For instance, consider the following sentences:

- A *paralegal* should type up *her* notes immediately after a client interview.

- An *attorney* should type up *his* notes immediately after a client interview.

- *Everyone* should type up *his* notes immediately after a client interview.

Such construction is frowned upon because it assumes that paralegals are generally female while attorneys are generally male. Also, the third sentence can be problematic because it could be read to imply that women do not have to type up their notes immediately. Today, it is considered antiquated and even offensive to use the masculine version of the pronoun in such situations. When writing informally, and in spoken English, many people attempt to get around this issue by using a plural pronoun even though the antecedent is singular. However, this construction is grammatically incorrect and should not be used in legal writing.

- **Incorrect: A paralegal should type up their notes immediately after a client interview.**

- **Incorrect: Everyone should type up their notes immediately after a client interview.**

The first sentence is grammatically incorrect because "a paralegal" is clearly a singular antecedent and "their" is clearly a plural pronoun, and this sentence sounds very awkward to most people. The second sentence is also grammatically incorrect because "everyone" is a singular antecedent and "their" is a plural pronoun. However, this sentence does not sound awkward to most ears because "everyone" sounds like it could be plural, and this construction has become very common in more informal writing. However, the second sentence should be avoided in legal writing despite being acceptable in spoken English and less formal writing.

Some writers will use "his or her" in order to work around this issue.

- **Everyone should type up his or her notes immediately after a client interview.**

- **Each tenant is responsible for paying his or her rent on the first of the month.**

However, while grammatically correct, using "he or she" or "him or her" throughout a document can become cumbersome and distracting. It can also cause confusion in legal documents, particularly if a writer forgets to use one form of the pronoun in a sentence. Some writers attempt to get around the problem by alternating "he/him" or "she/her" throughout the document. This practice should never be used in legal writing because it could create ambiguity in a legal document such as a contract. Additionally, it is jarring to most readers to see pronouns used this way.

Other solutions to the gender problem include: rewriting the sentence in such a way that the use of the pronoun can be avoided; structuring the sentence so that plural antecedents and plural pronouns are used; or repeating the noun.

- **A paralegal's notes should be typed up immediately following the client interview.**

- **Paralegals should type up their notes immediately following the client interview.**

- **A paralegal should type up the paralegal's notes immediately after the client interview.**

However, the third example creates the same stilted, repetitive language that pronouns are designed to eliminate in writing and should be used sparingly.

© 2019, 2020, 2021 NALA, Inc. All rights reserved.

Sentences

A sentence is a group of words that expresses a complete thought. Additionally, the sentence must contain a subject (the actor in the sentence) and a predicate (a verb and the object of the verb). Sentences begin with a capital letter and end with a punctuation mark. Sentences can be simple or complex.

- **The attorney argued.**

- **The attorney argued well on behalf of the plaintiff, but the jury rendered a verdict for the defendant.**

A clause is a group of words that contains a subject and a predicate. However, not all clauses are sentences. Independent clauses can stand alone as a sentence, but dependent clauses are not sentences because they lack a complete thought.

- **Independent clause: The judge instructed the jury.**

- **Dependent clause: After the judge instructed the jury**

In the second example, even though there is a subject and a verb, the use of the word "after" at the beginning of the clause leaves the thought incomplete because the writer does not tell the reader what happened after the judge instructed the jury.

Sentence fragments (incomplete sentences) and run-on sentences are the most common errors made when writing a sentence. A sentence fragment usually occurs when the sentence lacks a subject or predicate or when the writer uses a dependent clause without combining the dependent clause with an independent clause.

- **The juror, getting more tired by the minute**

This is an incomplete sentence because it lacks a verb. The phrase "getting more tired by the minute" is an adjective that is being used to describe the juror. A correct way to write the sentence is: The juror was getting more tired by the minute.

- **The plaintiff's attorney rose to his feet. Objecting to the admission of the exhibit into evidence**

The first sentence is a complete sentence, but the second sentence is incomplete because it lacks a subject. The sentence can be corrected as follows: The plaintiff's attorney rose to his feet objecting to the admission of the exhibit into evidence. Alternatively, the writer can turn the fragment into a complete sentence that stands on its own. The plaintiff's attorney rose to his feet. He objected to the admission of the exhibit into evidence.

- **Unless the attorney objects to the admission of the exhibit into evidence**

This last example is an incomplete sentence because it does not complete the thought; the sentence fragment leaves the reader wondering (unless what?). This type of fragment is fairly common when the writer begins the sentence with a subordinating conjunction. Subordinating conjunctions provide transitions between two ideas in a sentence and clue the reader as to which of the two clauses is more important.

- **Unless the attorney objects to the admission of the exhibit into evidence, the jury will see a highly prejudicial photograph that is irrelevant as to guilt or innocence.**

In the sentence above, there are two ideas being connected: the attorney should object to the admission of the photo, and the jury is liable to be prejudiced by viewing an irrelevant photograph. The fact that

---

 © 2019, 2020, 2021 NALA, Inc. All rights reserved.

the jury will be prejudiced is the more important point in the sentence. When starting a sentence with a subordinate word or phrase, writers must be very careful to make sure that they actually complete the thoughts that they are trying to convey in the sentence.

Run-on sentences occur when the writer combines two independent clauses into one sentence without the proper punctuation. As stated above, an independent clause contains a subject and a verb, and it expresses a complete thought. The independent clause can stand alone as its own sentence, be joined together with a dependent clause, or be joined together with another independent clause. However, when two independent clauses are joined together, the writer must use correct grammar and punctuation to avoid confusing the reader. The following example is a run-on sentence:

- **The attorney rose quickly to his feet he argued that the photograph was irrelevant.**

In this example, there are two independent clauses ("the attorney rose quickly to his feet" and "he argued that the photograph was irrelevant"), but the lack of any punctuation leaves the reader confused as to where one idea ends and the other begins. This example is known as a "fused" sentence because the writer has fused together two complete sentences without any punctuation or a coordinating conjunction. (Coordinating conjunctions such as "and," "but," or "so" connect words, phrases, and sentences.) There are several ways to correct this sentence. The writer can either add a comma and coordinating conjunction; separate the two sentences with a semicolon; or rewrite the sentences as two separate sentences.

- **Good: The attorney rose quickly to his feet, and he argued that the photograph was irrelevant. (Note, the use of he is not sexist in this example because one particular attorney is being described and that one attorney will be either a he or a she.)**

- **Better: The attorney rose quickly to his feet; he argued that the photograph was irrelevant.**

- **Best: The attorney rose quickly to his feet. He argued that the photograph was irrelevant.**

A run-on sentence can also occur when two independent clauses are joined together by a comma without a coordinating conjunction. This error is called a comma splice. A comma by itself is used to join a dependent clause to an independent clause, but when two independent clauses are joined together, the comma must be followed by a coordinating conjunction.

- **Incorrect: The attorney argued that the document should not be admitted into evidence, the judge overruled the objection.**

- **Correct: The attorney argued that the document should not be admitted into evidence, but the judge overruled the objection.**

Capitalization

Capitalization means writing a word with the first letter capitalized and the remaining letters in lower case (as opposed to ALL CAPS). The rules can be complex, and an exhaustive treatment is well beyond the scope of this chapter. Additionally, style manuals differ as to certain rules of capitalization. Inexperienced or unsophisticated writers tend to overcapitalize words by capitalizing general nouns such as police, suspect, or attorney, while those writing in a hurry without proofreading tend to forget the basic rules of capitalization, such as capitalizing the pronoun "I" or the first word in a sentence. A few of the general rules of capitalization are:

- **Capitalize the first word in a sentence and the first word after a period.**

- Capitalize proper nouns such as names of persons (Brian McDonald), days of the week (Wednesday), holidays (Memorial Day), specific geographical regions (Africa, Texas), brand names (Pepsi Cola), and organizations (the Philadelphia Eagles).

- Capitalize the part of proper adjectives that are derived from a proper noun such as: French literature, Russian dressing, and German shepherd.

- Do not capitalize the seasons: summer, fall, winter, and spring.

There are some specific capitalization rules that apply to legal writing. When referring to a court, the writer should capitalize any court that is named in full or any reference to the United States Supreme Court. In addition, the writer should capitalize "court" when addressing a specific court in a written document such as a motion or brief.

- Pennsylvania Superior Court Supreme Court (when referring to U.S. Supreme Court)

- This honorable Court should...

When the terms for parties such as plaintiff, defendant, appellant, or appellee are used, the rule is to use lower case when the term follows the word "the" and to capitalize when the word takes the place of the name of the party.

- In his brief, the plaintiff argued that the defendant breached the contract.

- In his brief, Plaintiff argued that Defendant breached the contract.

The words judge or justice should be capitalized when used as part of a title with a person's name, and the title precedes the name, but to use lower case in other situations.

- Judge Afesha Pierce

- Justice Ginsberg

- The judge ordered the spectators to stop shouting.

- The circuit court judge was elected by a slim margin.

- Here comes the judge.

Numbers

There is some disagreement among style guides with regard to numbers, and some authorities leave the choice to the individual writer. The most important point is for the writer to choose a style and to be consistent throughout the document. Do not, for instance, write "12" in one sentence or paragraph and switch to "twelve" in another sentence or paragraph. According to Strunk & White, when numerals appear in quotation marks, it is best to spell the number out.

The preference in legal writing is to spell out numbers zero through ninety-nine and round numbers such as one thousand. Other numbers are written as numerals such as 100, 678, 1001, etc. However, many legal writers, including those who write court opinions, do not follow this rule. Instead, they follow the more common rule which is to spell out zero through nine, and to use numerals for everything else. Paralegals should consult with their supervising attorneys and or court rules to determine if there is a preference. Again, the most important point is to stay consistent within the document.

 © 2019, 2020, 2021 NALA, Inc. All rights reserved.

RESOURCES

Print resources

- Deborah Cupples and Margaret Temple-Smith, *Grammar, Punctuation & Style: A Quick Guide for Lawyers and Other Writers*, West Publishing Company (1st ed. 2013)

- William H. Putman, *Pocket Guide to Legal Writing*, Delmar Cengage Learning (1st ed. 2005)

- William Strunk, Jr. and E.B. White, *The Elements of Style*, Longman (4th ed. 2000)

Electronic resources

- Grammarbook.com (The Blue Book of Grammar and Punctuation)

- Owl.purdue.edu (The Purdue Writing Lab)

© 2019, 2020, 2021 NALA, Inc. All rights reserved.

Spelling

Written by Christy Powers, Esq.

© 2019, 2020, 2021 NALA, Inc. All rights reserved.

In legal writing, the importance of how words are spelled and their usage are top priorities. Studies show that most readers do not read the letters, but the word as a whole. When a legal professional reads a document that was poorly drafted, the issues with the writing commonly are due to misspelled or misused words. Unfortunately, while software features are helpful, autocheck and spellcheck can be a disservice to legal writers. Drafting legal documents requires frequently proofreading the work for appropriate vocabulary, as well as errors and/or omissions.

While this section provides significant assistance for the student, examinee, and paralegal, there are many easily accessible resources to assist in spelling, vocabulary, and word usage. Some of the top resources for legal writers include but are not limited to Strunk & White's *The Elements of Style*, *Black's Law Dictionary*, U.S. Courts Glossary of Legal Terms, and The Merriam-Webster Dictionary.

According to The Merriam-Webster Dictionary, orthography is defined as a part of language study that deals with letters and spelling. Paralegal programs all over the country generally suggest and/or require at least two legal research and writing classes. These classes teach students word usage and proper word pronunciation for legal writing. It is also essential to remember there are many Latin terms which require one to turn to a Latin dictionary. Many say, "Latin is the language of the law." Accordingly, a legal professional should familiarize themselves with Latin terminology.

In the endeavor to understand common spelling rules, practice is the key. The rules and principles outlined in the grammar and punctuation sections will assist the examinee to prepare for portions of the Skills Exam.

COLLOQUIALISMS

Colloquialisms are words or expressions that are informal and typically used in ordinary conversational settings. For example, the word irregardless is commonly misused. Irregardless is a redundant and improper use of the word regardless. Additionally, should of is the inappropriate use of should have. Colloquialisms are very similar to slang or words which may be inconsistent with standard definitions. For example, the expression "cool down" may not refer to body temperature but instead, a level of anger. Colloquialisms and slang should be avoided in legal writing.

COMMONLY MISSPELLED AND MISUSED WORDS

Some of the common mistakes in legal writing are spelling related. Because spellcheck is not always correct, be cautious not to rely on it. The testing site's computer will have spellcheck, grammar check, and other editing features disabled during the skills portion of the exam.

Clear and concise writing requires the examinee to recognize variances in words that are pronounced alike but have different meanings (homonyms); words that are spelled the same but have a different meaning (homographs); and words that have a different spelling and pronunciation (synonyms). Mindful use of common legal vocabulary and terms is crucial to legal writing. Although not an exhaustive list, the following words are commonly misused and/or misspelled:

 © 2019, 2020, 2021 NALA, Inc. All rights reserved.

WORD - DEFINITION	CORRECT USAGE
accede - to assent, agree, or accept a demand or request	He told me to accede the offer made by the plaintiff.
exceed - be greater in number or size, to go beyond	I do not want to exceed the amount of time allotted for closing argument.
accept - consent to receive willingly, give an affirmative answer	I told my client to accept the offer that was provided by the plaintiff.
except - not including, other than	I was okay about the guilty verdict except for the sentence to house arrest.
air - the invisible gaseous substance surrounding the earth	The air was hot, humid, and muggy.
heir - a person legally entitled to the property or rank of another on that person's death	I am the legal heir of the decedent.
allude - to hint or to mention indirectly	He would allude to the fact that I was incompetent in medical malpractice law.
elude - to evade or escape	The child was able to elude the kidnapper by unlocking the door.
allowed - give (someone) permission to do something	The dissident was allowed to leave the country.
aloud - audibly; not silently or in a whisper	He read the suicide letter aloud.
aural - relating to the ear or the sense of hearing	She preferred using aural modalities to learn legal terms.
oral - by word of mouth; spoken rather than written; relating to the mouth	They had reached an oral agreement.
bail - the temporary release of an accused person awaiting trial, sometimes on condition that a sum of money be lodged to guarantee the accused person's appearance in court	He has been released on bail.
bale - a bundle of paper, hay, cotton, etc., tightly wrapped and bound with cords or hoops	The fire destroyed 500 bales of hay.
bait - food used to entice fish or other animals as prey	Herrings make excellent bait for pike.
bate - to moderate or restrain; to lessen or diminish	The loss of the motion to dismiss was a setback that bated his hopes for a quick resolution.
board - a long, thin, flat piece of wood or other hard material; get on or into (a ship, aircraft, or other vehicle)	Loose boards in the judge's chambers creaked as I entered.
bored - feeling weary because one is unoccupied or lacks interest in one's current activity	The jurors got bored with the testimony of the forensic accountant.
break - separate or cause to separate into pieces as a result of a blow, shock, or strain	I have been able to break the window many times.
brake - a device for slowing or stopping a moving vehicle, typically by applying pressure to the wheels	The hit-and-run driver never stepped on her brake before hitting the victim.

© 2019, 2020, 2021 NALA, Inc. All rights reserved.

WORD - DEFINITION	CORRECT USAGE
compliment - a polite expression of praise or admiration	I must compliment the court reporter for accuracy of the transcript.
complement - a thing that completes or brings to perfection	The husband's testimony complemented the plaintiff's and added validity to the loss of consortium claim.
council - a group of people called together or chosen for discussion or to make decisions	The council for the youth met yesterday at the town hall.
counsel - advice, especially that given formally; the lawyer or lawyers conducting a case	The counsel for the defense addressed the Court.
creek - an inlet in a shoreline, a channel in a marsh, or another narrow, sheltered waterway	The defendant realized with the guilty verdict that she was up a creek without a paddle.
creak - (of an object, typically a wooden one) make a harsh, high-pitched sound when being moved or when pressure or weight is applied	The old chairs in the deposition room creak as participants shift in boredom.
descent - an action of moving downward, dropping, or falling	The plane had gone into a steep descent prior to the emergency landing.
dissent - hold or express opinions that are at variance with those previously, commonly, or officially expressed	Two members of the court dissented from the majority.
desert - abandon (a person, cause, or organization) in a way considered disloyal or treacherous	He deserted his wife and daughter and gave up his parental rights.
dessert - the sweet course eaten at the end of a meal	The death row inmate wanted key lime pie for dessert.
die - stop living	If you do not take care of yourself, you will die.
dye - a natural or synthetic substance used to add a color to or change the color of something	The defendant dyed her hair blonde to avoid being recognized.
effect - something that inevitably follows an antecedent (such as a cause or agent); something designed to produce a distinctive or desired impression	The tension during the deposition had an effect on the court reporter's ability to concentrate.
affect - the conscious subjective aspect of an emotion considered apart from bodily changes; also: a set of observable manifestations of a subjectively experienced emotion	The tension in the room affected everyone's mood.
ensure - make certain that (something) shall occur or be the case	The client must ensure that accurate records be kept.
insure - arrange for compensation in the event of damage to or loss of (property), or injury to or the death of (someone), in exchange for regular advance payments to a company or government agency	The decedent was insured for $2,500,000.

© 2019, 2020, 2021 NALA, Inc. All rights reserved.

WORD - DEFINITION	CORRECT USAGE
feet - a unit of length; plural form of foot	He was three feet away when he shot the police officer.
feat - an achievement that requires great courage, skill, or strength	Her argument with the judge was a courageous feat.
hall - an area in a building onto which rooms open; a corridor; a large room for meetings, concerts, or other events	My torts class will be held in Vanderbilt Hall.
haul - (of a person) pull or drag with effort or force; (of a vehicle) pull (an attached trailer or load) behind it	His truck was hauled to the impound lot.
I'll - (contraction) I shall, I will	Now go away or I'll call the police.
aisle - a passage between rows of seats in a building such as a church or theater, an airplane, or a train	There is no sitting allowed in the aisle.
isle - an island or peninsula, especially a small one	The church sent missionaries to the Isle of Man.
its - (determiner) belonging to or associated with a thing previously mentioned or easily identified	The complaint would not fit in its file.
it's - (contraction) it is	It's a good day for a sentencing hearing.
mite - a minute arachnid that has four pairs of legs when an adult, related to the ticks; many kinds live in the soil and a number are parasitic on plants or animals	My poor dog was infested with mites.
might - used to express permission, liberty, probability, or possibility in the past, or used to say that something is possible	The jury might come to a decision before midnight.
morning - the period of time between midnight and noon, especially from sunrise to noon	Advisory hearings in the Sixth Circuit are early in the morning.
mourning - the expression of deep sorrow for someone who has died, typically involving following certain conventions such as wearing black clothes	She is still in mourning after the death of her husband.
need - require (something) because it is essential or very important	The 911 operator heard: I need help now!
knead - work (moistened flour or clay) into dough or paste with the hands; massage or squeeze with the hands	She kneaded her sore shoulders after the tough legal battle.
no - used to indicate that something is quite the opposite of what is being specified	It was no easy task persuading her to take the stand.
know - be aware of through observation, inquiry, or information	Most people know that acting out in court can lead to contempt of court.

Word - Definition	Correct Usage
peek - look quickly, typically in a furtive manner	The witness peeked at the photos that were moved into evidence.
peak - reach a highest point, either of a specified value or at a specified time	The tension in the courtroom peaked with the victim's testimony.
pique - stimulate (interest or curiosity); feel irritated or resentful	Has the prosecutor's case piqued the jury's interest yet?
please - cause to feel happy and satisfied; take only one's own wishes into consideration in deciding how to act or proceed; used in polite requests or questions	Please address the letters to the Editor.
pleas - a formal statement by or on behalf of a defendant or prisoner, stating guilt or innocence in response to a charge, offering an allegation of fact, or claiming that a point of law should apply	He changed his pleas for the counts of the indictment to not guilty.
read - look at and comprehend the meaning of (written or printed matter) by mentally interpreting the characters or symbols of which it is composed	I usually read all the deposition transcripts before the trial.
reed - a tall, slender-leaved plant of the grass family that grows in water or on marshy ground	The reeds by the lake at the crime scene obscured important evidence.
right - morally good, justified, or acceptable	I hope we are doing the right thing in this case.
rite - a religious or other solemn ceremony or act; a social custom, practice, or conventional act	The rite of communion was revoked upon excommunication.
root - the basic cause, source, or origin of something; the part of a plant that attaches it to the ground or to a support	Love of money is the root of all evil.
route - a way or course taken in getting from a starting point to a destination	The most direct route to prison is the three strikes law.
scent - an odor	I love the scent of a criminal's desperation.
sent - to have conveyed or delivered	Brad sent his partner the pleadings yesterday.
cent - a unit of money equal to 1/100th of a dollar in the United States	The dispute started with the theft of 49 cents.
seas - (plural) the expanse of salt water that covers most of the earth's surface and surrounds its landmasses	Turbulent seas are often the cause of marine accidents.
sees - perceive with the eyes; discern visually	I do not think he sees well enough to provide an accurate description of the victim.
seize - take hold of suddenly and forcibly	The police officers will seize his property.
shore - the land along the edge of a sea, lake, or other large body of water	The courthouse was situated by the shore.
sure - confident in what one thinks or knows; having no doubt that one is right	Are you sure you want to plead *nolo contendere*?

© 2019, 2020, 2021 NALA, Inc. All rights reserved.

Word - Definition	Correct Usage
sight - the faculty or power of seeing	He lost his sight as a baby.
site - an area of ground on which a town, building, or monument is constructed	The site where the malicious mischief occurred was irreparable.
cite - to quote as authority; to name	Remember to cite only those statutes that apply directly to the case.
through - moving in one side and out of the other side of (an opening, channel, or location)	She had to walk through the crowd protesting the trial.
threw - past tense of throw	The District Court threw out the lawsuit last year.
toe - any of the five digits at the end of the human foot	The toe was removed after the accident.
tow - (of a motor vehicle or boat) pull (another vehicle or boat) along with a rope, chain, or tow bar	A tow truck driver was reportedly killed in the accident.
tore - past tense of tear	She tore the document in half.
tour - a journey for business, pleasure, or education often involving a series of stops and ending at the starting point	I joined the tour of the prison.
tort - a wrongful act or an infringement of a right (other than under contract) leading to civil legal liability	Due to so many people bringing lawsuits to court in order to make easy money, officials are attempting to reform the way to win a case involving a tort.
torte - a sweet cake or tart	My grandma battered my grandpa for sneaking a taste of her delicious torte.
trial - a formal examination of evidence before a judge or jury in order to decide guilt (in criminal cases) or liability (in civil cases)	The trial court found the defendant guilty of murder.
trail - a mark or a series of signs or objects left behind by the passage of someone or something	The trail of evidence led directly to the defendant.
there - in, at, or to that place or position	I know there is truth to what you are saying.
their - belonging to or associated with the people or things	Their testimony was not factual.
they're - (contraction) they are	They're very good witnesses.
two - number, equivalent to the sum of one and one	The two of us walked to the courtroom.
too - in addition; also	Meg enjoyed the concert too.
to - expressing motion in the direction of (a particular location)	He walked to the electric chair silently.
waist - the part of the human body below the ribs and above the hips	The police officer grabbed her around the waist to keep her from falling.
waste - (of a material, substance, or byproduct) eliminated or discarded as no longer useful or required after the completion of a process	Ensure that waste materials are disposed of responsibly.

WORD - DEFINITION	CORRECT USAGE
week - a period of seven days	The RICO trial lasted sixteen weeks.
weak - lacking the power to perform physically demanding tasks; lacking physical strength and energy	She was recovering from her hospital stay and was too weak to testify.
whether - expressing a doubt or choice between alternatives	He seemed undecided whether to plead guilty or no contest.
weather - the state of the atmosphere at a place and time as regards heat, dryness, sunshine, wind, rain, etc.	The weather was nasty on the evening of the accident.
who's - (contraction) who is	Who's your Public Defender?
whose - belonging to or associated with which person	Whose turn is it?
wield - have and be able to use (power or influence)	The circuit judge wields a great deal of influence over the proceedings.
wheeled - (of a vehicle or other object) having wheels to enable it to move over the ground	The vintage two-wheeled vehicle was destroyed in the fire.
wright - a person who creates, builds, or repairs something specified	He was a wonderful and skilled playwright.
write - mark (letters, words, or other symbols) on a surface, typically paper, with a pen, pencil, or similar implement	He was asked to write his name on the paper for the handwriting expert.
your - belonging to or associated with the person or people that the speaker is addressing	What is your name and date of birth?
you're - (contraction) you are	You're part of a larger criminal organization.

© 2019, 2020, 2021 NALA, Inc. All rights reserved.

CHAPTER 12

Punctuation

Written by Elizabeth W. Marchioni

© 2019, 2020, 2021 NALA, Inc. All rights reserved.

Punctuation consists of the marks and symbols, such as periods, commas, and quotation marks, used to clarify meaning in writing. Punctuation marks are used to signal the end of sentences as well as to offset or stress certain words or phrases within sentences. Just as speakers use inflection, tone, volume, and rate to communicate meaning and nuance, writers use punctuation to do the same. Read the following three sentences aloud and think about the different meaning the writer is trying to convey.

- James caused the accident.

- James caused the accident!

- James caused the accident?

The importance of punctuation in legal writing cannot be stressed enough. Good legal writing should be clear, concise, precise, consistent, and unambiguous. In addition to correct grammar and spelling, good legal writing requires correct punctuation to achieve these goals. Courts will examine punctuation when interpreting ambiguities in statutes and legal documents such as contracts. Punctuation has been known to affect the outcome of a case. Incorrect punctuation not only has the potential to confuse the reader, but it tends to make the writer look careless at best or, even worse, uneducated.

The rules of punctuation are complex and numerous, and it would take an entire book to cover all of them. This section will cover some of the basics, particularly in areas where errors often occur, but the reader may want to consult additional resources such as those listed at the end of this chapter. Also, there are some areas in which punctuation is optional or style manuals disagree with each other as to the rule. An example is the use of the Oxford Comma (also known as the serial comma) which is placed immediately before the coordinating conjunction in a series of items. In such instances, this manual will follow the rule used most often in legal writing even if the rule differs from other forms of writing such as a journalistic style of writing.

There are 14 punctuation marks that are generally used in English writing. While many of the marks are common in legal writing, a few, such as the exclamation point, dash, or slash, are rarely used in legal or other formal types of writing. The 14 marks are:

1. Periods **.**

2. Question marks **?**

3. Exclamation points **!**

4. Commas **,**

5. Semicolons **;**

6. Colons **:**

7. Apostrophes **'**

8. Quotation marks **" "**

9. Ellipses **…**

10. Parenthesis **( )**

11. Brackets **[ ]**

12. Hyphens **-**

© 2019, 2020, 2021 NALA, Inc. All rights reserved.

13. Dashes —

14. Slashes /

PERIODS

Periods (also called full stops) are used to mark the end of a sentence that is a statement as opposed to a question or exclamation. The period signals to the reader that the writer has expressed a complete idea, and the reader naturally stops at the period before moving on to the next sentence.

- The paralegal filed the brief.

- The defendant appeared in court, but the plaintiff missed the trial.

Periods should also be used at the end of a sentence that is an indirect question.

- The paralegal asked the attorney where the file was.

- They asked who the witness was.

Periods are also used after most abbreviations.

- Dr. (doctor)

- Co. (company)

- Dec. (December)

- 6:00 p.m. (post meridiem)

However, periods are not used for commonly known acronyms such as FBI, NASA, or NFL. Finally, if a sentence ends in an abbreviation that takes a period, do not use more than one period.

- The Supreme Court is located in Washington, D.C.

QUESTION MARKS

Question marks should be used at the end of direct questions. If the question is part of a longer sentence that ends in a direct question, a question mark should still be used.

- Did the jury reach a verdict yet?

- She asked her attorney, "Did the jury reach a verdict yet?"

- I know I've asked you this before, but did the jury reach a verdict yet?

However, a period should be used at the end of an indirect question.

- She wondered if the jury had reached a verdict yet.

- She asked the attorney whether the jury had reached a verdict yet.

EXCLAMATION POINTS

Exclamation points (also called exclamation marks) are used at the end of a sentence for emphasis or to convey excitement. However, exclamation points are rarely used in legal writing and should be avoided unless they are part of a direct quotation.

COMMAS

A comma is a punctuation mark that indicates a pause in a sentence but not a full stop. Commas are the punctuation mark that seem to give the most trouble to writers, and people tend to overuse them in legal writing. Many people do not know all the rules pertaining to commas, and they try to place them in sentences where they sound good to their ears. One of the most important ways to ensure quality legal writing is to keep sentences simple and straightforward with limited use of descriptive language such as adverbs. However, such writing can become choppy and difficult to read. It then becomes necessary to vary sentence length. Commas, among other things, are used to pause between clauses in compound and complex sentences, to offset unnecessary information, and to separate items in a series. The main rules regarding commas are set forth. Refer to Appendix A for a judgement based on comma.

Items in a Series

Commas should be used to separate three or more items in a series.

- The attorney brought her notes, the case file, and a computer to the courtroom.

The comma before the conjunction "and" is called the Oxford Comma (another name is serial comma), and some writers choose not to use the final comma. However, the omission of the Oxford Comma can cause confusion, and it should be used in legal writing. The placement, or lack thereof, of an Oxford Comma can lead to different interpretations of legal documents or even statutes.

Linking Two Independent Clauses with a Coordinating Conjunction

If a sentence contains two independent clauses (a clause that expresses a complete thought or idea), use a comma and a coordinating conjunction to link the two independent clauses. Do not use a comma to separate two independent clauses without a coordinating conjunction. This is a grammatical error known as a comma splice.

- Correct: The paralegal researched the issues, and the attorney drafted the brief based on the research.
- Incorrect: The paralegal researched the issues, the attorney drafted the brief based on the research.

Nonessential Words, Phrases, and Clauses

Commas should be used to offset nonessential words, phrases, and clauses in a sentence.

- The client, however, refused to cooperate with the paralegal.
- The paralegal, who just graduated last week, started work today.

© 2019, 2020, 2021 NALA, Inc. All rights reserved.

However, a comma should not be used if the information is necessary to identify the noun as one out of several persons, places, or things. In the first sentence below, the words "who looked guilty" are set off by two commas, and the phrase is describing a single defendant who apologized to the plaintiff. In the second sentence, the words "who looked guilty" are being used to describe one among two or more defendants, and the phrase is not set off by commas. This is an example of when the use of commas helps to clarify the meaning of the sentence: was there one defendant who looked guilty as he apologized to the plaintiff, or were there multiple defendants, only one of whom apologized to the plaintiff.

- The defendant, who looked guilty, apologized to the plaintiff.
- The defendant who looked guilty apologized to the plaintiff.

Introductory Words, Phrases, or Clauses

Use commas to set off introductory words, phrases, or clauses.

- According to the client, the landlord failed to repair the heater even after repeated requests to do so.
- Unfortunately, the client did not show up for her interview today.

Appositives

An appositive is a word or words that refers to another noun in a sentence; usually the appositive provides additional information about the noun, but it is not essential.

- The attorney, a father of two, had to hurry home right after the trial ended.
- Anne, my sister, was driving when the other driver swerved into our lane.

Dates

Commas should be used to set off the year in a date.

- The client's birthday is March 10, 1970.
- September 11, 2001, is a date that few will forget.

If a day of the week is used in the sentence, the entire date should be set off.

- The hearing on Friday, October 8, 2018, should be interesting.
- The meeting is set for Tuesday, December 12, 2019, at 3:00 p.m.

Do not use a comma if the date contains only the month and the year.

- The trial will begin in August 2018.
- The accident occurred in March 2015.

Quotations

Use commas before or after quotations unless the quotation ends in a question mark or exclamation point. In American English, the comma should be placed within the quotation marks if the quotation comes at the beginning of the sentence.

- The witness said, "I saw the green car run the light."

- "I saw the green car run the red light," the witness said.

Salutations and Closings

Use a comma after the salutation of an informal letter (but not a formal letter, see below where a colon is used when you do not know the recipient personally), and after the closing (also referred to as valedictions) of every letter. Remember for salutations, it is important to capitalize each word before the comma is placed. For closings, it is important not to capitalize the words that follow before the comma is placed.

Salutations:

- Dear Mom,

- To Whom It May Concern:

Closings:

- Sincerely,

- Very truly yours,

SEMICOLONS

A semicolon is a punctuation mark that indicates a pause in a sentence which is longer than the pause of a comma but shorter than a full stop indicated by a period. Semicolons are mainly used to separate two independent and related clauses that could stand as complete sentences, but they have some other uses as well. Modern writers of fiction, journalism, and advertising tend to avoid semicolons, but they are still used in more formal types of writing such as legal writing and scholarly writing.

Linking Independent Clauses

A semicolon is used to link two independent but related clauses. Each of the clauses could stand alone as a complete sentence, but the semicolon is used to link them.

- John went to the courthouse two hours before trial to meet the client; Jordan stayed behind in the office until just before the trial started.

- The defendant's attorney was prepared for the trial; the plaintiff's attorney needed more time to gather evidence.

Separating Items in a Series

A semicolon is used to separate items in a series when the items already contain commas or when the items in the series are very long.

 © 2019, 2020, 2021 NALA, Inc. All rights reserved.

- A paralegal should know how to research thoroughly; be able to write clearly, precisely, and concisely; and possess the skills necessary to interview clients and others.

COLONS

A colon is used to direct attention to something such as a list, explanation, or quotation. It is also used to separate minutes from hours in expressions of time.

Introducing an Item or List of Items

Use a colon to introduce an item or a list of items as long as the colon will not interrupt the flow of the sentence. Do not capitalize the first item of the list unless it is a proper noun.

- He got what he wanted: a guilty verdict.
- I want an assistant who can do the following: take clear notes, interview clients, and conduct legal research.

Do not use a colon when the list follows a verb or preposition.

- Correct: The answer was in the statute.
- Incorrect: The answer was in: the statute.
- Correct: He saw the car fly through the stop light, crash into the plaintiff's car, and speed away from the accident scene.
- Incorrect: He saw: the car fly through the stop light, crash into the plaintiff's car, and speed away from the accident scene.

The Salutation of a Business Letter

Use a colon after the salutation of a business letter or other formal letter even if the letter begins with a person's first name.

- Dear Mr. Grimaldi:
- Dear Jim: (for a business letter)

Time

Use a colon to separate the hour from minutes in time.

- 4:00 p.m.
- 7:45 a.m.

APOSTROPHES

Apostrophes are used mainly to indicate possession and to form contractions.

© 2019, 2020, 2021 NALA, Inc. All rights reserved.

Possession

With singular nouns, possession is formed by adding an apostrophe followed by the letter *s*. In legal writing the *s* should be added after the apostrophe even when the word ends in the letter *s* such as in the third example.

- The client's car.

- The judge's ruling.

- The class's assignment.

The writer must be particularly careful with last names that end in "s."

- Mr. Jones's land.

With plural nouns, if the noun ends in *s* or *es*, the possessive is formed by adding an apostrophe after the *s*.

- The clients' bills.

- The paralegals' computers.

- The Jones' land.

With irregular plural nouns that do not end in *s* or *es* the possessive is formed by adding an apostrophe and an *s*.

- The children's basic needs.

- The women's books.

Compound Words

If the subjects of the compound word jointly possess the object, there should only be an apostrophe after the last word of the compound word.

- Mr. and Mrs. Smith's car was wrecked in the accident.
- Juan Gomez and Maria Gomez's property was subject to the deed.

If the subjects of the compound word possess the object individually, use an apostrophe after each word.

- Juan Gomez's and Will Black's cars were wrecked in the accident. (Each person's car was wrecked in the accident.)

Personal Pronouns

Many writers make the mistake of using an apostrophe to show possession for a personal pronoun such as "its" and "whose." Do not use an apostrophe with personal pronouns.

- A brief is only as good as its writer makes it.

- Whose computer is this?

© 2019, 2020, 2021 NALA, Inc. All rights reserved.

Contractions

Apostrophes are used to take the place of omitted letters in contractions such as *don't* (do not), *it's* (it is), and *can't* (cannot). However, contractions should not be used in legal writing unless they are part of a direct quotation.

QUOTATION MARKS

Quotation marks are used to indicate the exact words of a speaker. These are known as direct quotations.

- The defendant said, "I am going to kill you unless you pay me."

- "I will never pay you child support," he said.

If a direct quotation is 50 words or more, the quotation should be offset with block indentation instead of quotation marks.

Ellipses

An ellipsis (plural ellipses) is a punctuation mark consisting of three dots (it looks like three periods in a row), that is used in legal writing to indicate that some words have been removed from quoted material. In more informal or creative types of writing, an ellipsis may be used to indicate hesitation, but it should not be used this way in legal writing. Ellipses are particularly useful when writing memos or briefs which contain long quotations from cases or statutes. An ellipsis is used to shorten the quote and include only the pertinent material.

Here are two quotations from the Delaware Code's statute on third degree assault. Assume the client has only been charged with the second section (acting with criminal negligence). In the second example, the irrelevant section of the code has been omitted and replaced by an ellipsis.

- "A person is guilty of assault in the third degree when: (1) The person intentionally or recklessly causes physical injury to another person; or (2) With criminal negligence the person causes physical injury to another person by means of a deadly weapon or a dangerous instrument." 11 Del. C. §6011.

- "A person is guilty of assault in the third degree when: … (2) With criminal negligence the person causes physical injury to another person by means of a deadly weapon or a dangerous instrument." 11 Del. C. §6011.

PARENTHESES

Parentheses, which are round, are used to set off information that is not essential to the meaning of the rest of the sentence. The information in the parentheses interrupts or clarifies something in the sentence. Parentheses are also used to introduce abbreviations after a full name is given.

- Kim Lee (who really did not like the apartment) signed the lease.

- He would like to volunteer as a Court Appointed Special Advocate (CASA).

© 2019, 2020, 2021 NALA, Inc. All rights reserved.

Parentheses are also used in legal writing as part of case citations and to denote subparts of a citation to a statute or other numerical rule.

- *Texas v. Johnson*, 491 U.S. 397 (1989)

- Fed. R. Civ. P. 12(b)(6)

BRACKETS

Brackets, which are square, are used less frequently than parentheses. Brackets are used when the writer inserts something into quoted material, usually for clarification. They should also be placed around the first letter of a quoted sentence if the writer changed the letter from uppercase to lowercase or vice versa.

- The defendant said, "I didn't do it. Paul [the co-defendant] killed her."

- The relevant statute states "[a] person is guilty of assault in the third degree when: … (2) With criminal negligence the person causes physical injury to another person by means of a deadly weapon or a dangerous instrument."

HYPHENS

A hyphen (which differs from the longer dash) is used to connect words together when the words form a single idea. Hyphens are also used when certain numbers are written out.

Compound adjectives

Hyphens are used between compound adjectives that modify the next word.

- She suffered an employment-related injury.

- The law student lived in an off-campus apartment.

Age-related terms

Hyphens are used to tell the ages of people or things.

- The plaintiff is a two-year-old child.

- The contract was for a 50-year-old vintage car.

Compound numbers

Compound numbers between twenty-one and ninety-nine should be hyphenated when they are written out.

- The defendant had twenty-two dollars in his pocket.

- The check was for one thousand nine hundred and twenty-five dollars.

© 2019, 2020, 2021 NALA, Inc. All rights reserved.

DASHES

The dash, which is longer than a hyphen, is used to set off or draw attention to a part of a sentence. Dashes can take the place of commas, parentheses, or colons. However, dashes are considered to be informal, and should not be used in legal writing.

SLASHES

The slash (also known as a virgule) has several meanings including *and*, *or*, or even *per*. Due to its various meanings, the slash can lead to confusion and should not be used in legal writing.

RESOURCES

Print Resources

- Deborah Cupples and Margaret Temple-Smith, *Grammar, Punctuation & Style: A Quick Guide for Lawyers and Other Writers*, West Publishing Company (1st ed. 2013)

- William H. Putman, *Pocket Guide to Legal Writing*, Delmar Cengage Learning (1st ed. 2005)

- William Strunk, Jr. and E.B. White, *The Elements of Style*, Longman (4th ed. 2000)

Electronic Resources

- Owl.purdue.edu (The Purdue Writing Lab)

© 2019, 2020, 2021 NALA, Inc. All rights reserved.

Appendix A

Article: For Want of a Comma

In the case *O'Connor v. Oakhurst Dairy*, 851 F.3d 69 (1st Cir. 2017), a group of delivery drivers in Maine sued a dairy for failing to pay them overtime wages under statutory law. The trial court granted summary judgment in favor of the dairy, and the drivers appealed. The First Circuit Court of Appeals reversed the grant of summary judgment and remanded the case for trial. The Appellate Court began its opinion by stating, "For want of a comma, we have this case."

Generally speaking, Maine law required an employer to pay any employee who worked more than 40 hours a week time and half. However, a statute listed some exceptions to the law. The statute exempted the following activities from the overtime requirement: "The canning, processing, preserving, freezing, drying, marketing, storing, packing for shipment or distribution of: (1) Agricultural produce; (2) Meat and fish products; and (3) Perishable foods."

The issue was whether the words *packing for shipment or distribution of* should be read as one activity or two distinct activities because the statute could be interpreted two different ways. The drivers argued that the last activity in the series of exempt activities was *packing* (whether such packing was for shipment or for distribution) and the word *or* should be read to modify the word packing. In other words, packing was exempt from overtime whether the packing was for the shipment of products or whether the packing was for the distribution of the products. The drivers argued the statute did not exempt distributing (delivering) the products at all, and so they should have been paid overtime. On the other hand, the dairy argued that *packing for shipment* was an activity distinct from *distribution* of the products, and that the last item in the series of exempt activities was actually *distribution* of the products. Under this interpretation, distribution of the products was also exempt from overtime payment, and so the drivers should not have been paid overtime.

While the trial court read the statute to clearly exempt distribution from overtime, the Appellate Court disagreed. The Appellate Court stated that the lack of the serial comma, among other things, created ambiguity in the statute. The Court further stated that ambiguous provisions in the state's wage laws should be liberally construed to further benefit the purposes for which they are enacted, and therefore, should be read in favor of the drivers because the purpose of the law was to provide for overtime except for certain narrow exceptions. The Appellate Court reversed the trial court's grant of summary judgment and remanded the case for trial.

The case was never tried because the parties agreed to a settlement in which the dairy would pay the drivers five million dollars in overtime (as a group, not individually). Additionally, the Maine legislature revised the statute, replaced the commas with semicolons, and clearly exempted distribution of the named goods from overtime. The revised statute now reads: "The overtime provisions of this section do not apply to: ... The canning; processing; preserving; freezing; drying; marketing; storing; packing for shipment; or distribution of: (1) Agricultural produce; (2) Meat and fish products; and (3) Perishable foods."

O'Connor v. Oakhurst Dairy, 851 F.3d 69 (1st Cir. 2017); O'Connor v. Oakhurst Dairy, 2018 WL 3041388 (D. Me. 2018); 26 M.R.S.A. § 664.

© 2019, 2020, 2021 NALA, Inc. All rights reserved.

Clarity of Expression

Written by Nancy L. Jordahl, ACP, FRP, FCP

"If you can't explain it simply, you don't understand it well enough."

- Albert Einstein

© 2019, 2020, 2021 NALA, Inc. All rights reserved.

In this this chapter, the paralegal will learn to:

- Identify the different types of communications used in the legal profession

- Analyze how communication is affected by its purpose and intended audience

- Evaluate the effects of technology on communication

- Understand the role that preparation, content, word choice, and style play in clear communication

- Convert opaque communication to clear communication

In its simplest sense, clarity of expression means clear writing. The Skills Exam portion of the Certified Paralegal (CP) Examination consists of a written assignment. Precise, simple writing is necessary to complete the assignment in a timely manner. Even beyond the scope of the Skills Exam, it is crucial for a paralegal to write with clarity in all aspects of the profession.

TYPES OF COMMUNICATION IN THE LEGAL PROFESSION

All forms of communication are central to the legal profession. Verbal, nonverbal, written, and visual communication all play a role. This chapter focuses on written communication, but it is important to keep in mind the other forms of communication at play in the legal field.

Legal writing can be formal or informal. A letter to the judge may begin with "Your Honor" and end with "Respectfully yours." A letter to a well-known client might begin with "Dear Steve" and end with "Sincerely." But a text to your attorney probably will not have a greeting or closing.

Legal writing may be analytical, objective, and/or persuasive. An example of analytical writing would be an interoffice memorandum which contains an analysis of a fact pattern and a presentation of argument(s) regarding the facts. An example of objective writing would be a summary that is as neutral as possible and uses facts and statistics. An example of persuasive writing would be a settlement demand letter. Drafting legal documents such as contracts or wills are another form of legal writing.

There are aspects of legal writing that are unique to the law such as the use of citations. Another aspect of legal writing unique to the law which should be avoided is "legalese." Legalese is the specialized language of the legal profession that is hard for nonlawyers to understand. An example of legalese is: "Respondent moves that this Honorable Court impose a penalty, in an appropriate amount, pursuant to Section 2704, based upon the fact that petitioner has instituted these proceedings primarily for the purposes of delay and/or petitioner's position is frivolous and groundless." To help avoid legalese, avoid using Latin phrases unless necessary. If it is not a word that you would say in the normal course of conversation, do not write it. Would you use the word aforementioned in conversation?

EFFECT OF TECHNOLOGY ON COMMUNICATION

Legal writing has been impacted by technology. Keyboards have replaced typewriters, emails are more prevalent than letters, and many attorneys review documents on screen as opposed to "hard copies" on paper.

With changes in technology comes changes in written communication. According to https://www.pewresearch.org/internet/fact-sheet/mobile/ 97% of Americans own a cellphone and 85% own a smartphone. Now the legal profession communicates by texts, emails, apps/software, and emojis/

 © 2019, 2020, 2021 NALA, Inc. All rights reserved.

abbreviations. The forms of communication have changed, but the need for clear expression has not changed.

KNOWING YOUR AUDIENCE/PURPOSE OF COMMUNICATION

The first step to clarity of expression is to determine what you want to say and why. Questions you will want to ask yourself include: Who are you trying to communicate to (who is your audience)? What is the point of your communication? Is it to tell someone what to do? Is it to provide information? Is it to create a record?

A paralegal will not necessarily use the same style to communicate to a boss, a co-worker, a client, or a judge. Knowing the audience is key. In all legal communication, be professional and courteous. It is also important to keep in mind the amount of legal knowledge the intended audience may or may not have. A boss and co-workers or the judge will typically have more legal knowledge than clients. Depending on the area of law a paralegal specializes in, a client may not speak or write English.

Part of a paralegal's responsibilities include drafting legal documents. Pleadings, briefs, and discovery responses require familiarization with and compliance with the court required formats for submitting the legal document. It is also crucial to use the correct legal terminology when preparing those documents.

All correspondence will benefit from clarity of expression. This includes, but is not limited to: letters, emails, handwritten notes/sticky notes, memorandums, or chronologies. Everyone is busy and needs to use time effectively. A paralegal should try to communicate the most information swiftly but accurately. Of course, it is important not to be too brief and possibly exclude vital information. A good practice tip may be for a paralegal to ask the boss for feedback about how much or how little to include in certain communications. Look at examples that other articulate paralegals in the workplace have created.

ETHICAL COMMUNICATION

As legal professionals, paralegals have another component of communication and that is professional ethics. Periodically review the NALA Code of Ethics and Professional Responsibility, the ABA Model Rules of Professional Conduct, and the state ethics guidelines for ethical updates that affect all legal communications.

Confidentiality is the backbone of the law. Take steps to keep all appropriate legal communications confidential and privileged. Attorney-client and work-product privilege may be forfeited by inadvertent communication. A paralegal's own personal bias should not intervene into legal communications. With the onslaught of social media, many people are more accustomed to broadcasting their opinions on topics that should be private. Workplace communication should not be through Facebook, Instagram, Twitter, and the like. Although some attorneys prefer to advertise on social media, it is not the place to disclose private, workplace communications.

PRACTICAL STEPS TO IMPROVE CLARITY

Prepare for Your Communication

Lack of preparation creates more work in the long run and the potential for confusion or misunderstandings. To prepare for communication, organize thoughts or create a written outline. It may be best to start with a simple draft of thoughts and considerations. Write down everything that comes to mind even if it seems trivial, irrelevant, or off point. Then go back again to organize and focus it. Start with a goal in mind and check in periodically to make sure that you are staying on track. One way to organize is to go from general to specific.

Follow a Structure

Begin with an introduction, fill in the information in the body, and wrap it up with a conclusion. The main/most important idea must be first and then provide all the necessary supporting details. Use short sentences and simple words. If appropriate, use bullet points or numbering. Follow the rules of composition. Grammar, spelling, and punctuation were addressed in other chapters, but it is crucial to keep all three in mind for clear expression in writing.

Use an Active Voice

Active voice describes a sentence where the subject performs the action stated by the verb. Passive voice describes a sentence where the subject is acted upon by the verb.

- **Active voice**: Jennifer sipped champagne.

- **Passive voice**: The champagne was sipped by Jennifer.

Transitional Words and Phrases Usage

Transitional words and phrases connect words, phrases, or paragraphs together. This makes the text easier to read by giving the text logical organization and structure. Transitions may be additive, adversative, causal, or sequential. Examples of transitional words and phrases are: however, subsequently, next, for example, and finally.

Use Concrete Words

Concrete words identify things that can be observed and measured (touch, smell, hear, taste, and see). Instead of stating "sometime soon," use words that give the exact meaning such as "next Saturday."

Do Not Use Double Negatives

Double negatives are two negative words in the same sentence. The combination gives the clause a positive meaning instead of a negative meaning. An example in legal writing would be instead of "not uncommon" say "common" or instead of "not insignificant" say "significant."

 © 2019, 2020, 2021 NALA, Inc. All rights reserved.

Parallel Construction

Parallel construction is a balance within one or more sentences or phrases that have the same grammatical structure. It makes the information easier to process. "I came, I saw, I conquered" is an example of parallel construction.

Do Not Use Excessive Words

For example, the italicized words are redundant and should be omitted: They were *both* alike. The vote was *completely* unanimous. That citation was *previously* found. Watch out for adverbs (loudly, happily), adjectives (bad, important), and other words that are just filler (perhaps, just, maybe) that are not serving any purpose in your sentence other than taking up space.

Pronouns Can Replace a Noun

A vague pronoun will confuse readers unless the referent for each pronoun is obvious. "This," "these," and "it" are simple pronouns that can create the most trouble. Make sure that a pronoun clearly refers to something.

- **Vague**: Macie went with Mary to her mother's house.

- **Clear**: Macie went with Mary to Macie's mother's house.

Word Choice and Vocabulary Matter

If a paralegal does not know precisely what a word means, do not use it. There is no excuse for not knowing the definition of a word. There is always a dictionary available on a cellular phone or computer. Of course, examinees will not be allowed to use a cellphone or dictionary during the Skills Exam so be careful during the exam to use the proper word. It is particularly important when using legal terminology to use the correct word and also to explain terms if they are not common knowledge. If you write "I literally died laughing," you do not understand the definition of the word literally.

Always Proofread and Rewrite

Remove unnecessary sentences and unnecessary words. Never use two words when one will do. Take advantage of the internet to assist with proofreading. Websites like grammarly.com can check your (non-privileged) communications for errors. Also, it is good practice to have a trusted person proofread your work. Keep in mind that examinees do not have access to the internet or spell/grammar check on the exam.

Practical Suggestions to Improve Clarity

If paralegals are not confident in their legal writing skills, there are many ways to improve. One of the easiest ways to write better is to read. Some items to read for pleasure are: novels, newspapers, biographies, technical articles, magazines, or even the cereal box as you are eating your breakfast. Read books about how to be a better writer like *Bird by Bird: Some Instructions on Writing and Life* by Anne Lamott. If you are an audio/visual learner, watch a YouTube video (there are hundreds available from just a quick search with terms like "clarity legal writing"). Another way to improve your legal writing skills is to write more often. Contribute an article to NALA's *Facts & Findings* magazine, volunteer to prepare a memorandum on a legal topic at work, start a journal, or write a summary of a recent event for your local paralegal association newsletter. Practice helps both beginner writers and accomplished authors. After initially writing, do not fear constructive criticism. Ask a friend or family member to read the work and (providing it does not contain confidential information) to provide feedback on ways to improve.

Words/Phrases Associated with Improved Clarity

- **Focus/stay on topic**. Only communicate about one thing at a time. The reader will be confused when there are too many different topics in one communication. This is especially important when communicating via email. When changing the topic mid-stream in an email string, it may be best to create a new email with a new subject line.

- **Blunt/direct/confident**. Do not be passive-aggressive, but state what you want said and support the statement. Do not be vague.

- **Concise/precise/sharp/specific**. There is no need for unnecessary elaboration or superfluous details. Do not be redundant.

- **Sincere.** Speak from the heart, be passionate, and maintain a desire for communications to be the best they can. To be the best also means to be clear.

- **Lucid/transparent**. To be lucid is to be clearly understood.

- **Intelligent/logical.** Most legal professionals, whether attorneys or paralegals, are smart. It is not a career for the dull-minded. Make sure all communication reflects sound logic and reasoning.

- **Slow.** Do not be in a hurry. Clear writing takes time.

- **Consistent**. www.merriam-webster.com defines consistent as "marked by harmony, regularity, or steady continuity, free from variation or contradiction... showing steady conformity to character, profession, belief, or custom." This is the goal for legal writing.

- **True**. Be truthful about facts. Be true to yourself and your writing style.

Clarity of expression is just one component of successful legal writing. Decision-making, analysis of information, reading comprehension, punctuation, spelling, and grammar are also important skills for the paralegal to master to improve legal writing.

Resources

- *The Elements of Style* by William Strunk, Jr., and E.B. White
- *NALA Manual for Paralegals and Legal Assistants*, Sixth Edition
- Federal Rules of Civil Procedure

© 2019, 2020, 2021 NALA, Inc. All rights reserved.

Critical Thinking

Written by Christy Powers, Esq.

© 2019, 2020, 2021 NALA, Inc. All rights reserved.

The legal profession requires paralegals and lawyers to engage and employ a variety of skills and expertise. Critical thinking is a necessary skill all paralegals must learn and continuously refine regardless of the area of practice or employer.

This chapter will provide a brief introduction to critical thinking for those taking the Certified Paralegal (CP) Exam. Specifically discussed are the concepts related to critical thinking that are utilized in the Skills Exam section of the CP Exam. Upon completion of this chapter, readers will be able to:

- Explain the definition of critical thinking.

- Understand the role of critical thinking in the legal profession.

- Identify the components of critical thinking in legal analysis and decision-making.

According to the National Council for Excellence in Critical Thinking, critical thinking can be defined as "the intellectually disciplined process of actively and skillfully conceptualizing, applying, analyzing, synthesizing, and/or evaluating information gathered from, or generated by, observation, experience, reflection, reasoning, or communication, as a guide to belief and action." The Skills Exam assesses the ability of the examinee to identify the relevant facts provided, to analyze those facts against the legal authority provided, and to formulate a conclusion based on that analysis.

ROLE OF CRITICAL THINKING IN THE LEGAL PROFESSION

In most paralegal programs, students are taught the importance of critical thinking by demonstrating their ability to: communicate, problem-solve, evaluate, analyze, synthesize, and reflect. Paralegals apply their critical thinking skills to a variety of real-life situations upon entering the legal profession.

The Skills Exam consists of a written assignment completed within a 120-minute time frame. The examinee is presented with a fact pattern in memorandum format. The attorney-paralegal work relationship relies on this method of communication, which is frequently utilized as an initial case assessment. When an attorney is retained for a legal matter, they typically have a discussion with, or generate a memorandum to, the paralegal outlining the facts and the potential research required. The paralegal is then able to formulate tasks to be completed from that discussion regarding the memorandum. This could be a variety of items, ranging from researching further potential issues to locating relevant legal authority.

Effective problem solving is an essential skill paralegals and lawyers must possess to address client issues as they arise. Paralegals must be able to identify diverse ways to solve a problem effectively. Every paralegal develops their own process of metacognition to ascertain the best way to approach a matter through educational training and/or experience. According to Merriam-Webster's Dictionary, metacognition is defined as the "awareness or analysis of one's own learning or thinking processes." Not all problems are created equal. Accordingly, the approach to these problems varies from attorney to attorney and from paralegal to paralegal.

A paralegal must evaluate the client's options and assist in locating course(s) of action each time a legal matter is presented. The Skills Exam may present a variety of legal authority for analysis, including statutes, regulations, case law, and other legal references. It is up to the examinee to objectively review the information from both sides to discern what may or may not be relevant. Although the examinee knows which side the attorney represents in the fact pattern, all relevant facts and legal authority must be reviewed objectively.

 © 2019, 2020, 2021 NALA, Inc. All rights reserved.

Analyzing legal matters can be complex depending upon the paralegal's knowledge of the subject matter involved. Comparing the law to the relevant facts to determine the potential outcome(s) is the nucleus of the Skills Exam.

Examinees should carefully read through their work after completion of their essay/memorandum response. NALA allows two hours to complete the Skills Exam. It would be wise to allow at least 10 minutes to review the Skills Exam before final submission.

Components of Critical Thinking in Legal Analysis and Decision-Making

In the following chapters, the examinee will learn how to utilize effective reading comprehension skills to understand assignments. The examinee will use methods such as fact finding, analyzing legal authority and theories, formulating legal issues, and examining legal outcomes and conclusions. The Decision-Making chapter will address how to use various methods in decision-making to determine the best course(s) of action to communicate to the attorney on behalf of the client.

CHAPTER 15

Reading Comprehension

Written by Christy Powers, Esq.

© 2019, 2020, 2021 NALA, Inc. All rights reserved.

Passing the Skills Exam portion of the Certified Paralegal (CP) Exam requires examinees to use reading comprehension skills by evaluating a set of facts to a set of law(s)/legal authority. An examinee will confront two main functions in the Skills Exam. One function is to locate the necessary and relevant facts to assist in typing your exam answer. The second function is to assess the necessary and applicable law and explain how it applies to those facts. Upon completion of this chapter, readers will be able to:

- Understand the role of reading comprehension in the legal profession

- Recognize, sort, and recite the necessary and relevant facts

- Understand and recognize the applicable legal authority

The definition of reading comprehension is the ability to understand and process information provided to the reader. According to the National Research Council's Committee on Learning Sciences, some of the fundamental skills required in reading comprehension are the following: a working knowledge of legal vocabulary; the ability to understand the meaning of a word from discourse context; the ability to follow organization of a passage and to identify antecedents and references in it; and the ability to draw inferences from a set of facts and legal authority. The legal profession requires paralegals to read with purpose. The skill of reading comprehension is developed in paralegal classes and refined in practice while working under the supervision of an attorney. Discerning facts from opinions is a refined skill that takes practice through interaction with clients and their respective case(s).

An article published by *The Legal Education Review* stated, in part, that critical legal reading comprises three core sets of skills: mechanical, strategic, and critical. Mechanical skills involve decoding, such as knowing how to break a text down into its constituent parts, and comprehension, such as understanding how those parts have legal impact or effect. Strategic skills involve the ability to deploy appropriate techniques to read a text efficiently and with purpose. Critical skills involve bringing an interrogatory observation both to the text and to its position in a broader environment.

All legal analysis begins by reviewing the instructions/call of the case, the facts, and the legal authority provided. An inherent part of refined reading comprehension involves maintaining a large legal vocabulary. Remember, if the definition of a word, term, or phrase are unknown, it becomes necessary to define it before moving forward with reading and analysis. Although vocabulary is not tested as a separate section on the CP Exam, it is important to memorize as many legal terms and commonly used words in the legal profession as possible.

FACT FINDING

Recognizing, sorting, and reciting the relevant and necessary facts are integral in creating your "Facts" section of the Skills Exam portion of the CP Exam. The initial information provided in an "Internal/ Interoffice Memorandum" will look similar to this:

INTERNAL MEMORANDUM

TO: Paralegal Examinee

FROM: Jennifer Smith, Supervising Attorney

DATE: February 1, 2021

RE: Katie Jones, New Client File

 © 2019, 2020, 2021 NALA, Inc. All rights reserved.

When typing your heading for the exam, a few items are important to note here. Your "name" is "Paralegal Examinee." Never use your real name when creating your heading when typing your response. Additionally, Katie Jones appears to be a "new client." This may or may not be relevant in typing your exam, but it is important to take note of even the smallest of details during your fact-finding process.

As a reminder, most comforts of the regular software programs and word-processing functions have been removed on the CP Exam. A very helpful tool will be the ability to cut and paste. But in doing so, you must hover the mouse over the information and utilize the "cut/copy" function. NALA states that the use of ALT, CTRL, or TAB on the keyboard may cause the computer workstation to freeze. Most examinees find it easiest to hit "CTRL + C" to copy an item. That function should be avoided.

After reading the set of facts presented and the corresponding law(s)/legal authority, the examinee will begin to sort out what facts may or may not be relevant. Additionally, some facts may be missing and/ or unknown. A paralegal's job in refining and restating facts for the examiner, employer, and/or attorney must be concise and relevant.

Examinees will find that the fact patterns lack some amount of "discovery." Discovery is an information gathering process. As stated in the Civil Litigation section, discovery is the entire efforts of a party to a lawsuit and their attorneys to obtain information before trial through demands for production of documents; depositions of parties and potential witnesses; written interrogatories (questions and answers written under oath); written requests for admissions of fact(s); examination of any scene or location; and the petitions and motions employed to enforce discovery rights.

There may be missing or unknown facts. This might have an examinee asking themselves the following questions:

- "What is missing from this fact pattern that may be relevant?"

- "What unknown facts might sway an assessment in favor or in opposition to the client's case?"

- "If I knew X or Y fact(s), this may be helpful in making a clearer decision."

There also may be irrelevant facts. For writing purposes, the facts that do not seem to offer any relevancy in relation to the legal authority should be written without heavy detail. It is best not to assume anything.

For example, consider the following sample fact pattern regarding an alleged theft, the law provided, and a model of potential sample facts. NALA expects that you will create a set of "facts" for your Skills Exam. Inherently, you will need to pare down the facts as given and provide to NALA a set of relevant and dispositive facts. As you read the facts below, then consider how you might refine the facts for your NALA Skills answer.

Facts (as provided by NALA):

Jenny and Jake, a happily married couple, went to the movies. They enjoyed watching shows every other weekend on the live screen as a way to get some well-deserved time away from their seven children. Jenny's favorite place to attend the movies was at a ritzy theater in downtown New York. On January 13th, the couple treaded out into snowy conditions to get to the theater. Upon arriving to see the show, *Always a Never*, the couple checked their coats into the coat check and received tickets with a coat number.

The theater packed out at 300 attendees. The movie theater provided food and drinks to the attendees for a special showing of the newly released movie. Another couple who lived nearby, Katie and Jimmy, also attended a movie that evening. They, too, were parents who needed a night out on the town. Katie and

Jimmy checked their coats in to the same coat check as Jenny and Jake had that evening.

Throughout the evening, the coat check was monitored by one person. Only a few people left the theater early that evening. After the show ended, Jenny and Jake grabbed their coats and drove home. Upon arriving home, the babysitter noticed that Jenny's coat was a very expensive brand and was "made just for her," referring to the embroidery on the sleeve. At that time, Jenny realized that it was not the coat she wore to the theater. She decided to hang the coat and call the theater in the morning. Also, the prior evening, Jenny's friend Katie was not given the same coat as the number on her ticket and had argued heatedly with coat check monitor.

The next morning, Jenny woke up late. She rushed to get her two children to school. It was a cold morning. She grabbed the coat and left the house. While walking her youngest son to his preschool class, Katie, a mom of another child, noticed the coat Jenny was wearing. Katie knew that the coat was hers because she attended the theater the night before and, at coat check, was given a coat that was not hers. Katie decided to confront Jenny about the coat. From her phone, Katie showed Jenny pictures of Katie wearing the coat. Katie also informed Jenny that her coat was very expensive and originally cost $600.00. Jenny apologized and gave the coat back. Katie informed Jenny that, because it was disgusting and smelled horrible, she threw Jenny's coat away. Jenny grabbed Katie's coat back and proceeded to walk out the door. In shock, Katie notified the school resource officer who was able to catch Jenny in her car. Jenny was texting her husband regarding what just happened. The officer arrested Jenny. Jenny has come to our office for representation in the matter.

Please review the attached statutes and prepare a memorandum to me concerning what steps, if any, can be taken to assist our client with this matter.

Statutes

- **SS 410.200 Theft defined**: the carrying and taking away of personal property with the intent to deprive the owner permanently.

- **SS 410.203 Petty theft:** the theft of property valued at $500 or less is considered a Class A misdemeanor (as long as the property is not taken directly from the person of another).

- **SS 410.213 Class 2 felony**: theft of property valued at less than $500 taken from the person of another; or if property is valued at between $500 and $10,000 in value and the theft is committed in a school, in a place of worship, or if the property belongs to the government.

- **SS 410.214 Class 3 felony**:

  (a) theft of property valued at more than $500 and not more than $10,000.

  (b) property that is the subject of the theft is valued at less than $500, the offense is a Class 3 felony if the property is taken from the person of another.

  (c) any retail theft of property with a retail value of more than $300 is a Class 3 felony.

- **SS 410.500 Penalties**:

  (a) a Class A misdemeanor convictions hold a sentence of imprisonment for less than one year and a fine of no more than $2,500 for each offense, plus payment of restitution for losses associated with the theft.

  (b) a Class 2 felony conviction can result in a sentence of imprisonment ranging from three to seven years and a fine of not more than $25,000, plus payment of restitution for losses

© 2019, 2020, 2021 NALA, Inc. All rights reserved.

associated with the theft.

(c) a Class 3 felony conviction results in a sentence of two to five years of imprisonment, a fine not to exceed $25,000, plus payment of restitution for losses associated with the theft.

Model Sample Facts (the examinee's recitation of the relevant facts after reading the law):

On January 13th, Jenny and Jake attended a movie at a ritzy theater in downtown New York. The couple checked their coats into the coat check and received tickets with a coat number upon arrival at the theater. The theater had 300 attendees that evening. Katie and Jimmy, a couple who lived nearby, also attended a movie that evening and checked their very similar coats into the same coat check.

The coat check was monitored by one person throughout the evening. Only a few people left the theater early that evening. Jenny and Jake grabbed their coats and drove home after the movie ended. The babysitter commented on Jenny's coat upon Jenny's arrival home. The babysitter noticed that the coat was a very expensive brand and was "made just for her" upon pointing out the embroidery on the sleeve. Jenny realized that it was not her coat she wore to the theater. Jenny decided to hang the coat and call the theater in the morning. Around the same time, Katie discovered the coat she was given by the coat check did not match her ticket. Upset at the situation, she commented that the coat was "trash" in her opinion.

The next morning, Jenny woke up late and rushed out the door to get her two children to school. It was a cold morning, and Jenny grabbed the coat as she left the house. Jenny walked her youngest son into his preschool class. Katie, whose son attended the same preschool, also walked him to class that same morning. Upon entering the room, Katie noticed the coat Jenny was wearing was her missing coat. Katie knew that the coat was hers because she attended the theater the night previous and was given a coat back that was not the one she wore to the theater. Katie confronted Jenny about the coat by showing Jenny pictures on her phone where Katie was wearing the coat. Jenny immediately apologized and gave the coat back, then Katie informed Jenny she threw away Jenny's coat because it was disgusting and smelled horrible. Jenny grabbed Katie's coat back and walked out the door. Katie then notified the school resource officer who caught Jenny in her car texting her husband about the situation. The officer arrested Jenny. Jenny has come to our office for representation in the criminal matter.

READING LEGAL AUTHORITY

The ability to understand and recognize the applicable legal authority starts by identifying what type(s) of legal authority is presented to the examinee. From the scenario provided, the examinee is required to read and discern relevant facts as well as interpret the legal authority provided. Most exam scenarios present statutes or laws and possibly case law. Other common types of legal authority on the Skills portion are the following: rules, regulations, annotations, ordinances, and other possible combinations of each.

All legal authority needs to be assessed and considered. Some examinees find it helpful to read the facts first and figure out the parties, anticipate issues, and then apply the legal authority. Other examinees find it helpful to read the law(s)/legal authority first before reading the facts. This may provide an opportunity to breakdown the elements of the law(s)/legal authority without immediately assessing how the facts relate. In both instances, the examinee will match relevant facts to elements and/or case law provided in the legal authority. Additionally, examinees will find that certain facts are missing, omitted, and/or do not apply.

If case law is presented as part of the Skills Exam portion, it will be necessary for the examinee to analyze the case law by identifying the relevant facts, the issue(s), the holding, reasoning, and any concurring/dissenting opinions. Utilizing the skill of case briefing will assist the examinee in extracting the information in order to see how it may/may not apply to the relevant facts and law(s)/legal authority. While reading the case law provided, an examinee may find it helpful to type out the case brief in the answer screen. This brief, in turn, may be reduced to paragraph form to make it easier to analogize and/or distinguish from the scenario facts and legal authority provided on the exam.

Whether taking the CP Exam or working in the legal profession, comprehending and summarizing relevant facts and law(s)/legal authority starts with close attention to detail and an analytical mind. As many legal writing authors have stated, a good rule of thumb in reading comprehension is a combination of a superior command of the English language and an extensive legal vocabulary.

In the chapter on analysis of information, the examinee will learn how to utilize effective reading comprehension skills to analyze the information provided by assessing legal authority and theories, formulating legal issues, and assessing legal outcomes and conclusions.

RESOURCES

- Committee on Learning Sciences: Foundations and Applications to Adolescent and Adult Literacy; Division of Behavioral and Social Sciences and Education; National Research Council (2012); *Improving Adult Literacy Instruction: Options for Practice and Research*. National Academies Press. p. 41. ISBN 978-0-309-21960-0. Archived from the original on 2018-05-04.

- Steel, Alex; Galloway, Kate; Heath, Mary; Skead, Natalie; Israel, Mark; and Hewitt, Anne (2016). "A Critical Legal Reading: The Elements, Strategies and Dispositions Needed to Master this Essential Skill," *Legal Education Review*: Vol. 26: Iss. 1, Article 9. Available at: https://epublications.bond.edu.au/ler/vol26/iss1/9

Analysis of
Information

Written by Christy Powers, Esq.

© 2019, 2020, 2021 NALA, Inc. All rights reserved.

This chapter will provide the necessary tools to successfully navigate through the essay exercise assessment. Weighing all potential options for the client(s) is necessary to demonstrate the ability to be impartial. Upon completion of this chapter, examinees will be able to:

- Recognize, sort, and categorize applicable legal authority

- Isolate and recite the potential legal issues presented by the relevant facts and applicable legal authority

- Assess the client's potential legal outcomes and conclusions supported by the relevant facts and applicable legal authority

Consider the fact pattern provided earlier regarding an alleged theft in order to work through the legal authority and the potential issues presented.

FACTS (as provided by NALA):

Jenny and Jake, a happily married couple, went to the movies. They enjoyed watching shows every other weekend on the live screen as a way to get some well-deserved time away from their seven children. Jenny's favorite place to attend the movies was at a ritzy theater in downtown New York. On January 13th, the couple treaded out into snowy conditions to get to the theater. Upon arriving to see the show, *Always a Never*, the couple checked their coats into the coat check and received tickets with a coat number.

The theater packed out at 300 attendees. The movie theater provided food and drinks to the attendees for a special showing of the newly released movie. Another couple who lived nearby, Katie and Jimmy, also attended a movie that evening. They, too, were parents who needed a night out on the town. Katie and Jimmy checked their coats in to the same coat check as Jenny and Jake had that evening.

Throughout the evening, the coat check was monitored by one person. Only a few people left the theater early that evening. After the show ended, Jenny and Jake grabbed their coats and drove home. Upon arriving home, the babysitter noticed that Jenny's coat was a very expensive brand and was "made just for her," referring to the embroidery on the sleeve. At that time, Jenny realized that it was not the coat she wore to the theater. She decided to hang the coat and call the theater in the morning. Also, the prior evening, Jenny's friend Katie was not given the same coat as the number on her ticket and had argued heatedly with coat check monitor.

The next morning, Jenny woke up late. She rushed to get her two children to school. It was a cold morning. She grabbed the coat and left the house. While walking her youngest son to his preschool class, Katie, a mom of another child, noticed the coat Jenny was wearing. Katie knew that the coat was hers because she attended the theater the night before and, at coat check, was given a coat that was not hers. Katie decided to confront Jenny about the coat. From her phone, Katie showed Jenny pictures of Katie wearing the coat. Katie also informed Jenny that her coat was very expensive and originally cost $600.00. Jenny apologized and gave the coat back. Katie informed Jenny that, because it was disgusting and smelled horrible, she threw Jenny's coat away. Jenny grabbed Katie's coat back and proceeded to walk out the door. In shock, Katie notified the school resource officer who was able to catch Jenny in her car. Jenny was texting her husband regarding what just happened. The officer arrested Jenny. Jenny has come to our office for representation in the matter.

Please review the attached statutes and prepare a memorandum to me concerning what steps, if any, can be taken to assist our client with this matter.

© 2019, 2020, 2021 NALA, Inc. All rights reserved.

Statutes:

- **SS 410.200 Theft defined**: the carrying and taking away of personal property with the intent to deprive the owner permanently.

- **SS 410.203 Petty theft**: the theft of property valued at $500 or less is considered a Class A misdemeanor (as long as the property is not taken directly from the person of another).

- **SS 410.213 Class 2 felony**: theft of property valued at less than $500 taken from the person of another; or if property is valued at between $500 and $10,000 in value and the theft is committed in a school, in a place of worship, or if the property belongs to the government.

- **SS 410.214 Class 3 felony**:

  (a) theft of property valued at more than $500 and not more than $10,000.

  (b) property that is the subject of the theft is valued at less than $500, the offense is a Class 3 felony if the property is taken from the person of another.

  (c) any retail theft of property with a retail value of more than $300 is a Class 3 felony.

- **SS 410.500 Penalties**:

  (a) a Class A misdemeanor conviction holds a sentence of imprisonment for less than one year and a fine of no more than $2,500 for each offense, plus payment of restitution for losses associated with the theft.

  (b) a Class 2 felony conviction can result in a sentence of imprisonment ranging from three to seven years and a fine of not more than $25,000, plus payment of restitution for losses associated with the theft.

  (c) a Class 3 felony conviction results in a sentence of two to five years of imprisonment, a fine not to exceed $25,000, plus payment of restitution for losses associated with the theft.

ASSESSING LEGAL AUTHORITY

The Skills Exam poses a variety of legal authority. The potential types of legal authority provided on the exam are the following: laws, statutes, rules, regulations, annotations, ordinances, case law, and other possible combinations of the items listed. For purposes of the Skills Exam, all of the legal authority provided must be assessed and considered. For example, the definition of theft as, "the carrying and taking away of personal property with the intent to deprive permanently," could potentially describe both Jenny's and Katie's behavior. Jenny may have committed theft by grabbing Katie's coat and leaving the classroom. Katie may have committed "theft" by throwing Jenny's coat away, as it deprived Jenny permanently of her personal property. As indicated above, the examinee will have to assess and consider all the statutes/rules that relate to the cost of the coat or Jenny's intent when she took Katie's coat back. In summation, the examinee must have the ability to segregate relevant facts, identify issues, and apply those relevant facts to reach a conclusion in a concise analysis.

LEGAL ISSUES

There are a few ways an examinee may identify issues. There will always be more than one issue. Issues can be determined by reviewing the legal authority provided and examining its applicability.

When drafting issues, it is best to use a question format beginning with words such as "Whether," "Did," "If," "What," and/or "How." For example, the following are a few viable issues:

1. <u>Whether</u> Jenny committed theft? *yes*

2. <u>If</u> Jenny committed petty theft, would she be guilty of a Class 2 felony, and/or a Class 3 felony?

3. <u>If</u> Jenny committed any forms of theft, what might be the penalty?

2-5 years of imprisonment, fine not to exceed $25,000, restitution of losses associated w/ theft

LEGAL OUTCOMES AND CONCLUSIONS

Writing the conclusion for the essay requires the examinee to scrutinize the client's situation in order to evaluate outcomes and potential results. Based on the situation above, one could conclude that Jenny would be charged with theft if it was her intent to permanently deprive Katie of the coat.

Later in the textbook, decision-making will be covered which will provide the examinee a process by which to analyze the relevant facts and determine how they relate to the statutes provided.

Decision-Making

Written by Penelope Long-Leahy, ACP

© 2019, 2020, 2021 NALA, Inc. All rights reserved.

To pass the Skills Exam portion of the Certified Paralegal (CP) Exam, paralegals must be confident in their decision-making skills. In the legal world, decisions often must be made promptly and without hesitation. Exercising the best judgment in these situations can be challenging. Rather than approach decision-making impulsively and/or emotionally, it is important to establish a method by which to deduce the best course of action.

Decision-making is a prominent part of the Certified Paralegal (CP) Exam. In addition to the many options to choose from when answering multiple choice questions in the substantive (Knowledge) section, the Skills section of the exam provides a complex essay writing exercise that requires an objective analysis. For the essay, the examinee is given a memorandum from an attorney which contains a set of convoluted facts (hypothetical scenario) and a collection of statutes (or "rules"), and/or case law. The fact pattern contains many "red herring" facts for the purpose of challenging the paralegal to sort through and identify only the facts essential and relevant to the issue(s). At the end of the facts section of this memo, the attorney asks a question: a problem the paralegal must analyze to reach a conclusion. The paralegal must weed through and decide which facts are specifically relevant to the question asked in the memo. The examinee must be able to negate those statutes and apply the pertinent facts to the relevant statutes. In doing this, it is helpful to reason/decide why each statute should be applied or negated. Thus, excellent decision-making and sharp analytical skills are crucial to passing this portion of the exam.

Often, a paralegal's self-reflection into their typical decision-making process can assist with improving bad habits, such as overcomplicating the facts or making impulsive decisions. Once the paralegal is aware of those behaviors and learns the tools to make competent and informed decisions, the paralegal should be able to cast those unproductive habits aside, work through the relevant data, and come to a logical conclusion.

FORMS OF ANALYTICAL REASONING

Making sound decisions requires analyzing the situation at hand and assessing the best approach to problem solving. There are three types of analytical reasoning.

1. **Deductive Reasoning** is a logical process in which a conclusion is based on the similarities of multiple premises that generally are assumed to be true. Deductive reasoning is sometimes referred to as top-down logic or syllogism. It is a type of logic where general statements are used to form a conclusion.
   For example:
   All apples are fruits, and a Granny Smith is an apple. Therefore, the Granny Smith must be a fruit.

2. **Inductive Reasoning** proceeds from specific premises to a general conclusion.
   For example:
   The chair in the living room is red. The chair in the dining room is red. The chair in the bedroom is red. Therefore, all chairs in the house are red.

3. **Analogical Reasoning** is the ability of an individual to analyze a situation, formulate a step-by-step method to evaluate the alternatives, eliminate the options that do not fit, and find a solution that best matches the problem. Questions requiring analogical reasoning make up a significant section of the Law School Admission Test (LSAT). An example of analogical reasoning is when one thing is understood (X) and another is not (Y), to conclude something about Y.

 © 2019, 2020, 2021 NALA, Inc. All rights reserved.

Example: (from *https://www.indiabix.com/logical-reasoning/analogies/*)
Odometer is to mileage as compass is to

A) *Speed*
B) *Hiking*
C) *Needle*
D) *Direction*
Answer: Option D

Explanation:
An odometer is an instrument used to measure mileage. A compass is an instrument used to determine direction. Choices A, B, and C are incorrect because none is an instrument.

Because analogical reasoning compares the first to the second and uses that comparison to conclude the comparison of another similar scenario or situation, it is the same method used in the principle of *stare decisis*. *Black's Law Dictionary*, 2nd Ed. defines *stare decisis* as "the doctrine that requires that judges abide by the prior decisions on the same issues (usually courts within the same jurisdiction and of equal or higher level)." It is the law of precedence. This is why it is important to have a solid comprehension of analogical reasoning when analyzing a fact pattern against a set of statutes or rules.

SEVEN STEPS TO THE DECISION-MAKING PROCESS

Generally, there are seven major steps to the decision-making process. Because this decision-making section is focused on the Skills Exam, the process will be examined using the essay as an example.

Ultimately, the essay exercise that makes up the Skills section of the CP Exam requires the examinee to answer a question or questions. To competently analyze this question, which is put forth by an attorney in memorandum format, the examinee must make decisions. The decision process can be broken down into the following seven steps:

1. **Identify the problem for which a decision must be made.**
   What needs to be achieved by this decision? What are the issues presented by the question?

2. **Gather all facts and data required to solve the problem.**
   What are the relevant facts? To ascertain the relevant facts, one must determine which facts are not relevant to the problem.

3. **Identify decision alternatives as they pertain to the fact pattern and the statutes provided.**
   Narrow down the options.

4. **Weigh the evidence within the fact pattern.**
   Which relevant facts directly affect the problem outcome? Which available statutes relate directly to the facts provided?

5. **Choose the alternative.**
   Once the fact pattern has been reduced only to relevant facts and then applied to the appropriate statutes ("rules") and/or case law, it is time to write an analysis. Why does this statute apply? As mentioned above, it is beneficial to the examinee to also ask why a specific statute does not apply, although it is not a requirement to address all alternatives and negate those that do not apply. Noting or thinking about which statutes must be negated will assist in understanding which statutes do apply and why.

© 2019, 2020, 2021 NALA, Inc. All rights reserved.

6. **Now it is time to conclude by putting together all the above steps.**
   The conclusion should be concise and must answer the question asked by the memorandum.

7. **Finally, review the analysis and conclusion.**
   Have all the relevant facts been addressed? Have all the relevant statutes been applied? Proofread the essay for spelling, punctuation, and sentence structure. Has the problem been resolved? Was the attorney's question in the memo answered? If not, it is time to dig a little deeper as to why there was not a desirable outcome and repeat the steps.

ETHICAL CONSIDERATIONS IN DECISION-MAKING

Most paralegals can recite the profession's ethical guidelines in their sleep. These guidelines, along with additional protocols enumerated in the Model Rules of Professional Conduct for attorneys, dictate the considerations a paralegal must consider when faced with a decision-making task for which there is an ethical dilemma.

The paralegal professional basic guidelines mandate that a paralegal shall not:

- Enter an attorney-client relationship

- Negotiate fees with a client

- Appear in court on behalf of a client

- Give legal advice

Paralegals must be mindful of these ethical boundaries when faced with decisions in or outside the workplace. In everyday life, paralegals are confronted with ethical decision-making. Examples include a neighbor requesting assistance with contract terms, or a friend asking for advice concerning a divorce or other legal matter. These are common occurrences in the life of a paralegal. It is difficult to say no to a trusted friend or neighbor. However, it is essential that paralegals consider ethical obligations in their personal lives as well as at work. Even seasoned paralegals may believe they know the correct answer or how to fill out a form, but ethically, the appropriate course of action would be to refer the friend or neighbor to a licensed attorney. An example of a workplace decision-making challenge might be when the (boss) attorney asks the paralegal to sign a pleading, or to send out a contract without the attorney's oversight (review). Following the seven steps of decision-making, the paralegal's moral compass, and the perimeters which govern the profession, should lead the paralegal to an ethically sound conclusion.

To conclude, it is important to understand how emotions can get in the way of sound decision-making. Learning to identify emotional triggers and to consider consequences of a decision leads to good judgment and analytical ability when faced with tough decisions.

© 2019, 2020, 2021 NALA, Inc. All rights reserved.

Practice Skills Exam
- Sample Essays

Sample Skills Exam Question #1

Answer the following question. You will be graded on your ability to identify which facts are relevant and state them concisely and accurately; identify the threshold or main legal issue and any secondary issue(s); and identify the relevant legal authority and apply it to the facts and draw persuasive logical conclusions. Do not rely on any other authority or your knowledge of the law; only use what is given in the question. Your answer should be in the form of a memorandum to the attorney including the following: Facts/Issue(s), Discussion/Analysis, and Conclusion. Pay attention to clarity, composition, conciseness, and organization.

MEMORANDUM

TO: Paul Paralegal

FROM: Andrew Attorney

DATE:

RE: Client Linda Hill - Inheritance

Linda Hill would like us to review two documents she brought in today and to give our opinion on what she may expect to inherit from her uncle's estate. Linda relayed the following:

Kenneth Blue, Linda's uncle, and his wife, Elaine, met late in life. They had no children. Elaine was an only child, and her parents died soon after her marriage to Kenneth. Kenneth has six nieces and nephews. Linda, Larry, and Lance Hill are the children of Kenneth's sister Jean. The other nieces and nephews are the children of Kenneth's sister Ella. They are Brian Cross, Liz Green, and Donna Cross.

Elaine died in 2009. After Elaine's death, to alleviate his loneliness, Kenneth spent more time with the six nieces and nephews. He had his attorney, Sarah Swift, draw up a will, in which he left his estate in equal shares to the six nieces and nephews. Kenneth signed the will on October 1, 2010. His signature was witnessed by Swift and her assistant. The will named Donna Cross as executor of the estate. He told the six nieces and nephews about the contents of the will and said they should notify Ms. Swift when he dies. He said she would handle everything then.

Kenneth was diagnosed with a terminal illness in January 2012. Fearing that the day might come when he would not be able to manage his own financial affairs and wanting to be free of financial worries while fighting his illness, Kenneth asked the court to appoint Sarah Swift conservator of his estate. This would give her the authority to manage his assets and to pay his bills, beginning with the court's appointment on June 2, 2012, and ending on his death or when Kenneth successfully petitioned the court to terminate the conservatorship. Pursuant to the laws governing conservators, on July 10, 2012, Sarah Swift filed an inventory of Kenneth's assets with the court, which listed miscellaneous personal property, two bank accounts with balances totaling $4,500, and 30 shares of Baker Holiday Class A stock. After Swift used the $4,500 in Kenneth's accounts to pay some of his medical bills, she sold one (1) share of the Baker Holiday stock on July 30, 2012; the sale price was $120,000.

Kenneth fought his illness bravely but died at home on July 7, 2013. A few days after the funeral, Linda and her cousins met with Swift at Swift's office. Swift told the nieces and nephews at their meeting that Kenneth had 29 shares of Baker Holiday stock and $102,500 cash in the bank when he died. Swift reviewed the will Kenneth had signed in 2010 and said she would draft the documents necessary for

---

                                      © 2019, 2020, 2021 NALA, Inc. All rights reserved.

probate proceedings. Swift hired a company specializing in estate sales to dispose of Kenneth's personal property. A company representative showed up in Swift's office on July 20, 2013, and handed her a paper found in a drawer of Kenneth's desk. The note, in Kenneth's handwriting, said:

"When I die, my niece Linda Hill gets all my Baker Holiday stock. Everything else goes to my nephew Brian Cross. Donna Cross should be the executor of my estate. (signed) Kenneth Blue, January 1, 2012."

Linda brought copies of both the 2010 will and the handwritten note with her today and left them with us. Please review them and the applicable statutes and prepare a memorandum setting out the relevant law and your conclusions on what Linda's share of her uncle's estate will be, if anything.

Selected Statutes

2-2301 Definitions.

(a) **Conservator** - a person who is appointed by a court to manage the estate of a protected person.

(b) **Devise** (noun) - a disposition under the provisions of a will of real or personal property; devise (verb) - to dispose of real or personal property by will.

(c) **Devisee** - the person designated in a will to receive a devise.

(d) **Estate** - the property of the decedent or the protected person whose affairs are subject to the provisions of this Chapter 2.

(e) **Executor** - the person appointed by the court to administer the estate of a deceased person.

(f) **Protected** - is a minor or other person for whom a conservator has been appointed.

(g) **Testator** - the maker of a will.

2-2327 Execution. Except as provided for holographic wills, every will is required to be in writing, signed by the testator, and signed by at least two individuals who witnessed the signing of the will.

2-2328 Holographic will. An instrument which purports to dispose of a person's property upon the individual's death but does not comply with section 2-2327 is valid as a holographic will, whether or not witnessed, if the signature, the material provisions, and an indication of the date of signing are in the handwriting of the testator.

2-2332 Revocation by writing or by act. A will is revoked by a subsequent writing which qualifies as a will under either Section 2-2327 or 2-2328, so long as it expressly revokes a prior will or wills or which has terms inconsistent with a prior will or wills.

2-2345 Change in securities. If the testator makes a specific devise of certain securities, the specific devisee is entitled only to as much of the devised securities as is a part of the estate at the time of the testator's death.

2-2346 Specific devises. Preservation of specific devises in certain case of sale by conservator or guardian.

(a) If a testator makes a specific devise of certain property, the specific devisee is entitled to as much of the specific devise as is a part of the estate at the time of the testator's death.

(b) If specifically devised property is sold by a conservator or guardian, the specific devisee has the right to a devise equal to the net sale price, less that part of the net sale price expended by the conservator or guardian for the benefit of the protected person.

2-2350 Conversion of assets by a conservator or guardian. A specific devisee may recover from a conservator or guardian damages of triple the amount of any of the net sale price of specifically devised property which said conservator or guardian converts for personal gain or expends for purposes other than for the benefit of the protected person during the protected person's lifetime.

© 2019, 2020, 2021 NALA, Inc. All rights reserved.

MEMORANDUM

TO: Andrew Attorney

FROM: Paul Paralegal

DATE:

RE: Linda Hill's Inheritance

Kenneth Blue ("Blue"), uncle of our client Linda Hill, died July 7, 2013. Ms. Hill wants our opinion on what she will inherit from him.

FACTS:

In October 2010, Blue made a will leaving his estate in equal shares to six nieces and nephews, one of whom is our client, Linda. The will was drafted by attorney Sarah Swift, signed, and properly witnessed. The will named niece Donna Cross executor. Blue's wife had predeceased him.

Blue was diagnosed with a terminal illness in January 2012. For assistance in managing his financial affairs, Blue petitioned the court to have attorney Swift appointed as his conservator. Following the court appointment in June 2012, Swift filed an inventory of Blue's assets, as required by law. The assets were miscellaneous personal property, bank accounts with balances totaling $4,500, and 30 shares of Baker Holiday Class A stock. As conservator, Swift sold one share of the Baker Holiday stock on July 30, 2012.

Blue died July 7, 2013. At a meeting with the nieces and nephews held soon after Blue's funeral, Swift reviewed the 2010 will and informed them Blue had died with $102,500 in the bank and 29 shares of Baker Holiday stock. Swift said she would draft papers to open probate.

On July 20, 2013, a representative of the company hired to dispose of Blue's personal property delivered to Swift a paper found in a drawer of Blue's desk. The note, in Blue's handwriting, appeared to be a will leaving all Baker Holiday stock to niece Linda Hill, and everything else to nephew Brian Cross, and naming Donna Cross executor. It was signed and dated January 1, 2012.

ISSUES:

1. Does Kenneth's writing dated 1/1/2012 qualify as a valid holographic will?

2. Does the 1/1/12 will revoke the prior will?

3. Who inherits the Baker Holiday stock and the funds in the bank account?

Discussion/Analysis

Blue's 2010 will was signed by the maker and witnessed by two individuals, as required by Section 2-2327. A writing that does not meet the requirements of Section 2-2327 for execution of a will, but that directs disposition of the maker's property, and is signed by the maker with an indication of the date of signing, all in the maker's handwriting, will qualify as a holographic will under Section 2-2328. The discovered document dated January 1, 2012, stated how Blue wanted his estate distributed, and named an executor, all in Blue's handwriting, and was signed by Blue. The January 1, 2012, writing is a valid holographic will.

Section 2-2332 states that a will is revoked "by a subsequent writing which qualifies as a will under

© 2019, 2020, 2021 NALA, Inc. All rights reserved.

either Section 2-2327 or 2-2328 so long as it expressly revokes a prior will or wills or which has terms inconsistent with a prior will or wills." The 2010 will left Blue's property equally to six nieces and nephews. The holographic will written in 2012 leaves property to only two people: the Baker Holiday stock to our client Linda Hill and the residue to Brian Cross. Because the holographic will written by Blue in 2012 has terms inconsistent with the 2010 will, the holographic will revokes the 2010 will.

The holographic will left Linda all of Blue's Baker Holiday stock. Accordingly, she will inherit the remaining 29 shares under Section 2-2346(a). At issue is the one share sold by Swift while she was Blue's conservator. Section 2-2346(b) directs that the devisee (Linda) is entitled to the net sale price of specific property left to a devisee, less that part of the net sale price expended for the benefit of the will's maker, if it was sold by a conservator. When Swift was appointed conservator, Blue had $4,500 in the bank. After those funds were expended on Blue's care, Swift sold the share for $120,000. When Blue died, he had $102,500 in the bank. This bank balance was the remaining net sale proceeds of the share sold by a conservator, and, pursuant to Section 2-2346(b), should go to Linda.

Conclusion

The 2012 writing is a valid holographic will, which effectively revoked the 2010 will. Under the terms of the 2012 holographic will, Linda inherits the remaining 29 shares of Baker Holiday stock and the $102,500, because it is the balance of the net sale proceeds of the share of Baker Holiday stock sold by Swift as conservator.

© 2019, 2020, 2021 NALA, Inc. All rights reserved.

SAMPLE SKILLS EXAM QUESTION #2

Answer the following question. You will be graded on your ability to identify which facts are relevant and state them concisely and accurately; identify the threshold or main legal issue and any secondary issue(s); and identify the relevant legal authority and apply it to the facts and draw persuasive logical conclusions. Do not rely on any other authority or your knowledge of the law; only use what is given in the question. Your answer should be in the form of a memorandum to the attorney including the following: Facts/Issue(s), Discussion/Analysis, and Conclusion. Pay attention to clarity, composition, conciseness, and organization.

MEMORANDUM

TO: Chris Garcia, Paralegal

FROM: Cynthia Chan, Attorney

DATE:

RE: Animal Attack at Sacks Assisted Living for Lions (SALL)

After years of research and training, Beverly and Dan Sacks turned their cattle ranch into a wild animal sanctuary dedicated to giving quality care to elderly and sick lions from reputable circuses and zoos around the United States. Located in the California Sierra Nevada foothills, the sanctuary is known as "Sacks Assisted Living for Lions" (SALL).

The sanctuary houses over 50 lions that roam freely in a highly secured, fenced, natural habitat. Eligible animals include circus lions which have reached the age of retirement, typically 18, or lions that are physically unable to perform the circus tricks mastered at a young age. About one-third of the lions have come from zoos. Some of the lions are blind or suffering from illnesses associated with old age.

SALL is open to visitors for a fee during daylight business hours, Thursday through Sunday. Trained staff members drive visitors in protected vehicles, either an SUV or minivan, through the 200acre sanctuary, stopping along the way to allow the visitors to enjoy unobstructed views of the lions resting or rolling in the grass and playing together. Although the lions spend most of their time resting, they are inquisitive and social by nature. Occasionally, a few lions may approach the tour vehicles and rub against the bumpers like big house cats. The lions have used their claws to scratch the rubberized, plastic bumpers, requiring replacement. During the 10 years that SALL has been open, no lion has ever attacked a visitor or staff member. However, under statutory and case law, the lions are still considered "wild animals" and should be considered "wild animals" for your analysis.

Neighbors Greg Thompson and Sam, his adult son, were often paying visitors to the sanctuary. After several years, the Sacks let Greg and Sam visit the sanctuary during business hours without paying. Sometimes Greg or Sam even drove the tour vehicles among the lions without Beverly or Dan along, often with paying visitors in the vehicle. Sam also has helped with upkeep of the vehicles including replacing the animal damaged bumpers. Sam liked to entertain visitors with stories about the lions and their prior days as circus performers.

Late one night, Sam and a friend James were drinking beer and watching television. Sam started talking about the lions. James had never been to the sanctuary and wanted to see the lions. Knowing that the lions can be active during the night hours, Sam offered to take James over to the sanctuary. Sam told James that they could enter SALL at night without Beverly or Dan ever knowing, but they would have to scale a 12-foot fence to gain access.

© 2019, 2020, 2021 NALA, Inc. All rights reserved.

Sam and James scaled the fence. Sam knew where the tour vehicle keys were kept, and he took one to drive around the sanctuary. Beverly and Dan saw the lights of the tour vehicle from the ranch house but assumed that it was one of the hired staff who came in the evening several times a week to check on the lions' water supply and food.

Sam and James drove into the sanctuary. Some of the lions came up to the vehicle and started rubbing against the door and bumper. In an attempt to impress his friend with how well he knew the animals, Sam stopped the vehicle and got out. He reached over and tried to feed an elderly lioness. In the process, he stepped on the lioness's foot, causing the lioness to bite Sam twice on the forearm. When Sam screamed, James panicked. James slid over to the driver's seat and started the vehicle. He quickly pulled Sam and his mangled arm back into the tour vehicle, but in the process the lioness clawed James's arm.

James managed to drive the tour vehicle to the ranch house where Beverly and Dan promptly called 911. An ambulance arrived shortly and transported Sam and James to a local hospital. James was treated for his injuries and released from the hospital after several hours. Sam was treated and admitted to the hospital. He was later transferred to another hospital and underwent several surgeries during a 10day hospital stay.

Our clients, Beverly and Dan Sacks, wonder if Sam and James would succeed in a lawsuit against SALL. Please review the statutes relating to these potential claims and prepare a memorandum to me, evaluating the legal aspects and stating whether Sam and James would succeed in a lawsuit against SALL.

Selected Statutes

Section 1001. For the purposes of this Chapter, Sections 1002 to 2010, a wild animal is a living creature that is not a plant, that has not been tamed or domesticated, is traditionally thought of as being wild, and in its natural state or running unrestrained in a natural environment.

Section 1002. A wildlife refuge, also called a wildlife sanctuary, may be a naturally occurring sanctuary, such as an island, that provides protection for species from hunting, predation, or competition, or it may refer to a protected area, a geographic territory within which wildlife is protected. Such wildlife refuges are generally officially designated territories, created by government legislation or licensing, although the land itself may be publicly or privately owned.

Section 1003. The Federal Wildlife Service is responsible for designating, licensing, and regulating wildlife sanctuaries, including wildlife refuges and territories or areas.

Section 1004. It is a federal crime for any person to house, feed, or care for wild animals without a federal license issued by the Federal Wildlife Service.

Section 2001. The possessor or owner of a wild animal is subject to liability for the resulting harm caused by the wild animal even though it would not have occurred but for the unexpected, innocent, negligent, or reckless conduct of a third person.

Section 2004. Notwithstanding Section 2001, if a person injured by a wild animal voluntarily subjected himself to the wild animal, with knowledge of the danger, that person may not recover compensation for his injuries from the animal's owner.

Section 2008. Notwithstanding Section 2001, a trespasser, one who has no permission from the landowner to come on the land, may not recover for damages resulting from injuries when the trespasser comes willingly onto the land and suffers injuries as a result of those things the trespasser knows or should have reasonably known to exist on the land.

 © 2019, 2020, 2021 NALA, Inc. All rights reserved.

SAMPLE SKILLS EXAM ANSWER #2

MEMORANDUM

TO: Cynthia Chan, Attorney

FROM: Chris Garcia, Paralegal

DATE:

Re: Animal Attack at Sacks Assisted Living for Lions (SALL)

You have asked me to review certain statutes and determine if Sam and James would be able to succeed in a lawsuit for their injuries against our clients Beverly and Dan Sacks.

Facts

Our clients Beverly and Dan Sacks operate and own the Sacks Assisted Living for Lions (SALL), a 200-acre wild animal sanctuary for elderly lions retired from circuses and zoos. The sanctuary is a natural habitat where the lions roam freely, but the area is secured and fenced. For a fee, visitors are given tours of the sanctuary and the lions in protected tour vehicles during daylight business hours.

Sam Thompson, a neighbor of the Sacks, has many times toured the sanctuary, has assisted in giving tours, and has helped with repairs to vehicles caused by the clawing of the animals. One night, Sam was entertaining his friend James and suggested they go over to the sanctuary to see the lions. Sam assured James that he could get on the property without Beverly and Dan being aware of their presence, but they had to get over a 12-foot fence.

Sam and James went onto the property and took a tour vehicle. Sam stopped the vehicle near a lioness and got out. He stepped on the lioness's foot. The lioness attacked and injured Sam. James was also injured when he came to Sam's assistance. Dan and Beverly Sacks are asking if SALL could be liable for the injuries to Sam and James caused by their lioness.

Issues

Main Issue: Is SALL liable for injuries to Sam and James?

Secondary Issue A: Did Sam voluntarily subject himself to the wild animal with knowledge of the dangers, thus preventing him from recovering damages?

Secondary Issue B: Are Sam and James considered trespassers, and thus both precluded from recovering damages?

Discussion

Under statutory and case law it is settled that lions are considered wild animals. Under Section 20-01 the Sacks, as possessors of wild animals, would be liable for the resulting harm that occurred to Sam and James.

Although the Sacks are liable under Section 20-01, the actions of Sam and James will create a complete defense. Sam was very much familiar with the wild animals and the sanctuary. He had visited the

---

© 2019, 2020, 2021 NALA, Inc. All rights reserved.

sanctuary a number of times, assisted in tours, and helped with repairs to tour vehicles caused by the clawing of lions. He also knew what the lions could do when provoked. Under Section 20-04 if a person "…injured by a wild animal, voluntarily subjected himself…with the knowledge of the danger… [he]… may not recover compensation for his injuries." Sam knew the dangers and voluntarily chose to leave the vehicle, which led to the attack and the injuries.

In addition, both Sam and James are considered trespassers who have no permission to come on to the land under Section 20-08. That provision states: that a "…trespasser comes willingly onto land and suffers injuries…" from things he "…knows or should have reasonably known to exist…" may not thus recover compensation. Sam and James did not ask permission to come onto the land. Furthermore, Sam assured James that Beverly and Dan would not know they were taking a night tour, and that they would have to scale a 12-foot fence to gain access to the property. Sam and James were well-aware they were coming onto property with wild animals without permission of the owners.

Conclusion

Under Section 20-01, Beverly and Dan Sacks, who own and operate SALL, are liable for injuries caused by the wild animals they keep. However, under the facts presented, the Sacks have a complete defense because of the actions of Sam and James. Sam is precluded from recovering since he knowingly encountered the potential danger of being near a wild animal under Section 20-04, and he was a trespasser with knowledge of the wild animals under Section 20-08. Although James had not been to the sanctuary before, he is precluded from recovery under Section 20-08 as a trespasser with knowledge of the existence of wild animals.

© 2019, 2020, 2021 NALA, Inc. All rights reserved.

SAMPLE SKILLS EXAM QUESTION #3

Answer the following question. You will be graded on your ability to identify which facts are relevant and state them concisely and accurately; identify the threshold or main legal issue and any secondary issue(s); and identify the relevant legal authority and apply it to the facts and draw persuasive logical conclusions. Do not rely on any other authority or your knowledge of the law; only use what is given in the question. Your answer should be in the form of a memorandum to the attorney including the following: Facts/ Issue(s), Discussion/Analysis, and Conclusion. Pay attention to clarity, composition, conciseness, and organization.

MEMORANDUM

TO: Stanley Dorite, Legal Assistant

FROM: Wilma Wonka, Staff Attorney

DATE:

RE: Stewart Carr Disciplinary Proceeding

Stewart Carr is a sole practitioner and a longtime attorney in this city. One of this firm's senior partners, Edwin Tuttle, has been asked to work with the Counsel for Discipline of the Utopia State Bar Association as a special prosecutor in a matter regarding Mr. Carr. Mr. Tuttle promised the Counsel for Discipline that we would take a look at the case.

One of Carr's clients purchased a toy chest at an estate sale. Several years later, she found six Series E United States savings bonds in the chest. The bonds had been issued to Hans and Louise Brinker as joint tenants. After attempting unsuccessfully to cash the bonds, the client employed Carr to find the owners and to obtain a reward or a finder's fee. The client told Carr that she wanted a reward of one-third but would take less. She said that if she did not get a reward, she would light her fireplace with the bonds.

In December of last year, Carr located Dick Brinker, a grandson of the original owners, both of whom were deceased. Carr told Brinker that his client wanted a reward of one-third and would kindle her fireplace with the bonds if she did not get a reward. Brinker contacted Earl Ludlow, a lawyer practicing in a nearby city. After negotiations between Carr and Ludlow, Dick Brinker agreed to pay a finder's fee to the client.

Approximately one month later, Dick Brinker contacted another attorney, Steve Guenzel, and requested a second opinion about the arrangement he had made with Ludlow.

Guenzel called Carr and, among other things, discussed Utopia Stat. 35-514 with him. That statute provides:

> A person who comes into control of property of another that he knows to have been lost or mislaid commits theft if, with intent to deprive the owner thereof, he fails to take reasonable measures to restore the property to a person entitled to have it. Any person violating the provisions of this section shall, upon conviction thereof, be punished by the penalty prescribed in the next lower classification below the value of the item lost or mislaid pursuant to Section 38-518.

Carr responded to this discussion by repeating his demand for a reward. Attorney Ludlow withdrew from the case.

Next, Guenzel called Carr and withdrew Brinker's previous agreement to pay a finder's fee.

Gladys Watson, Dick Brinker's sister, upon learning of the bonds' existence, filed a complaint against Carr with the Counsel for Discipline of the Utopia State Bar Association. Later, a police officer suggested that Watson call Carr and record the conversation.

Watson took the officer's advice and recorded the conversation. Instead of Stewart Carr, however, she spoke with Carr's legal assistant, Jack Fehrman. Fehrman related that Mr. Carr was out of the office; that they were no longer involved with the Brinker bonds; and that they had closed their file on the matter. Rather than discontinuing the conversation, however, Fehrman continued to talk to Watson. During that conversation, Fehrman said, "So, our client would rather light her fireplace with them if she does not get some money out of this. . .and if she decides to light her fireplace with them, I'm going to applaud her. You people are so greedy that nobody wants to pay her anything."

The entire matter, including the recorded telephone conversation, has been referred to the Counsel for Discipline and is now the subject of a pending hearing before the Committee on Inquiry. Carr is being charged with violating Canon 7-102(A)(7), which states, "A lawyer shall not assist a client in conduct the lawyer knows to be illegal," and Canon 9, which states, "A lawyer must avoid the appearance of impropriety."

Upon his admission that he had the telephone conversation with Watson, Fehrman was fired by Carr. Carr believes he should not be held responsible for Fehrman's statements, which were made without his knowledge or consent.

Please prepare a memorandum that discusses this case in light of existing statutes, ethical rules, and case law.

Selected Case Law

State of Utopia Ex Rel. Utopia State Bar Association,
Relator, v. Alex M. Krist 232 Utop. 445
Filed June 9, 1989 No. 87-546

Original action. Judgment of Disbarment.

The facts are that on or about April 30, 1986, the Counsel for Discipline received a written letter of complaint against the respondent by Mrs. Roy Butternut concerning respondent's handling of a bankruptcy matter. On May 1, 1986, the respondent received notice that he was the subject of a complaint made to the Counsel for Discipline, with an attached copy of Mrs. Butternut's complaint. He was further notified that he had fifteen (15) working days to respond. The letter from the Counsel for Discipline went on to state that if respondent failed to respond, the Rules provide that this failure alone shall be grounds for discipline.

On or about February 21, 1986, the Counsel for Discipline received a written letter of complaint against the respondent by Ms. Judy Scriven on behalf of Scriven, Quill, and Scriven, a freelance court reporting firm, asking for "help and/or advice" in collecting several unpaid deposition bills. The Counsel for Discipline forwarded the complaint to respondent and stated, "In my opinion, (Scriven's) letter does not set forth sufficient facts to file a complaint against you. I would appreciate, however, a written response from you addressing the issues raised." On April 24, 1986, May 20, 1986, and June 11, 1986, the Counsel for Discipline again notified the respondent by letter that he was the subject of a complaint by Ms. Scriven and requested an immediate response.

In his first amended answer to formal charges, respondent affirmatively alleged that he had timely responded to any notices of complaints he received from and after February 21, 1986, and stated:

© 2019, 2020, 2021 NALA, Inc. All rights reserved.

1. For further defense, Respondent denies that violation of a duly imposed procedural rule of this Court states facts sufficient to constitute a cause of action for violation of a substantive Disciplinary Rule of the Canons of Ethics as adopted by the Court.

2. For further defense, Respondent alleges that the Committee on Inquiry found that the failure to pay a disputed deposition bill did not form the basis of a substantive complaint against a member.

3. That such substantive complaint should have been dismissed if received by the Counsel on Discipline since such conduct, if true, has never been understood to form the basis of a disciplinary violation.

Respondent testified as to his personal problems, overwork, and extensive travel in 1986, and that he was not in his office on a daily basis commencing in May or June of that year. He became aware that his secretary, Ruth Johnson, often neglected to do the work he gave her and did not perform her duties while he was out of town, but he did not fire her because he did not want to train another secretary. Respondent also testified that Johnson took some of his files from the office while he was out of town after she had difficulty cashing one of her paychecks. Respondent testified that after Johnson quit in August 1986, a new secretary discovered a bundle of documents belonging to respondent, including his responses to the Butternut and Scriven complaints.

At the hearing before the referee, Betsy Boop, an attorney who shared an office with respondent, testified as to Johnson's general incompetence. Boop stated that she would not allow Johnson to do work for her. She also testified that after the new secretary was hired, they discovered old mail and notes which had been placed between two books on a table. Boop did not read the mail but noted that many of the items belonged to Krist.

Respondent was required to respond to the complaints pursuant to Utop. Ct. R. of Discipline 9(E) (rev.1986). A reasonable attorney would understand that the type of conduct is prohibited and adversely reflects on his fitness to practice law. The record supports a finding that respondent violated the Canons of Ethics in this respect.

We note that respondent was not charged with failure to provide management, supervision, and control of his office staff and procedures as required by Canon 1-102(A)(6). Respondent's own testimony suggested, however, that his failure to respond to the Butternut and Scriven complaints is the fault of his secretary, who he knew to be incompetent.

Even though we conclude that the referee's finding that respondent violated Canon 1-102(A)(6) by failing to provide management, supervision, and control of his office staff and procedures was in error, respondent's reliance on secretary's alleged incompetence as a defense is entirely misplaced. While respondent's failure to properly supervise his employee was not charged against the respondent, such conduct does not constitute a defense to the misconduct charged. A lawyer may not avoid responsibility for misconduct by hiding behind an employee's behavior and may not avoid a charge of unprofessional conduct by contending that his employees are incompetent.

The preliminary statement in the Canons of Ethics as adopted by this court states, "A lawyer should ultimately be responsible for the conduct of his employees and associates in the course of the professional representation of the client." "A lawyer also has responsibility to be aware at least of the major areas of responsibility and the actual work habits of employees and to exercise effective supervision." C. Wolfram on Modern Legal Ethics 16.3.1. at 893 (West 1986).

In *State ex rel. USBA v. Statmore*, 218 Utop. 138,356 E.W. 2d 875 (1984), we said: "A lawyer's poor accounting procedures and sloppy office management are not excuses or mitigating circumstances in reference to commingled funds. (Citations omitted.) Similarly, "[A]n attorney may not escape responsibility to his clients by blithely saying that any shortcomings are solely the fault of his employee. He has a duty to supervise the conduct of his office." *Attorney Grievance Comm v. Goldberg*, 292 Md. 650, 441A.2d 338 (1982). We hold that a lawyer is ultimately responsible for the conduct of his employees and associates in the course of the professional representation of the client.

Respondent's testimony shows only that his failure to supervise his employee directly contributed to his failure to timely respond to the Butternut and Scriven complaints. He may not use his secretary's alleged incompetence to shield him from the consequences of his unprofessional conduct.

The record clearly demonstrates that respondent has violated his oath of office and the disciplinary rules cited by the referee. We have no confidence that a public reprimand, or even a suspension, would serve to modify respondent's attitude or to protect the public. We recognize that disbarment is a harsh penalty. We conclude that in the circumstance of this case, a judgment of disbarment is appropriate. JUDGMENT OF DISBARMENT.

© 2019, 2020, 2021 NALA, Inc. All rights reserved.

MEMORANDUM

TO: Wilma Wonka, Staff Attorney

FROM: Stanley Dorite, Legal Assistant

DATE:

RE: Stewart Carr Disciplinary Proceeding

You have asked me to review existing statutes, case law, and ethical rules concerning the pending disciplinary proceedings involving Stewart Carr. Mr. Tuttle has been asked to serve as special prosecutor on behalf of the Utopia State Bar Association against Carr.

Facts

One of Carr's clients purchased a toy chest at an estate sale and later found six Series E United States savings bonds in the chest. The bonds had been issued to Hans and Louise Brinker as joint tenants. After attempting unsuccessfully to cash the bonds, the client employed Carr to find the owners and to obtain a reward or a finder's fee. The client told Carr that she wanted a reward and that if she did not get a reward, she would light her fireplace with the bonds.

Carr located Dick Brinker, a grandson of the original owners, both of whom were deceased. Carr relayed his client's demand to Brinker who, in turn, retained an attorney. Carr negotiated a finder's fee for his client. Later, Brinker sought a second opinion from Steve Guenzel. Guenzel discussed the provisions of Utopia Stat. 35-514 with Carr, who repeated his client's demand. Guenzel withdrew the offer of reward.

Gladys Watson, Dick Brinker's sister, learned about the bonds and filed a complaint with Counsel for Discipline of the Utopia State Bar Association. She called Carr's office and recorded her conversation with Carr's legal assistant, Jack Fehrman. Fehrman repeated the threat of Carr's client to use the bonds as kindling if she did not receive a reward for them.

Issues

1. Must Stewart Carr bear professional responsibility for the wrongful statements made by his legal assistant?

2. Did Stewart Carr violate any ethical rules, independent of the statements made by his legal assistant?

Discussion/Analysis

Stewart Carr's demand on behalf of his client violated Utopia State Statute Section 38-514, which states that anyone who comes into control of property he knows to have been lost or mislaid commits theft if he fails to take reasonable steps to restore the property to its owner. Even if Carr did not know of the existence of this statute at the time the original demand was made, he repeated his demand for a reward after the statute was pointed out to him.

Canon 7-102(A)(7) provides that "[a] lawyer shall not assist a client in conduct the lawyer knows to be illegal." Carr knew the demand he made on behalf of his client was illegal. As such, he is subject to appropriate disciplinary action.

Although the statements made by Carr's legal assistant are superfluous given Carr's own conduct, the point should be made that he cannot absolve himself of the misconduct of his employees. Jack Fehrman's wrongful statements must be attributed to Carr. Canon 1-102(A)(6) requires that "[a] lawyer must provide management, supervision, and control of his office staff." When faced with this issue in relation to a legal secretary, the Utopia supreme court stated:

> Such conduct does not constitute a defense to the misconduct charged. A lawyer may not avoid responsibility for misconduct by hiding behind an employee's misconduct and may not avoid a charge of unprofessional conduct by contending his employees are incompetent. *State of Utopia ex rel. USBA v. Krist*, 232 Utop. 445 (1989).

Although the specific sanctions that may be imposed cannot be reviewed without more thorough background information concerning Mr. Carr, it seems clear that he has violated specific Canons of ethical conduct, based both upon the conduct of his employee, Jack Fehrman, and upon his own conduct, independent of his employee.

Conclusion

Stewart Carr is professionally accountable for the conduct of his employee, Jack Fehrman. Independent of Jack Fehrman's conduct, however, Carr personally violated Utopia State Statute Section 38-514, Canon 7-102 (A)(7), and Canon 9 when he made an illegal demand on behalf of his client.

© 2019, 2020, 2021 NALA, Inc. All rights reserved.

Practice Questions
Answer Key

A B C D

© 2019, 2020, 2021 NALA, Inc. All rights reserved.

Chapter 1: United States Legal System Answer Key

1. **C. English common law**
    English common law is a system in which laws develop through the courts by case decisions. Common law is generally uncodified, meaning that there is no centralized compilation of court opinions, although cases are often published chronologically.

2. **D. *Stare decisis***
    The doctrine of *stare decisis* is the proposition that when an issue has been previously considered by a court and a ruling has been issued, the court will defer to its previous decision. This creates predictability and consistency for subsequent parties similarly situated involving the same legal issues.

3. **C. Right to safe housing**
    During the adoption process of the United States Constitution, the original document was amended to include specific guarantees of individual rights relating to liberty, justice, and the reservation of unenumerated rights and powers. These amendments (1-10) came to be known collectively as the "Bill of Rights."

4. **B. Preemption**
    The preemption doctrine holds that state regulation is precluded or invalid by federal regulation in three situations: 1) when Congress expressly states its intent to preempt state regulation; 2) when a state law is inconsistent with federal law, even though no express preemption has been made by Congress; and 3) when Congress, by its enactment of a comprehensive legislative scheme, sufficiently occupies a field so that it is reasonable to infer that it left no room for the states to supplement the federal law.

5. **B. Administrative branch**
    In setting up the structure of the federal government, the Founding Fathers applied the theory of separation of powers. Influenced by the social and political philosopher Montesquieu, the framers of the Constitution divided the federal government into legislative, executive, and judicial branches. Each branch is separate from the other and was established with specific duties and methods of selection.

6. **A. True**
    Congress can override a veto by a two-thirds vote of both houses. Both the veto power and Congress's ability to override a veto are examples of the system of checks and balances intended by the Constitution to prevent any one branch from gaining too much power.

7. **D. Six years**
    Senators serve six-year terms. Only one-third of the Senate is subject to election each two-year cycle.

8. **D. Lifetime**
    Members of the Supreme Court are nominated by the president of the United States and confirmed by the Senate. Federal judges serve for life, subject to retirement or removal from office through impeachment by Congress.

© 2019, 2020, 2021 NALA, Inc. All rights reserved.

9. **B. Two years**
   Members of the House of Representatives serve two-year terms, and the entire House of Representatives is subject to election every two years.

10. **A. Four years**
    The president serves a four-year term of office subject to a term limit of 10 years. The 22nd Amendment provides for a limit of two terms of office plus two years or less if a person serves part of the last president's term.

11. **A. The Electoral College**
    The president is not directly elected by the people, but rather is elected through an Electoral College process where each state is apportioned electors based on their representation in Congress, both the House and Senate.

12. **B. *Marbury v. Madison***
    The exact nature and scope of the review of the federal courts was originally vague. That changed in 1803 with *Marbury v. Madison*, a Supreme Court case which established the Court's power of judicial review, by which the courts determine the constitutionality of executive and legislative acts. Judicial review is another key example of the checks and balances system in action.

13. **A. Legislative**
    The legislative branch is responsible for enacting laws and providing the money necessary to operate the government.

14. **B. Executive**
    The executive branch is responsible for implementing and administering the laws enacted by the legislature.

15. **D. Judicial**
    The judicial branch is responsible for interpreting the Constitution and laws and applying these interpretations to cases and controversies brought before the courts.

16. **D. Declare war**
    The United States Constitution creates a limited and defined federal government of enumerated powers, not one of general powers such as those of the states. Article II, Section 8 of the Constitution sets forth the enumerated powers specifically delegated to the federal government, including declaring war.

17. **B. Legal digests**
    Primary sources of law provide first-hand, original information from bodies or individuals with legitimate law-creating authority. Secondary sources are not first-hand sources with binding authority but rather are analysis or reviews of the law by legal scholars or indexes and finding tools used to assist in researching the law. Legal digests are secondary sources of law.

18. **A. Quasi-Legislative**
Administrative agencies have a "quasi-legislative" function under which agencies generally follow specific procedural steps in adopting and issuing regulations. These steps usually include public notice, public comment, adherence to general guidelines, and explanation of the legislative source of the agency's authority for enforcing statutes and regulations.

19. **B. Quasi-Executive**
Administrative agencies perform "quasi-executive" functions in enforcing the regulations they have passed. Agencies investigate complaints and identify conduct they deem violate their regulations. Agencies commonly investigate activities subject to their regulations and may issue citations for violations, as well as issue advisory opinions stating generally how the agency views particular conduct.

20. **B. The Administrative Procedures Act**
In 1947, Congress enacted the Administrative Procedures Act (APA), which governs the process by which administrative agencies create and enact regulations.

21. **A. Personal jurisdiction**
Personal jurisdiction is the authority of a court to hear and decide a dispute involving the particular parties before it. Personal jurisdiction is geographical. Courts have personal jurisdiction over parties who reside or do business within a particular country, state, district, circuit, or county.

22. **B. Subject matter jurisdiction**
Subject matter jurisdiction is the authority of a court to hear and decide a particular dispute before it.

23. **D. Exceeds $75,000**
Federal court jurisdiction is limited to cases provided for by the Constitution or specifically authorized by Congress. This includes cases between citizens from different states when the amount in controversy exceeds $75,000, which is referred to as "diversity" jurisdiction.

24. **C. The locality where the crime occurred**
In criminal cases, proper venue is the locality where the crime occurred.

25. **C. Civil lawsuit**
Alternative dispute resolution refers to the processes that can be used to resolve conflicts or claims without having to go to court. This includes negotiation, case evaluation, mediation, arbitration, and mini-trial.

© 2019, 2020, 2021 NALA, Inc. All rights reserved.

CHAPTER 2: CIVIL LITIGATION ANSWER KEY

1. **A. Preponderance of the evidence**
   The burden of proof in most civil cases is the preponderance of the evidence. Clear and convincing evidence is used in civil cases where issues of greater importance, such as termination of parental rights, are at stake. Beyond a reasonable doubt is used only in criminal cases.

2. **A. Admitted**
   This discovery tool can be used to establish a fact, a legal theory, or the genuineness of a document. When a party does not timely respond to a request for admission, the fact, theory, or document is deemed admitted. There is no need to provide further proof.

3. **B. Summons**
   The summons is the document that orders the defendant to respond to the complaint and provides the deadline for an answer. A subpoena is a court order compelling an individual to appear and testify. An affidavit is sworn testimony used to support a motion or opposition. Proof of service is the document filed by a process server that evidences the date, time, and recipient of legal documents.

4. **B. FRCP 8**
   FRCP 8(c) lists the affirmative defenses that may be asserted. In responding to a preceding pleading, a party shall set forth affirmatively accord and satisfaction, arbitration and award, assumption of risk, contributory negligence, discharge in bankruptcy, duress, estoppel, failure of consideration, fraud, illegality, injury by fellow servant, laches, license, payment, release, *res judicata*, statute of frauds, statute of limitations, waiver, and any other matter constituting an avoidance or affirmative defense.

5. **C. Respondeat superior**
   Respondeat superior is a doctrine of vicarious liability, usually applied to an employer for the negligence of an employee. Contributory negligence, *res judicata*, and statute of limitations are common affirmative defenses in civil litigation.

6. **A. Court may dismiss case**
   The harshest penalty for failure to participate in discovery is the dismissal of the case. This remedy is used sparingly, usually with repeated offenses, disregard for court orders, or flagrant disrespect for the court.

7. **D. Motion for summary judgment**
   A motion for summary judgment asks the court to enter judgment as a matter of law if the moving party proves there is no genuine dispute as to any material fact and is entitled to the relief requested.

8. **D. Opening statement**
   The opening statement informs the jury what evidence each side will present during the trial.

9. **A. Deposition**
   Depositions may be used to gather information from parties, lay witnesses, or expert witnesses. Other discovery methods are limited to parties only.

---

10. **B. Supplemental jurisdiction**

Supplemental jurisdiction is a way for the federal court to hear a matter for which it would not normally have jurisdiction. If the matter has a substantial relation to a federal issue in addition to state issues, a case may be brought in federal court. An example would be the Exxon Valdez oil spill. The incident occurred in state waters and many Alaskans suffered damages as a result of the oil spill, putting the jurisdiction in state court. However, the U.S. Constitution places all admiralty (or maritime) matters within the jurisdiction of federal court. The federal court would have supplemental jurisdiction to hear claims related to the oil spill.

11. **D. The attorney believes the juror is uneducated**

An attorney may use a peremptory challenge to remove a potential juror for any reason, including the attorney's belief that a juror is uneducated. A reason does not need to be stated. In this question, the attorney may remove a juror who is biased or knows a party for cause. However, the U.S. Supreme Court has held that peremptory challenges cannot be used to systematically strike prospective jurors from the jury panel on the basis of race (*Batson v. Kentucky*, 1986).

12. **B. Motion for Default**

When a defendant fails to answer a complaint, the plaintiff may motion the court for a default judgment. A Motion to Compel is used to make a party comply with a court order or requirement, such as participating in discovery. A Motion to Strike is used to amend a pleading. A Motion for Summary Judgment is a dispositive motion that will end litigation.

13. **A. Answer**

When a counterclaim is asserted, the appropriate response under FRCP 7 is an answer. A cross-claim is asserted by one party against a coparty. A reply is typically used in motion practice. A third-party answer is the response to a third-party complaint.

14. **C. Special verdict**

In a special verdict, the jury issues findings as to each issue in dispute, as well as indicating the prevailing party and any award. A directed verdict is a ruling entered by a trial judge after determining that there is no legally sufficient evidentiary basis for a reasonable jury to reach a different conclusion. A general verdict simply indicates the prevailing party and possibly any award. A unanimous verdict is used only in criminal trials.

15. **A. The defendant**

Because the defendant asserts an affirmative defense in the answer, the defendant also has the burden of proving the defense. A plaintiff could only assert an affirmative defense in response to a counterclaim, cross-claim, or third-party complaint.

16. **B. Challenge jurors**

The trial scheduling conference occurs before the jury pool is brought together for voir dire. In the trial conference, the parties confirm the issues in dispute, agree to or resolve any evidentiary challenges, and confirm the length of trial, number of witnesses, and plan the admission of evidence.

 © 2019, 2020, 2021 NALA, Inc. All rights reserved.

17. **D. Issue a final judgment**

Before the entry of final judgment, the court will hear arguments, issue jury instructions, and rule on evidence. After the jury issues its verdict, the court then issues the final judgment. The judgment may be oral or written, becomes part of the official record, and becomes appealable to a higher court. This is the final act of the court at the trial level.

18. **D. Permissive joinder**

Permissive joinder allows a party, whose presence in the litigation is not required, to join if there are issues of fact or law common to all parties arising out of the action, and each plaintiff is entitled to relief. Compulsory joinder is mandatory when that person's involvement is required to grant complete relief, or the party has an interest in the litigation and their presence is required to protect those interests.

19. **B. A party lacks standing**

In situations where a party dies, becomes incapacitated, or is removed from public office, a substitution of parties is appropriate. When a party lacks standing, they do not have a legal right to sue for relief. A party must have incurred damages or the loss of a legal right to have standing.

20. **A. An indispensable party**

An indispensable party is one whose participation in the litigation is necessary in order for the court to render a decision that completely resolves the dispute. A permissive party is one who may be joined in the litigation if there is a question of fact or law in common, and the permissive party has a separate and individual right to relief. A third-party is a non-party who is joined through a third-party complaint after the court grants permission for third-party inclusion.

CHAPTER 3: CONTRACTS ANSWER KEY

1. **A. Revocation**
   Revocation is the recall of some power (authority, or thing granted) making void of some deed that had existence until the act of revocation.

2. **C. Void**
   An agreement is void when it is illegitimate and unenforceable from the moment it is created.

3. **C. Bilateral**
   A bilateral agreement involves two parties each promising to do (or not do) something.

4. **A. Breach**
   A breach occurs when a contract has been broken by a party to the promise.

5. **D. Implied**
   An implied contract is a legally binding obligation formed by the actions, conduct, or circumstances of one or more parties in an agreement.

6. **A. Rejection**
   Rejection occurs when one party decides not to accept the offer that was made, or accept goods as promised.

7. **C. Seriously intended**
   There are three requirements of a valid offer: communication, serious intent, and definite terms.

8. **D. Fraud**
   Fraud is the wrongful act or deception intended to result in financial or personal gain.

9. **B. Duress**
   Duress is a threat, violence, or other action done to compel someone to do something against their will or better judgment.

10. **C. Undue influence**
    Undue influence is excessive persuasion or domination that causes another person to act (or refrain from acting) by overcoming that person's free will and results in inequity.

11. **B. Remedy**
    Remedy is the way a right is satisfied by a court when some harm or injury (wrongful act) is inflicted upon an individual.

12. **A. Fraud**
    He commits fraud because his deception is intended to result in financial or personal gain.

13. **D. Something of value is being exchanged by the two parties**
    Consideration must be of value (at least to the parties) and exchanged for the performance or promise of performance by the other party.

© 2019, 2020, 2021 NALA, Inc. All rights reserved.

14. **A. Incidental**
These are costs and expenses incurred by the non-breaching party to avoid other direct and consequential losses caused by the breach and are not incidental nor direct damages due to the breach.

15. **B. Void**
Illegal contracts are void because they are illegitimate from the moment of creation.

16. **A. Yes**
A contract can only be terminated by parties to the contract.

17. **C. Performance**
Successful performance of a contract will discharge the person bound to do the act from any future contractual liability.

18. **D. Liquidated damages**
Both parties to a contract agree on the amount of money one party pays to the other upon breaching the agreement.

19. **C. Nominal damages**
Small sum awarded as damages where a legal right has been infringed, but no real or substantial loss has been proven to have occurred.

20. **B. Compensatory damages**
These damages are paid to a plaintiff when a loss has occurred as the result of criminal or negligent behavior.

21. **A. Misrepresentation**
When a false representation has been made recklessly or knowingly without belief in its truth.

22. **C. Seal**
There are three key elements of a binding contract: offer, acceptance, and consideration.

23. **B. Novation**
This is a complete transfer of all rights, duties, and obligations of a contract to a third party that will replace a party to the original contract.

24. **C. Rescission**
Rescission is a legal remedy allowing a party to cancel a contract and is the unwinding of a contract.

CHAPTER 4: CORPORATE AND COMMERCIAL LAW ANSWER KEY

1. **A. Limited partner**
    A general partnership does not have a limited partner. A limited partner is only found in a limited partnership. A general partnership will also need to apply to the IRS for a Federal Employer Identification Number and should enter into a partnership agreement with all its partners.

2. **B. Not timely filing tax returns**
    The remaining answers are typically reasons why a court may determine that the corporate veil has been pierced.

3. **B. Are personally liable for debts of the corporation**
    If the court pierces the corporate veil, then the shareholder(s) become personally liable for the debts and actions of the corporation.

4. **C. The election of officers**
    Under Section 7.32 of the Model Business Corporation Act, Shareholder Agreements are authorized to let shareholders dispense with the formality of a Board of Directors (which includes holding an annual meeting of the Directors) and holding annual shareholder meetings. This section of the Act does not allow for the Corporation to dispense with officers.

5. **C. An initial public offering**
    An initial public offering (IPO) is the first sale of stock by a private company to the public. IPOs are often issued by smaller, younger companies seeking the capital to expand, but can also be done by large privately-owned companies looking to become publicly traded.

6. **B. Partnership**
    An S corporation is taxed as a partnership for federal tax purposes. An S corporation is called "a small business corporation" but this is not a tax classification.

7. **B. False**
    A nonprofit corporation must apply to the Internal Revenue Service and meet certain qualifications in order to become tax exempt. The tax exemption is granted by the IRS.

8. **D. 990**
    IRS Form 990 is annually required to be filed for a tax-exempt organization. If the nonprofit is not tax exempt, then it would file IRS Form 1120 and pay appropriate taxes. Form 8832 is a tax election form for LLC, and IRS Form 2553 is a form used to elect small business corporation status.

9. **D. General partnership**
    A limited liability company, limited partnership, and nonprofits are all incorporated businesses. A general partnership does not have to be formed by filing an incorporation document.

© 2019, 2020, 2021 NALA, Inc. All rights reserved.

10. **A. Duty of care and duty of loyalty**
    The "primary" fiduciary duty for a Director is duty of care and duty of loyalty. Duty of good faith, duty of confidentiality, and duty of disclosure are additional fiduciary duties that courts may impose.

11. **A. True**
    The Sarbanes-Oxley Act was enacted as a result of various major corporate and accounting scandals of larger corporations in the 1990s.

12. **A. In an informed basis, in good faith, and in the honest belief that the actions taken were in the best interest of the corporation**
    Directors and officers must always act in their fiduciary capacity and in the best interest of the corporation (never in their best interest and not only the best interest of the shareholders).

13. **B. False**
    Under this rule, courts will generally refrain from questioning the directors' judgment so long as their judgment can be attributed to some rational corporate purpose. This rule is designed to protect directors and officers of a corporation from making a decision that turns out badly. In the event a business decision of the directors is challenged and taken to court and the court determines that the director(s) did not act within the business judgment rule (they breached one or more of their fiduciary duties), a court may judge in favor of a plaintiff. It is imperative that directors uphold their fiduciary duties to the Corporation at all times.

14. **C. Is a set of amendments to the Clayton Antitrust Act**
    The HSR Act was a set of amendments made to the Clayton Act. The HSR Act only requires certain types of mergers or transactions (relatively large in size) to file with the Department of Justice.

15. **D. Sherman Antitrust Act**
    The Sherman Antitrust Act was the first Federal antitrust act enacted in the U.S.

16. **D. The value of a company's brand name and the reputation of the company**
    Goodwill is an intangible asset that arises when one company purchases another for a premium value. The value of a company's brand name, solid customer base, good customer relations, good employee relations, and any patents or proprietary technology represent goodwill.

17. **B. False**
    The sale of assets of a business does not result in a change of owners of a business. The buyer purchases the assets of the company and is not purchasing the ownership interest in the company.

18. **C. Two businesses merge to offer similar or compatible products or services in the same market**
    A horizontal merger occurs when two or more businesses that offer similar or compatible products or services in the same market combine under a single entity. The driving force for this type of merger is a desire to obtain a larger market share.

19. **D. Two businesses merge who produce compatible products or services for a specified finished product**

A vertical merger occurs when two or more companies who produce compatible products or services for a specific finished product. The object of this type of merger is to create an entity that is more efficient in its operation.

20. **D. Dissolution**

A dissolution is the closing down of a business. Vertical, horizontal, and consolidation are all types of mergers.

21. **B. Single member LLC is taxed as a sole proprietorship**

Under the Internal Revenue Code, the default taxation rule for a single member LLC is as a sole proprietorship.

22. **A. Multiple member LLC is taxed as a partnership**

Under the Internal Revenue Code, the default taxation rule for a multiple member LLC is as a partnership. The multi member LLC can make an election to be taxed as something other than a partnership.

23. **A. Members.**

Owners in an LLC are called members. Managers can be members of the LLC but are not required to be members. Shareholders are owners of stock in a corporation, and partners are owners of interests in partnerships.

24. **B. Elect the Directors of the Corporation**

The shareholders of the corporation elect the directors. The directors of a corporation elect the officers. The registered agent is typically appointed by the incorporation or the directors of the corporation. The directors will also authorize the bank account(s) of the corporation.

25. **D. President, Secretary, and Treasure**

Under the model business corporation act and most state statutes, the minimum officers that must be elected each year are: President, Secretary, and Treasurer. State statutes allow for any other officers to be elected as determined by the corporation (i.e., Vice President, Assistant Secretary, Assistant Treasurer, etc.)

© 2019, 2020, 2021 NALA, Inc. All rights reserved.

CHAPTER 5: CRIMINAL LAW & PROCEDURE ANSWER KEY

1. **A. Treason**
   Remember the mnemonic: MR. & MRS. LAMB for common law felonies (murder, rape, manslaughter, robbery, sodomy, larceny, arson, mayhem, burglary). Common law crimes are actions against the state. Treason is an attempt to overthrow or betray a national government in favor of a foreign power.

2. **B. False**
   The unreasonable search and seizure and right to a speedy trial are protections under the Fourth and Sixth Amendments. The Fourth Amendment provides protections from unreasonable search and seizure. The Sixth Amendment provides the right to a speedy trial.

3. **B. False**
   Paul's confession was coerced and obtained under duress causing it to be involuntary. Pursuant to the Fifth Amendment, an involuntary confession violates due process and cannot be used against him. Additionally, the evidence obtained pursuant to the involuntary confession, and evidence derived thereof, cannot be used against Paul which is sometimes referred to as "fruit from the poisonous tree."

4. **D. Fourth Amendment**
   The Fourth Amendment protects a person's privacy and right to freedom from unreasonable government intrusion into their persons, homes, business, and property including search and seizure by police.

5. **B. False**
   Passion killing is an example of second-degree murder. The elements of first-degree murder include premeditation and deliberation. Second-degree murder does not require those two elements. Passion killings involve in the heat of the moment acts without a forethought.

6. **C. Conspiracy**
   Robbery, forgery, and larceny are crimes against property, wherein conspiracy involves another person to create the criminal act.

7. **C. Duress**
   Duress involves a threat from another human being of death or serious bodily harm if a person does not perform a specific act.

8. **A. True**
   The Exclusionary Rule also applies to violations of the Fifth and Sixth Amendments. The Exclusionary Rule precludes use of evidence obtained pursuant to an illegal search and seizure against a person at trial, and subsequent evidence derived thereof, as "fruit of the poisonous tree."

9. **B. False**

   Not only is evidence that is the product of an illegal search inadmissible in court, but so is additional evidence that was derived from the initial evidence. This principle is known as the fruit of the poisonous tree doctrine. The "tree" is the evidence that the police illegally seize in the first place; the "fruit" is the second-generation product of the illegally seized evidence. Both tree and fruit are typically inadmissible at trial.

10. **B. False**

    Border searches are exempt from Fourth Amendment protections. Border searches require no warrant, probable cause, or a degree of suspicion.

11. **B. 14 days**

    This is pursuant to Federal Rules of Appellate Procedure §4(b).

12. **B. Without the permission of Owner, Defendant takes Owner's motorcycle with the intention of driving it 100 miles to a casino and back. Defendant is charged with larceny.**

    The defendant did not return the motorcycle. In all the other scenarios, the motorcycle was returned to the Owner.

13. **A. True**

    An ambiguous statute is one that is capable of two or more equally reasonable interpretations. The rule of lenity holds that ambiguity in a criminal statute should be resolved in favor of the defendant.

14. **A. True**

    Strict liability acts produce outcomes that are punishable regardless of state of mind.

15. **B. Two witnesses**

    A person can be convicted of treason only by the testimony of two witnesses or by confession in open court pursuant to Article III, Section 3 of the U.S. Constitution.

© 2019, 2020, 2021 NALA, Inc. All rights reserved.

Chapter 6: Estate Planning and Probate Answer Key

1. **B. Jerry Smith and Anne Smith, as joint tenants**
   Joint tenancy is a form of ownership by two or more parties having an equal share and right to the property. Upon the death of one party their interests in the property transfers to the remaining parties.

2. **C. Statutory will**
   A statutory will is basically a "fill in the blanks" will that is based on your state's statutory provisions for making a will and is not tailored to the testator's needs.

3. **A. The property passes in accordance to the intestate statute of the decedent's state of domicile**
   In cases of decedents passing without a will, the state of their domicile determines their will for them and leaves the decedent's personal and real property to their closest blood relative(s).

4. **A. An advance health care directive**
   An advance health care directive allows someone to express desires and preferences of medical and life support decisions, including donations of organs and designation of primary physician.

5. **C. Betty Nichols took Kevin Molina to his doctors' appointments and ran his errands for him; she threatened to quit if he did not change his will and leave his estate to her.**
   In cases concerning duress or undue influence the testator does not act freely or is convinced by a person in a close position to execute a will favorable to them.

6. **A. 9 months after the date of the decedent's death**
   IRS Form 706 Generation-Skipping Transfer tax returns are for large estates that exceed the threshold for paying federal estate taxes. This return is complex and includes many schedules relating to assets, deductions, and credits.

7. **B. Life estate**
   With a life estate the holder does not actually hold title to the property in a manner that they can transfer it to another person. They only hold ownership of the property for the duration of their life.

8. **A. Delegate the performance of trust duties**
   The Trustor sets out in the trust the name of the Trustee. This Trustee must carry out the duties of the trust personally for the benefit of the trust and the beneficiary.

9. **C. Die without a valid will**
   In the event a person dies intestate, their assets will be passed to their closest blood relative(s) as determined by the intestate succession laws of their state.

10. **A. Health Insurance Portability and Accountability Act**
    Signing a HIPAA release allows a personal representative to have rights to access protected health care records and treatment information. Further, it allows the personal representative to communicate with health care professionals and insurance companies.

---

11. **A. A lifetime of income from the CRT assets during the settlor's life or a specified number of years**

In a Charitable Remainder Trust the trustee sells the assets paying no capital gains taxes, reinvests the assets, and generates income. Upon the death of the donor, the named charity inherits the remainder of the trust.

© 2019, 2020, 2021 NALA, Inc. All rights reserved.

CHAPTER 7: REAL ESTATE AND PROPERTY ANSWER KEY

1. **C. Fee tail estate**

   Most jurisdictions have abolished or modified the fee tail estate. The fee tail estate was essentially the same as the fee simple estate, but it could only be inherited by the issue of the owner as specified in the deed conveying such estate. The most common freehold estate in use today is the fee simple estate, which contains all the rights that can possibly relate to land. The life estate terminates upon the death of the holder and therefore cannot be inherited. The life estate is rarely seen today in most jurisdictions. Trusts are not estates in real property, although they are often used to accomplish the same results as the life estate.

2. **D. Long-term ground lease**

   The holder of a long-term ground lease has a nonfreehold estate in that they have possession, but not ownership, of the real property leased. The holder of a life estate has a freehold estate in that they have both possession and ownership of the real property, although the ownership is limited to a specified period of time. An investor in a real estate investment trust or a member in a real estate cooperative owns an interest in those entities, not a direct interest in the real property owned by those entities.

3. **A. Option to lease**

   Elizabeth would want to include in the lease an option to lease additional space. This would provide the right to lease certain specified space in the building if it becomes available. Elizabeth would want to make sure this includes the specific terms for such option, including the amount of notice required from tenant when electing to exercise the option and the amount of rent to be paid for the additional space. A renewal option would permit Elizabeth to extend the length of the term of the lease of her original premises subject to specific provisions. An option to purchase would provide Elizabeth with the right to purchase the entire property in which the leased space is located, under specified terms, including the purchase price. A right of first refusal means that, if at any time during the term, the landlord shall receive an acceptable offer to purchase the entire property, the landlord would be required to provide Elizabeth with notice of the terms of such offer. Elizabeth would then have a specified period of time in which to notify the landlord in writing that she intends to enter into a contract with the landlord upon the same terms and conditions.

4. **D. Special warranty deed**

   A special warranty deed includes warranties such as a covenant of the right to convey and a covenant of quiet enjoyment but limits those warranties to claims of an interest in the real property under the grantor. A general warranty deed includes such warranties as they pertain to claims of an interest under the grantor, but also under all of grantor's predecessors. A quit claim deed contains no warranties. A sheriff's deed is used to convey title following foreclosure on a mortgage or a court ordered sale for a judgment and contains no warranties.

5. **B. Covenant against encumbrances**

   In a covenant against encumbrances, the grantor represents that there are no encumbrances against title such as mortgages, easements, and tax liens. A covenant of right to convey is a representation of the grantor that the right to transfer interest in the real property. In a covenant of quiet enjoyment, the grantor warrants that the grantee will be able to enjoy the real property against the claims of third parties, and in a covenant of warranty, the grantor covenants to warrant and defend the grantee's title against such claims of third parties.

6. **B. Gross lease**
Under a gross lease (also known as full-service lease) rent is all-inclusive. This means that the landlord pays all expenses or "nets" (taxes, insurance, and common area maintenance) associated with the property out of the rent received from tenants. Utilities and janitorial services are also included under a gross lease. Under a single net lease, the tenant pays a base rent amount, plus its proportionate share of one of the "nets." Under a triple net lease, the tenant pays a base rent amount, plus its proportionate share of the three "nets." A modified gross lease (also known as a modified net lease) is similar to a gross lease in that the rent is paid in one lump sum, which can include any expenses agreed upon by the landlord and the tenant, but utilities and janitorial services for the premises are typically excluded from the rent and paid directly by the tenant.

7. **C. Use restriction**
The landlord could include a use restriction in other tenants' leases which would prevent them from engaging in certain activities such as opening a music store. A right of first refusal, an option to lease, and a termination clause would relate to the other tenants' rights to purchase the retail center, lease additional space within the retail center, or terminate their leases, respectively.

8. **A. Joint tenancy with right of survivorship**
A joint tenancy with right of survivorship may arise when two or more owners are conveyed equal interests in real property at the same time, through the same grant. Upon the death of one of the joint tenants, the surviving joint tenant(s) inherits the interest. Tenants in common may take at different times through different conveyances, and they may have unequal interests in the property. Tenancy by the entirety is a form of joint tenancy, with the additional requirement that the co-owners be a married couple. Community property is not a concurrent estate, although it is another form of ownership by multiple parties.

9. **B. Appurtenant**
A gross easement benefits a particular party while an appurtenant easement benefits a particular parcel or parcels of land. A court may grant an easement in necessity when a conveyance of real property results in a parcel with no access to a roadway. A negative easement prohibits the owner of the servient estate from engaging in activities the individual would otherwise be permitted to do.

10. **D. Non-exclusive**
An adverse possession claimant must possess the subject property exclusively; if multiple parties use the subject property, no single one of them can claim ownership. The possession of the subject property must be hostile, meaning without the permission of the record owner. The possession must be continuous for the intended use of the subject property for the period of time required by the statute of limitations. The subject property must be possessed in an open way that would be obvious to a record owner showing reasonable attention to the property.

11. **C. Bundle of rights**
The bundle of rights is a concept in real property law stating that an owner possesses certain rights in the real property owned, including the rights to possess, lease, mortgage, convey, use and enjoy, and exclude others. The bundle of rights is not a specific instrument affecting property that would be included in a title commitment. The information contained within title commitments includes instruments affecting the ownership interest in the property, including mortgages, easements, and tax liens.

    © 2019, 2020, 2021 NALA, Inc. All rights reserved.

12.   **B. Deed of trust**

Under a deed of trust, the borrower grants ownership of the real property to the trustee to hold on behalf of a lender until the loan is satisfied. A trustee's deed is used to convey property when a trustee sells real property pursuant to the power of sale provisions of a deed of trust. A bill of sale is used to transfer ownership of personal property. A security agreement grants a secured party an interest in personal property of a debtor.

© 2019, 2020, 2021 NALA, Inc. All rights reserved.

CHAPTER 8: TORTS ANSWER KEY

1. **C. Consideration**
   Consideration is an element of a contract. Causation is the missing element of a tort in the sample question.

2. **B. Preponderance of the evidence**
   Beyond a reasonable doubt is the burden for a criminal case. Clear and convincing requires 70-75 percent confidence that the facts support the decision. Conclusive is just a random word meaning serving to prove a case.

3. **D. The unexpected frailty of the injured person is not a valid defense to the seriousness of any injury that is caused to them**
   Answer "B." refers to the zone of danger. Answer "C." refers to *rex non potest peccare*.

4. **A. Employment**

5. **B. Dram shop law**
   Criminal law would require prosecution by the state. Premises liability is for an injury that occurs on the premise. Social host liability is for a private individual.

6. **D. A bystander case**
   The impact rule requires that something contact or "impact" the plaintiff as a result of the defendant's negligent act, even if the impact is minor. The "zone of danger" requires that the plaintiff be close enough to the defendant's negligent act that the plaintiff was at immediate risk of physical harm. The "foreseeability" rule finds that a defendant must have been able to reasonably predict that their actions could result in the negative consequence experienced by the plaintiff.

7. **B. Joint and several liability**
   Primary liability is an obligation for which a party is directly responsible. Strict liability does not depend on negligence or intent to harm. Vicarious liability is when someone is held responsible for another person's liability.

8. **C. Police report**
   If properly authenticated employment records, medical records, and school records can be allowed as evidence at trial.

9. **A. Dog bite**
   Under the strict liability rule, a person must pay compensation for damages even if they are not at fault. In a dog bite case, the person is not at fault, but the dog is. Slip and fall, medical malpractice, and negligent hiring are all examples where they are a person at fault.

10. **B. An intentional tort**
    It is not a negligence tort because it is caused by an intentional act. It is not a strict liability tort because there is fault. It is not a personal injury tort because there is not bodily injury involved.

© 2019, 2020, 2021 NALA, Inc. All rights reserved.

11. **D. Comparative fault**

Consent, self-defense, and necessity are all defenses to intentional torts.

12. **C. Negligence per se**

Civil negligence per se is a legal doctrine where an act is considered negligent because it violates a statute or regulation and causes harm to the defendant such as speeding. Product liability and premises liability are different torts, and the Lincoln Law applies to the False Claims Act.

13. **A. A manufacturer**

Product liability is the area of law to sue manufacturers, distributors, suppliers, retailers, and others who make products available to the public for the injuries those products cause. Doctors, employers, and condominium associations are not any of those.

14. **C. There must be recreational use**

For premises liability to apply: (1) the defendant must possess the premises/land; (2) the plaintiff must be an invitee or a licensee; and (3) there must be negligence. Recreational use is not necessary. Recreational use statutes are a defense to premises liability claims.

15. **D. To deter the defendant**

Punitive damages are not meant to compensate the Plaintiff but are intended to reform or deter the defendant and others from engaging in the same conduct. They are meant to punish not reward.

CHAPTER 9: PROFESSIONAL AND ETHICAL RESPONSIBILITY ANSWER KEY

1. **D. Working or knowing about a case where one's prior law firm represented the opposing party**
    Possession of information about a former case (such as attorney strategies, thought processes, work-product, and/or privileged client information) may cause irreparable harm, injury, or prejudice to the opposing party. The general canon of ethics adopted by the National Association of Legal Assistants, Inc. (NALA), Canon 8 states, "A paralegal must disclose to an employer or prospective employer any pre-existing client or personal relationship that may conflict with the interests of the employer or prospective employer and/or their clients."

2. **B. At times, they fail to communicate with the client regarding the status of their case**
    Failing to communicate with a client is one of the most common causes of legal malpractice suits and complaints to state bars. Attorneys have a legal duty to maintain "professionally adequate" communication with clients. See ABA Model Rules of Professional Conduct 1.4: Communications.

3. **D. All the above**
    One of the paralegal's duties is to keep the attorney focused and on task. It is perfectly acceptable for the paralegal to engage in all tasks listed above. The general canon of ethics adopted by the National Association of Legal Assistants, Inc. (NALA), Canon 2 states, "A paralegal may perform any task which is properly delegated and supervised by an attorney, as long as the attorney is ultimately responsible to the client, maintains a direct relationship with the client, and assumes professional responsibility for the work product."

4. **C. A paralegal giving a legal opinion to a friend**
    It is considered an unauthorized practice of law (UPL) when a paralegal gives a legal opinion to anyone (no matter who the paralegal is speaking with). The general canon of ethics adopted by the National Association of Legal Assistants, Inc. (NALA), Canon 4 states in part "A paralegal… must not render independent legal judgment in place of an attorney…"

5. **A. An ethical wall is a screening mechanism that protects a client from a conflict of interest**
    The ethical wall prevents other lawyers within the same firm from participating in any matter involving the client, including restricting access to that client's files, in order to protect that client's information from potentially being disclosed to other clients that may profit from the information.

6. **A. The law firm can be disqualified**
    An attorney has a duty to disclose any conflicts of interest in order to preserve professional judgment on behalf of the client. Failing to disclose may adversely affect the representation of a client. See ABA Model Rules of Professional Conduct 1.7: Conflict of Interest: Current Clients. "There is a significant risk that the representation of one or more clients will be materially limited by the lawyer's responsibilities to another client, a former client or a third person or by a personal interest of the lawyer."

© 2019, 2020, 2021 NALA, Inc. All rights reserved.

7. **B. Conflict of interest was discovered at a later time and eventually caused the law firm to be disqualified**

A paralegal worked extensively on this case and knew the Plaintiff for several years. She later left the firm and worked for the firm representing Urfa-Sexton, although she did not immediately know that at the time. The Georgia Rules of Professional Conduct 1.9 (c) state in part "a lawyer who has formerly represented a client in a matter or whose present or former firm has formerly represented a client in a matter shall not thereafter: (1) use information relating to the representation to the disadvantage of the former client…" The court also applied this to nonlawyers who work under the supervision of an attorney. The Court remanded to the Court of Appeals to remand to the trial court for a hearing to determine if the paralegal's current firm had given proper written notice to the Plaintiff and her counsel at the paralegal's old firm.

8. **C. Yes, if the state bar association has suspended or disbarred their membership**

When an attorney is disbarred or their license is suspended, they are prohibited from practicing law. This usually occurs after the state bar determines that a lawyer is unfit to continue practicing law, typically after numerous complaints by clients, other lawyers, or judges. For instance, if an attorney practices law while suspended or disbarred by the Bar Association, then they fall under "UPL."

9. **D. A conflict of interest is a situation when the consideration of one party is to the detriment of another**

There is a significant risk that the representation of one or more clients will be materially limited by the lawyer's responsibilities to another client, a former client, or a third person or by a personal interest of the lawyer. See ABA Model Rules of Professional Conduct 1.7: Conflict of Interest: Current Clients.

10. **C. Know about the state's laws or statutes concerning paralegal requirements**

The general canon of ethics adopted by the National Association of Legal Assistants, Inc. (NALA), Canon 10 states, "A paralegal's conduct is guided by bar associations' codes of professional responsibility and rules of professional conduct." See also NALA's Model Standards and Guidelines for Utilization of Paralegals, Section V. Guidelines. Note that for some states, paralegals should first abide by state statutes and regulations governing paralegals, to be followed by local state bar associations' codes of professional responsibility, and rules of professional conduct.

11. **A. The work-product doctrine protects materials prepared in anticipation of litigation from discovery by opposing counsel**

For many reasons, the paralegal should type in the "Subject" line of the email (or on the top of the email): "ATTORNEY WORK-PRODUCT." The work-product doctrine protects materials prepared in anticipation of litigation from discovery by opposing counsel. Attorney work-product are the products that paralegals can create for the attorney that are confidential, such as notes, memoranda, reports on conversations with the client or witness, research, and confidential materials that reflect an attorney's or paralegal's impressions, conclusions, opinions, or legal research, and suggested legal strategies or theories.

12. **C. Learn about law updates and which legal procedures and practices are being implemented and utilized in the law firm**

Communications with a paralegal's legal team is very significant for a number of reasons. A paralegal should be proactive with their communications with all members of the legal team to not just receive specific directions for their multiple projects, but to also learn about law updates and which legal procedures and practices are being implemented and utilized in the law firm. As a paralegal, it is important to keep abreast with the laws as well as current and upcoming legal practices and technology trends within the legal field.

© 2019, 2020, 2021 NALA, Inc. All rights reserved.